Tradition and Identity in Changing Africa

Tradition and Identity in Changing Africa

Mark A. Tessler
The University of Wisconsin—Milwaukee

William M. O'Barr
Duke University

David H. Spain
University of Washington

Foreword by Ronald Cohen
Northwestern University

HARPER & ROW, PUBLISHERS
NEW YORK, EVANSTON, SAN FRANCISCO, LONDON

For Pat, Jean, and Cathie

Sponsoring Editor: Walter H. Lippincott, Jr.
Project Editor: William Monroe
Designer: June Negrycz
Production Supervisor: Valerie Klima

(Title).
Tradition and Identity in Changing Africa

Library of Congress Cataloging in Publication Data
Tessler, Mark A
  Tradition and identity in changing Africa.

  Includes bibliographies.
    1. Ethnology—Africa. 2. Social change—
Case studies. I. O'Barr, William M., joint author.
II. Spain, David H., joint author. III. Title.
GN645.T47   301.29'6   73-7207
ISBN 0-06-046591-3

Contents

PART FIVE   Conclusions

Foreword

All over the earth life is changing, evolving, moving, developing, modernizing, radicalizing, or being exhorted to do so. The stability of yesterday is seen today not in terms of peace and tranquility but rather in the light of the injustice, the oppression, and the inequality that went along with colonialism and the general dominance of western cultures on the world scene. Intellectuals, social scientists, politicians, ideologists and others look to this tumult and ask themselves what it is all about. Can we make some sense of all this rapid change? Is it simply the playing out of the industrial revolution as it now spreads itself around the globe? Is it man becoming too populous and writhing in a Malthusian nightmare of ecological destructiveness? Or is it the result of centuries of white racism now finally getting its come-uppance from the earth's darker-skinned peoples who are on their own march to equality or even ascendancy? Possibly it is all these things and more. Whatever it is, change is upon us with a vengeance; and somehow we try as best we can to adapt in that most human of all ways—by understanding. This is the context that informs this book and indeed much of the emphasis on change in scholarly work.

With more complex political systems and the increasingly advanced technology devised by modern science, the pace of change accelerates and the threads that tie the past to the future become taut with tension and pressure. It is almost as if man advances, whatever that means, by becoming more insecure, less sure of what he really is, or was, or will be. When change is great enough, then the past fails to inform the future and must either be rejected or reinterpreted.

Under such conditions individuals, groups, or nations as wholes, experience a crisis in identity. It is extremely difficult to desire change and yet continue to set one's own past as a guide for the future. Then along with modernization goes a haunting, albeit false, syllogism: the "less developed" must become like the "more developed" in order to achieve what they desire. To become **more** like others is to become less like one's self, and so rapid **social** change has as one of its possible costs a harrowing side effect— that of a possible denial of the worthiness of one's own **cultural** heritage. The result can be a sense of inferiority which is **only** assuaged by becoming as much like the goal objects of change **as** possible so that self-confidence becomes limited to the degree to which there is self-denial. Identity can then only be future- oriented since the past is busily being shed, yet it is always there producing a tension in identity. Are we what we wish to become, or what we were, or are we both even though they may be unre- lated or even contradictory?

The problem is made sharper by the fact that a large range of very tangible goals tend to validate the so-called "developed- underdeveloped" continuum. Modern manufacturing, electrifica- tion, transportation, housing, adequate health facilities, education, and hosts of correlated consumer goods are more plentiful in some countries and much less widely distributed in others. These latter are, however, dedicated to achieving more of such goods, services, and the means to produce them. Thus contemporary social change does divide the world into those who have more and those who have less material wealth and technologically advanced productive capacities. And those who have less, but want more, are dubbed "underdeveloped," since they wish to obtain more of these particular values for themselves.

As the process of change proceeds, a question soon arises as to how broad the changes must be. It is one of the terribly thorny issues for which as yet there are very few firm answers. Russia, Japan, and China are often referred to as models from which contemporary nations can learn a great deal. But each of these societies is *still* in the throes of change, so that how much or how little they will become or remain uniquely tied to their own traditional past is in no way clear as yet—possibly it never will be. Japan industrialized without westernizing; yet today in such areas as the family and the role of women, Japan *is* taking on forms of social structure that are more like those of the West than they have ever been before. On the other hand interest in, and support of, traditional culture in Japan is a popular mass movement. The question emerges: in order to have modern technology must a people take on the social structure, political ideology, cultural style, and other cultural attributes, such as religion, of those who already have these things? Since the correlation between these things is not clear we cannot provide pat answers to questions about what things from tradition must be relinquished and what things modified or preserved in order to provide continuity in the historical experience of a people.

For most people living through such changes much of this conflict may be unconscious or even irrelevant. Still, they experience difficulties over their desires for what often turn out to be conflicting things, as the cases here very aptly point out. But in the end they do make choices—because they must. They have to decide whether to move to the city for good or to maintain some long-term interest in the rural area from which they come. They must decide, consciously or unconsciously, about a large range of things that determine whether they will become "new men" or members of a traditional group unchanging in its ways. For leaders and intellectuals who wish to create an ideology for the people such problems are more difficult. It is from these groups that we can see the various strategies of adaptation emerging.

One strategy is that of rejection of tradition. Generally this seems to be associated with the preindependence periods and even then to be seen as a form of self-rejection. Colonial officials often stimulated such reactions by rewarding those in the conquered territories who were most like themselves. And such a reward system creates its own tradition so that even when independence is achieved it is hard to get over the idea that what is foreign is modern and, by a false definition, "better" as well. This idea applies even within countries among groups trying to achieve better status and greater equality. Thus for nearly a hundred years American blacks who were most like the dominant white middle class were more acceptable and generally seen as more successful than the majority who were culturally somewhat divergent.

But the assimilationist strategy is dependent upon differentials of power that are unbridgeable. Only if there is no other way to obtain the desired ends of social change will individuals, groups, or nations resort to such sharp breaks with their own past. Otherwise the realization is inevitable that one cannot gain a genuine identity by shedding a heritage. Indeed, self-confidence and pride demand an affirmation of one's own uniqueness and the contribution of one's history to the present. In Africa, Nkrumah (among others) spoke of the "African personality," and Nyerere sees in local African tradition a sense of cooperation and community that is a guide for contemporary nationalist ideology. In Nigeria scholars have found viable and complex political philosophy in the writings and practices of precolonial governments in West Africa.[1] Bourguiba of Tunisia and Senghor of Senegal, as well as others, have discussed these issues. In short, leaders see their people modernizing in terms of technology—living in electrified housing, listening to radios, sending children to schools, and so on. But they will be doing so in their own idiom, searching for personal and social goals that are adapted from and guided by their own traditions.

I suspect that as comparative work continues, the search for identity, viewed as a dependent variable, will be found to be significantly affected by the nature of traditional sociopolitical systems, by religion, and by the peculiarities of the colonial intrusion. Peoples whose precolonial societies were already in the form of centralized states generally have traditions of statecraft, diplomacy, administrative skills, and political ideology that can be looked back upon not only with pride, but as a source of inspiration. Where such large-scale systems did not exist, contemporary writers are reinterpreting comparative categories so that nationhood is in fact part of their tradition. Thus Igbo political cultures, often seen as acephalous, are now being viewed as a series of local city-states having an indigenously developed concept of African democracy. And where even this much organization was lacking, the quality of past social relations rather than complexity of organization can be looked to as a guide for the future. What Radcliffe-Brown characterized as the solidarity of siblings in African societies, for example, can become instead the traditional basis for a modern ideology of brotherhood among all members of a nation—or even among all Africans.

Religion serves similar functions from a different perspective. In Islamic Africa the traditional religion is recognized as one of the great worldwide religious movements with a highly developed background of law, criticism, and literacy. This has stimulated a search for indigenous Islamic scholarship, as reflected in the establishment of many local institutes of Islamic studies, and a feeling of solidarity with the wider Moslem community. Although sometimes the object of reformist efforts, Islam is generally

---

[1]See, *Nigerian Administration Research Project: First Interim Report,* Institute of Administration, Ahmadu Bello University, Zaria, Nigeria—especially the article by Mahmud Tukur, "Philosophy, Goals and Institutions of the Sokoto Caliphal Administration: A Preliminary View."

regarded as an extremely important link to the past and to the very roots of identity. Christianity in Africa has created more of a crisis in identity since it is foreign and antagonistic to indigenous religions. To be a Christian in Africa is to be a person who has given up his past, or at least its unique cultural roots. It is interesting in this respect to observe the growth of indigenous African Christian religion such as the Jamaa movement in Zaïre (Fabian 1971) and the Aladura movement in Nigeria which is now rapidly spreading from the Yoruba area to such peoples as the Kaje and the Kagoro in middle-belt Nigeria. These peoples claim that the newer forms of Christianity allow them to bring African ideas, rituals, and beliefs into church, making them feel more comfortable and giving the religion itself a more definable African identity.

Although it is fast disappearing, the colonial intrusion has also shaped the search for identity. In some places it was considered the height of success to cultivate an Oxford accent, while in others to obtain the Legion d'Honneur served a similar purpose. To a significant degree, this phase has passed. The generation now reaching adulthood in many African countries grew up entirely in the postcolonial period. But wisps of this peversity remain, even though much of Africa is well into the second decade of independence. In many states, for example, the national language is still the language of the colonial power. Unknown to much of the populace and only a second language to most of the rest, linguistic patterns thus constitute an aspect of identity that keeps many African nations cut off from their past and tied to their former colonizers.

The search for identity goes on and will, in my view, be a major theme in African political and social philosophy in the years to come. At times it may seem odd to the unsophisticated outsider, as when a young woman is arrested in Uganda for wearing a miniskirt. But this book, and my few remarks here, are an attempt to show what complex and important issues lie behind such acts. Modernization may mean taking on a new and foreign technology, but it does not mean that Africans should or must at the same time drop their concepts of proper dress, as if to say the only person who can use modern technology is one who acts, dresses, thinks, and behaves like the people from whom the technology is obtained.

There is a final aspect to the problem of identity. The painful awareness that income gaps between the rich and poor nations (as between the rich and the poor within nations) will not close readily or in the near future is beginning to sink in and is a stimulus to a new aspect of the identity crisis. In view of a long road ahead in which relative economic positions in the world may change very little if at all, continued position near the bottom of world economic status faces many African nations and their intellectuals. Instead of looking only to their own conditions, their own past, and their own identity as an explanation for this continued lower international position, some are now looking outward as well. Throwing over the western concept that a country is a developing unit whose *infrastructure* is the primary ingredient in its development, they are taking up A. G. Frank's (1969) idea that unequal development is primarily a function of the worldwide structuring of economic and military power. It follows then that their relative poverty is due to the structure of international political and economic relationships rather than their own internal "backwardness." I am not wise enough in the intricacies of development economics to comment intelligently on the validity of this notion. However, it is well designed to serve as a rebuttal to the proposition frequently advanced in the west that nations are poor largely because of the poverty of their cultural traditions.

If this assessment is correct, then several things can be predicted. Studies of international exploitation of the newer countries of Africa and Asia will proliferate, especially in the newer countries themselves. This is all to the good since it ultimately will determine just what role outside forces do play in curbing development. According to this view, development is not only a means of creating change *within* nation-states, but also *between* them so that exploitative relations can be rearranged to become redistributive. If this is the case, we can look to a growth of zenophobic reactions to foreign aid and a greater set of claims for outright write-offs of loans. We can also expect nationalization of foreign investment without compensation. The nationalizing state claims this is logical and just since the profits previously taken out of the country were used to develop not the local economy but that of the richer investing country. In sum, the identity crisis lends to a search for outside as well as inside reasons for low economic status, and this contributes to national dignity and pride by shifting some of the burden elsewhere. The result is antagonism to the richer nations, especially those with economic ties to the poorer countries, and a set of ideological claims for redressing the balance as an additional stimulus to development.

The extent to which such reactions will occur is a function of the degree of exploitation actually taking place, the rate of development within the poorer country, and the functional utility of increased isolation from the richer nations. If it is clear and documentable that international trade agreements are to the serious detriment of the poorer nations, then the shoe fits and blame for relative national poverty can be placed squarely upon the shoulders of the richer nations. There is also a spillover effect as well, since the ideology itself propagates the view that development requires not simply bootstrap efforts, and foreign loans, but redistribution of wealth between nations as well. Thus, for example, terms of trade favorable to poorer nations must be part of international agreements even where exploitation is not so clearly obvious on a bilateral basis.

In the very few cases where development rates are fairly high, or seen to be relatively successful, as with Ivory Coast and Nigeria, such ideology is less attractive. Because these countries are doing fairly well, there is a quite understandable tendency not to rock the boat. An expanding middle class with a newfound stake in this growth tends as well to provide support for a less aggressive international stance. Even this more conservative position can change if local radical opinion mobilizes and takes over the government, as occurred in Chile. However, the existence of opposition in the middle class and the real contribution made by foreign-managerial efficiency, plus the punitive moves made by richer nations whose investments have been nationalized, provides a sober and somewhat somber result to such acts.

Finally, there is the functionality of isolationism. As with Japan in the past, and China and Cuba more recently, a growing number of African countries, starting with Tanzania, have entered a period of isolation, especially from ex-colonial western nations. Older colonial links are effectively broken and new often profitable ones are set up. Certainly the concentrated contacts with the former colonial power are very significantly narrowed and international linkages are much more widely spread and controlled. In doing all of this, a new identity is being created in which the nation as a whole is a much freer agent in the international arena. The cathexis toward the older colonial power in terms of identity is diffused and a newer national identity can be more easily created. Antagonism to the richer nations helps provide a rationale for these more restrictive policies to ex-colonial powers.

And so the identity crisis has both an internal and external face.

This book deals primarily with its internal side. Future work in this area will have, as well, to see the international relations of the poorer nations from the perspective of identity creation and crises. Who we are in terms of our own past and future and in relation to others has become a vital force in the world today. For social scientists it is a perspective that sheds much-needed light on what seem often to be irrational acts in the nonwestern world or even among minority groups at home. Yet when seen in terms of the identity problem, much that at first seems illogical becomes clear and even predictable.

This brief and overly general posing of the wider ramifications of the identity problem implies an important methodological point. The authors of this book have dealt with three cases that seem at first sight to be noncomparable. These include two ethnic groups and a modern nation-state. One of the ethnic groups is acephalous and situated in East Africa, the other is an ancient African kingdom of West Africa, and the modern nation is in North Africa. Since these societies are of very different orders, it might appear that comparisons among them simply confuse the issues being studied. But a careful reading of these cases shows the exact opposite is in fact true. By varying the scale so drastically the authors have shown that the identity and tradition problem is present in today's world at many levels of social and political activity. Indeed I have gone beyond their comparisons and suggested that it is present among individuals *and* at the international level as well. Thus the diversity of cases presented here serves in an epistemological sense as a control for scale differences which are assumed, then demonstrated, to make less difference than one would at first believe. In all these societies, the question "Who are we?" is of paramount importance and centers on attempts to resolve inconsistencies between answers to the questions "What have we been?" and "What are we in the process of becoming?"

Ronald Cohen

Preface

This book grows out of a number of experiences the three of us have shared in recent years. One of the most significant experiences has been our association with Ronald Cohen, Professor of Anthropology, Political Science, and African Studies at Northwestern University, whom we shared as a mentor. During the early 1960s, his seminars kindled and sustained our interest in social change and modernization. We are grateful for the innumerable hours of tutorials in which he guided our study of these processes in the African context.

Another formative influence has been our association with the Program of African Studies at Northwestern. First in the guiding hands of the late Professor Melville J. Herskovits, and now of its current director, Professor Gwendolyn Carter, the program instills in its students not only an enduring passion for the study of Africa but also a firm grounding in an intellectual tradition that emphasizes the multidisciplinary study of African societies and cultures. To Professor Carter and the faculty of the program, we owe a special debt.

The people in Tunisia, Tanzania, and Nigeria with whom we lived and worked in the course of our research have contributed beyond measure to this volume. It is they who directed us to the issues we have focused upon and who untiringly instructed us in the myriad ways of their cultures.

Our students at the University of Wisconsin—Milwaukee, at Duke University, and at the University of Washington have also contributed significantly to the form and content of this book. They have encouraged us by providing helpful comments and constructive criticisms in our efforts to provide them, and students elsewhere, with a single concisely written volume that examines the changes engulfing traditional Africa. We have endeavored in this book to document general trends that our studies suggest are in evidence in widely differing parts of Africa. At the same time, we have tried to provide readers with the data, both qualitative and quantitative, upon which these generalizations are based. And finally, we have attempted to bring to life the many individuals lumped together in tables or other aggregate descriptions. Nevertheless, no book as brief as this one can express fully the results of more than five years of combined field work in North, East, and West Africa.

A few individuals must be singled out for special thanks: the members of the Department of Sociology at the University of Tunis; Ruben Ezekiel, Juma Issa, and Jackson Mrendoko in Tanzania; and Malam Ibrahim Walad in Nigeria. Without their help and guidance, our work would have been much more difficult. For their help during the final phases of the preparation of the manuscript, we thank Robert and Jean Fox whose lakeside cottage in Indiana provided a pleasant retreat where we were able to work together. Finally, we thank our wives for their continual encouragement and support—both in the field and at home. As faithful companions and critics, we could have asked for no more.

M. A. T.
W. M. O.
D. H. S.

ACKNOWLEDGMENTS

Several people deserve special thanks for their helpful comments on the Pare chapters: Jerry Barkow, Patricia Beaver, Muriel Smith, Jean O'Barr, and Pam Richardson. The fieldwork on which these chapters are based was conducted in Tanzania from August, 1967, through November, 1968, supported by National Institute of Mental Health predoctoral fellowship (5-F01-MH37229-03). Financial support from the Council for Intersocietal Studies of Northwestern University and the Duke University Research Council aided in the analysis of the field materials. The Wenner-Gren Foundation for Anthropological Research provided travel funds to attend a conference at the Afrika-Studiecentrum, Leiden, the Netherlands, in December, 1970, where some of the materials were presented in an earlier version. The section of Chapter 5 dealing with language has been published in a slightly different version in *Anthropological Linguistics,* 13:289–300, June, 1971.

The research discussed in Part Three was supported financially by a grant and fellowship from the Foreign Area Fellowship Program, and by faculty research grants from the University of Washington. This support is sincerely acknowledged. Portions of these chapters were improved by the critical comments of my colleagues John A. Brim, Charles F. Keyes, and L. L. Langness. The computer assisted portions of this analysis were tirelessly engineered by my research assistant, Daniel D. Eggars. Their valuable help is greatly appreciated.

The fieldwork on which the Tunisia chapters are based was conducted in 1964–1965 and 1966–1967. Survey research during the 1966–1967 period was made possible by a grant from the Council for Intersocietal Studies of Northwestern University. Related work at the University of Tunis in 1964–1965 was supported by the Program of African Studies of Northwestern University and by the American Friends of the Middle East. The generous assistance of each of these agencies is gratefully acknowledged. Sincere thanks are also extended to Abdulwahab Bouhida and Paul Sebag, who read the manuscript and offered valuable comments. Some of the material in Chapter 14 appeared in *World Affairs*, 133:183–200, December, 1970. Some of the data presented in Chapter 15 have been published in *Social Science Quarterly*, 52:290–308. This material is included here with the permission of these journals.

PART ONE

Introduction

1

Tradition and Identity
in Crisis

In the latter half of the twentieth century, most African societies
are struggling to resolve conflicts between the forces of tradition
and change. In contrast to Westerners who found their societies
mercilessly ravaged by the Industrial Revolution a few generations
earlier, contemporary Africans are more self-aware and conscious of the revolution restructuring their lives. And many hope
this awareness will make it possible for them to play a greater
role in controlling change and in shaping their ways of life in
the future.

Defining ways of life that will unite the technological and
material advantages of the present age with the precious heritage
of African cultures is an urgent problem, perhaps the most urgent
of all in contemporary Africa. Increasingly, the African continent
is alive with change. Both rapidly growing metropolitan centers
and rural African villages teem with anticipation and excitement
about the future. But there is also a desire to preserve esteemed
traditions. Most Africans are witnessing in their own lifetimes a
revolution of society and culture whose proportions are potentially
Copernican; and the specter of such radical change produces
its own antithesis, an intense struggle for continuity in the midst
of change. This dialectical tension between continuity and transformation, this concern for assimilating the best of an emerging
world culture without in turn being assimilated by it—in short,
this juxtaposition of two deeply felt but only partially compatible
desires—is the dynamic of social change in contemporary Africa.

The agents of acculturation that call into question traditional
normative systems are well known. For one thing, there has been
an explosion of information everywhere in Africa. In remote oasis
towns and in lofty mountain villages, the school and the transistor
radio increasingly promote an awareness of the world at large.
They provide the ideas and images by which individuals compre-

hend and relate to their own lives a world taking shape beyond the traditional nexus; and, eventually, they lead to a modification of people's views of their own society.

Urbanization is also transforming many African societies. Throughout the continent, men are migrating to cities in search of employment, motivated in part by the centripetal pull of urban life and in part by the need for cash to send back home. In the villages, the men's absence creates dislocations, modifying patterns of societal organization, and requiring redefinitions of moral codes. For the men themselves, employment and urban life require the playing of roles that exacerbate alienation from traditional values. Even as unskilled laborers participating marginally in the affairs of a city, they acquire new conceptions of time, of work, of social relations with colleagues and kinsmen, and much more. When migrations are temporary or seasonal, the return of workers to rural communities becomes an additional force for change. When families follow the men to a city, the scope of Africa's social and psychological revolution expands even further.

The forces for change are everywhere much the same, but their impact on individuals varies considerably. For some, the erosion of traditional life portends an optimistic future. Freed from the constraints of tradition and oriented toward a different world, the members of this vanguard welcome the opportunity for new political and cultural destinies. To others, however, the possibility of change is fearful. Almost instinctively, these individuals realize that the experience they have acquired over a lifetime will count for little should time-honored ways of life disappear. Backed by their conservatism, many of the traditional societies are putting up a determined and extraordinary fight for survival. Attachments to old orders are strong, and, in the final analysis, even highly acculturated individuals are often ambivalent about new values which threaten to displace ancient and venerable traditions.

The tension generated by a confrontation of ancient and modern values does not exist in a political vacuum. The leaders of many African nations believe they must sweep away whatever aspects of traditional life threaten developmental efforts. The achievement of independence was the overriding goal of African nationalists following World War II; self-government with danger was preferable to stability under another's tutelage. But now, with most of the continent liberated from colonial rule, concerns of nation-building and economic growth assume paramount importance. Most national leaders believe the citizenry must be educated to play its part in the emerging new order. The acceptance of a political formula that binds the periphery to the center and that transcends parochial loyalties is necessary for the creation of a national and participatory political culture. Similarly, the modification of long-standing attitudes toward work, wealth, and productivity is needed in order to achieve economic goals. In short, time-honored traditions having to do with language, religious beliefs, ideas of success, family organization, and much more have become legitimate objects of official concern. Official attempts to mobilize masses and to forge a national and progressive cultural system are thus another factor disrupting traditional Africa.

Many political programs seek to promote new ideas. Most political parties in Africa, for example, perform socialization as well as recruitment functions. Moreover, since the content of education and the communications media is often at least partly state controlled, these too are frequently vehicles for the articulation of deliberately chosen national values. Nevertheless, official attempts to manage social change do not necessarily mean that little of the old order will remain. Political leaders in Africa are fully aware that efforts to mobilize the populace will be more effective if couched in familiar images, comfortable idioms, and meaningful symbols. Therefore, by their very efforts to foster development, national leaders strengthen at least some aspects of tradition. Moreover, the survival of traditional norms is far more than an instrumental concern. It is an ardently desired social value that many nationalists earnestly pursue. Having struggled to preserve their cultural integrity during the colonial period, and living today in a world that frequently describes their countries as underdeveloped, the leaders of Africa seek for their peoples the dignity that comes with maintaining their own authentic cultural heritages. They share with a growing number of African intellectuals a preoccupation with the study of history and with the definition of their historic identity.

A quest for continuity, for the preservation of tradition, for new identities that do not neglect ancient loyalties lies at the heart of the social revolution engulfing Africa. Equally important, however, is the incorporation of new elements, including the most awesome of all, an institutionalized capacity for continual transformation. Reconciliation of the inevitable personal and political conflicts that arise from this clash of cultures continues to be one of Africa's greatest challenges.

THE THREE CASES

The chapters that follow tell the stories of three African societies, of greatly differing size and complexity, whose divergent histories have only recently become entangled. Yet the dilemmas of these peoples who are experiencing the effects of far reaching social and cultural change echo as familiar themes across the African continent and beyond into the Third World generally.

One case concerns the people of the Pare highlands of Tanzania, a relatively small-scale agricultural and herding society that had no overarching political organization prior to the colonial period. In broad terms, the people of Pare represent the so-called stateless societies of Africa which have been incorporated with varying degrees of success first into European colonial structures and more recently into the nation-states of independent Black Africa. Part Two of this book examines the responses of this egalitarian people, both collectively and individually, to a series of changes which have altered the basic patterns and symbols of their sociocultural identity.

By contrast, the Kanuri people of Bornu in northern Nigeria have had an encompassing political organization for centuries, with a kingdom which continues today, as in the past, as the dominant element in the area. In general terms, Bornu exemplifies the state-level societies of pre-colonial Africa. Part Three of this book focuses on the response of the Kanuri to changes in patterns of social mobility—changes that have undermined the institution of clientship, a primary *modus operandi* for individuals in this society for generations and a principal basis of their sociocultural identity.

Different from both Pare and Kanuri society is the nation of Tunisia, an historically well-known sociopolitical entity that achieved political independence from France in 1956. In its broad outlines, Tunisia typifies the newly independent nations of Africa. Part Four of this book analyzes responses of various Tunisian social classes to the change process. It suggests how the values and attitudes individuals hold are changing and affect, in turn, the culture and identity of the entire nation.

The three cases presented here offer the advantage of both national and subnational perspectives on changing Africa. In all three societies, there is pronounced individual and collective interest in preserving valued traditions as bases for contemporary and future identities. At the same time, however, there are increasing pressures for change from within and without. Thus a desire both to embrace the new and to preserve the old characterizes the people of Pare, Bornu, and Tunisia. The remainder of this chapter provides a brief background for the central issues of each case, setting the stage for the more detailed analyses in later chapters.

THE PARE

One of the most important aspects of nation building in Tanzania is gaining the support and loyalty of the country's more than twelve million people. Tanzanians speak more than one hundred different languages. Over 90 percent of them live in the rural hinterland and many of these are nonliterate. For generations, the bases of primary loyalty and social identification have been extended families, clans, "tribes," language groups, and other relatively small-scale communalities. Developing a single national identity among these culturally diverse peoples is no easy matter. At least two significant reconciliations must take place: first, the traditional enmity of many neighboring groups must be overcome and, second, the legacies of colonialism must be reconciled with the African heritage. Nevertheless, no goal is more important to the leaders of Tanzania than developing a common identity among the peoples who live within the borders of this new nation. Having recaptured their independence from Europe in 1961, the leaders are seeking to build this identity from the common African heritage of their people and on the premise that many of the problems they share can best be solved through collective action.

For the majority of Tanzania's peoples who continue to make their livings through farming, herding, fishing, or some combination thereof, the goals of the national leaders are filled with uncertainties. They often hear about *maendeleo* ("development") and *ujamaa* ("brotherhood") on the radio, from their children who have gone to school, through the newspapers they occasionally read, and at public meetings. But understanding the meaning of national political and economic goals is for many a slow and evolving process. Their leaders have proclaimed them "children of the country," citizens of Tanzania. Yet, many remember that among their fellow Tanzanians are peoples who were their most dreaded enemies only a few generations ago. The policies of *ujamaa* socialism, outlined by President Nyerere most dramatically in the Arusha Declaration of 1967, declare old-fashioned and out-of-date many long-standing customs. There has been a redistribution of surplus land, for example, over-turning traditional procedures for allocating and inheriting farming and grazing areas. Another significant policy is the relegation to secondary status of local vernaculars. The already widely known Swahili language has been elevated to the status of national and official language, becoming thereby an important symbol of Tanzanian identity. Local languages, by contrast, are prohibited in all public meetings, all government business, and in schools. But more than a few people are skeptical about the wisdom and value of overturning well-entrenched and familiar conventions. And the inertia of traditionalism and the friction generated by persons seeking to maintain the status quo sometimes impede the national leaders as they seek quick realization of their goals.

Part Two of this book is a study of the effects of social and political change on the collective identity of one of Tanzania's peoples, the Pare, who live in the northeastern part of the country. Multifaceted changes that began during the colonial era have brought about transformations in means of livelihood, material culture, life styles, social relations, and in the very bases of Pare identity. Only a generation or two ago, being Pare meant living in the highlands of the Pare Mountain Range, speaking the Pare language, and ordering the succession of the stages of one's life according to traditional rituals. But while these ideals of identity retain significance in the lives of many people, the funda-ments of Pare ethnicity have been shifting in recent years. More-over, the scope and rapidity of change have accelerated since independence as a result of the policies of the Tanzanian gov-ernment. Even those who dwell in the most remote pockets of the Pare mountains are keenly aware of the changing nature of their society—though they sometimes understand little about the genesis of the changes and are often passive in shaping their future. The contrast between indigenous and introduced is to be found in most parts of the culture, in a coexistence of old and new that is at times peaceful and at times uneasy.

People worry about the future of the life they have known and whether they will be secure in the world *maendeleo* is bringing. For some, change portends a happy liberation from the con-straints of tradition. For others, however, it undeniably means agony and intense personal suffering. The nature of their col-lective existence, the essence of their ethnic identity, cannot be set apart from the life styles of the individuals who make up the communities of highland Pare and from the beliefs held by these individuals. And as people learn new ways and ideas, the fate of Pare culture is inevitably questioned. Will the men who go to the city and will the children who go to school continue to speak the Pare language? Will the rituals that mark the transitions of life for Pare people pass out of existence? Will the land itself retain its significance and its centrality to those who learn about the outside world? These questions, because they ask about the classic fundaments of Pare identity, inevitably occur to those who pause from time to time to reflect on the issues of change in the broader perspective of the society as a whole. The differing perspectives of men and women, children and adults, the educated and the illiterate, the outmigrant and those who remain at home affect both the perception of the rate and the evaluation of the significance of the changes. To nation-builders in the capital who think in national terms, parochial identities and loyalties appear unprogressive and are believed to threaten national integration. To many of the old people of Pare, the conventions of their traditional society are familiar and valued; it is unthinkable that they should not resist changes in them. To many of the younger people, especially those with several years of formal schooling and experience outside Pare country, many of the changes are much too slow in coming. But whatever their position in the flux of social and cultural change, there are few Pare people indeed who do not seek some of both worlds. Solving this paradox is one of the greatest dilemmas they face in life.

The chapters dealing with the Pare will elaborate these issues. Chapter 2 examines the effects of the change process on the lives of a few Pares. Data in Chapter 3 on the locale of the study, the community of Usangi in the highlands of the North Pare mountains, lay the groundwork for an examination in Chapter 4 of the bases of Pare ethnic identity before the intensive changes brought by the colonial period. Chapter 5 probes the crises of identity brought on by decades of change, and Chapter 6 assesses the future of Pare ethnicity in a continually changing world.

THE KANURI

"To keep Nigeria one is a task that must be done." This slogan was the clarion call of the late 1960s, during the agonizingly long and bitter Nigerian civil war. Ultimately, in a formal political sense, unity was achieved with the ending of the war in January of 1970. But like most multicultural nations of Africa, while

Nigeria may be "one," it is certainly not homogeneous. Indeed, recognition of Nigeria's cultural diversity has long been fundamental to understanding her past, and we may expect it will continue to be important for anticipating her future. Today, though Nigerian leaders pursue the task of welding a strong, viable nation out of highly diverse cultural entities, most of these groups seek to maintain their separate ethnic identities. They do this not only to preserve links with their proud heritages, but also as a basis for meeting the social and economic challenges to which national leaders exhort them.

Part Three of this book is a study of efforts to balance pressures for continuity and change operating on the system of authority and status mobility that undergirds one of Nigeria's oldest political entities, the kingdom of Bornu in the northeastern corner of the country. The structuring of authority and the regulation of power relationships are at the heart of not only the political system in Bornu, but of all sectors of society. They provide the cultural, social, and psychological bases for individual mobility and they define the quality of life that is the essence of Bornu's collective identity.

For centuries, foreigners visiting what is today the northern part of Nigeria have been deeply impressed by the well-developed patterns of status and authority they found; and nowhere has this been more true than in the 1000-year-old kingdom of Bornu. European travelers who visited this Moslem state in the nineteenth century wrote vivid accounts of a mighty feudal-like empire supported by agriculture, trans-Saharan commerce, and a powerful army. By the twentieth century the power of the Kanuri king of Bornu had been eclipsed, first by a Sudanese invader-conqueror and then by a shift in patterns of long-distance trade away from the Sahara. Moreover, Britain took advantage of these circumstances and established colonial hegemony over the area. Nevertheless, the reigning king of Bornu is still viewed by his more than one-million Kanuri subjects as a vital spiritual leader, and power and pomp are still important motifs in this corner of Nigeria. Upon seeing row after row of brilliantly clad horsemen riding in celebration of the great Islamic festivals, Id-el Kabir and Id-el Fitr, one realizes that much of the grandeur of an earlier age survives in the present.

But much more than gallant horsemanship remains as a reminder of ancient Bornu. The very fabric of Kanuri society centers on an institution that has been of great importance in the past as

well as the present. This is the institution of clientship—a pattern of social relationships based on a premise of inequality. As the principal basis for social relationships and social mobility, it forms the core of the Kanuri authority structure. The institution of clientship gives to each man a place in society and, at the same time, a means to better his position. By having clients, a man commands valued resources. He has subordinates to do his bidding and to assist him in rendering service to others in return for their favors. By being a client, a man shares in the wealth and prestige of his patron. He may use these to further his own purposes and, perhaps, to begin to acquire clients of his own. Nevertheless, while the resulting hierarchy of superior-subordinate relationships is well established, the currents of change flowing across Africa are making their influence felt in Bornu and are challenging the traditional system of authority.

The Nigerian civil war cast into gaunt relief the disdain with which Kanuri traditions, along with those of other such kingdoms in northern Nigeria (e.g., the Hausa), are viewed in other parts of the country. And a particularly common target of criticism was the institution of clientship. Clientship is seen by many in southern Nigeria as a basis for social, political, and economic conservatism. Indeed, in the heat of the war, some influential southern politicians accused Bornu and the rest of the North of "sycophancy, deference support, and a pathological craving for praise." Such stereotypic views were greatly exaggerated during this tense period of Nigeria's history, but they nevertheless reflected a long-standing and continuing contempt in the South for many northern institutions. Moreover, such views were prompted not only by a belief that the feudal traditions of the North were out of date, but by more specific and practical issues as well. Many were then and are now convinced that Nigeria needs a populace of productive men, each contributing to the growth of the entire country, but that Hausa and Kanuri society are made up of cohorts of client-followers who blindly support their patron-benefactors in the hope of being rewarded with political office and a life of luxury. This hardly seems to be the way for a people to serve the national quest for progress, and in this context, the lagging pace of development in Bornu and other parts of northern Nigeria is no surprise to these critics. They view the proud Kanuri legacy and its continuing vigor as being purchased at the cost of lingering illiteracy and stunted economic growth.

People in Bornu have their own images, both of themselves and of their "progressive" critics. First, they do not consider themselves unprogressive. They point with pride to their efforts to modernize and expand the social services and economic institutions of the kingdom, and they express disappointment that their accomplishments are not more widely known and respected. Second, from the vantage of some in Bornu, an endemic problem in many parts of Nigeria outside the northern tier of states is over-ambition and a general lack of respect for authority. In their own society, persons who reject client relationships and who instead display an undue penchant for individualized ambition earn the pejorative epithet *yamgama bultu qai,* "he who is ambitious like a hyena."

Many in Bornu are also disturbed by the challenges to long-standing aspects of Kanuri identity emerging within Bornu itself. They are convinced that the number of "hyenas" in Bornu is on the rise. At a minimum, they know that a growing number of young men, especially the more educated among them, are explicit in their wish to avoid becoming involved in patron-client relationships. Young men say such a system abuses them; one who has been to school ought to be able to find better ways to achieve security and status. Moreover, the growing and increasingly cosmopolitan towns of Bornu offer an enticing array of new, emancipating opportunities where clientship is often not a prerequisite for success.

It remains to be seen whether the traditional Kanuri clientship system will be able to perpetuate itself in the face of mounting criticism inside and outside Bornu. But it is certainly too early to record its demise. Even the young people who reject clientship are aware that the old system is still well established. They know that many of their peers continue to utilize the system in pursuit of status and other goals, and therefore, in spite of their own skepticism, it is an open question as to whether they will be able to reject completely the older ideals. If they are able to do so, however, and if they grow in number, there may be a dramatic transformation and redefinition of the bases of ethnicity and identity in Bornu. Thus, the chapters in this volume dealing with Bornu ask about the future of the traditional system of clientship. Following an introduction, in Chapter 7, to some basic themes in Kanuri culture, the social and historical context and symbols of Kanuri identity are outlined in Chapter 8. Chapter 9 illustrates the way clientship and superior-subordinate relationships pervade Kanuri society, providing a basis for individual mobility and a

foundation for collective identity. Chapter 10 then examines contemporary Kanuri attitudes toward clientship, occupational prestige, and achievement in order to provide a basis for discussing,
in Chapter 11, the economic, political, and cultural future of Bornu.

THE TUNISIANS

In February of 1960, Tunisia's President, Habib Bourguiba,
shocked his countrymen by drinking a glass of orange juice in
public during the daylight hours of Ramadan. Bourguiba's ges-
ture launched a national campaign against the traditional observance of this Moslem month during which believers must
neither eat nor drink from sunrise to sunset. As the President
broke the fast, he told the nation that a rupture with tradition
was necessary to overcome stagnation and weakness. He observed
that the productivity of most who fasted was greatly reduced and
that the country could ill afford to throw away the gains of eleven
hard months in an annual ritual of slothful days and indulgent
nights. Announcing that government offices and schools would
no longer conform to the special schedules usually in effect
during the month of Ramadan, the President declared that Tunisia
was engaged in a war against poverty. Soldiers, he asserted,
cannot do battle on an empty stomach.

Many defended Bourguiba's action. They argued that the traditional observance of Ramadan was simply not compatible with the
needs of a modern nation. But others were dismayed that the
President of a Moslem nation should so blatantly defile the teachings of the religion. They recalled that only a few years before,
Bourguiba and other nationalists had opposed the French in the
name of Islam. Bourguiba himself organized demonstrations when
colonial officials attempted to suppress Moslem institutions, and
the party he helped to found held meetings in mosques and
called upon people to pray five times a day for national martyrs.
Indeed, the constitution written at independence formally rejected
Western secularism and proclaimed Islam the religion of state.
How then could Bourguiba ask the Tunisian people to suspend
observance of one of the five basic pillars of Islam? Was it not a
defense and a rejuvenation of Tunisia's Moslem personality that
the nationalist revolution had been all about?

Organized opposition to Bourguiba's program began almost
immediately. The rector of the Islamic university of Tunis and
the Grand Mufti of Tunis both publicly condemned the attack

upon Ramadan. Religious leaders in the holy city of Kairouan, as well as other interior towns, expressed displeasure in a more novel way. Rejecting Bourguiba's scientific determination of the lunar month in favor of the Cairo calendar, they began and ended the Ramadan fast one day later than the rest of the country. Early in 1961, popular opposition culminated with mass rioting in Kairouan. An angry crowd, shouting "Allah is great, He will not depart," converged on the house of the regional governor, burning cars and entering the residence. Eight persons were killed and it took twenty-four hours to quell the rioting (Moore 1965:59).

Each side in the Ramadan controversy was able to offer convincing arguments in support of its position; and that, in fact, is Tunisia's problem. Bourguiba made a good case when he argued that Ramadan and other aspects of Islam impede the construction of an economic and social system appropriate to the needs of a modern nation. Many conservatives acknowledge this. But the President's critics struck an equally responsive chord by retorting that economic development has historically been an instrumental goal in the Arabo-Moslem world, sought in order that the community of believers might better defend its ancient civilization from the challenge of the infidel. The thought that sacred traditions might be sacrificed for material gain has long been inadmissible. Bourguiba himself acknowledges that the country must find a way to discredit outmoded beliefs without rejecting the classical legacy of Arabism and Islam.

The Ramadan controversy illustrates a more general Tunisian problem. The nation needs and desires both a movement away from sacred traditions—a rupture with the past for the sake of social and economic development, and a renewed interest in those traditions—a reaffirmation of the past for the sake of dignity and symbolic fulfillment. In its totality, of course, traditional culture is not confronted with so impossible a fate. Some aspects undoubtedly will remain inviolable because of their special significance in the quest for dignity and identity. Others will have to be disavowed because they intolerably threaten more temporal objectives. But, like the observance of Ramadan, many traditional normative patterns are centrally linked to both the temporal and the metaphysical goals of the nationalist revolution, to both the rational and the romantic elements of the society's own definition of the good life. They are thus at the center of a poignant national controversy and their future is the subject of Part Four of this book.

Tunisian ambivalence about the future of traditional culture is evident in a number of important areas. The nation finds itself rationally compelled to reject time-honored social codes relating not only to religion but also to women's rights, child-rearing, professional life, and language. A change in the traditionally inferior status of women is necessary if the labor force is to be expanded, if the home is to be run by an educated woman, and if there is to be a general lessening of the individual authoritarianism that stifles initiative and ingenuity. Liberalization of traditional child-rearing practices is necessary for the same reasons. Long-standing attitudes toward work must be modified if workers are to be induced to enter vital professions and to work harder and more productively. And the use of French as a national vehicular language is necessary, for the present at least, because Arabic is plagued by structural difficulties and because educated Tunisians have been trained to do their best work in the colonial language. Nevertheless, such a broad range of normative traditions cannot be substantially modified unless individuals are prepared to alter fundamentally their own identity and that of their society; and this many are unwilling to do. Tunisians did not oppose colonialism only to accept now its doctrine of the inferiority of Tunisian culture. There is widespread agreement that the quest for material progress must not be permitted to bring about the reorganization of society along purely European lines.

The need to balance material and spiritual needs is not a dilemma for elites and politicians alone. In the decade and a half since independence, the percentage of literate Tunisians has jumped from less than 15 to more than 40 percent, and students continue to pour out of the nation's schools by the hundreds of thousands. The Destourian Socialist Party is also spearheading a vigorous assault on ignorance and apathy. More than 1200 territorial and professional party cells meet regularly to discuss the problems of the nation. Thus, as a nation, Tunisia is rapidly passing from a traditional to a modern political culture, characterized by high rates of citizen concern and citizen participation in the affairs of state. But the mobilization of Tunisia's population has not mitigated the cultural dilemma before the nation. It has, if anything, increased the scope and intensity of the national debate over the future of traditional norms and values.

The chapters focusing on Tunisia will explore the implications of this debate, beginning with an examination in Chapter 12 of the cultural attitudes of four young Tunisians. The review of major themes in Tunisian history in Chapter 13 lays the foundation for an examination, in Chapter 14, of five key cultural issues: language, religion, women's rights, patterns of child-rearing, and professional life. Chapter 15 presents survey data on the attitudes of middle- and lower-middle class Tunisians toward these issues, and Chapter 16 utilizes these data to make projections about the future of Tunisia's traditional normative inner order.

The chapters that follow examine the future of traditional identities in three changing African societies. Despite differences between them, the traditions of each society are being called into question by the same kinds of planned and unplanned agents of change, and all three are experiencing similar tensions and dilemmas as a result. This book is about the response of these societies to changing conditions. In presenting and discussing each case in the subsequent parts of this book, a common format has been employed. First, a series of incidents or biographies introduces the dominant concerns of the people in each society. Second, relevant social, cultural, and historical data about the setting of each study are provided. The third and fourth chapters dealing with each case introduce and analyze key issues of the society's collective identity. The final chapter in each part comments on the future of traditional culture and asks whether age-old identities will survive Africa's social revolution. At the conclusion of the third case, a final chapter (Part Five) discusses common themes that emerge from the cases and considers the Pare, Kanuri, and Tunisians in the larger perspective of socio-cultural change in Africa.

PART TWO

The Pare
of Tanzania

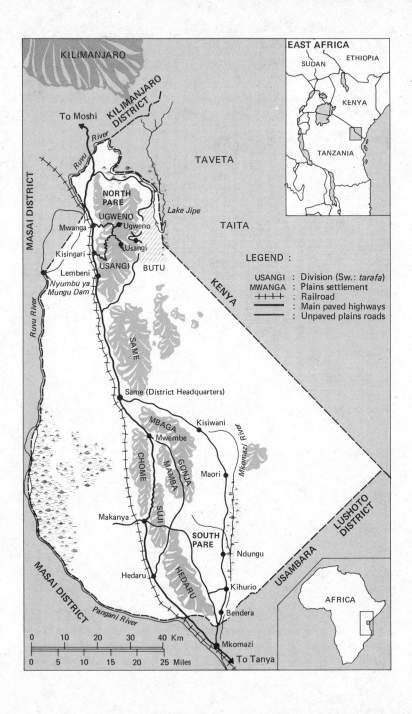

KILIMANJARO

To Moshi

KILIMANJARO DISTRICT

Ruvu River

MASAI DISTRICT

TAVETA

NORTH PARE

UGWENO
Ugweno

Mwanga

Usangi

Kisingari

USANGI   BUTU

Lembeni
Nyumbu ya
Mungu Dam

Lake Jipe

TAITA

KENYA

Ruvu River

SAME

Same (District Headquarters)

MBAGA
Mwembe

Kisiwani

CHOME

MANBA

GONJA

Mkomazi River

Maori

Makanya

SUJI

SOUTH PARE

Ndungu

HEDARU

Hedaru

Kihurio

LUSHOTO DISTRICT

USAMBARA

Bendera

MASAI DISTRICT

Pangani River

Mkomazi

To Tanya

EAST AFRICA

SUDAN   ETHIOPIA

KENYA

TANZANIA

LEGEND :

USANGI : Division (Sw.: tarafa)
MWANGA : Plains settlement
++++ : Railroad
──── : Main paved highways
──── : Unpaved plains roads

AFRICA

| 0 | 10 | 20 | 30 | 40 Km |
| 0 | 5 | 10 | 15 | 20 | 25 Miles |

2

The Human Dimension in
Social and Cultural Change

Karim opened the brown envelope carefully. He was a bit disappointed that it was not larger. A correspondence course of ten lessons on "Upgrading Your English" had cost him almost a month's wages and he had high expectations. Karim had stopped his schooling after seven years. Although he had wanted desperately to be one of those fortunate few who manage to pass into secondary school, he had not been chosen. Karim's father had died when he was young. Being the oldest son, he felt a special responsibility to share his wages with his mother and to help pay the primary school fees of his two younger brothers and a sister. Karim had left home, a remote mountain village, to look for a job in a nearby city. He had hoped to find work as a clerk in a government office, perhaps in the post office, but all he was able to find was a job as houseboy to a family of Asian shopkeepers. Karim did not like the work, but he washed their clothes, cleaned their house, and went to market for them without complaining. There were others from his village who couldn't even find jobs as houseboys. Finally, he had saved enough money to order the correspondence course. After English, he planned to do courses in bookkeeping and practical mathematics. Perhaps then he could get a clerical job.

Karim sat in the small, sparsely furnished room he shared with two relatives from his village who worked in the same city. It was not as good as he had hoped, but he didn't like spending money on rent. He pondered over the instructions and looked at the English sentences he was to examine and correct. It was not an easy lesson, but he was determined to master it. Karim had grown up speaking the Pare language. When he entered school, he began to learn Swahili. His native language is spoken by less than 200,000 people and there are virtually no books published in it. Swahili had not been difficult for him. It was, in fact, very similar to the Pare language. During the third year at school, he began to learn English. At that time, Tanganyika was still a British territory and if he were to go on to secondary school, he would have to know English. But his five years of English had ill prepared him to cope with the first lesson of his course.

He was asked to explain what was wrong with the sentence, "A grate fire was roaring in the grate," and with another that read "Her hands were blew from the cold." Karim knew that "blew" was a verb and thus he wrote that it was "out of place in the sentence." The other sentence had stumped him. Although he recognized *great,* he had never seen *grate* before. He wrote in his best English in the space provided: "This sentence obviously does not make sense. It should be 'A great fire was roaring.' "

He puzzled through the remaining eighteen sentences and mailed the first lesson back to the correspondence college the next day. He had checked the mail every day afterwards, but it was over two weeks before the corrections and the next lesson reached him. Karim took the letter to his room and carefully opened it there. He read the reader's comments:

You must be more careful in your lessons. I suggest you consult an English dictionary for the meaning of such words as "grate." Had you understood its meaning, you would have easily seen the errors in Sentence No. 1. . . .

And so it went. Karim read the comments sadly. Of the twenty sentences, he had got only three correct. The explanations of his mistakes were disheartening. Soon his humiliation turned to bitterness. He read the comments again and thought to himself: "After all, this isn't England. How was I supposed to know that the white hands of the English turn *blue* when it's cold?"

Karim's frustrations are shared by many Africans who view many of the social and cultural changes that have taken place in their societies as European cultural imperialism. His entire schooling had been largely insensitive to local conditions. He had been taught mostly about Europe and European ideas. And the view of Africa he got in school was that of discovery and improvement by Europeans. In his own life, Karim is perhaps powerless to overcome the passivity he continually feels. But he is not alone in his helplessness, for a great many Africans are seeking to overcome this passivity in the change process. It is not change that they resist, but denigrating change. Even the most ardent of African nationalists, like Tanzania's Julius Nyerere, argue for the adoption of certain foreign ways. But such changes, they argue, need not mean abandoning all tradition. What must be achieved is a synthesis—the best of both worlds—the good things from indigenous and foreign cultures. And in making the choices about what is desirable, Africans themselves want the right to make the decisions.

Sometimes the choices that must be made are simple and the decisions are easy. Few Africans, for example, deny the greater utility of hoes over digging sticks, of automobiles and bicycles over walking, and of piped water over carried water. But many decisions are not so simple and individuals are consequently faced with having to make difficult and trying choices. The following story of Yonaza illustrates one such conflict-ridden situation.

One night during the evening meal, Yonaza complained to his wife about the unusual amount of grit in the food. As the bottom of the dish from which they ate came into view, he discovered large fragments of glass. Apprehensively, Yonaza examined the stores of food for clues as to the source. To his horror, he found glass in most of the food supplies, including the salt and sugar, the tea leaves, and even in the powdered milk they used for the baby. There could be no question—someone had tried to poison him and the ten or so members of his household.

When Yonaza considered the evidence, it seemed that only a member of his household could have had liberal enough access to the supplies to have done it. "But how could that be," Yonaza asked himself, "for have we not all eaten the poisoned food?" He queried each person in turn but no one would admit having done it. The old man, who had been a church member for years, decided to ask God to reveal the culprit. The members of his household fell to their knees as he began to pray. Before long one of the boys, who was about fifteen years old, spoke up claiming to have poisoned the food. Yonaza pressed the boy to reveal his motives, but to no avail.

The entire household, the boy included, set out for the local medical facility a mile or so away. That night the medical assistant examined them, prescribed preliminary treatment, and asked the family to return the next day for further examination.

Early the next morning, a crowd of about two hundred people assembled at the local dispensary. This was clearly a serious matter, for such large crowds are rare in the highlands. The medical assistant was preparing to send the family to a hospital for more extensive examinations when the boy, who had been quiet and subdued to that point, rushed out from one of the rooms. The crowd parted as he moved into its midst, swinging above his head a pillow case containing a few heavy objects. He stood alone and yelled garbled phrases which no one seemed to understand. Several men lurched at him and eventually pinned him to the ground while the medical assistant prepared and administered a sedative. In moments, the boy was again subdued.

The family was taken to a hospital some twenty miles distant where they were placed under observation. A few days later, when it had been determined that the finely ground glass had caused no apparent internal injuries, all were allowed to return home except for the boy who was taken by police to await trial at district headquarters. Some weeks later, he was brought to trial and given a sentence of a few years in jail.

The motives which lay behind the boy's actions became the subject of great speculation. At length, a single interpretation of the facts gained wide acceptance in the community. The boy, it turned out, was not the biological son of the old man, Yonaza. Rather, he was the son of Yonaza's deceased brother, who, along with his siblings, had come to live in the old man's household following their father's death. Were it not for the fact that the boy's mother was missing from the household, such an arrangement would have been in perfect accord with local customs. To have followed tradition precisely, Yonaza should have inherited his brother's wife as well as his brother's children. He had, however, refused to inherit the widow on the grounds that his church prohibits polygamy and to have done so would have resulted in his excommunication. Many people took the fact that the boy had himself eaten poisoned food to indicate that spirit possession was involved, since, they argued, no sane person would do so of his own volition. The boy's mother, it was said, had, in her anger at being returned to her family instead of being inherited, bewitched the boy and caused him to attempt to kill her husband's brother and his family.

Although the particulars of this case are extraordinary, Yonaza himself is typical of the many individuals in changing African societies who find themselves caught in a cross fire of conflicting demands stemming from their various loyalties. In his particular case, the conflict came between the church and the traditions of his people. Since Yonaza could not both inherit the widow and remain in the church, there was no way out of making a choice. Having to select among a wide range of identities and modes of action is by no means limited to the area of life crisis events such as marriage and widow inheritance. Similar choices must be made by Yonaza and others like him in many areas of life.

Social and cultural transformation, because all aspects of a system do not change in synchrony, produces dislocations and conflicts. Individuals who live in the midst of change must develop ways to cope with the inevitable conflicts if their lives are not to be consumed and destroyed by the change process. A common way of dealing with such conflicts is maintaining a stance of compartmentalizing one's thoughts and actions. Keeping each thing in its proper place, and not trying to resolve all the conflicts, is proving to be a successful *modus vivendi* for many Africans in adapting to the contemporary world, a mode which works reasonably well when connections among the many spheres in which individuals operate are maintained and when movement among them is possible.

Issa managed reasonably well in keeping his several worlds apart from one another. His job as a clerk in a large government hospital was not much like the life he had known as a child growing up back in the highlands of Pare. Issa liked his job, for it provided him with the cash income which he needed to support his wife and three small children who alternated seasonally between residing in the house he had built for them in Pare and the two rented rooms he occupied in the city where he worked. Issa tried to save as much of his salary as he could in hopes that he would be able to return permanently to the highlands some day.

Issa had been a sickly child. Recently, his attacks of asthma had returned. Moreover, at the hospital where he works, the pains in his side were diagnosed as a liver infection and were becoming increasingly worse despite the medication that he had been given. In addition to the pains and the wheezing, Issa was occasionally affected by the loss of his normal personality.[1] Sometimes he would cry out in the night that he was dying. But by daybreak he usually had recovered his senses. Physically, his condition worsened. Finally he stopped taking the medicines he had been given by the doctor since they seemed to do him no good.

[1]This was described in Swahili as *akili yake iliruka*, meaning "his mind flew away."

Issa became more convinced that his end was near. He began to leave his work for a day or two at a time to return to Pare to be treated with traditional medicines. But none of these helped him either.

Since the attacks were more severe in nonworking hours, Issa managed to keep his job at the hospital. Having tried both hospital and traditional medicines, he engaged the services of a Pare diviner. This doctor, before Issa and his assembled relatives, performed an elaborate and dramatic divination replete with the stabbing of live goats through their hearts and a ritual eating of the charred flesh of the sacrificial animal by all those present. At length, the diviner announced the results of his divination to Issa and his relatives. Issa's problems were said to result from a debt which his mother had incurred while Issa was still in her womb. She had owed a few shillings to a Masai, but since he was a foreigner, she had been reluctant to pay him. The man had cast his spell over her, causing a genie to enter her body. The genie settled in the fetus, unknown to the mother, and was continuing to cause Issa trouble. Both mother and son were given advice on how to oust the genie. They did as they were told, but Issa's relief was only temporary.

Issa's family spent a great deal of money on the traditional curing. The divination was costly—involving the slaughter of several animals, the preparation of large quantities of beer, and cash fees for the diviner. Issa was in some respects luckier than many of his fellows who live in the highlands, for he and his family could afford the expense of traditional curing rituals. Nowadays, many poor people are limited to the use of hospital medicines, since they are free. Issa, who was well acquainted with the ways of the hospital, much preferred the less-impersonal traditional curing practices. He especially liked having his kinsmen show concern for him by helping pay the cost of the divination and participating in it.

When I interviewed Issa, we talked about his illness. I discovered that he saw no conflict in his own life between the two curing systems. As a Westener, I had been thinking of the hospital as waging an ongoing battle with traditional medicines. Issa tried to set me straight. It was not a case of either/or.To him, each was valid and had its own domain. Issa explained that the hospital was most useful for certain kinds of ailments, especially cuts, sores, bruises, prenatal and maternity visits, sick children, and so on. For the more diffuse and harder to treat conditions, he preferred traditional medicines. Sometimes, he claimed, he would try one and then the other.

Compartmentalization, as noted earlier, works well when the paths of movement between the various spheres of action are kept open. It is not, however, always the case that such channels are kept open as they are in Issa's case.

The kind of sociocultural changes that have been going on in Africa are wide in scale and are not limited to just one or even a few areas of life. Changes in one aspect of the system are often out of step with changes in others. This discoordination can produce serious problems of adjustment at both societal and individual levels. Shortly after I arrived in Pare country, I found my own life agonizingly entangled with that of a man who found it impossible to maintain the compartmentalization he so desperately wanted.

It was a moonless night, and I was working at my writing table. Already, I had grown accustomed to the voices of people passing in the night. My house had no window panes, only shutters, and I seldom had occasion to see the moving figures or the lights of the passersby. For some reason on that particular evening, the voice I heard alarmed me. I stopped writing and moved near the door to listen. As the voice grew closer, I realized that I was hearing English rather than either Swahili or the Pare language. I listened silently as the speaker grew closer to my house. The words I could make out from the repeated phrases made me shiver in the coldness of the mountain's crisp night air.

"Some people think I am crazy," the voice said, "but they are not right." Then, in the dark, the speaker arrived at my door. Had it not been for the words he spoke next, I would have felt that I was listening to a Shakespearean actor in soliloquy. As he spoke I was snatched back from my anachronistic musings to the time and place where I stood at that moment. The voice cried out, each phrase reverberating in the air. "Not for a second," he paused. "Not for a minute," he paused again. "Nor for an hour will I ever understand." He spoke as though he knew I stood behind the unopened door. "Tell me, *Mzungu*,[2] why the American government sends guns to kill the Vietnamese but won't send tractors to help the Tanzanians?"

I have no idea how long a clock would have measured the silence that followed. I recognized the voice as belonging to

[2]The Swahili term for European or "white man."

Elia, the son of the old man who lived near me. I was shocked by what I had heard, and impotent to answer. I never moved to open the door. What could I say? I stood there a long time wondering how he expected me to respond or whether he expected any response at all.

As he moved on toward his house, his voice faded away in the dark. Still I hardly slept that night. The next morning I learned that many people think Elia is crazy.[3] I was told he spends whatever money he has in the local bars. He had probably been returning from one of them when I heard him. Others told me that Elia is nearly forty and still lives with his parents since he has never married. Most days he has so little money he has to beg others for the cigarettes he smokes.

I found that Elia had not always been this way. For several years he had worked in Nairobi as a driver, which explained his knowledge of spoken English. He had come home after losing his position in the reforms that followed Kenyan Independence. He had been unable to find a job back in Tanzania. So he did the inevitable—he returned to his childhood home and took up farming. Shortly after that, Elia's spells of madness began. People said he is given to doing unusual things and to speaking unintelligibly. His father once arranged through local government officials and the community medical facility to send Elia to a mental hospital, where he spent a year or so. People said he had been better for a while, but when I knew Elia his spells of madness had returned.

The social factors that precipitated Elia's difficulties are easy to understand: he had moved from a traditional childhood in a rural farming community into a semimodern role in the city; he had become accustomed to urban life and to a certain style of living; then, suddenly, he lost his job—through no apparent personal fault except that he was a foreigner—and could not find another one. He was reduced in the end to returning home to his father, to giving up the style of life to which he had become accustomed in the city, and to resuming a life of farming. When I knew him, Elia was having difficulties readjusting to the humdrum of a rural existence and to being very poor. He escaped whenever he could—sometimes through drink, when he could afford it; other times psychically. Although Elia had demonstrated

---

[3]The Swahili term *kichaa* was used, for which the Johnson Swahili-English dictionary offers these English equivalents: craziness, lunacy, madness.

a concern that extended beyond himself to the problems of mankind, he was himself a casualty of a wide-scale human process. Change had prepared him for a different kind of existence, had allowed him to live it for a while, but would no longer permit him to do so. His simple aspiration of finding a job as a driver proved to be too difficult for the system to satisfy and Elia's identity faced crisis.

Sociocultural changes raise inevitable questions about traditional identities and their relevance in altered environments. In many parts of the African continent, uniformities in the patterns of change can be discerned. Traditional religions of small scale are giving way to membership in Christian and Islamic sects, which in turn become new bases of loyalty which crosscut traditional ethnic, language, and even national boundaries. The once relatively standardized life cycles of many African societies are giving way to a myriad of new careers, which share only a few similarities with one another. Migration to urban areas, even if only for short periods of time, has itself made Africans more aware of the cultural differences among them. Within any particular society, the absolutes and givens of yesterday are today's variables. For individuals and for societies, such changes often precipitate crises of identity. It is to the study of this crisis of identity that these chapters dealing with the Pare highlanders of Tanzania are devoted. In Chapter 3, the historical, cultural, and geographical setting for the study will be examined. In Chapter 4, the significance of ritual, land, and language, the basic symbols of the ethnic identity of the Pare people will be probed. In Chapter 5, the ambiguities that the contemporary world has produced in these bases of ethnic identity are examined as a basis for considering, in Chapter 6, the future of Pare ethnicity.

3

The Usangi Highlands

Pare District (also known as Same District after the name of the village which serves as its headquarters) is diverse in both land forms and culture. The mountains that form the core of the district rise forbiddingly from a dusty plain for nearly one hundred miles along Tanzania's northeastern border. This narrow, broken range is an impressive land form in its own right. Yet it continually suffers invidious comparison with Mt. Kilimanjaro, whose more spectacular peaks lie perpetually snow-capped only a few miles to the northwest in equatorial East Africa. A plain surrounds the mountains on all sides and forms the peripheries of the district. Ordinarily arid, the plain is not generally suited to agriculture except in the few regions that have water from either mountain streams or irrigation devices. The plain provides instead a vast open space where farmers can herd their livestock. From the plain, the upper slopes and high plateaus of the Pare Mountains give little indication that they are indeed more lush and fertile and are home to more than one hundred thousand people.[1]

This study focuses on Usangi, one of six administrative divisions within the district. Located in the North Pare Mountains, Usangi is considered throughout the district to be the most changed and developed sector. Let us consider the factors that have combined to give it this quality.

---

[1]Preliminary figures for Same (Pare) District, Kilimanjaro Region, from the August, 1967, population census showed the district population to be 149,732 (Central Statistical Bureau 1967:22). No breakdown is given by tribe or language group; nor is it possible to separate the residents of the highlands from the plains settlements on the basis of published data. Pare District covers an area of about 3,050 square miles with an estimated population density of 49.1 per square mile in 1967 (Central Statistical Bureau 1967:9). Such a figure, however, does not adequately represent the differences between the often overpopulated highlands and the almost barren plains.

HISTORY

Usangi's oral traditions[2] include accounts of how the ancestors of the present inhabitants began migrating into the area many centuries ago. Oral traditions and archaeological evidence suggest that this movement, which eventually resulted in the replacement of an earlier Bushmanoid hunting-and-gathering population by Bantu-speaking agriculturalists, had certainly begun by the thirteenth century A.D. and quite possibly several centuries earlier (Kimambo 1969a:39). Immigrants came from the Taita Hills to the north in what is now Kenya and from nearby Kilimanjaro, Usambara, and the Nguu Mountains in present-day Tanzania. Highland communities increased in size through the continual incorporation of newcomers, a process that has continued even into the nineteenth and twentieth centuries.

The two major divisions of the highlands, today known as North and South Pare, reflect the history of the Pare range. In the middle of the eighteenth century, North and South Pare appear to have been separate linguistic communities with Gweno[3] being spoken throughout the North and Asu being the language of South Pare. Kinship connected certain clans in the two areas, but there were few significant political, economic, or ritual linkages between North and South. By the eighteenth century, North Pare had developed a complex political organization with its center in Ugweno. In the South, only small-scale political organizations had evolved and the connections among them were cultural and linguistic rather than political.

During the final years of the eighteenth century, the Gweno chiefdom began to lose effective control over its southernmost district, Usangi. To break out from the hegemony of Gweno rulers, the people of Usangi solicited the aid of certain Asu-speakers from South Pare. The success of the revolt resulted in the Asu allies being given land lying in the buffer zone between Ugweno and the newly independent Usangi. This strategic placement of the Asu-speakers from the South between Usangi and Ugweno insulated the residents of Usangi from interaction with other northerners. The incorporation of the southern allies into Usangi

[2]Kimambo's articles and books listed in the bibliography contain his published works on Pare history.
[3]For the convenience of English readers, Bantu language prefixes have been dropped. *Gweno* is thus an abbreviated form of *Kigweno* as *Asu* is an abbreviated form of *Chasu*.

brought significant changes: Asu either became or was reestablished as the first language of all the Usangi people after a few generations,[4] and members of indigenous and immigrant clans married one another. Real amalgamation of the two societies, however, was blocked by the fact that the immigrants were denied permission to participate in the male initiation rites and were required instead to return to the South to do so.

During the nineteenth century, the North continued to fragment politically. The once-strong Gweno chiefdom grew weaker, giving rise to a number of small, autonomous political units. Political fragmentation also occurred in South Pare. In both cases, the coming of Arab and Swahili caravans in the nineteenth century appears to have been a primary factor in the demise of the eighteenth-century political systems. In order to participate in the caravan trade, many district rulers and village headmen ignored the traditional authority systems and dealt independently with the traders. The result by the final decades of the nineteenth century was a series of petty chiefdoms spread throughout the Pare Mountains area (Kimambo 1968:25–31).

When the Germans arrived in the late 1800s, they found no large-scale political organizations in Pare. In their efforts to bring the area under colonial administration, the Germans attempted to identify local leaders and give them official certification. In Pare, a very large number of people were given certification as indigenous rulers, including many of the trading entrepreneurs of previous years. This reached its extreme when a certificate was issued to one man who claimed only five subjects (Kimambo 1968:33). The Germans dealt with the local rulers through middlemen known as *akidas,* who were not usually of the groups they ruled. The akidas had certain magisterial powers and were responsible to the Germans for the maintenance of law and order and the collection of taxes in the areas under their jurisdiction. They were aided by locally appointed headmen, called *jumbes.*

The British assumed responsibility for Tanganyika Territory in 1918 under a League of Nations mandate. Because cultural and

---

[4]Kimambo has argued in his history of Pare that the North and South were separate linguistic communities prior to the eighteenth century. Some of my informants, however, claim that Ugweno's influence over Usangi was relatively short lived and that prior to the attempt to incorporate Usangi into the Gweno state, Asu had been the language of Usangi. The recapturing of their independence from Ugweno resulted in the reinstatement in Usangi of Asu as the only language of importance.

linguistic similarities in North and South Pare seemed to suggest a natural ethnic group, Pare District was created in 1928 to facilitate indirect rule through indigenous authorities. The Germans had, it will be recalled, "created" many chiefdoms through their attempts to identify local leaders. The extension of indirect-rule policies by the British to Tanganyika had the effect in Pare, as in many other societies, of enlarging and strengthening otherwise small spheres of influence and in some cases stimulating the development of structure where there had been little before. On several occasions during their colonial administration which ended in 1961, the British attempted to reshuffle boundaries and to amalgamate some of the chiefdoms that had been recognized by the Germans. These recombinations laid the groundwork for the six administrative divisions that exist in Pare District today.

Tanganyika became an independent nation in 1961. Two years later, President Julius Nyerere effected a merger of his country with the island of Zanzibar, giving the name Tanzania to the union. Shortly after independence, traditional chiefs were abolished throughout the country. Today's governmental institutions in Pare District are local-level components of the national political infrastructure. Pare District, one of sixty units of local-government administration, is headed by an area commissioner who serves both as head of local government and secretary of the political party in the district. Below him are six administrative divisions and a number of party branches. The boundaries of the divisions within Pare District often follow lines of agreement reached during the colonial period. North Pare's two divisions are Ugweno and Usangi. In South Pare, four districts were formed through amalgamations of many of the petty chiefdoms that arose in earlier years.

LIVELIHOOD

In the Usangi highlands, as elsewhere in the mountains of the district, hoe cultivation is the primary subsistence activity. Most families have garden plots at several different elevations, thereby taking advantage of differences in rainfall, climate, and growing conditions and providing insurance against localized crop failure. In addition to a cow or two kept in highland homesteads for milking, those families that own large herds of livestock typically herd them on the lower plains. Often, several families cooperate in the herding ventures by pooling their animals and each in turn taking the responsibilities for overseeing the welfare of the animals. Farming and herding are both important parts of the Pare means of livelihood. Farming is considered by the large majority to be their ancient and honored way of life, preferable to alternatives that have presented themselves in recent decades. Herding is also an important part of Pare subsistence activities. Cattle, sheep, and goats enter traditional rituals and sacrifices, are important stores of wealth, and continue to be essential parts of the bridewealth. During the colonial period, two factors combined to upset the traditional patterns of livelihood. First, population pressure on the land in the Usangi highlands increased, and second, the colonial government levied taxes. These two factors in combination brought about significant changes in the ways in which Usangi people make their livings.

There are a number of indicators that point out the nature of the land-scarcity problem in Usangi. First, the Pare system of land use requires a father to divide his farming lands among his sons so that each has enough to support himself and his dependents. The youngest child of each wife is expected to accept the responsibility of caring for his mother after the father's death, and consequently it is he who inherits her house and any gardens she may own at the time she dies. Otherwise, all children are due equivalent amounts of farm land. Ideally, a father gives his sons their initial plots. Theoretically thereafter, farms may be increased by cutting virgin lands and by obtaining plots from agnatic or uterine kin, from affines, or even from nonrelatives. For many years now, land has been in such short supply in Usangi that some men are unable to obtain usage rights to enough land through any or even all of these means.

Throughout Pare country, people claim that they once kept large numbers of cattle in the highlands. The fact that intertribal raiding for livestock is unknown today means that animals can be herded on the adjacent plains. Nevertheless, a few cattle continue to be kept in most highland homesteads for milking. The typical way such milch cows are kept in Usangi differs from other parts of the district. In Usangi, where grazing land is almost unknown, cows are kept inside and grasses are brought to them. In contrast, in many parts of South Pare, a man can keep a few cattle in the highlands (though never a large herd) and still expect to pasture them near his house. This difference points again to the relative scarcity of land in Usangi when compared to other parts of the district.

In considering Usangi's land scarcity, it should be emphasized that the crisis is not only one of absolute scarcity in the sense that the present population exceeds the carrying capacity of the land given the current technology, but it is also a crisis brought on by inequities in the present distribution of land among those who live in the area. Unused pieces of land do exist in Usangi. Yet would-be users are told that the plots are earmarked for sons and brothers who will soon begin to build houses on them. In other cases, residents who have relatively large amounts of land, but who also see that they or their kinsmen will surely need it in the future, often plant long-term crops like coffee and then tend it poorly or hardly at all. Such practices indicate the crisis is both a shortage in general and an inequitable distribution of what land there is.[5]

Taxation of colonized peoples was employed all over Africa not only to finance colonial governments but also to induce Africans to give up traditional subsistence activities and to turn instead to wage-employment in European-owned enterprises. The labor force had to be created if the country was to develop according to the plans of the colonists. And Africans had to be induced into the money economy. The people of Usangi, because of their problems at home, were particularly susceptible and many were quick to take up the alternatives that the colonial economy provided for them. One alternative was to undertake cash-earning activities at home. The other, and more common, was to look outside for ways to earn the needed cash.

In Usangi, some people took up cash cropping, primarily coffee. But the relatively high population pressure left little land for such enterprises in North Pare. In South Pare, where land was more plentiful, cash cropping was, and continues to be, a more viable alternative for the majority of the population. On the plains surrounding the North Pare mountains, cereal crops are grown for sale in those areas where there is sufficient water. Cash crops are usually sold through cooperative societies to the marketing board rather than on an individual basis by those who produce them. Government officers and the mass media are encouraging Tanzanians to grow more crops in the 1970s, but land is too scarce to allow for much expansion in Usangi. Both eastern

---

[5]In 1969, the national government set up a land tribunal to investigate land-holding practices in Pare and other parts of the country aimed specifically to combat such situations as these.

and western plains are either now or have been the sites of large alienations of land to European farmers who generally raised sisal, a fibrous cactus used primarily in rope making. In former years when the world market for sisal was better than it is today, these estates provided jobs for many of the men from mountain areas of the district as well as for many laborers coming from far away—even from outside East Africa.

There are no large-scale industrial enterprises of any sort within the district with the exception of less than a dozen primary-processing plants of agricultural products (like sisal and sugar-cane) and minerals (like gypsum and magnesium). A large hydroelectric plant, designed to supply the urban areas of Moshi and Arusha to the north with electricity, is under construction on the Ruvu River on the western plains of the northern part of the district. But these actually provide income for only a few high-landers.

Most Usangi men have been forced to look elsewhere, particularly to the cities and to plantations away from Pare, for the means of earning cash. Although land shortage was one of the primary precipitating factors in the development of wide-scale labor migration in Usangi, it is only one of the reasons why today almost every Usangi man spends at least a few years of his life engaged in cash-earning activities away from home. Many must work to marry since cash is an acceptable, often preferred substitute for the livestock of the traditional bridewealth. Not to be overlooked or minimized in assessing the factors that motivate young men is the wanderlust which is continually kindled by the tales told by those returning to the highlands. Entering into such ventures is often viewed nowadays as a proper way to mark the movement of a boy from childlike dependence on others to independence as a man of means. Whatever reasons motivate specific individuals to leave the highlands, so common is the trend that it has profound consequences for the nature of Usangi society, as will be seen in Chapter 5.

INTRUDERS INTO THE USANGI HIGHLANDS

During the last one hundred years or so, many kinds of intruders have sought to penetrate the mountain country of highland Pare, including not only Europeans but Arabs, Asians, and other Africans as well. All these peoples had different aims and methods. And significantly, the consequences of their efforts were different.

Arabs came in search of ivory and slaves. The Pare Mountains themselves were not the ultimate goals of Arab caravans, at least during the early years. In their push to the interior of East Africa, the Arabs who camped in the Pare foothills traded with the people of Pare. In addition to the foodstuffs they needed to sustain their journey, the caravans began to exchange trade goods for local slaves and ivory in Pare. Along the paths of the caravan routes in the foothills of the entire range and in the northern highlands (Usangi and Ugweno), the Arabs left behind them large numbers of Islamic converts and significant imprints of Swahili culture.

In contrast to the Arabs is the experience of the Asians who have come to Pare. When compared to other parts of East Africa, one of the most striking characteristics of Pare is that Asian shopkeepers never lived in the highlands. An Asian shopkeeper once moved his family to Usangi and tried to run a shop there for a few years. But boycotts forced him to close and move away. Another Indian owned a bus that made a daily round trip from Usangi to Moshi. When a second bus was started under African ownership, the Indian bus owner was boycotted until he agreed to join forces with the Africans and this also set a strong precedent against Asian economic incursion in highland Pare.[6]

Asians have met with relatively greater success in the towns along the base of the mountains and in Same, the district headquarters. But in none of these places is there a large group of Asian settlers. Where there are a few (as there are in Same for example), they are likely not to be of the same cultural background. Their interests and spheres of social interaction are directed not simply to other people of Asian descent nearby but to people who are like themselves even though they may be geographically distant. Wherever they live, their participation in the community is reserved. They play few social roles and at present tend to limit their participation to their economic roles as traders and employers.

The contacts and intrusions of other Africans were more complex and are therefore more difficult to comprehend. Many non-Pares now living in the district are Chagga, Shambala, and Masai whose homelands border on Pare country and with whom interaction has been more intense due to their close proximity. The re-

---

[6]Near the end of my fieldwork, a government officer of Asian descent was assigned to Usangi. He apparently met with greater success than had his predecessors. This may, however, be related to his noneconomic role.

lations between Pares and other Africans have improved since the Pax Britannica. Intertribal warfare and raiding in the area were intense in precolonial times. Pares had elaborate sets of defensive tactics when raiders came. These included the cry of *yoweh* (a loud cry reserved for trouble), underground tunnels to hide in, fortified villages, and community emergency procedures used in times of raiding.

Pares give the Masai special recognition as powerful warriors although Chaggas and Shambalas took large tolls as well. In Usangi, the serious raiding of earlier generations has been replaced by ritual joking relationships, called *utani*[7] in Swahili, between Pares and their former enemies. Nowadays there are a number of Chaggas working in Usangi as lumberjacks. The relationship between these men and local residents is a friendly, but chiding, joking relationship. Should a Chagga wear his hat backwards for example, a Pare may touch it with his hand which has been wetted with saliva and claim it for his own. Theoretically, Chaggas can exercise the same kind of claim over the property of Pares who behave in any extraordinary way.

The Masai, uninterested in settling down, pose little threat to Pare land holdings. Traditionally, they raided Pare for women and cattle and today their interests have not turned to farming. Both the Chaggas (from the north) and the Shambala (from the south) have, however, threatened Pare land holdings by migrating into the area.

During 1968 there were discussions among Pares in Usangi about a few Chaggas who were moving into the fertile Usangi plains at Butu. Pares, not wanting to move permanently to the lowlands, feel threatened by the Chaggas who have come to Butu and established farms. The threat of land alienation at a place like Butu seems severe to the Pares because they too are experiencing land scarcity. Unlike lands taken earlier for sisal estates on the western plains of Usangi, the land at Butu is especially important for the people of Usangi as farmland.

In South Pare, encroachment by other Africans onto Pare land has followed a different pattern. Shambalas and others have been in the foothills of the Pare Mountains for a long time. In places like Kisiwani, which existed as a town since caravan routes began

---

[7]Joking relationships are familiar in the anthropological literature. See Beidelman (1966) for example of an extended treatment of the *utani* relationship among the Kaguru of Tanzania.

passing through the area, Shambalas and others moved first into the towns. Later they began establishing farms nearby and marrying Pare women. The result is that these people are now so intertwined with Pare people that expelling them would mean driving out sisters and daughters as well. The pattern these people followed, basing themselves in towns or on sisal estates while establishing farms gradually, and then marrying Pare women, allowed footholds to be gained quietly but firmly. Today the only ways in which Pares can get rid of these intruders once they have reached the highlands is through witchcraft or sorcery accusations backed up by large numbers of Pare supporters.

The main difference between the impact of Europeans and other intruders has been a difference of organization and goals. Westerners came better organized, with multigoals and multimeans to achieve them. Europeans pushed into Pare country as missionaries and as doctors, as plantation owners and as large-scale farmers, as colonialists and as agents of foreign governments. The content of the interactions of Europeans with Pare people centered around many things—government, education, health, and religion.

The intrusion of Europeans in Usangi resulted in the development of new governmental institutions linking the chiefdom of Usangi with the district, the capital, and the European metropole. In educational facilities, Europeans set up both government- and mission-sponsored schools so that today Usangi has a total of fifteen primary schools. In health, Usangi has the only government-run medical facility outside district headquarters—a large hospital headed by a doctor who is assisted by a staff of several nurses and dressers.

In the area of religious institutions, Europeans brought missions, churches, schools, and medical facilities. Both Christianity and Islam are so well established in contemporary Usangi that it is difficult to find people who do not belong, at least nominally, to one group or the other. Usangi has a large Friday mosque. Throughout the highlands of Usangi, there are several smaller daily mosques where the devout say the customary five daily prayers. A few can even boast of having made their pilgrimage to Mecca. Two Christian denominations have established themselves firmly in Usangi—the Lutherans, whose first mission station in North Pare was established in the first decade of this century, and the Roman Catholics, who came in the 1930s. In Usangi, at least, the domains of the two denominations are fairly well established and there is little open competition between the two groups.

Thus, each kind of people who intruded into the Usangi highlands had its own peculiar effects. Arabs left their religion in pockets throughout the hinterland of Tanganyika as they moved inland along caravan routes. They made no attempts to settle in Pare country, although they camped in the foothills from time to time. Asians had less impact on highland peoples per se. They settled permanently in the lowlands and opened shops that brought new material goods into remote areas. Other Africans formerly raided highland Pare for women and cattle. More recent relations with them have been less hostile, but migrants from other tribal groups are seen by the Pares as threats to their land holdings. Few precedents have evolved for concerted efforts in dealing with other intruders as was the case with Asian shopkeepers. In considering the transformation of Pare traditional society and culture, it is important not to forget that other intruders besides Westerners have left their indelible marks. Not all the change agents have been Western, although many have been. This is a fundamental reason why change in Pare has not simply been Westernization.

CONTEMPORARY USANGI

One of the most noticeable things about Usangi is its narrow, all-weather road, which has been intricately carved into the convoluted western slopes of North Pare. Local residents proudly tell the story of how this road was built. Their accounts claim that Pare traders returned home in the early decades of this century telling of newly built roads over which motor vehicles carried both people and goods into and out of the Chagga and Shambala highlands. The people of Usangi and Ugweno cooperated in drawing up a plan for building a road to connect the North Pare highlands with the plains, hoping that such a road would bring similar economic advantages to their own areas as it had to the Chagga and Shambala peoples. First, the men of each chiefdom built a road running from the *baraza,* or local court, in their own chiefdom to a common point in the highlands. Then, they cooperated in building a single road running from that point to the plains. The people claim that they spent about ten years building the road during which time they received no technical assistance from the colonial government. On June 6, 1936, the British District Officer traversed the entire length of the road to open it officially. Some years later, a technical advisor was sent by the government to suggest changes in the course of the road to eliminate the more hazardous corners. Today, one can hardly expect to climb the thirteen miles from the hot, dusty settlement at Mwanga, where the road branches off the Moshi-Tanga highway, without seeing one of the half a dozen or so vehicles that carry goods to the many highland shops or without meeting one of the four buses that connect the center of Usangi each day with the town of Moshi some fifty miles away and with the district headquarters at Same.

In ascending from the plains into the highlands along this road, one notices a gradual shift in the natural flora and in the cultivated crops. Land on which maize grows well gives way to a zone in which plantains, cassava, and beans prosper. A few miles up the road population density increases dramatically and houses are closer to one another, separated by garden plots and occasional groves of trees instead of expanses of arid wasteland. The herds of several dozen cattle that graze on the plains are not to be found in the highlands. Instead, most families keep a single milch cow, or perhaps two at most, inside their houses. Due to land shortage, cattle are not taken to pasture in the highlands of North Pare. Instead, grasses must be cut and carried to the animals, most of which are seldom taken outside the houses in which they are kept.

A typical homestead consists of at least a single building of wattle-and-daub construction, usually shaped like a beehive and partitioned inside into kitchen, cattle-keeping, and sleeping areas. More affluent households have a second building, usually rectangular in shape but of the same construction as the first. The second building usually contains a formal sitting room and one or more bedrooms. The formal sitting room is not used much except on special occasions: weddings, funerals, and entertaining visitors. Women and children prefer sitting around the hearth. They are often joined at night and during the rainy seasons by the adult men of the household. Sheets of corrugated iron have replaced the traditional thatched roofs in perhaps as many as half of the homesteads in the Usangi highlands. A small number of communally owned water mains supply a large number of households with piped water whose sources are the springs that rise high on the upper slopes of the mountains. A few affluent households have water outlets inside their houses; others must depend on outlets they share with a few other families; but there are still many households in which women and girls must spend a substantial portion of their working day fetching water from a distant stream. Electricity has not yet made its way into Usangi. Hearth fires, kerosene lamps, and flashlights provide artificial light at night.

Most families have a garden plot or two adjacent to their homestead. The typical crops planted in such plots are plantains and coffee, the latter being grown in a small quantity as a cash crop. The plantain grove is located just downhill from the house in which the cows are kept, making it easy to utilize the animals' manure for fertilizer. It is a rare family whose fields are all located near the homestead. Farms and garden plots belonging to a household are likely to be widely dispersed, even to the extent of being a few miles apart. Not only is land itself scarce today in the parts of the highlands where people prefer to live, but most farmers recognize the advantage of diversifying their farming sites both for insurance against localized drought or damage and because some crops yield better within certain ranges of elevation. The flood plain at the base of the eastern slopes is especially fertile and most Usangi highlanders also farm there. Women do most of the agricultural labor, not because the people of Usangi have any special prohibition against men engaging in such work, but because so many men work away from home in order to earn cash, a phenomenon which will be considered more extensively in Chapter 5.

Feeder roads stretch out from the main road in all directions, climbing even farther into the high peaks that surround the floor of the mountain valley that forms the center of Usangi. At the end of the bus line are about thirty shops, most of which sell general merchandise. A few are specialized: a carpenter, a butcher, a couple of tailors, and a restaurant or two. At present, nearly every household depends on the local shops for such essentials as kerosene, soap, cooking oil, salt, spices, tea leaves, matches, and sugar. More affluent families buy cigarettes, sodas, candies, flashlights, jewelry, cloth, readymade clothes, yarns, shoes, and such toys as rubber balls for their children. When farm produce runs low, even ground maize meal and wheat flour are bought in the shops. In addition to their retail businesses, a few of the keepers of the larger shops buy sufficient quantities of goods when they go to town to act as wholesalers to the many small shops in the more remote parts of the Usangi highlands.

Only a short distance from the bank of shops at the end of the bus line is the *baraza*. Although the court is itself in session only a few days each year, people go to the *baraza* for a number of reasons. The offices of the Divisional Executive Officer and other government officials stationed in Usangi are located there. The post office (which has daily deliveries by bus from Moshi) operates in an adjoining building. Sometimes men just go to sit on one of the low walls of the open-sided court building to chat with one another or to pass the time of day with those who come to the post office or to the government offices. A short walking distance from the *baraza* is the office of the Tanganyika National African Union (TANU), the political party of mainland Tanzania. Many Usangi residents are dues-paying members of the party and attend its regular meetings. The TANU office sponsors community-development projects, particularly the *Umoja wa Wanawake* (literally, "Unity of Women"), a women's organization that promotes the extension of skills among women, and the Ward Development Committee, which fosters self-help and other development projects.

In contrast to other parts of the district as well as to Tanzania as a whole, Usangi has relatively abundant social services, a good road, many schools and shops, a large medical facility, and a generally outward-looking and progressive population. The rather substantial changes that have taken place in Usangi in the last several decades are the result of the coalescence of the efforts of early missionaries and Islamic proselytizers, heavy investments by the British colonial government, an acute land shortage, and a few forward-looking individuals in the local community. In the next chapter, some of the characteristics of Usangi society before the transformations brought by more recent changes will be reconstructed and used later to assess the nature and significance of changes during Tanzania's colonial and independent periods.

4

The Bases of Pare Ethnic Identity: Ritual, Homeland, and Language

Ethnic identity, contrary to the views expressed by some social scientists, is not stable and fixed. Rather, as this chapter and the two which follow attempt to demonstrate, ethnicity is flexible and shifting, emerging and changing in response to the contexts in which it is expressed. Certain situations call for the expression of a particular identity, while other contexts make it appropriate to submerge, forget, or even deny the same identity. This chapter examines the genesis and nature of Pare ethnic identity. The two following chapters examine the contemporary status of this identity and inquire into the prospects for its survival in a changing world.

THE GENESIS OF PARE

Unlike many African societies, Pare is not an ancient collectivity. The oral traditions of these people make no assertion of autochthony but tell instead a history of migration, both into and within the Pare highlands, and of the gradual coalescence of Pare as a meaningful social and cultural unit. At the beginning of the colonial period, the inhabitants of the Pare Mountains spoke several dialects of at least two nonintelligible languages. The existence of relatively similar cultures among the peoples of the Pare Highlands and of a homeland, geographically separate and distinct from the arid plains and neighboring mountain ranges, provided important bases for the development of a collective identity in the contact period. Nineteenth and twentieth century changes in the surrounding sociocultural environment placed premiums on unity, not divisiveness and thereby fostered the growth and significance of Pare as a unit. Table 4.1 provides a schematic summary of the evolution of Pare.

In the precontact period, the most significant units of the social

Table 4.1 The Evolution of Pare

Period	Early Precontact (ca. 1300–1750)	Later Precontact (Mid-18th to Mid-19th Centuries)	Contact and Colonial (Mid-19th to Mid-20th Centuries)	Post-Independence (1960s–1970s)
Largest or Most Significant Unit(s) of Social Organization	Clans.	Clans. Asu versus Gweno.	Pare.	Pare.	Tanzania.
Major Characteristics of Period	Asu and Gweno are separate linguistic communities; North and South Pare are not connected.	Formalization of ties between North and South; Asu speakers move into North.	Pare evolves as a meaningful unit; Asu and Gweno merge in the face of incursion by outsiders.	Pare is a recognized ethnic group in the new nation of Tanzania.	Identity as Tanzanians supplements regional and local ethnic identities.
Symbols of Identity	Totems, taboos, some occupational specialties.	Initiation rites, language (Asu versus Gweno).	Land, language (Kipare), and life-crises rituals.	Land, language (Kipare), and new or changed life-crises rituals.	History, language (Swahili), indigenous culture.

organization were clans,[1] most of which tended to be localized but not necessarily exogamous. The clans of northern Pare were Gweno-speaking while those in the southern parts of the highlands were Asu-speaking. Neither sector of the highlands was politically unified until at least 1500 and no political bonds of any significance developed between the North and the South until late in the colonial period.[2]

In the early precolonial period, the most relevant units in an individual's life were his household, his close relatives (particularly those on his father's side), and his clan. Though an individual relied first upon his patrikinsmen, he tended to think next of his mother's relatives when he was in need of assistance. Despite a patrilineal bias, matrilateral relatives were not insignificant since, outside his father's and his mother's patriclans, there were no suprafamily units such as age sets to which the individual could turn.

Some clans claim to have originated from migrations into Pare country from Taita to the north; some came from the Nguu Mountains which lie in the direction of the coast; others emigrated from the nearby countries of the Chagga, Shambala, and Mbugu peoples. Still others came into Pare from more distant places. In addition to clans originating through migrations into Pare country, frequent fragmentation and division within existing clans gave rise to new clans—or at least to subclans. When clan fissioning occurred, often the splinter group moved some distance away from the core, yet typically remained in the Pare highlands. As a consequence of their diverse origins, culture varied significantly from clan to clan. Some had totemic associations with animals and observed special food taboos. Others were associated with particular craft specialties, such as smithing. Prior to the changes stimulated by the advent of caravans in the nineteenth century, there was little regional specialization in the Pare area beyond salt production and iron working. Salt, iron, and iron tools were traded by those who produced them with agriculturalists and herders in exchange for the products of their labors. This sporadic trade was concentrated in Pare although it was not limited to that

[1]The term "clan" is used for these groups following Kimambo (1969a). For an early description, see Guth (1932).

[2]Dating follows Kimambo (1969a, 1969b) who has conducted extensive research on the history of the Pare Mountains area.

area alone. North Pare iron workers traded their products for Chagga and Masai livestock. In the South, livestock were traded with people from Usambara in exchange for *mpaa* (gazelle) hides needed for certain Shambala rituals. Migration between North and South Pare during the precontact period produced some clans in the two sectors of the highlands that claimed relations to one another, but such relations were ordinarily not significant in daily interaction because of the distances involved.

Some time after the year 1500, important changes in spheres of influence and control took place within the highlands. South Pare never developed beyond a number of small-scale polities, but in the North a complex, centralized political structure evolved in Ugweno and encompassed all or most of North Pare. As part of the reforms brought about as a result of this development in the North, the formerly clan-based male initiation rites were brought under central control. For the first time in history, there emerged an organization which crosscut the localized clans and integrated the disparate districts of North Pare. Men from different communities were taught together the ways of adult men, including the methods and lore of collective defense against the raids of neighboring groups. Female initiation rites typically remained limited to girls of a single clan.

As noted in Chapter 3, the clear association of North Pare with Gweno-speakers and South Pare with Asu-speakers became confused in the latter half of the eighteenth century as a result of the Asu-speaking southerners who assisted Usangi in its revolt against Ugweno remaining in the North. Allying themselves with the southerners who had been placed strategically in a buffer zone between Usangi and Ugweno proper, the original residents of Usangi gradually adopted or returned to Asu as their native language but denied the immigrant southerners access to the male initation rites in Usangi and thereby prohibited total cultural amalgamation and integration between immigrants and indigenes. Until the time when the initiation system fell into disuse in the twentieth century, the immigrants in the North continued to send their young men back to the South to be initiated. Although the South and the North became closely entangled as a result of the movement of Asu speakers into Usangi, the complete integration of the southern allies did not occur. Independent Usangi never developed any equivalents of the community-wide rituals that the Gweno polity had sponsored, and their separate ritual lives served to remind the residents of Usangi that they were two peoples, not one.

It was the colonial era which brought about the changes that forged Pare as a meaningful unit. Faced with the incursion of outsiders, the peoples of the Pare highlands often found it useful to ignore their internal differences in order to present a united front to the outside world. Following the practice that developed during the colonial period, the term *Pare* is used today by outsiders to refer to the inhabitants of the Pare highlands, whether Asu- or Gweno-speaking.

There are two separate theories as to the origin of the outsider's term, *Pare.* The theory most widely held among northerners is that the name comes from the Chagga *mpare,* meaning "hit" or "strike." According to this theory, the word was used by the Chagga as a battle cry when they raided the inhabitants of North Pare. Through an unexplained process, the term was extended to all the inhabitants of the Pare Mountains.

A different story is told more often in South Pare about the origin of the name. It is reported that Arab traders were told by the Shambala people that the inhabitants of the mountains that lay to the north were *Vampare.* This was, in fact, the name of a clan whose homeland is the southernmost part of the Pare range. Informants claim that the clan's name was misapplied by foreigners to all the people living in the mountains that lay between Usambara and Mt. Kilimanjaro. Regardless of the actual origin of the term *Pare* as a name for the inhabitants of the mountain range that today also bears that name, the significance of both stories is the same—*Pare* is an outsider's designation, not a self-appellation.

Through a process which is not as yet fully documented, most people in North Pare had learned to speak Asu by the time of German contact in the late nineteenth century. In the case of Usangi, it appears that the indigenes, formerly Gweno-speakers, adopted or returned to Asu as their native language and ceased using Gweno almost entirely. Many place names, however, are of Gweno origin. In Ugweno proper, both men and women learned Asu as a second language but the reasons behind this remain to be explained. When the Germans arrived, they found most people of the Pare Mountains area speaking Asu (although for some it was only a second language) and spoke of the area as inhabited by the *Vasu,* or the Asu-speakers. In the German colonial period,

North Pare was administered with Kilimanjaro, the South with
Usambara. To the British who took over the administration of
Tanganyika Territory after World War I, the Pare Mountains appeared to be a natural unit for colonial administration under
indirect rule. In 1928 a number of political boundaries were rede-
fined within the highlands, some small chiefdoms were consolidated into larger ones, a district political structure was created,
and Pare became politically unified for the first time. The British
employed the term *Pare* rather than *Vasu,* which the Germans
had often favored. The language of the highlanders was called
Pare (in English) or *KiPare* (in Swahili), but in actuality it was
nothing more than the Asu language. Told that they were a "tribe"
and administered as such, a consciousness of Pare-ness developed
among the highlanders during the British period. The formerly
disparate clans of the Pare Mountains often tended to overlook
their differences and to emphasize instead their many similarities,
especially in opposition to the colonial regime itself. Indeed, the
first collective action on the part of all Pare peoples occurred in
the 1940s as a popular revolt against certain aspects of the
colonial taxation system (Kimambo 1971).

Pare became a new and important unit of social and cultural
identification for the peoples of the highlands. Drawing on communalities in their heritage, three symbols or sets of symbols
emerged in this period to set Pares apart from other indigenous
peoples of the British East African colonial arena. These symbols
were: the Pare Mountain range, their geographically isolated and
distinctive homeland; the Pare language, actually the Asu language but spoken by most highlanders as their native language
and by others as a second language; and a number of rituals,
not rituals of collective solidarity since few of these existed even
in previous periods, but rituals of the life cycle that despite some
variations within the Pare area were construed as culturally distinctive, especially in contrast to other peoples. Ironically, at the
very same time these symbols were emerging as the primary symbols of Pare ethnicity, new forces—themselves brought through
contact—were undermining the symbols of this developing ethnic
identity. In the remainder of this chapter, the contributions of
homeland, language, and ritual to Pare ethnic identity are examined. The description here is a generalized and ideal account
of this identity in Usangi during the early colonial period. These
symbols have undergone dramatic, sometimes revolutionary,

changes in the last several decades, and it will be to these changes and their effects on Pare ethnicity that we turn our attention in Chapter 5.

PARE RITUALS

At the beginning of the colonial period, neither North nor South Pare—and certainly not all of Pare—had important community-wide rituals. With few exceptions, ritual life was either clan-based or limited to members of closely related clans. Therefore, as Pare identity developed during the colonial period, there were few significant supraclan rituals to utilize as Pare rituals. Instead, life-crisis rituals were seized upon and employed as symbols of Pare identity. Although the indigenous cultures of North and South had varied in small ways in the handling of rites of passage, these differences became insignificant. What mattered was that Pares, and those aspiring to be Pares, commemorated the passage of their lives through various stages according to certain distinctive ritual prescriptions, thereby signifying their identity as Pares. The most significant rites were: birth, circumcision, initiation, marriage, and death.

Birth

An event of great significance for the course of an individual's life took place before his birth—the marriage of his parents. The giving of bridewealth by the groom and his close agnatic kinsmen to the family of the bride signified marriage and meant that her children would become members of the patriclan of her husband, their *pater* or sociolegal father. Although there had been differences in local customs within the highlands, the Pare District Council—the local government authority composed of the district chiefs—standardized bridewealth early in the British period so that customarily throughout Pare it consisted of four cows (two of each sex) and a male and a female goat. Informants today believe this was the appropriate amount for precolonial Usangi. The *fingirua,* as the male goat was called, sealed the marriage. It was not necessary to transfer the entire bridewealth in order to give the children a claim to clan membership. Only the *fingirua* had to be given for the children to become members of their father's clan automatically at birth.

It sometimes happened that a child was born before the *fingirua* had been given. In such a case, the child's clan membership was not resolved. When the *genitor* was known, people would say that the child would belong to his clan if he were to give the *fingirua*. But until such a time as it was actually given, the illegitimate child remained the ward of his mother's father. In those cases where a man did not want to marry a woman with whom he had sired a child, it was possible to incorporate the child into his clan by giving to the child's grandfather whatever amount of wealth the old man would agree to accept in return for the child. Until the *genitor* either made such arrangements or gave the *fingirua* (thereby marrying the child's mother), such a child was *kakaye wa mbweheni,* or "child of the house."

It was often difficult for illegitimate children to find sponsors willing or able to help them. Their maternal grandfathers usually had several children of their own and typically a large number of legitimately descended grandchildren who were members of their own patriclans. For illegitimate male children, the old men were often unable to play major roles in amassing the boys' bridewealth and in helping them out on other occasions. If the illegitimate child was female, however, the *genitor* usually came forward wanting to make the child a member of his clan so that her bridewealth would go to him at the time she was old enough to marry.

A woman in childbirth was attended by some of her own and her husband's close female relatives. Men were excluded from the event and were told only that a child had been born. The child's sex would not be revealed to the father and other men until the naming ceremony took place four days later. Following the delivery, the mother was permitted to remain at home for a long period of time (the exact number of days varied in different parts of the highlands). The women who assisted her in giving birth would then take care over her cooking, farming, and housekeeping responsibilities. She reciprocated as each of them gave birth on other occasions.

When a child's father had already given the *fingirua* for his mother, a ritual on the fourth day after birth symbolized formal recognition and incorporation of the child into his father's clan. This ceremony, called *kula mchumbi wa mwana* or "cleansing of the child," was described in 1922 by the German missionary Ernst Kotz who witnessed it many times. He noted that the father was allowed to enter the house for the first time on the fourth day after the child was born. Four men accompanied him. One of the women who was assisting the mother presented the father with the child, mentioning the name the women had selected for the child. Usually this name referred to events surrounding the birth of the child (Kotz 1922:27–28). This was not the only name the child was to receive. Each child was given the name of a member of the grandparent's generation, beginning with the patrilateral side for the first child of each sex and then alternating between matrilateral and patrilateral names for each successive male and female child. In recalling the significance of the cleansing ceremony which took place on the fourth day, informants claim that the festivities, which always included beer drinking and feasting on special foods, was the father's way of expressing his joy in recognizing the child as his own and receiving him into his clan.

Circumcision
Traditionally circumcision of both sexes took place before the onset of puberty, usually between the ages of six and twelve years. The operation was performed by specialists of the same sex as the child. Children of both sexes were often circumcised on the same day. Sometimes several men arranged to have all their children circumcised together—sharing in the gifts for the operators and in the preparation of food and drink for the guests. The circumcision ceremony was called *ngasu ya kaa* meaning "the ceremony done at home." Those who were circumcised together had no special relationship to one another as they do in some other societies where it provides the basis for membership in common age sets.

Puberty Ceremonies
Both male and female puberty ceremonies were periods of instruction in proper adult behavior and symbolized the beginning of social maturity. The character of the rites for the two sexes differed greatly. The female ceremony, often held on a small scale for only a few girls at a time, was called *kueka*. It was performed at home under the direction of an old woman who was knowledgeable in the secrets of instruction and responsible for teaching them. After several days of seclusion, the girls emerged on a final day of celebration when they were socially recognized as having "grown up."

For boys, instruction by elders in the affairs and secrets of men took place in special ritual forests. The ceremonies, which often lasted as long as two weeks, were called *mshitu* (literally, "forest"). The *mshitu* was a clan ritual, except in North Pare where late in the precontact period it was used by a group of indigenous clans to exclude immigrants from the south.

Marriage
Some time after a young man's initiation, his family took the initiative in arranging his marriage. A suitable woman was found, and her family was approached by a relative of the prospective bridegroom. Following the initial discussions, a long period ensued in which each family investigated the other and contemplated the consequences of such a marriage. In addition to the customary bridewealth (four cows and two goats), the groom gave the bride's mother a special gift if he discovered that her daughter was a virgin. In order for his bride to come to live with him, it was only necessary for the *fingirua* to have been given. Several years might pass before he was able to give all the wealth to his wife's family. Not only was it usually difficult to amass all the wealth at once, but giving it in small amounts periodically allowed him to determine how stable the marriage was over time. As each child was born, the wife's family probably insisted that additional wealth be given until the amount originally agreed upon was finally reached.

Death and Burial
Shortly after an individual died, his body was buried in the floor of the house in which he had been living. It was buried in an upright position beneath the surface of the ground, except for the head, which was supported on poles placed across the opening of the grave. The protruding head was covered with straw and sealed over with clay. Much later, after the body had decomposed and the skull had separated from it, a second burial took place. At this time, the skull was removed, the hole containing the body was filled in, and the skull was cleaned and taken with great ceremony to be placed in the ancestral shrine of the individual's clan, usually a grove of trees or a shallow cave. For a woman, this meant that her skull was returned by the husband's family to her clansmen who were responsible for placing it among the skulls of other deceased members of her clan.

By the early colonial period, these rites had come to signify Pare identity. Internal differences between North and South and among various local traditions were ignored, especially when dealing with such outsiders as colonial officers and missionaries. This set of passage rites emerged as uniquely Pare.

RESIDENCE IN THE PARE HIGHLANDS

The Pare people think of themselves as highlanders, an aspect of their identity that has deep roots in their culture history. In precolonial times, the rugged terrain of their mountainous country helped insulate the residents of the Pare highlands from their neighbors and from outsiders. But a greater inhibition to free movement between highlands and plains was the frequent raiding of Pare country by the Chagga, the Masai, and other peoples who looked to the area as a source of cattle and women. The highlanders of Pare developed many defenses. Some lived in fortified settlements of several households. Others depended on hiding in caves and underground tunnels during the raiding. Whatever ventures the highlanders made into the surrounding plains were of short duration and limited scope: hunting, collecting medicinal herbs and roots, and the like. As indicated earlier, some limited trading with neighboring groups did occur prior to the eighteenth century, but it was the advent of the Swahili and Arab caravans that brought an expansion of trading interests outside the highlands (Kimambo 1968). Following the pacification of the area during the colonial period, farming and herding activities of the highlanders gradually expanded to the plains. But even today few Pares are willing to relinquish their highland homesteads. They commute instead between mountains and plains.

In the Pare (Asu) language, they call their highland homeland *vwasu* and contrast it with *nyika,* the adjacent plains. A true Pare always lives in *vwasu* and would never think of living in *nyika.* Consider the symbolic opposition of *vwasu* and *nyika* in the following description of the punishment of a *kighiria* through banishment from the highlands.

According to tradition, a girl should not become pregnant before passing through the puberty rite. A ritual correction such as a public shaming was considered appropriate punishment for the violation of incest between initiated adults, but not sufficient punishment for a *kighiria,* as such a girl was called. A *kighiria* was expelled from the highlands in a manner employed only in the punishment of her offense. The small drain hole, used for the manure and urine of the animals kept inside the round house, was enlarged and the *kighiria* was forced to pass through it alone. The obvious symbolism here indicates the heinous nature of the offense. She was told to leave the highlands forever and to go instead to live among the wild animals of the *nyika* wilderness since she had behaved as though she were one of them. Her father claimed a cow from the one who impregnated her, if he was known, and the animal was butchered in an unusual fashion, further indicating the seriousness of this offense. Instead of removing the animal's hide (which traditionally had great value as clothes), it was left on the carcass to be consumed in the roasting process so that nothing would remain to remind her family that she once lived. When she died, her skull was not placed among those of her ancestors in the clan shrine.

This drastic treatment of the *kighiria* demonstrates in its symbolism the traditional sentiments of the Pare people toward their country. The highlands and the plains stand as symbolic opposites of one another. One is deemed the proper preserve of people; the other is fitting habitation for wild animals and those who behave like them.

The significance of their mountain homeland for Pare identity is great. Both Northerners and Southerners shared a common devotion to highland residence, even before the beginning of Arab and European contact. The struggle to keep their distinctive homeland their own provided a common rallying point for the highlanders as the colonial period unfolded.

THE PARE LANGUAGE

Gweno and Asu, the ancient languages of North and South Pare respectively, are not mutually intelligible with one another. Bryan, who has worked out a classification scheme for the Bantu languages in this part of East Africa (1959:122), considers them to be distinct languages and placed each with a different group of related languages. Gweno-speakers claim intelligibility with certain Chagga dialects spoken in the Kilimanjaro area. Asu speakers are not generally aware of any such closely related language to their own.

In a multilingual environment, language is a ready and powerful symbol of ethnic identity. By the beginning of the colonial period, all Usangi residents—whether immigrants or indigenes—had become native speakers of Asu. In their refusal to continue speaking the Gweno language, the original inhabitants of Usangi had dissociated themselves from Gweno after their successful revolt. By adopting the language of their Asu allies from South Pare, the people of Usangi assumed a vital part of Asu identity, a part that ironically was to become a base of yet another identity in the twentieth century as Asu was to assume the role of the Pare language.

The dialects of Pare (Asu) spoken throughout the district are so varied as to not always be easily intelligible with one another. But in most cases, the dialects of adjacent communities are similar enough not to impede communication.

Following the advent of Arab caravans in the nineteenth century, many people of the Pare Mountains area began to learn to speak Swahili. Using Swahili as a vehicle of intertribal communication, of government administration, and of education, highland Pare communities became increasingly bilingual during the late nineteenth and twentieth centuries.

Becoming Pare

Being a Pare at the beginning of the colonial period thus involved participating in the prescribed life-crisis rites, living in the highlands of the Pare Mountains, and speaking the Pare language. It did not involve another criterion that is often considered by other peoples to be a *sine qua non* of ethnic membership. It was not necessary for an individual to be born of Pare stock for him, or surely for his descendants who embraced the three symbols of ethnicity, to become Pare. A generation or two was usually required to demonstrate the intention of an immigrant family to remain in the Pare highlands, to learn Pare (Asu) as their primary language by forgetting any other ancestral language, and to adopt Pare ritual commemorations of their lives through the various stages.

Two cases demonstrate the apparent ease with which it was possible for immigrants of serious intent to become Pares.

THE CASE OF SAMWELI

Samweli's father was born in Chagga country. He came to live in the North Pare highlands with early Lutheran missionaries for whom he worked as a cook. He married a Pare woman and lived the remainder of his life in the Pare highlands. After the old man died, his son Samweli became the missionaries' cook. Samweli, who was born in the Pare highlands and grew up speaking the Pare language, knows the place in Chagga country where his father was born and has visited it a few times. Now an old man himself, Samweli claims that he is a Pare of the Chagga clan.

This case illustrates the way in which a new line can be started through immigration into Pare country. Although the son of an immigrant, Samweli maintains no formal ties with any kinsmen in Chagga country. There is nothing in his behavior to suggest that he does not consider himself wholly Pare. Nobody would dispute his right to call himself Pare.

THE CASE OF ALI

Ali was born in Shambala country. As a boy, he moved to a market town in the Pare foothills where he worked at a sisal estate. Ali married a Pare woman whom he met at the marketplace. After giving bridewealth to her family, he moved his residence to the highlands. Every now and then he leaves his wife and children in order to return to Shambala country.

Few people are willing to call Ali a Pare. Although he lives in the highlands and speaks the Pare language fluently, people consistently refer to him as a Shambala. It is said that he has not lived in the highlands long enough to embrace Pare culture to the exclusion of Shambala customs. His children, who were born in the Pare highlands, are culturally indistinguishable from other children of the same age. Yet they are seldom considered Pares since their father is a Shambala and there always remains the possibility that he might take them to live with his people in Shambala country. Ali's commitment to Pare customs and to continued residence in Pare country is not yet firmly established.

Although contact precipitated the development of Pare ethnic identity, nearly one hundred years of colonialism has not left this ethnicity untouched. The introduction of Christianity and Islam, of schools, and of labor migration has resulted in wide discrepancies between the models of the rites of passage described here and the way they are practiced today. Long-term cash-earning ventures outside the highlands have disturbed the close and automatic association between residence in the Pare highlands and Pare identity. And the formerly monolingual populations of most highland communities have become bilingual. In the next chapter, these changing facets of ethnic identity in contemporary Usangi will be examined.

5

The Crises of Change—Ethnic Identity in Contemporary Usangi

The middle and later decades of the colonial period brought about a number of far-reaching social and cultural transformations in the communities of the Pare Highlands, including many in the very fabric of Pare identity itself. Of the three symbols considered in Chapter 4, passage rites have changed most. Many old rites are no longer practiced; some have even been replaced by such new rites as going to school and participating in labor migration. Further, the formerly close association between Pare identity and residence in the highlands has been made less absolute because of the fact that most men spend considerable portions of their adult lives working away from home. And, because most Usangi people are now bilingual speakers of Pare (Asu) and Swahili, the centrality of the Pare language is threatened.

This chapter examines the changes that have taken place in the symbols of Pare ethnic identity and attempts to answer a number of questions that arise as a result of these changes: How do people view changes in the symbols of their ethnic identity? What significance do such changes hold for ethnic identity itself? With apparently substantial erosion in the cultural manifestations of Pare identity, how is such an identity maintained, if indeed it is? And, finally, what identities are alternatives to Pare ethnicity? For answers, we return to the village of Usangi in the highlands of North Pare and focus our attention upon ritual, homeland, and language and upon the significance of ethnicity in contemporary Usangi.

The data on which this chapter is based were collected during eighteen months of field research in 1967 and 1968. In addition to conventional ethnographic techniques, survey interviews were conducted in Usangi during the early months of 1968 among a set of related kinsmen. All those who resided in Usangi at the time were interviewed there. The remaining individuals who lived and worked away from home were sought out and interviewed at their residences or places of work. Interviews with this latter category of individuals, both outside the highlands and often later in Usangi, provided great insight into the nature of the cash-earning experience itself.

The set of individuals who were interviewed constituted a genealogy-based sample. Briefly, the procedure involved interviewing a group of kinsmen. The first step was finding a suitable informant who could also act as field assistant. Then, his genealogy (including both patrilateral and matrilateral kinsmen) was collected for as many generations as necessary to give a "sample" of the required size, which, in the case of Usangi, was a set of 199 individuals, 99 of whom resided outside the highlands at the time the interviews were conducted. Finally, each individual was sought out for interviewing. Of those residing in Usangi, 96 percent were actually interviewed. Distance and time limitations resulted in only 65 of all those living away from home being contacted.

Genealogy-based sampling is especially useful in field situations where random sampling is not possible. Elsewhere, it has been shown that the set of individuals generated by this procedure represented remarkably well the age, sex, educational, and occutional distributions in the population of the Pare highlands (O'Barr 1973).

RITES OF PASSAGE

Pressures from Christian missionaries, Islamic proselytizers, and the two colonial governments altered the Pare rites of passage. Once more or less uniform for all Pare people, the rites no longer operate on anything like a universal basis. Some of the ancient ways are only memories in the minds of old people; others have undergone transformations to such degrees that they bear little resemblance to practices at the beginning of the colonial period; none have remained unaffected. New rites of passage have been incorporated into Usangi's social life—especially going to school and spending time in cash-earning stints outside the highlands. But whether looking at introduced rites or the remnants of the old ones, the overriding theme, which cannot be overlooked, is that diversity, variety, and alternatives now characterize all stages of the life cycle.

Although most parents continue to give traditional names to their children, the traditional birth celebration is seldom held.

The efforts of both Christians and Moslems to replace it with religious celebrations have done much to undermine the traditional cleansing ritual, but other factors have also contributed to its demise. For one thing, many men work away from home and consequently are not present on the fourth day after birth when the cleansing ceremony should take place. Moreover, the common practice of submitting to prenatal examinations at the local medical facility has removed a great deal of the secrecy traditionally associated with childbirth, and the father, if he should be home, is not required to wait until the fourth day to see his child.

Circumcision rites illustrate well what has happened to one of the traditional rites of passage as a result of contact. Some agents of change, namely the Moslems, have required circumcision of males as part of their own ritual life. Others, particularly the early German missionaries, found circumcision of both sexes unnecessary, condemned the practices as pagan, and refused to allow them to be practiced in mission dispensaries. This difference in approach by the two religious groups has never been very well understood by most Usangi villagers. From their perspective, they have seen a once universally accepted custom become a cultural dividing line.

The church's position on circumcision has relaxed somewhat in recent years, but Christians are still told that they ought not consider it important. Yet most Pares consider male circumcision not only important but also a *sine qua non* of adulthood. Many men whose parents follow the church's teaching on circumcision choose to be circumcised as adults. A considerable number of families no longer practice clitoridectomy because, they say, they are convinced of its relation to difficulties in childbirth. Some elders think it is bad to have stopped circumcising females. They cite the lower incidence of the practice among younger women as a chief cause of the larger number of illegitimate children they feel are being born today.

Although a chief function of circumcision is to distinguish an individual as a member of society who bears a symbol of his social identity, the church often failed to appreciate this aspect of its significance. Perhaps with the zeal of Paulist evangelism, they were reacting against both what they considered to be a pagan ritual which ought to be replaced by its Christian counterpart (i.e., baptism) and also the history of this curious custom and its significance in early Christianity. At least one priest has invited the traditional circumcisor into the mission dispensary from time to time. He argues that since children become Christians through the rite of baptism, they should also be allowed to become full members of their society through participating in those traditional rituals which are not specifically forbidden by Christianity. Clitoridectomy is not allowed in the dispensary because of the negative medical evidence which has accumulated against its practice.

Christian and Islamic religious leaders in Usangi tried to convince their followers that God does not approve of their participating in such pagan celebrations as the traditional puberty rites. Today, many elders who have knowledge of these rituals refuse to participate on the grounds of conflict with their religion. The British colonial government was also instrumental in curtailing the rites by requiring that they be licensed. The *mshitu* and *kueka* rites held today are highly abbreviated versions and only a small number of children enter them. Celebrations of the rites are often clandestine due to the criticism they receive from members of the religious organizations.

Bridewealth was one of the few Pare traditional customs to receive wide sanction by the agents of change. Both religious groups and government accepted it as the basis of the marriage contract. But this tacit acceptance should not be taken to mean that the traditional institution remains intact.

Substituting cash for the traditional items of bridewealth has undermined the collective action of the patrikin in arranging marriages and given young men the power to make marriage arrangements directly with the families of their prospective brides. Old men, having few ways to obtain cash, often prefer it to livestock. The fact that the traditional names for the parts of the bridewealth (such as *fingirua*) are retained and applied to the cash should not obscure the fact that the shift from the dependence of sons on fathers to independent action in arranging their marriages marks a radical departure from the traditional Pare marriage institution.

Despite the fact that its significance had been altered, the custom of giving bridewealth went unquestioned in past decades while other rites of passage (especially those surrounding birth, circumcision, and initiation) were under heavy fire from agents of change. But the stability of the practice has recently been threatened by a different force—young people who claim that the custom means buying wives and who argue for marriages based on romantic love and arranged only by the partners. Pare elders have countered them by saying that, without bridewealth, young people are likely to change their minds as quickly as they decide to marry and this would, they contend, reduce marital stability.

Traditional Pare mortuary practices have been replaced by corresponding Christian and Islamic rituals. Among Christians the peals of the church bell announce a death among the parishioners. The faithful gather for a funeral ceremony in church, after which the body is buried in the church cemetery. Moslems perfume and wrap the body of the deceased in expensive grave cloths before burying it in the banana grove near the house in which the person lived. No longer are the skulls of either Christians or Moslems taken to ancestral shrines, and, although most shrines remain intact, veneration of ancestors through clan rituals is largely a thing of the past, replaced by Islamic and Christian funerary rites.

Over the past several decades, the life cycle has diversified through incremental changes to the point where it is virtually impossible today to describe a typical life cycle for the people of Usangi. Instead of, or sometimes in addition to, some of the traditional Pare rites of passage, other events mark stages of maturation of the individual. Going to school is the most significant of these new stages. Working outside the highlands is another important passage rite for many young men. Schooling and its significance is considered in the next section. A discussion of out-migration is postponed until after we can consider the symbolic importance of residence in the highlands.

Going to School—A New Rite of Passage

Usangi has fifteen schools with more than three thousand students enrolled in them.[1] Primary consequences of schooling are exposure to nontraditional ideas, learning new kinds of skills, becoming literate, and gaining a knowledge of a much wider range

[1]About 13 percent of the population of Usangi were students in the year 1967. According to official figures there were 3,349 students in a total population of 25,942. Data on the students were supplied by the District Education Officer, in Same, on November 8, 1968; population figures were abstracted from the 1967 national census (Central Statistical Bureau 1967:9.) Calculated on the basis of students per household, two out of every three households averaged a student in primary school in 1967. Census figures show Usangi with 4,937 households. Households are officially defined as "a group of persons living together and sharing their living expenses. Usually it includes the husband and wife and children" (Central Statistical Bureau 1967:9).

of foreign places and things than was typical in the past. The end result of even a few years schooling is the transformation of children into new kinds of individuals who share significant similarities with children in other parts of the world going through the same kind of educational experiences. And these are, of course, quite different from the values and experiences they share with their grandparents and, in many cases, with their own parents.

Schooling is important to the people of Usangi. Most parents want their children to attend school since being educated provides the major key to alternative life styles to peasant farming. But like parents everywhere, many fail to appreciate that, along with learning the practical skills, schools open new possibilities to the students. And as can be expected, Pare parents become deeply concerned when they see their children changing in ways they deem undesirable. Nevertheless, Usangi's facilities even during primary years are hardly sufficient to meet the needs of the number of children sent to school by their parents. Significant land shortage in Usangi has caused many Usangi parents to make every effort to educate their children. Schooling does not hold such great significance in some other parts of the district where the population pressure on the land is not so great.

Fashioned after a British model instituted in the colonial period, Usangi's schools are divided into lower primary (first through fourth years, called *standards*) and upper primary years (standards five through seven). At the end of standard four and again at the end of standard seven, the student faces rigorous examinations which determine whether he will be allowed to continue. Quite a considerable number of those taking the examination at the end of the fourth year are allowed to continue. The bottleneck comes at the end of standard seven when only 10 to 15 percent are allowed to enter secondary school. All parents are keenly aware that few children actually enter secondary school. Yet most of them are ill prepared to think their own children, especially their sons, will be among the ones who fail to go on. In the past, the school system was structured to favor not the majority who spend only a few years in school, but the small minority who were to become the educated élite. This legacy from the colonial period is being changed by the post-independent government.[2] Despite policy changes that require a long time to take effect, the overriding idea of the educational system is for students to con-

---

[2]See Nyerere's policy statement, *Education for Self-Reliance* (Nyerere 1967a).

tinue through secondary school. Consequently, the people of Usangi try to maximize the chances for their children. For example, it has become the common practice to send a child to standard one when he is as old as ten or eleven, the belief being that older children have a better chance to succeed. This practice receives support from teachers who argue that by starting late, the children who do not go on beyond primary school will be old enough to assume young adult roles after completing their education.

In choosing the school to which a child is to be sent, the most important criterion seems to be the availability of space in the school. Also important (when there is opportunity to choose among several schools) is the family's estimate of the level of success in examinations of students at that school. The supporting agency appears to make little difference in choosing the school. Once a child is in school, however, his parents may try to switch him to another school where he will receive proper religious instruction consonant with his own denomination, but religious affiliation seldom seems to be a primary criterion in the selection of a school.

The people of Usangi see a crisis in their educational system today. They are convinced of the value of education and of the likely success of the educated. Those who complete secondary school stand good chances of being employed in the civil service or of finding jobs in business. A few fathers, wanting so much to send their children to school, have even resorted to bribery to obtain places for them. Many send their children to repeat standard seven, hoping they will pass the examination the second time around or pass it with higher scores and be allowed to continue. When the children fail to enter secondary school (as most inevitably do since the opportunities are so few), disappointment is intense. Having failed to go on means either that they must take up farming or look for work in a city.

For the people of Usangi, a success for one member of the family is a success for all. The child who does succeed in entering secondary school will be expected to help his parents and siblings more than others who will not have had all the same opportunities. Thus, parents wanting their children to be successful are also hoping to share in the success of their children.

Even before the emergence of Pare identity in the early colonial period, ritual was often a divisive rather than unifying force in the life of highland communities. Although many elders contend that the traditional passage rites are important parts of their cultural heritage, these ideals are seldom achieved. Not only are there new passage rites, such as going to school and participating in labor migration, but most Usangi residents also tend to embrace Christianity or Islam with greater fervor than they do the old passage rites. As a consequence, the disappearance of many of the old customs surrounding the life crises is not always viewed as a loss. Members of the organized religious groups have reinterpreted and incorporated some of the passage rites (e.g., bridewealth) into their own ritual lives and replaced others with their Moslem and Christian counterparts. Being Pare today for many Usangi people is not inconsistent with being good Christians and Moslems, for only a few families in the most remote parts of Usangi do not claim allegiance to one or the other of these groups.

HOMELAND

In recent years, the close relationship between Pare identity and residence in the Pare highlands (*vwasu*) has been called into question by two related factors—increasing land shortage in the highlands and the cash-earning stints which most men spend away from home. But instead of forsaking their identity as highlanders, those who must leave have evolved a variety of mechanisms which help them maintain close ties with those who remain at home in the highlands.

A common response among those who have some land, but not enough to support their families, is to seek additional plots on the adjacent plains. People in such circumstances typically commute to lowlands farms during planting, growing, and harvesting seasons, but maintain their homesteads in the mountain community and thereby their identity as highlanders.

Commercial ventures present another alternative for those whose farming lands are inadequate. Given the land pressure, cash-cropping as a commercial enterprise is not practiced on a large scale in the Usangi highlands. Coffee is the only cash crop planted in North Pare and, in contrast to many parts of South Pare and to Kilimanjaro, the amounts seem petty and insignificant. Two kinds of commercial activities, however, are practiced extensively in the highland: shopkeeping and marketing of locally produced pots. As evidence of the extensiveness of shopkeeping in the highlands, figures abstracted from official records show Usangi to have about one shop for every forty-four households.[3] With respect to the pot trade, a locally owned co-operative buys pots from the peasant women who produce them. When they have accumulated a large number of pots, the men hire a truck to transport them to markets in Moshi, Arusha, and other cities. These same men then act in turn as retailers.[4] However, the most common alternative for those who find themselves with insufficient farm land is leaving home in order to engage in cash-earning activities elsewhere.

About three out of every four Usaugi men leave the highlands. They fall into three categories, differentiated from one another by the nature of the subsistence activities and the ties maintained with home and kin. These categories and their relative proportions are: first, the wage earners and petty businessmen who maintain strong ties (the largest of the categories accounting for about 85 percent of the out-migrants); second, men who continue in the traditional subsistence activities of farming and herding and who typically maintain some ties with the homeland (approximately 10 percent of the migrants fall in this category); and third, disenchanted, alienated men, usually cash earners who maintain few if any ties with home and kin (accounting for only about 5 percent of the men residing away from home). Each of these situations and its effects on highland residence as a primary symbol of Pare ethnicity are considered in turn.

WAGE-EARNERS AND BUSINESSMEN

Most men go to work either in a city where there are varied opportunities to earn cash, or they work on a plantation or for a company where many men work at similar jobs. Working for a plantation or a company usually means living quite some distance from the nearest city, yet both environments share certain similarities that stand in strong contrast to life in Usangi. Both kinds of situations are multiethnic in composition, are typically characterized by relatively large flux of population, and offer opportunities to earn cash in amounts almost unprecedented for those

[3]These figures were abstracted from the Trading Licenses Register in the Revenue Office of the Pare District Council in Same on November 7–8, 1968.

[4]Although precise records were not kept on production cycles, informants describe the production of pots in Usangi in a remarkably similar fashion to that described by Nash (1961) where production tends to peak near festival days when the extra cash is needed. Pots are made by Usangi women when they have the time and when they need the cash.

who remain at home. Men leaving the highlands to earn cash tend to go to places where kinsmen and/or friends are already working and thus where they can get some assistance in getting settled. Nowadays Usangi men work in so many different locations that the man seeking his first job can almost assuredly count on the assistance of some kinsman or acquaintance from Usangi in getting established wherever he elects to go.[5]

Most men working outside the highlands earn cash either as wage earners or as petty businessmen. The distinction is important to the men themselves, not so much because of the amounts of earnings or status since these vary considerably within each category, but because of differences in the flexibility of working arrangements in the two categories. The self-employed petty businessman has a sharp advantage over the wage earner in structuring working arrangements. This difference matters most when it comes to returning home to Usangi. The self-employed man can come and go more or less as he likes, taking into account of course the profits he may forego when he closes his shop or business. The wage earner, on the other hand, be he night watchman or government clerk, is likely to lose his job if he takes too many liberties in returning home as he pleases or in attending to domestic crises.

The life styles, living arrangements, relations with family, and so on of cash earners differ considerably. Much of this variation, however, is not a function of different types of cash earners but rather can be accounted for by a developmental model of the cash earner. The developmental cycle of working away from home is rooted in the individual's own life cycle and a different combination of attributes characterizes each of the stages, as shown in Table 5.1. Familial relations, especially the dependency

---

[5]Proportions of persons residing outside the highlands must be taken as an approximation because of frequent movement between the highlands and outside, making a firm count meaningless. Individuals were interviewed in the following places: Arusha (14 potential interviewees; 14 interviewed); Arusha Forest Reserve (5 of 5 interviewed); Moshi (9 of 9 interviewed); Rau/Kahe, Kilimanjaro District (5 of 8 interviewed); Arusha Chini, Kilimanjaro District (1 of 1 interviewed); Kisangara Chini/Nyumba ya Mungu Dam Site, Pare District (7 of 7 interviewed); Same, Pare District (11 of 11 interviewed); Dar es Salaam (6 of 11 interviewed); Tanga (6 of 10 interviewed); and miscellaneous places in South Pare (1 of 5 interviewed). Due to distance and time limitations, individuals in the following places were not interviewed: Mwanza and Bukoba (8); Dodoma (5); Iringa (1); Morogoro (1); and Lushoto (3). In all, 65 percent of the potential respondents living outside the Usangi highlands were interviewed. Information on many of the others was supplied by their kinsmen.

Table 5.1 The Developmental Cycle of Working Outside

Phase	Individual's Stage in Life Cycle	Individual's Stage in Cash-Earning Cycle	Residential Arrangements (Highlands)	Residential Arrangements (Outside)	Family and Dependency Relations
I	The young man has usually finished his years of schooling but has not yet married.	Goes out to look for work.	Has not built a house.	Lives with a friend or relative.	Depends on friends and relatives with whom he lives until he can secure a job.
II	Marries.	Accumulates sufficient bridewealth to marry.	Builds a house for his wife in the highlands where she is expected to farm.	Continues living with the friend or relative, or perhaps rents own room.	More economically independent now, he must attempt to pay his own way and to support his wife.
III	Becomes a father.	Continues working outside.	Must constantly choose between investment in the two places where his interests lie.		His wife, children, and other kinsmen depend on his earnings.

| IV | Becomes a mature man. | Continues working outside; begins grooming successor. | By now he usually has established his own independent living arrangements in both places. | Many others come to depend on him as they come to look for work or perhaps go to school. |
| V | Becomes an elder. | Returns home. | Moves back to the highlands to live in the house he has built there. | He comes to depend on his children (or his successors who have taken over his business ventures). |

of the cash earner on others or they on him, changes through the cycle. It begins with the individual leaving the highlands to seek a means to earn cash and ends with his eventual return to his home country. In the early phases he works to accumulate bridewealth to marry and to save in order to build a house of his own in the highlands. Following the midpoint of the cycle, he begins to formalize plans for returning home by grooming his successor. The cycle terminates with his return to the highlands.

Men who work away from home usually maintain two residences. One they build among their close agnates on land belonging to their clan; the other they must establish at the place where they work. For most men, closing one's house and moving one's family to the city is as unthinkable as it is infrequent. Nearly every cash earner who was asked about his rationale for building a house in his traditional village recited cases of men whose successful economic ventures outside the highlands turned to naught almost overnight, leaving them in the end able to return only to their traditional homes and investments there. Cash earners build their houses in the highlands as soon as they can manage. Often the two residences the cash earner maintains are very unequal—the usual pattern being that the better residence is located at home even though the cash earner may spend most of his time away from it.

The phase of a man in the cash-earning cycle determines the composition of his two residential units. For example, a young man looking for a job is usually not married. After he finds a job and establishes himself, he will build a house in the highlands and marry. In addition to long-term changes linked to the individual's life cycle, certain short-run factors may influence the composition of the residential units. The dependents of cash earners (wives and children in particular) spend various segments of the year in the two places where the household head's interests lie. The trend is for women to spend the planting and harvesting seasons in the highlands and other parts of the year with their husbands. But even this may be disrupted by other factors such as pregnancy, health, or number of small children.

In terms of familial relations, the cash earner becomes increasingly independent as he progresses through the cycle. Others come to depend on him for cash, assistance, and hospitality in much the same way as he was once dependent on those who preceded him.

There are two primary ways in which cash earners interact

with those who remain at home. One of these is through occasional visits in either direction. The other is through the sharing of earnings with kinsmen at home.

The men who work outside the highlands in places easily accessible by bus may return home frequently, perhaps as often as every week. Others, particularly those who live far away or those whose occupations make it difficult, may not return home for years. Visits of cash earners to their homes in the highlands provide an opportunity to examine the welfare of their dependents, their farms, and their livestock. Opinions and judgments of cash earners may be sought either through letter or personal contact, especially in matters in which they are expected to be involved financially. In addition to visiting relatives themselves, cash earners are usually happy to receive their relatives and friends from the highlands when they arrive in the city. Visiting and receiving visitors are important means of maintaining the ties between cash earners and their kinsmen.

In addition to face-to-face contact, other means of interaction keep cash earners in touch with home. The most widespread alternative means is through the single cash earner who acts as intermediary for others from his home area. Customarily any cash earner who intends to return to the highlands announces his plans among his fellows who then prepare letters to forward to their wives, parents, or children at home. Often the sealed letters are accompanied by cash in amounts ranging from a few shillings to a hundred or more. The man who acts as carrier is generally trustworthy, for he acts within a context of friends and relatives. Moreover, he will eventually need to rely on others to perform this same service for him when they return for visits.

Another institution that operates to maintain contact between wage earners and their kinsmen is the post office. Although mail arrives in the highlands nowadays five times a week, a large number of registered letters arriving in each mail attests to the fact that some cash earners depend on the post office to send money to their relatives. Nevertheless the cash earner returning to the highlands is preferred over the postal service. The fact that personal delivery is both quicker and cheaper is probably not the most important reason why it tends to be favored over the post office. A more significant reason lies in the advantage that personal delivery provides to both sender and recipient. The carrier functions as intermediary between the cash earner and his kinsmen, and can report personally to each about the welfare of the other. In a word, it is cash that both draws most men from their traditional homes into cities, and helps to maintain, through the sharing of earnings, the ties between those who go and those who remain behind.

A variety of mechanisms thus help the cash earner maintain solidarity with his homeland: visiting, receiving visitors, sending money, and establishing homesteads in the highlands. These mechanisms not only foster symbolic and vicarious identification among the men who work outside the highlands with what happens at home, but they often make the absentee husbands, fathers, and sons *de facto* participants in the social life of the Usangi highlands.

FARMERS/HERDERS

Perhaps as many as one out of every ten individuals leaving his country to engage in economic pursuits elsewhere becomes neither a wage earner nor a petty businessman but rather continues in the traditional subsistence activities of farming and/or herding. One reason that may motivate such people is the same one that motivates many who seek cash-earning occupations, namely the land shortage. Although some who emigrate under these conditions are probably able to find wage employment from time to time, many claim to prefer the greater economic security of agricultural and herding activities to the probable alternative of periodic unemployment in the city. A further factor is that many lack the minimum skills, particularly the education, often needed to obtain wage employment.

Another reason why some people emigrate from their country lies in social rather than in economic necessity. Informants mention individuals who had left the highlands after being suspected of witchcraft. Often before such individuals are accused publically, mounting social pressures make their situations so difficult that they leave the highlands, as it were, of their own volition.

Whatever their reasons for leaving, the life style of such emigrants is qualitatively different from that of the cash earner. Farmers/herders must build durable houses outside the highlands, for unlike the cash earners, all their subsistence activities tend to be conducted in the single location where they live. And unlike cash earners, the farmers/herders expect their wives and children to live with them, since all family members have important roles in the farming/herding domestic economy. The nature of the subsistence activities thus dictates to some degree the types of family organization that are most adaptive under various circumstances. One such difference can be seen in the fact that the farmers/herders cannot afford to send their wives to the highlands during the planting and harvesting seasons as do many cash earners—for this is the time when the wives' services are most needed in the fields where they live. Unlike cash earners, who typically maintain both residential ties (in the form of houses in the highlands) and kinship ties (through visiting in both directions, sharing of earnings, letter-writing, etc.), the farmers/herders usually do not maintain such strong ties. Many lack sufficient land in the highlands on which to establish homesteads, and the similarity of the rain, and hence the agricultural, cycles makes it impracticable to attempt to farm in the highlands.

Like cash earners, farmers/herders can expect to receive visitors from the highlands from time to time. And they too are welcomed in the highlands whenever they are able to return. But the interaction between highlanders and emigrants often does not stop here. When faced with shortages of grain crops (currently a common occurrence), highlanders often turn to their relatives who farm elsewhere as potential suppliers. This arrangement is advantageous to both parties, since the farmers can sell their crops to their relatives for more than wholesalers are prepared to pay, and highlanders obtain the grain at a lower price than is possible through any other source.

Although the nature of their subsistence activities dictates that farmers/herders spend most of their lives outside the Pare highlands, few forego their desire to return to it. When sick, many seek help in traditional Pare medicines and curing practices. Often very old persons return to the highlands to await death among their kinsmen. As with cash earners who die outside the highlands, the bodies of deceased farmers/herders are frequently taken back to the highlands for burial. Finally, farmers and herders maintain solidarity with the country from which they come through the perpetuation of traditional Pare rituals to celebrate the rites of transition, many of which are remembered better by those living away from home than by those who are in the highlands.

"DISENCHANTED" INDIVIDUALS

In addition to cash earners and farmers/herders, there is at least one other category of Pares who live outside the highlands. These people may be referred to as "disenchanted" individuals because, to a greater or lesser extent, they have cut both residential and kinship ties with the homeland. Many people probably feel this way some of the time, yet only a few remain permanently disenchanted. Some people appear to be already disenchanted when they leave the highlands in search of employment. Others become disenchanted as a result of the frustrations caused by life outside. But, in strict numerical terms, these alienated individuals account for only a small number of the people residing away from home.

Two brothers provide an illustration of such disenchanted individuals. Their father Masudi, who has twenty children by his two wives, gives little assistance to Rashidi and Juma who are middle sons, primarily because he has already given all the land he has to their older brothers. The older sons maintain ties with their parents and, although they work outside the highlands, have built houses near their father's. However, Rashidi and Juma are disenchanted with thoughts of returning home and at present have no plans for building houses in the highlands. Rashidi lives in Moshi; his brother in Dar es Salaam. Neither sends money home nor has much contact with kinsmen who work in the same towns. Both brothers are in their early twenties, and each feels he has plenty of time to mend the rift between himself and his kinsmen. Rashidi and Juma have cut themselves off; they have not been cut off by others. There will be a place for them as prodigal sons, even though it may be only a meager one. The father, though aware of his sons' whereabouts, has temporarily given up trying to communicate with either of them since they have not responded to his previous attempts.

A major source of disenchantment lies in the conceptions people living in the highlands hold about the nature of life outside. Those who return home periodically are the primary source of information about urban life. At times, a cash earner may exaggerate his success in the city, claiming for example to have a better job or living conditions than he in fact does. As a result, the conceptions that develop in the minds of their younger siblings or children may be far more favorable than the reality of the situation warrants. Many are disappointed when they go out on their own to learn that life in the city is neither so good nor so easy as they had been led to believe. This discrepancy between expectations and actual conditions doubtlessly accounts for some of the disenchantment to be found among Pares living away from home. Irrespective of the source of their alienation, the crucial difference between these individuals and the others who work as cash earners or farmers/herders is that the "disenchanted" cut (even if only temporarily) most ties with home. They neither build houses in the Pare highlands nor maintain relations with their kinsmen there.

Thus, cash earners, farmers/herders, and disenchanted individuals are differentiated from one another by the kinds of ties each maintains with the homeland. Cash earners maintain both residential and kin ties. Emigrant farmers/herders maintain only kinship ties, since they in effect move from the Pare highlands to establish residences elsewhere. And disenchanted individuals maintain neither residential nor kin ties. At different points in his life, an individual may move from an approximation of one of these models to another. A disenchanted young man may become reconciled to his homeland and his kinsmen, in which case he may resemble a typical wage earner. Alternatively, a wage earner who becomes discouraged with his inability to make good in the city can become disenchanted with both home and city—since he may be unable to fulfill obligations to his kinsmen or to realize his dreams. He may try his luck at farming or herding cattle and thereby establish a permanent residence outside the highlands. If he is successful in his venture, he may reestablish relations with his kinsmen.

Present trends indicate that Pare people working away from home, especially those in urban areas, are not likely to give up their strong allegiance to the homeland in favor of permanent urban residence. Even though, it might be argued, there would probably be a natural evolution over several generations in that direction, national government policies discourage movement to cities and encourage instead rural development—all of which tends to reinforce Pare skepticism in urban life. Despite the fact that significant numbers of Pares spend considerable portions of their lives away, ties to the homeland are maintained in a variety of ways.

Of the Pares living away from home, only cash earners have any substantial effect on the local society and economy. They provide significant cash inputs for the local economy, create important links to the outside world, serve as diffusers of information about faraway places and new ideas, and continue to play important roles either in person or by proxy in their kinship groups and neighborhoods. These people, who account for the vast majority of those who go outside the highlands, do not forsake their identity as Pare. Although seldom physically present in the highlands, these individuals show great commitment to kinsmen and homeland. There is little evidence to suggest that their cash-earning activities undermine their identity as Pare highland farmers—for most men keep in close touch with home and it is to such a life that most aspire to return.

LANGUAGE

As ritual and residential bases of identification become more confused, language serves increasingly as an unambiguous focus of Pare ethnic identity. For those living away from the Pare highlands, using the traditional vernacular serves as a symbol of identity, separating the culturally heterogeneous urban population into exclusive groups based on place of origin. For those who remain at home, the Pare (Asu) language is a ready badge to symbolize unity and set the Pare people apart from intruders. In the next few pages, we examine the current complexity of language use in Usangi, showing how contact and change have served to strengthen and invigorate rather than undermine the role of the Pare language.

Language Abilities

Pare (Asu) is the most widely known language in Usangi, spoken by most persons as their native language. A very small proportion of Usangi residents are not native speakers of the Pare language. These are primarily women who grew up speaking other languages but who married Pare-speaking men and have lived in Usangi long enough to become fluent speakers of their husbands' native language.

Since Arab caravans first moved through the Pare foothills in the mid-nineteenth century, Swahili has been gaining currency to the point where today about 80 percent of Usangi residents speak it fluently (see Table 5.2). Most of the remainder have some knowledge of the language since it is almost impossible not to know and use some Swahili in the contemporary cultural milieu of Usangi. Differences in age, sex, and literacy are related as follows to Swahili-speaking abilities (see Table 5.3).

Table 5.2 Speaking Abilities of Interviewees
In Pare (Asu), Swahili, English, and African Vernaculars

Language	Speaks Fluently	Speaks a Little	Doesn't Speak	Totals
Pare (Asu)[a]	>99% (158)	<1% (1)	— (0)	159
Swahili[b]	79% (127)	16% (24)	5% (8)	159
English[c]	3% (5)	29% (46)	68% (108)	159
Other African Vernacular[d]	———	16% (24)	——— 34% (135)	159

[a]All those who were born and grew up in Usangi are fluent speakers of Pare (Asu). The one person who "speaks only a little" Pare (Asu) was not born in Pare. I used my assistant's evaluation of a person's abilities in Pare (Asu) whenever there was any doubt.
[b]Ability to speak Swahili was evaluated differently. The individual's abilities in spoken Swahili was scored at the time of the interview according to the following criteria:
  Speaker of Fluent Swahili—those who report themselves to be fluent speakers of Swahili and/or cases in which Swahili was the language of the interview without posing difficulties for the respondent;
  Speaker of a Little Swahili—those who report themselves to speak less than fluent Swahili *and* when this was obvious in the interview (both conditions must obtain); in a few cases, I decided that a particular respondent had so much difficulty in responding to questions in Swahili that he should not be considered a "fluent speaker" even though he made this claim for himself;
  Non-Speaker of Swahili—those who report themselves to be unable to speak Swahili and cases in which the interview had to be conducted in Asu with the assistant acting as my translator since the Swahili of the respondent and my Asu were inadequate for effective communication; in a few cases, I decided that a person could speak a little Swahili although he did not make this claim for himself.
[c]Since no English was used in the interview, gauging the respondent's English abilities in the same manner his knowledge of Swahili was determined was not possible. However, with two of the five respondents reporting to be fluent speakers of English, I subsequently had long conversations in English. For those who report that they speak "a little English," I estimate that they know proportionately less than those who report the ability to speak "a little Swahili."
[d]No distinctions were made between those who know only a little bit of another vernacular and those who speak another African language fluently. Reported ability is the only criterion used here.

SEX

Usangi men almost universally tend to speak Swahili. This is not the case for women, more than one third of whom are judged to speak it less than fluently. Unlike the women, most Usangi men have spent time away from home working at wage-earning jobs in cities or on plantations, or perhaps serving in one of the world wars, where they learned Swahili. In the past men have had

Table 5.3   Swahili Language Abilities

	Speaks Swahili Less Than Fluently[a]	Speaks Swahili Fluently[a]	Number
Men	3%	97%	72
Women	35%	65%	87
Age below 27 years[b]	8%	92%	82
Age 27 or more	32%	68%	77
Has never written a letter in any language[c]	69%	31%	32
Has written a letter in Swahili[c]	10%	90%	98
Has written letters in Swahili and English[c]	0%	100%	27

[a]Criteria explained in footnote b of Table 5.2.
[b]Median age = 27 years.
[c]Based solely on individual's self-report.

greater exposure to educational institutions than women and they operate in more contexts in which Swahili is used than do their wives.

AGE

Younger people have greater facility in using Swahili than do older people. Both the increasing usage of Swahili in general and the greater exposure of young people to formal educational institutions contribute to this trend.

LITERACY

Facility with spoken Swahili is associated with literacy; the more literate a person is, the more likely he is to be a fluent speaker of Swahili. There are, however, fluent speakers of Swahili who are illiterate. Learning to read and write ordinarily takes place in Swahili nowadays; thus, it is almost impossible to be literate and not to know Swahili. No one was discovered who claims to have learned to read in Pare (Asu) in the early mission schools who is not now also able to read Swahili. Moreover, the paucity of published materials in the Pare language and the difficulties ordinarily encountered by native speakers who attempt to write it militate against exclusive literacy in that language.

English is being continually deemphasized as Swahili becomes more important as a symbol of Tanzanian nationalism. In Tanzania however, English remains important as a language of instruction in higher education (in secondary schools and at the university), in commerce (not only with non-African countries but also with close neighbors like Kenya and Uganda),[6] and in dealings with foreigners. Within Usangi itself, English is not used much and very few people are in fact able to speak English fluently. There are many however who claim to know "a little" English, but this usually means they have been taught some English at school or that they learned a few English phrases while working with Europeans.

Some of the older people probably had sufficient contact with German colonialists to have learned at least a few phrases from that language. German colonial policy, however, did not encourage Africans to learn German. Consequently, few Pares ever spoke this language to any extent. In recollecting colonial days, most Pares claim that the Germans learned the vernacular to a much greater extent than did the British after them.

Arabic forms the basis for many of the greetings used by the people of Usangi, especially the Moslems, many of whom say they are able to "read" the Koran. This usually means, however, that they are able to pronounce the words of the Koran. Most are dependent on a Swahili-language interpretation for the meanings of the passages whose words they utter.

Some Usangi residents claim abilities in speaking other African vernaculars[7] besides Pare (Asu). Most of those who make such claims say they learned these languages while living away from Usangi, are typically men with at least standard four educations and are fluent speakers of Swahili (presumably the vehicle of the learning). Knowing another African vernacular is almost by definition dependent on contact. But contact with non-Pares, even outside the highlands, does not necessitate a knowledge of other vernaculars since Swahili can and usually does serve as the

[6]Recent decisions of the Kenya Government to employ Swahili more widely in government and commerce may limit further the use of English in Tanzania's relations with its close neighbors. (See "Kenya Is Facing Language Woes" in the *New York Times,* November 26, 1970.)

[7]The language and frequencies with which they are mentioned are: Arusha (9), Bondei (2), Chagga (83), Digo (4), Gogo (1), Hehe (1), Kamba (1), Kikuyu (1), Massai (1), Shambaa (3), Taita (1), and Zigula (1). Of the 24 claiming to speak another African language, 19 named only one language, two named two languages, two named three languages, and one named four languages.

medium of communication. Many of those who live outside the highlands, especially women, live in enclaves of other Pares and tend to limit their social interaction to such people, in which case the Pare language is usually spoken.

Who then are those who report that they learn other vernaculars? Since Swahili is more likely to be used than any vernacular as the medium of communication between members of different ethnic groups, learning another tribal language or even bothering to use its greetings may be more an indicator of openness and sociability than of anything else. Some data support this hypothesis. Those individuals interviewed outside Usangi were asked whether they like their work and style of life. All those who say they do also report knowledge of another African vernacular. And interestingly, all those who say they dislike their work and way of life in the city do not report the ability to use any other vernacular. This rather striking correlation suggests that those who learn to speak other African vernaculars may have certain personal qualities (e.g., openness, willingness to learn, sociability, etc.) which those who do not bother to do so may lack.

The Domains of Asu and Swahili

Although about 80 percent of Usangi's population are bilingual in Pare (Asu) and Swahili, the two languages are not interchangeable with respect to appropriate times of use. Each language has rather clearly defined settings in which its use is more appropriate than the other. Inappropriate use in time or situation may bring the wrath of elders (if, say, children were to use Swahili in addressing their parents) or of the government (if, say, someone were to use Pare publicly in a development meeting).

Usangi residents were asked to name the situations in which Swahili is used (not "should be used") rather than another language. With reference to its use in Usangi, they responded: at the hospital (52 times); with people who do not speak Pare (Asu) (30); in the shops (22); at home (17); in school and/or reading (15);[8] in government/TANU meetings (14); at the court or post office (13);[9] and at the mosque (4). These data show that people

---

[8]The Swahili word *kusoma* (to read, to study) makes it difficult to distinguish between these two situations.

[9]The court and the post office in Usangi are adjacent to one another. Reference to one does not exclude the other in popular usage.

associate Swahili primarily with the government, the political party, with social services, with schools and literacy, with foreigners, and with commerce. Only a few people mentioned the use of Swahili at home. Swahili is in fact not used much in most Usangi homes, but the situations in which villagers do use it at home are worth noting.

Young people often speak to each other in Swahili—practicing what they are learning at school, as a way to tell secrets in front of their preschool siblings who speak little or no Swahili, and as an imitation of their parents, especially of their fathers. Sometimes men will speak to each other at home using Swahili—usually about matters of business or about affairs which concern neither women nor children. Occasionally younger women will speak to one another using Swahili, perhaps as a symbol to others of their education, or, as men do, to hide things from their young children.

Cross-status communication almost never takes place in Swahili. Men seldom are seen speaking to women in Swahili. Mothers rarely can be heard addressing their children in that language. When used at home, it seems most often to be in contexts in which speakers of similar statuses converse with one another. The most notable exception to this rule perhaps is that fathers can sometimes be observed speaking Swahili to their children with the intention of teaching these young children Swahili phrases before they start to school. But in this situation, and in other conversations between old and young people that take place in Swahili, the elder member of the dyad appears to initiate the use of the nonindigenous language. The content of such a dialog is often limited to superficial and mundane matters. In Usangi homes, things of importance tend to be discussed in Pare (Asu).

Thus far, we have been talking about spoken language. When it comes to writing, the use of language changes. All those who claim to have written a letter report that they have used Swahili for this purpose (see Table 5.4). Less than half of them have used Pare (Asu) for this purpose, and less than one fourth have written a letter in English. Swahili is used with much greater frequency in writing than is the Pare language. People who would ordinarily not speak to one another using Swahili (e.g., husband and wife, parent and child, etc.) will write to each other using that language. Several informants claim that most letters they write to other Pare speakers consist of Swahili sentences

Table 5.4 Writing Abilities

Language	Used to Write	Not Used to Write	Number[a]
Swahili	100%	0%	125
Asu	44%	56%	125
English	22%	78%	125

[a]Only 125 of the 159 individuals are able to write.

and employ Pare (Asu) words and terms for ideas which are hard to express in Swahili.

The people of Usangi believe that before the coming of Arabs and Europeans into their country, Asu and Gweno were sufficient for all situations involving language, and indeed were the only languages in use by the residents of highland Pare. Contact has, of course, necessitated the use of nonindigenous languages. Recollections of linguistic difficulties in early contact times can be found in the oral traditions of the highlanders. One often-told story concerns a man who was shot because the Germans, who could not understand that he was asking for permission to urinate in the bushes, thought he was trying to run away.

From one point of view, we might interpret Pare (Asu) as a residual language, continuing to be used where Swahili has yet to make serious incursion. We might argue on the other hand that it is not a residual language at all, but one which continues to be used in situations where it has always been used: in the kitchen, on the farm, at home, with friends, and in greetings. Since the early colonial period, it has had the additional important role of serving as the Pare language. In an increasingly multilingual environment, and as other symbols of Pare ethnicity wane in significance, their common language must play an even greater role as a symbol of Pare-ness.

Language Attitudes

Although no one seriously believes that Pare (Asu) will be forgotten in the near future, many people are concerned about the future of their language in the face of government policy decisions making Swahili the national language of Tanzania. During the colonial period, few people perceived English as a threat to the continued use of Pare (Asu) since so few Usangi residents had any facility with that language. Most people, however, speak Swahili readily, and the future relationship between local and national languages is not clear to them. Because English has been removed from its former position of prominence, its future too seems unclear. Several questions dealing with attitudes toward Asu, Swahili, and English were asked of residents.

Should Asu be the language of the home?　Many persons who express quite radical opinions concerning the validity of many Asu traditions hold firmly that their traditional language should continue to be used. When asked whether they would like to see Swahili used more in the home, almost all the respondents (94 percent) say flatly "no."

Should Swahili be the public language in Usangi?　When asked about their feelings with respect to the use of Swahili and Asu outside the home, just over half (51 percent) say they do not oppose more widespread use of Swahili than is current. Men express this view more than women (61 percent as opposed to 43 percent), indicating perhaps their greater facility with the language and their greater participation in the institutions where it is used most.

Should there be more books in Asu?　Since the end of German-run schools in the Pare highlands, few books have been published in Asu. Although the Lutheran Church has always used the vernacular in its services (unlike the Roman Catholics who chose Swahili), all church groups had used the Swahili Bible until 1967. In that year, the Lutherans in association with the Seventh Day Adventists published the first Pare (Asu) version of the New Testament. Expectations prior to its publication were high, but young people have found it difficult to read, despite its extensive glossary.

Of those asked, nearly two thirds (65 percent) say they would prefer to see books published in Pare (Asu) instead of in Swahili, a preference which is inversely related to amount of education and to fluency in Swahili.[10] Had the sample included some people who have completed secondary or university educations, the trends noted here might not continue to hold. Conversations with better-educated Pares, particularly secondary and university students, seldom reveal a preference for Swahili. Many prefer to

[10]For those with standard two educations or less, preference for books in Asu is 68 percent; for those with standard three or four educations, 69 percent; for those with standard five or more, 50 percent. Of those judged to be less than fluent in Swahili 93 percent prefer Asu books; this drops to 73 percent among those who speak Swahili fluently.

read and speak English, a language which they quite naturally associate with higher education. Some feel that written Pare (Asu) provides the best medium for the preservation of local traditions and history and they advocate a wider role for it. Many well-educated Pares claim that Swahili offers few of the challenges of English or Pare (Asu).[11]

Are those who use Swahili and English being disrespectful? Many Usangi residents (50 percent) feel that Pares who use Swahili or English in a homogeneous group of native Pare (Asu) speakers must be up to no good. These languages, perhaps imperfectly known to some of those listening, are sometimes used to communicate several levels of meaning at once, all of which may not be understood by everyone present. The use of foreign languages for this purpose can be quite complex, involving the backhanded forms of Swahili known as *kinyume,* in which even those who speak the language reasonably well under ordinary conditions can be tricked by the use of inverted meanings. These may be coupled with unfamiliar vocabulary or the patterned alternation of certain phonemes (as, for example, in the forms of English known as "Pig Latin"). Since most Pares tend to be clever in such uses of the Pare language, many people feel that those who use foreign languages in Usangi are making puns at the expense of others. In addition to such subtle uses of language, young people sometimes speak openly in Swahili or English about those people whom they judge not able to understand them.

One half (50 percent) of the respondents think that the use of Swahili in front of elders shows disrespect. Even more (62 percent) think such use of English is disrespectful. Such opinions are inversely related to degree of literacy.[12]

Is a knowledge of English necessary today?   The increasing national emphasis on the use of Swahili in education and government presumably will make knowledge of English less a necessity

---

[11]President Nyerere has suggested that the myth that scholarly books cannot be written in Swahili offers equally great challenges to young Tanzanians. See his *Dibaji* (Preface) to *Uchumi Bora* (Nyerere 1966).

[12]For Swahili, 63 percent of the illiterates say its use is disrespectful; 52 percent of those literate in Swahili say so; and 26 percent of those literate in both Swahili and English express this opinion. For English, the percentages are 72, 66, and 37 respectively.

for the ordinary Tanzanian than it has tended to be in the past. When asked whether a knowledge of English is necessary today, more than half (55 percent) of the respondents say yes. More men (70 percent) than women (43 percent) say so. And such a response is more frequent among the fluent speakers of Swahili (59 percent) than among those who know it less perfectly (41 percent).

Thus, responses to the attitudinal questions which may appear at first somewhat contradictory actually show Usangi residents are accustomed to multilingualism and have rather well-defined ideas about appropriate uses of each language (e.g., Pare [Asu], rather than Swahili or English, is the language of respect to be used before the elders; the Pare language is the most appropriate one for the home; both Swahili and English have uses in other situations; etc.). These attitudes support the current relationship between the Pare language and Swahili in which each language has a more-or-less clearly defined and separate functional domain: the Pare language is associated with home, farming, family, etc., while Swahili is the language associated with government, schools, literacy, social services, etc. This relationship between the two languages, which has been developing for many years, has been inextricably established through government directives that Swahili must be used in all primary schools and in all public meetings of government or party.

There are a number of indications, however, that suggest the present linguistic profile of Usangi is not stable. First, increased educational opportunities for both males and females, especially at the primary school level, is resulting in increased literacy among Usangi's residents and hence their greater facility in using both spoken and written forms of Swahili. Second, the analysis of attitudes toward language shows increasing literacy and greater facility with Swahili to be associated with more liberal attitudes toward the use of nonindigenous languages. Thus, increasing literacy can be expected to produce a more relaxed acceptance of Swahili.

Yet it does not follow that increased use and approval of Swahili will result in the loss of the Pare language. The Pare people show strong devotion to their language and there is no reason to believe that they will not continue to do so, at least in the near future. Desires and attempts to preserve Pare (Asu) are widespread: nearly everyone says it should continue as the language of the home; Seventh Day Adventists and Lutherans continue to employ it in their churches; some claim it should be written (e.g., certain church groups, well-educated people who think it would be useful in preserving traditions, and the majority of interviewees who think it should be used to publish more books). But if current trends may be taken as indications of what is likely to occur in the future, it appears that Pare (Asu) will not become a written language. This prediction is supported by the facts that Pare children are not taught to write Pare (Asu) in school, those who do try to write in the language claim it is difficult, and the recently published New Testament in Pare (Asu) has not been well received.

One can only speculate about the relationship of Pare (Asu) and Swahili in the years to come. Several factors, occurring with increasing frequency, would appear to militate against universal knowledge of the Pare language in the future: the intermarriage of Pare-speakers with non-Pare speakers; the long periods of time which many men spend away from the highlands while working in cities; and the inability of children of Pare parents who grow up away from Usangi to speak the Pare language. Despite such ominous and disruptive influences, emotional attachments to the Pare language are strong and immediate prospects for its survival seem very good indeed. Its role as a primary symbol of Pare ethnic identity is likely to keep the language, albeit changing and evolving, alive for many years to come.

Thus far in this chapter, we have seen that Pare ethnicity has not been undermined as a result of substantial changes in the symbols of this identity. In the case of ritual, the individual life crises have slowly and, for the most part, quietly been replaced by Christian and Moslem counterparts and new passage rites like going to school and participating in labor migration. Being Pare today is not inconsistent with being Moslem or Christian. While many Pares spend a lot of time away from their homes, most maintain close ties through a variety of means so that close association with the mountain homeland is still an important and viable part of Pare ethnic identity. And language continues to serve as a primary symbol of Pare ethnicity despite the fact that most Pares also speak Swahili. Thus, Pare ethnicity has evolved since the early colonial period. Though changed somewhat in content and symbolic expression, it is alive and well. Since independence in the early 1960s, Pares have been developing an identity as Tanzanians which supplements, but does not replace, Pare ethnicity.

IDENTITY AS TANZANIANS

Being Tanzanians is something unique for the indigenous peoples of this new nation. Belonging to a European-governed colonial territory is a far cry from being a citizen of a nation whose people have the opportunity to guide their own destiny. United first in struggling for *uhuru* ("independence"), the common efforts of Tanzania's peoples have been directed since independence to a new set of goals: overcoming poverty, ignorance, and disease. Tanzania's articulate spokesman, President Julius Nyerere, seeks support of the country's citizens, most of whom are rural farmers, by attempting to convince them that theirs is a set of common problems for which roughly similar solutions are appropriate. In just over ten years since Tanganyika gained its independence in 1961, Nyerere has worked hard to develop a sense of national identity among his people. With the assistance of many of his countrymen committed to the general goal of developing the nation, a set of symbols of Tanzanian identity has been forged. Although the number of specific symbols associated with Tanzanian national identity defies enumeration, three of those which the government has employed to signify Tanzanian identity will be examined. These are history, language, and indigenous culture.

HISTORY

During the colonial era, Tanzanian children were taught the history of the expansion of the British Empire and of the blessings wrought by the French Revolution. By implication, they were also taught that Africa had no history, save that written by Europeans about their explorations and conquests of the "dark continent," a perniciously ethnocentric epithet at best. Modern Tanzanian historiographers are part of a growing number of historians attempting to overcome such a view of Africa. They are now at work writing a different sort of history, one which spans the years from the dawn of man himself in Tanzania's Olduvai Gorge to the age of the Arusha Declaration and the growth of *ujamaa* socialism as the guiding philosophy of modern Tanzania. Many of the archives with which the new historians must work are living ones, for the elders of Tanzania's traditional societies are the repositories of the knowledge and wisdom of the ages, which has been transmitted orally from generation to generation. And the swift and far-reaching changes of recent decades have created a sense of urgency to collect the oral traditions that tell of Tanzania's history.

In addition to collecting oral history, writing a history of modern Tanzania and its origins calls for a reinterpretation of much that has already been written. It is significant to note the differences in interpretation between the essays in Kimambo and Temu's recently published *History of Tanzania* and conventional interpretations in the past. For example, no longer is 1961 spoken of as the year when mainland Tanzania gained its independence from Britain, but as the year when Tanzanians *recaptured* independence (Cliffe 1969:239). The Maji Maji wars of 1905 to 1907 are not viewed as some kind of colonial nightmare resulting from native unrest and discontent but rather as "one of the beginnings of the struggle for lost independence" which resulted from colonialism itself (Gwassa 1969:117). Agreeing in essence with those who argue that all history is interpretation, one of the editors of the volume has this to say of the Tanzanian interior before 1800:

Certainly it is becoming clear that the Tanzanians of that period were much more in control of their own affairs than has hitherto been allowed. They were able to create political ideologies which suited their own environments and needs. It is from the realization of such achievements that the Tanzanians of today must draw inspiration and courage as they strive in developing a modern nation founded on their own culture (Kimambo 1969a:33).

The Kimambo and Temu volume and a number of others either recently published or in preparation are aimed at revolutionizing the history curriculum in the schools of Tanzania and in the process making an Afro-centric history a source of pride for Tanzanians and a symbol of their common destiny.

LANGUAGE

Tanzania is more fortunate than most of Africa's new nations which must overlook the fact that their national languages must be English or French and search elsewhere for ancient symbols to serve the cause of national identity. Swahili's origin is coastal but by the advent of the German colonial period it was already an important *lingua franca* in the interior of mainland Tanzania and beyond. Relegated second place to English during the British colonial period, Swahili was seized upon by Nyerere as the vehicle of communication among Tanzania's African majority and as an indigenous symbol of independent Tanzania. During the British colonial period, Swahili was favored as the language of education and literacy over local languages, and it has come to have significance not only in interethnic communication but also among speakers of the same vernacular while operating in such nonindigenous arenas as schools, hospitals, churches, and governmental facilities. Its elevation since the early 1960s to the status of national language has made it even more important throughout rural Tanzania. And even in the most remote parts of the country, significant portions of local communities have facility in using the language.

To underscore its association with national identity, the government now requires all government and TANU meetings, from local councils through the national assembly, to take place in Swahili. Those who employ vernaculars in such situations are liable to fines. A massive campaign is underway in Tanzania's schools to make facility—both spoken and written—of highest priority for the young people of Tanzania. But for those who may not have attended schools and for those who are unable to use Swahili to its fullest, the government is also waging a teaching program on many fronts to upgrade knowledge of Swahili and to explicate the meaning of new terms and reinforce their usage. One primary way of doing this is through a variety of radio programs aimed to teach adults and interpret new policies and terms.

As a national language, Swahili closely reflects political culture. *Maendeleo* ("development") became a national catchword in the 1960s. People were told: *usiwe kupe* ("don't be a tick") meaning "don't subsist on the life blood of others") but learn *kujitegemea* ("to be self-reliant"). Terms like *ujamaa* ("brotherhood") and *ushirikana* ("cooperation") have entered the political vocabulary of Tanzanians. Radio Tanzania and the efforts of schoolteachers and government officers have done much to interpret their meanings to the masses. Slogans like *Uhuru na Kazi* connect the efforts of the 1940s and 1950s (*uhuru*, or "independence") to the goals of the 1960s and 1970s (development through *kazi*, or hard "work").

INDIGENOUS CULTURE
Most symbols of Tanzanian nationalism are drawn from the indigenous and the ancient rather than the European and the

colonial. A few newly created forms, such as Tanzania's distinctive national dress, have emerged and become quickly associated
with national identity.

Nyerere's policies of *ujamaa* socialism are based not so much
on borrowed ideas from other socialist countries but on what he
considers to be the essence of many of Tanzania's traditional
societies—cooperation, sharing, and egalitarianism. Upon these
are built new policies which may be seen as extensions of these
ancient ideals. Nyerere has skillfully built upon what there was,
not failing in the process to recognize shortcomings in the indigenous systems. In "Socialism and Rural Development" (Nyerere
1967b:106–144), he argues there is much of value in traditional
life. He points out two particular weaknesses in the indigenous
systems: the inferior status of women in many traditional societies
(which must be overcome if the country is to develop) and poverty (which resulted from ignorance and the small scale of operations in most traditional systems). Nyerere has shown himself time
and again to be a master craftsman in building a new national
identity on a firm foundation of indigenous culture expunged of a
few inherent faults. He takes his building materials wherever he
finds them, being careful first to make certain that African culture
truly lacks a suitable ingredient before borrowing from the East
or the West.

With independence came new national days. The anniversary
of the founding of TANU, *Saba Saba* (July 7), and Independence
Day (December 8) are among the most important national holidays. To celebrate them, the government is carefully forging a
national culture by molding together the indigenous *ngoma's*
(dances) of many ethnic groups into a collage that is uniquely
Tanzanian. And in contributing to this new national culture from
their ancient heritages most ethnic groups have shown a great
deal of pride. The mixing of dance and song of many ethnic
traditions has produced a collectivity that is truly more than the
sum of its parts.

Thus, as independent traditions are fused together in creating
Tanzanian national culture, we will probably hear Tanzania referred to as a melting pot of many different traditions, but not one
in which regional and local identities are always lost in the
process. Unlike the uprooting of Europeans, Africans, Asians, and
indigenes that occurred in creating America, most of Tanzania's
peoples have remained in place and ethnic identity has not been

consumed in the process of creating a national identity. Each identity, national and local, is called up in different situations. When appropriate to express their ethnicity, Pares have as ready symbols their highland identity and their traditional language. When appropriate to express their unity with fellow Tanzanians, a powerful set of symbols is at their disposal: history, language, and culture.

6

The Future of Pare Identity

The last several decades have produced a proliferation of units with which to identify. Overlaying the bonds of traditional kinship and clanship in Usangi are a host of new identities: Asu/Gweno/ Pare; tribesman/citizen of Tanzania; rural farmer/urban worker; Moslem/Christian/pagan; educated/illiterate—to name only a few of the most obvious. The result of these changes has been a transformation of society from one in which status and social position was determined by membership in a particular kinship group to one in which individuals play a variety of roles and assume different identities as they move among multiple arenas of action.

Colonialism created a new arena of action for many highlanders—the context of the Pare tribe. As an amalgam of Asu and Gweno peoples, the new unit was able to serve as a focus of regional identity vis-à-vis outsiders and to provide a necessary organizational base for resisting colonial incursions into traditional life. During the colonial period, what had been Asu or Gweno often became Pare. And today, when speaking of themselves in Swahili, native Asu-speakers are likely to call themselves *Pare* and stop at that. By doing so, they ally themselves with the Gweno-speaking peoples (who do the same thing when they speak Swahili). The result is often a submergence of the two ethnicities in Pare identity.

IDENTITY AND ITS EXPRESSION

A number of writers have dealt with the existence of multiple and varying identities. Writing over three decades ago of the Nuer, Evans-Pritchard asked:

What does a Nuer mean when he says, "I am a man of such-and-such a *cieng?*" *Cieng* means "home," but its precise significance varies with the situation in which it is spoken. If one meets an Englishman in Germany and asks him where his home is, he may reply that it is England. If one meets the same man in London and asks him the same question he will tell one that his home is Oxfordshire, whereas if one meets him in that county he will tell one the name of the town or village in which he lives. If questioned in his town or village he will mention his particular street, and if questioned in his street he will indicate his house. So it is with the Nuer . . . (Evans-Pritchard 1940:136).

The same sort of answers could, of course, be given for the highlanders of Usangi. There are some contexts in which clan identity is more important than Pare ethnicity; the converse holds in other situations; and so it is with other loyalties of individuals. The people of Usangi call their different identities into being through symbolic ritual actions involving language, demeanor, dress, and even the expression of appropriate ideas and attitudes. Leach (1954) made this point in his study of the Kachin Hills area of Burma by noting that speaking a certain language, wearing a certain style of clothes, behaving in certain fashion were all ritual expressions of identity. In Pare, when people speak Swahili they call up their national identity as Tanzanian citizens. When they speak the Pare language, they emphasize regional, ethnic, and local identity.

Identities shift in response to situational contexts. Those who share an identity in one context may be divided on other issues. For example, highlanders who are employed in cash-earning occupations away from home are likely to take a different stand on an income-tax issue from those who depend primarily on rural farming activities for their income. On another issue, such as how Islamic religious holidays should be celebrated, those who stood on opposite sides of the tax issue are likely to find that a common religion ties them together. Potential cleavages among Usangi highlanders are numerous. The way sides are likely to line up in a crisis can no longer be predicted on the basis of kinship and clanship since a large number of other interests (religion, education, occupation, and the like) crosscut the society. On some occasions, all internal differences in Pare may become insignificant and those who were previously divided on an issue unite in order to present a common front to outsiders.

It is tempting to think of the various identities which Usangi highlanders assume as representing more and less inclusive units. But in Usangi at least a precise hierarchical relationship does not obtain among the identities. For example, clans are smaller units than are the two categories of Asu- and Gweno-speakers, each of which is in turn smaller than the collectivity known as the

Pare people. While it is true that most native highlanders claim allegiance to clan, language, and tribal units, the three levels cannot be consistently ranked as more and less inclusive. Clans run across the Asu-Gweno division of Pare society. And, it is conceivable that on some occasions at least, Asu-speaking Mshana clansmen might feel closer connections with Gweno-speaking Mshana than they would necessarily feel with people who are just other Asu-speakers.

In spite of the lack of a precise overall relationship among identities, some persistently take precedence over others. For example, most highlanders side with their religious sect (Christian or Moslem) on issues involving conflict with traditional Asu customs. This is not invariably the case, but there is a strong and persistent tendency in that direction, as we saw in the case of traditional rites of passage like the traditional birth and burial ceremonies for example that tend to be neglected by almost everyone and replaced instead by Moslem and Christian celebrations of these life crises.

Another case in which there seems to be a persistent choice of one kind of identity over another involves the men who work away from home. When they must choose between investment in the two areas where their interests lie, in short, when they must choose between their identity as rural farmers and urban workers, they nearly always favor their identity as farmers. One highlander who was working in the growing city of Arusha expressed this sentiment in explaining why he considered the city to be less developed than Usangi:

The *maendeleo* ("development") you see all around us in the city—things like tarmac on the streets, electricity and running water in the houses, indoor toilets everywhere—this is only the *maendeleo* of the few who work here. What about their families back at home? If you follow most of these men to the places where they came from, you can find their houses on unpaved roads, you'll see that they lack electricity, piped water, and fancy toilets. This *maendeleo* is only superficial. What really counts is what's at home.

Through their persistent investment in their traditional villages, urban workers bolster their identity as rural farmers, an identity which often is difficult for them to realize in behavior because the exigencies of making a living in the contemporary world demand that they continue to reside away from Usangi.

Some identities interlock with ancient traditions more easily than others. Christianity and Islam met with different problems as each encountered Pare traditional culture. But in general, Christianity demanded more changes than Islam. For example, as Islam was incorporated into Pare culture, little if anything was done to change the manner in which the male circumcision was practiced—yet Moslems claim it as part of their religious rituals. Among Christians, it will be recalled, circumcision was discouraged, separating generations and creating a cultural dividing line where none had existed. Further, Islam reinforced Pare polygamy while the church demanded monogamy even to the point of requiring male converts to give up all but their first wives.

Thus, the changes of the last few decades have, in general, created more flexibility in Pare society. Many people look on these changes as good, as providing new possibilities and as opening opportunities. The introduction of mission stations, for example, provided an early opportunity for socially peripheral individuals (e.g., illegitimate children, *Kigharia* girls, and others who would have been short-changed in the traditional system) to be guided and helped into social maturity. While social and cultural changes mean new possibilities and new opportunities for a great many people, there are others for whom new importations are not seen as desirable alternatives. New roles, new arenas, and so on are confusing and contradictory. Some people lack the ability to make an easy transition, and become, as a result, social misfits, alienated individuals, and at times mentally ill. Change, particularly its uncoordinated aspects, plays havoc with social conventions. The lives of some individuals are inevitably caught up in cross fires of conflicting, irresolvable demands. Others, like Elia, are lead down blind-alleys.

CHANGE, CONFLICT, AND IDENTITY

The people of Usangi share with thousands of other third-world communities a great dilemma of change—how to borrow from the outside and yet retain their traditional ethnic identity. Like most Third-World peoples, the residents of Usangi do not deny the desirability of Western material culture over much of their own indigenous technology. Kerosene lamps, radios, umbrellas, and hundreds of other items that have been imported from the West are considered necessities of life by many Usangi people. There are of course a few people who wish to deny the importance of such nonindigenous culture, but the vast majority seek these aspects of imported Western culture. Many are concerned with the degree to which they must change the entirety of their lives in order to have the material things they desire so much. They ask: Is it possible to have both the material changes they want and yet retain the old cultural ways they value? To this question posed time and again by the citizens of the Third World and asked nearly as many times by social analysts, there are two kinds of answers.

One kind of answer is ideological. African politicians and poets have repeatedly answered in the affirmative, expressing the desire to retain the best of both worlds. In one sense this is what Tanzania's President Julius Nyerere is seeking a *ujamaa social-ism*—a development plan which calls for improved agriculture through the importation of the technology of scientific agriculture together with the retention of the patterns of indigenous social organization, cooperation, and sharing so basic to the ethos of so many of Tanzania's people and so foreign to the Western capitalist society in which scientific agriculture originally developed.

The other kind of answer to this question is empirical. For example, the degree to which it is actually possible for certain aspects of African family organization to be maintained on the salary of a factory worker no matter how much he may want to do is limited by empirical realities. It is likely to prove difficult if not impossible to maintain multiple wives and several children on the salary which a factory worker is paid in an African urban center. The adaptive advantage of large families in rural agri-cultural communities becomes maladaptive in the urban environ-ment where the additional wives and the many children add nothing to the production process while enlarging the demands upon the husband/father's meager wages.

Hence, both kinds of answers must be given to this dilemma of change. There are many who want to believe it is possible to maintain some of the best of African culture at the same time that the best of the West is incorporated. Yet these people cannot deny the empirical impossibility of certain combinations of the two ways of life.

The multiple identities of an individual sometimes conflict with one another. A frequent arena of this conflict has been the coming together of Pare traditions and the nonindigenous religions of Christianity and Islam. Yonaza in Chapter 2 could not both inherit his brother's widow and remain in the church; to satisfy the demands of either the church or Pare tradition would necessarily result in conflict with the other. But sometimes what appears to be conflict between various institutions and identities may be more in the eye of the observer than it is a reality to the observed. Consider, for example, the case of the introduction of the hospital into Usangi. To the European way of thinking, hospital and traditional medicines tended to stand as opposites to one another. The missionaries often saw the hospital as waging a continual battle against indigenous medicines and directed their actions and prayers toward gaining victories for the hospital medicines. Any statistical survey of the use of hospital facilities in the last few years (if the data were available) would surely show that hospital use has in fact increased—probably at the expense of traditional medicines. There are, however, many people in Usangi like Issa in Chapter 2 who do not view the hospital and traditional medicines as conflicting with one another. The two exist as alternative, but certainly not equivalent, institutions. Which one is to be used depends upon the situation—that is, on factors like the folk evaluation of the disease or ailment, the distance to the hospital or to the native doctor's house, the cost of treatment, the desires of the ailing person or his kinsmen, and perhaps other factors. To think of this as a choice between old and new, between indigenous and introduced is to view the matter ethnocentrically. For many people in Usangi, it is not a matter of traditional medicines and curing practices being replaced by "European" hospitals and facilities. Pare culture is managing to accommodate both forms. The new supplements the old; it has not replaced nor does it appear about to replace the indigenous curing practices.

These same points hold with reference to the sociolinguistic situation of Usangi. Swahili does not appear to be replacing the Pare language. Nor is there any apparent danger of languages like English, Arabic, and other African vernaculars replacing either Pare (Asu) or Swahili. Instead, Pare (Asu) continues to be used as the language of mothers and their children, of the kitchen, of farming, and of respect. Swahili is the language of recently introduced institutions like school, hospital, post office, the national government, and the political party. Both languages coexist and supplement each other. Each seems inappropriate when used outside its own social contexts. The social structure has accommodated both languages—each of which has its own special functional domain.

The most important means of resolving conflicts among various identities is *compartmentalization.* Usangi people nowadays live in many worlds and find many different, often seemingly contradictory, styles of behaving appropriate to their different roles and life styles. To survive under such conditions, they learn to compartmentalize their lives, to turn on and off aspects of their personalities, sets of attitudes, different roles, and the like as the exigencies of different situations demand. This ability is familiar and commonplace to most Westerners who operate as a matter of course in this fashion. It is becoming the same for many of Usangi's people. The man who works in the city must learn the argot and proper behavior to exhibit with both fellow workers and superiors; yet if he wishes to be successful at home in Usangi he must retain the proper demeanor: showing respect to his elders and concern for his various kinsmen. For Westerners this may seem a small change, but for a people whose entire lives were once constrained by a set of strict rules of etiquette, respect, and deference, the shift to multiple arenas of action is indeed dramatic and revolutionary.

In our analysis of change, we must take care not to be deceived by certain customs and aspects of the social structure which may appear to have remained intact, when indeed only the façade, the shell of the former significance, has been retained. The apparent retention of Pare bridewealth is a good example of such a change. Young men, as wage earners, control their cash income largely independently of their senior agnatic kinsmen. In earning the desired cash, young men have been freed from structural dependence on their seniors, which was a significant aspect of the traditional bridewealth institution. The fact that bridewealth continues to be given should not be taken to mean that a lot of changes have not gone on under the surface. In this case, the movement between different arenas of action (i.e., the rural highland of Pare and the urban centers where cash can be earned) has brought about a significant transformation of the old system. Nor should we be deceived by changes in the specific content (e.g., the symbols) but not in the reality itself (e.g., the ethnicity). Land, language, and ritual are raw materials for symbolizing Pare ethnic identity. They do not however constitute it; they serve instead as foci for its expression. Changes in the symbols do produce tensions and dislocations in the identity. But such changes do not necessarily result in changes in the identity itself; rather the modes of its expression change.

THE STUDY OF IDENTITY

Future studies must help answer important questions about ethnicity, not simply in urban contexts, but in the rural hinterland villages of the Third World. Some of the most important of these questions are:

What are the various identities which people assume and when is each expressed?　In Usangi, this is basically the question of when a person sees himself or herself as Asu, Gweno, or Pare; as Moslem, Christian, or practitioner of the old Pare religious ways; as a farmer or an urban worker; as a Pare tribesman or a Tanzanian citizen; or as any one of a growing number or identities. The highland community of Usangi is no longer stratified only by lines of kinship and clanship but is crosscut nowadays by multiple criteria which place people in numerous social categories and groups. The identities assumed by highlanders and the situations in which they are expressed are continually expanding.

Do one or more of these persistently take precedence over others?　Different identities are expressed in different situational contexts, but, in Usangi at least, there is a persistent tendency for identity as Moslems and Christians to take precedence over traditional Pare modes of behaving. Similarly, Usangi people who work outside the highlands persist in favoring their identity as rural farmers rather than as urban workers. These are the most clear-cut cases of persistent choice among varying identities in Usangi. In the arena of the nation of Tanzania, the government is attempting to foster a strong identity among the populace as citizens of this new nation and to encourage individuals to assign a high priority to such an identity. While the first decade of nation building in postindependent Tanzania has brought such an identity into the purview of millions of citizens it is nonetheless a slowly evolving process.

What are the conflicts among the various identities individuals assume and roles that they play?　A frequent area of collision between identities for the people of Usangi has been the coming together of traditional Pare culture on the one hand and Christianity and Islam on the other. At times, the demands of one of these is in serious conflict with the requirements of the other, forcing the individual to make a choice or live with the strains of conflict. Governmental and educational institutions have also not always accommodated Pare tradition comfortably. The courts, for example, have not always respected Pare traditions nor can the schools be said to instill ideas that interlock with Pare traditional culture in a happy coexistence. But as important as defining the areas of conflict is the necessity of recognizing that some areas which may seem to outsiders to be conflictual may indeed not be so for the Usangi villager. Swahili and Pare (Asu), for example, have rather well-demarcated functional domains and seldom conflict seriously with one another. Further, Pare traditional medicines and curing practices seldom conflict with the hospital and its medicines—at least from the point of view of the Usangi villager. Observers must take care not to impute conflict to situations where there is little or none.

Nyerere's attempts to build Tanzanian identity out of the raw materials of the African heritage has kept conflicts between ethnic and national identities to a minimum. Certainly there are points of conflict between Pare tradition and *ujamaa* development policies, but perhaps as much as any other African leader, Nyerere has searched out the genius of the African past and tried to utilize it in building the future.

How are conflicts among the various identities resolved?   The most common mode of resolving conflict is through compartmentalization or insulation of the various identities so that they can be expressed situationally and do not actually conflict with one another. This means, in effect, that the conflict is not actually reconciled. But since the two arenas are kept apart, friction is reduced and often kept to a minimum. There are, however, times when an individual is unable to compartmentalize or manage his conflicting identities. In such a case, he may suffer acutely under the stress, perhaps becoming psychically incapacitated when the pressures of conflict become too great.

And, finally, how are the identities themselves changed through individual roles players, who, in other contexts and situations, assume different identities?   Participating in multiple arenas and assuming different identities can have a feedback effect on the various identities an individual plays. In Usangi, we saw how the young men who have worked away from home as cash earners have altered the structure of village life and the content of cultural identity. Because old men are increasingly coming to desire cash rather than livestock for bridewealth, and because young men have direct access to cash through their work activities, the traditional institution of marriage is changing. No longer does the young man depend upon his patrikinsmen to amass the livestock of bridewealth, items to which his access would have been severely limited in the traditional social context. Consequently, this difference is helping to change marriage in the Pare highlands from a contractual arrangement between families to one between the young man, his fiancée, and her father. Another example of the feedback effect that results from role playing in multiple arenas comes from the interaction of Pare ethnic and Tanzanian national identities. Participation in national rituals (going to public meetings, celebrating national holidays, voting, speaking Swahili, etc.) not only strengthens collective national identity but also serves as object lessons to many of Tanzania's people showing that multiple identities are both desired by the nationalist leaders and possible in practice. Comprehending this weakens the exclusive grip of ethnic identity and enlarges the repertoire of identities which the highlanders of Pare assume.

PARE—PAST, PRESENT, AND FUTURE

When asking questions about the future of cultural identity in Pare we must recall that Pare identity is itself a relatively recent phenomenon which co-opted ancient symbols from the past. Recent decades have seen significant alterations in the symbols. Yet, Pare ethnic identity has been growing, developing, and increasing at the same time. In precolonial times, Pare unity and identity was unimportant; in fact, it did not exist. Pare "traditional" society, which some people call the "tribe," coalesced during the early colonial period and became a base for resisting the incursion of outsiders. Thus, what we think of today as Pare society and its cultural expression are in fact relatively recent phenomena. Pare society was created to serve important purposes as the sociocultural environment changed. Once developed, it continued to be an important entity throughout the colonial period and even today in postindependence Tanzania.

Almost since the very moment Pare ethnicity came into being, forces for change have been at work altering the symbols of Pare ethnicity, and present trends indicate that such changes will continue in the future. Pare life-crisis rituals have either been forgotten or seriously transformed as a result of years of interference by outside forces; association with the Pare highlands has been called into question by the increasing numbers of people who seek wage employment away from the homeland; and the equation of Pare people with speakers of the Pare language is no longer a solid relationship. Yet, paradoxically through it all, Pare ethnic identity has not been undermined. In fact, interethnic interaction has invigorated and strengthened Pare ethnic identity. People make efforts to speak the Pare language in situations where they feel it is appropriate—at home, with family, in traditional rituals, and the like. They express Tanzanian identity in the same fashion by using Swahili in public meetings, in governmental transactions, and so on.

Frequent comparisons of themselves with other peoples and increased interactions with the outside world have made Pare highlanders even more conscious of their own ethnicity than ever before in their history. The years to come are likely to see the persistence and invigoration of this ethnicity, despite changes in the conventional symbols that lie at its base.

PART THREE

The Kanuri of Nigeria

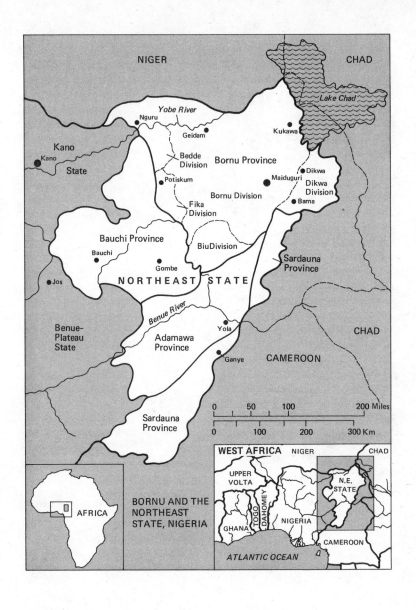

NIGER

CHAD

Lake Chad

Yobe River

Nguru

Geidam

Kukawa

Kano

Kano

State

Bedde
Division

Bornu Province

Dikwa

Potiskum

Maiduguri

Dikwa
Division

Fika
Division

Bornu Division

Bama

Bauchi Province

Biu Division

Bauchi

Sardauna
Province

Gombe

Jos

N O R T H E A S T   S T A T E

Benue–
Plateau
State

Benue River

Yola

CHAD

Adamawa
Province

Ganye

CAMEROON

0   50   100   200 Miles

0   100   200   300 Km

Sardauna
Province

AFRICA

BORNU AND THE
NORTHEAST
STATE, NIGERIA

WEST AFRICA   NIGER   CHAD

UPPER
VOLTA

N.E.
STATE

GHANA

TOGO

DAHOMEY

NIGERIA

CAMEROON

ATLANTIC OCEAN

7

Themes in Kanuri Culture

The soft early morning light was just beginning to filter through the trees, giving everything a sleepy yellow glow. The leaves made a gentle sound as they were jostled by a rarity for that time of year—a cool breeze. A woman busily frying bean cakes appeared to be the only one around to appreciate it; even the dogs were quiet in the Village Head's compound that morning. It was a good morning for sleeping. The woman had many cakes to fry, but she was not too busy to sit back and enjoy the momentary change in the weather. She sat and let her eyes close while the breeze curled around her.

As she sat, leaning against the wall of the compound, a lone figure on a bicycle came down the road. He was peddling with easy strokes and began to slow down as he approached the front of the Village Head's compound. Suddenly, when he reached the front of the compound, he stopped, got off his bicycle, and removed his shoes. Bending at the waist, he picked up his shoes with his left hand and walked the bicycle past the headman's house. Then, he stopped again, dropped his shoes, and slipped them onto his feet once more. In one easy movement, he remounted his bicycle and rode off down the street.[1]

The woman was still resting and had not seen the man, but Auno and Grema had. Sitting in the shadows of a house across the way, they had forced themselves out of bed at such an early hour on so pleasant a morning because they were on their way back to school after the long hot-season break. They were going

---

[1]Themes and events in this chapter, although presented as a single series of interrelated events, are based on separate incidents I observed in Bornu. The themes represented in these events are not to be seen as a summary of all the important themes in Kanuri culture. They are among the most important themes, however, and they are of central importance to the analysis in subsequent chapters. The people portrayed in this and subsequent chapters are composites and, although they bear common Kanuri names, they have no relationship to particular individuals.

early in order to have a free day in Maiduguri. There were things they must purchase in the canteens near the marketplace, and they were going to meet some of their friends at the cinema that night. With so many things to do, they had to get an early start.

The scene they had witnessed was very familiar to them. They had both grown up in this village and both had seen men take off their shoes as they passed in front of the houses of important people like the Village Head. It was a sign of respect and nearly everybody did it. But Grema and Auno had also been in Maiduguri a few weeks before when it had been announced that no longer would it be necessary—indeed, now it would be forbidden—to remove one's shoes when entering the office of a government official. The leaders in Kaduna, then the temporary political center for the northern group of states, had handed down a regulation which declared such behavior to be unnecessary in modern Nigeria. Removing one's shoes should be limited to the mosque and, for reasons of neatness and politeness, when inside the rooms of someone's house.

This ruling had caused considerable comment among young people such as Grema and Auno. Seeing this new ruling as a sign of progress, many students gave second thoughts to their previous disinterest in seeking positions with the government when they finished school. Some students had rejected such a possibility before because they simply did not want to have to continually bow and scrape to all the big men in order to get and keep a job. Such behavior, they felt, was far worse than having to remove one's shoes when passing in front of the house of a big man. With the new ruling, however, they could look forward to other changes, and Grema and Auno discussed the possibilities all the way to Maiduguri as they jounced along in the truck that took them there.

By the time they had finished all of their errands, there was barely enough time to get to the cinema. They were in a hurry because prospects for a delightful evening seemed very good, indeed. The film had been shown in Maiduguri before and although they had not seen it, friends assured them it was a very dramatic story. The excited crowd at the open-air theater only added to their anticipation.

After the heat of the afternoon, the open night sky above the crowd at the cinema was a cool and pleasant relief. Auno and Grema were only two of an audience of about three-hundred Nigerian men and a few women of all ages and classes. For them, the heat of the afternoon was only a memory. For the central figure in the film, however, the problems were just beginning to mount. The film—*She!* The situation—the initial phases of a palace rebellion by a small group of political subordinates in the tiny desert kingdom ruled by Haggard's famous character. Sensing impending disaster, the audience began to stir, becoming noticeably tense. Sitting resolutely on her throne, the queen argued sharply with her adversaries, but she seemed to be losing ground rapidly. Then, in the midst of their dispute, she rose from her throne and threateningly commanded, "You will not do such a thing. I am the *absolute power* here!" Almost to a man, the audience leaped up, shouting in resounding support as she asserted her supreme power.

By the time the film was over, Auno and Grema understood why their friends had recommended the film so highly. Grema and Auno were still excitedly talking about it when they reached the house of an uncle with whom they would spend the night. There were other students there, as well, but none of them had seen the film, so the two of them tried to convey some of the drama of the story as well as something of the power of the woman who had been at the center of it. The students listened with great interest, as did two younger boys who had been permitted to stay and listen—provided they would fan the others to keep them cool and to blow away the occasional mosquito.

Grema had finished with the last details of the film when Auno, who had always been the one with the vivid imagination, remembered one of his dreams—a dream he had been intending to tell Grema for a long time. It was an especially good dream, and with such an attentive audience, this was an appropriate chance to tell it.

"The dream began on the porch of the Secondary School and you, Grema, and all the rest of us were crowding around the notice board to see the results of the West Africa School Certificate Examination. Unfortunately, there were not many happy faces as the fellows read their scores, but Allah must have been with me as I looked and found I had received high passes in four subjects and a merit in history. Because of this, I found myself suddenly at the University in Zaria, and there I was again doing history. I was also doing studies in administration. Eventually, I received exceptional scores on all my tests so that when I was graduated, I was posted as the District Officer of Bornu Emirate."

Although accustomed to the tales Auno could tell, Grema still could not contain himself, so wonderful was Auno's fortune. Forgetting it was all a dream Grema burst out, "What about me! Did you see my score?" At this, the now tiring boys with the fans broke into laughter and brought Grema back to reality and Auno back to his story.

"Well, I had not been at my post very long before many of the famous people of Bornu began to visit me and pay their respects. I always welcomed them warmly and they soon loved me. Many men gave me hints about their daughters and so I began to think of marriage."

"Auno!" shouted Grema, "you are the most amazing storyteller. How can someone as homely as you expect to marry so beautiful a girl?...What happened next?"

"On the day of the marriage, I saw myself sitting in front of my large house, gorgeously dressed in a fine gown. In front of the house were thirteen multicolored carpets. They were large, thick, and costly. On these carpets and sitting very close together, so many were they, were thousands of my friends and other guests, playing cards and enjoying themselves."

"Whoy yo! Whoy yo!" cried Grema. "Surely this story could not have been dreamed even by you, Auno!" By this time, the young boys were too wide-eyed with admiration to say anything, not to mention having forgotten their bargain with the fans.

With an inward smile and outward seriousness, Auno began the climactic moments of his dream. "Every second of the day," he began, "people were flocking to my house with a feeling of jubilation. Some people were coming with drums beating and their young and beautiful women danced in front of them. When they came close, they greeted me respectfully and sang praises about my family, my wisdom, and my power. Other people came to greet me, as well, and everywhere there was pleasure and enjoyment. As a result, I was moved to dash [give] them something, so I called my servant who came quickly to my side. I gave him a key and told him to bring money from my room in the house. When he returned, I gave the drummers and dancers more than one-hundred pounds. With that, they began to praise me in melodious tones, and in this happy condition and beautiful setting, I awoke."

The thoughts and actions of Grema and Auno illustrate several key elements of Kanuri identity, at least for men and as seen from the vantage point of students. Some of these are general, recurrent, and time-honored themes in Bornu—the importance of showing respect, the need for reassurance as to one's popularity, an admiration of power, and a concomitant recognition of the dangers of insubordination. Others, though less pronounced, are emerging as important new themes—informal and official doubts about the necessity of traditional demonstrations of respect, and an interest in achieving social mobility through individualized skills—skills which are sometimes seen, to be sure, as prerequisites for appointment to political office. The older, established aspects of identity are being challenged by these new themes and, as a consequence, a question of major importance to Kanuri is the fate of traditionally dominant cultural patterns. At present, these themes remain the basis of Kanuri identity, but their centrality is being called into question by increasing numbers of people. And many who do so argue that such cultural characteristics impede efforts to stimulate economic growth.

Individuals vary greatly in their receptivity to fundamental changes in the symbols and patterns that mark their identity. This is true in regions of the world long exposed to rapid change as well as in areas where change is recent. The cost of such fundamental changes often is high and resistance to change may be great as a result. But Nigeria and many other African nations are investing heavily in projects designed to encourage indigenous entrepreneurial activity and economic growth. Government leaders and "experts" see such activity as necessary for the achievement of material development. Moreover, individuals who in the past had their ambitions stifled by traditional social systems are finding long-sought-after benefits in the push to development and are giving additional support to these programs. The net result is that traditional identities are under great pressure. Kanuri culture, especially those aspects most closely related to social mobility and clientship, is undergoing changes that may well mark the transition from an old to a new cultural basis for identity.

Nevertheless, it would seem prudent at the outset to remain cautious about both the economic and the cultural implications of the development trends just noted. Whether cultural changes that do take place will in fact produce the desired stimulus to economic growth, and whether pressure from new themes in Kanuri culture will in fact lead to a redefinition of what it means to be a Kanuri, are crucial but as yet unanswered questions in Bornu. They are not, moreover, questions that admit of an easy answer. Like the Nigerians involved, social scientists themselves disagree about the factors that are fundamental to either the achievement of economic development or the transformation of a culture and its attendant symbols of unity and identity. For example, many observers have been pessimistic about the potential of Nigerian entrepreneurship (e.g., see Andreski 1968, Kilby 1969, Proehl 1965, and Stopler 1962, among many others). Often, this pessimism is based on the apparent resistance to change of some of Nigeria's ethnic groups. But others have suggested that current weaknesses in entrepreneurship lie not with an unwillingness to respond to opportunities but rather with limitations of technical sorts unrelated to cultural patterns (see, for example, J. Harris 1968). And still others (e.g., A. Cohen 1969) suggest we may not even fully understand responses that are being made because our notions of what constitutes efficient entrepreneurial behavior are biased toward ethnocentric Western models.

All of this suggests the people of Bornu may be confronted by a double dilemma posed by the reciprocal but ambiguous relationship between traditional culture and development. The goal of these chapters is to shed light on two fundamental questions linked to that ambiguity. First, there is the question of the effect of traditional culture on development. It is possible that traditional Kanuri values significantly retard economic growth and development. Such a view has been voiced about other cultures, and increasingly, individuals in Bornu may be heard voicing similar views about their own culture. But others consider the sacrifice of values at the very heart of Kanuri identity to be an unacceptable price to pay for material gain. Moreover, they sometimes claim that Kanuri cultural patterns are but an insignificant item on the list of factors retarding economic growth. Social research cannot completely resolve this debate over priorities perhaps, but it can evaluate systematically the effect of particular cultural patterns on development. In so doing, each individual may be enabled to establish his own hierarchy of values with a reasonable knowledge of the implications of his decisions.

Second, there is the question of the effect of development on traditional cultural patterns, the other side of the social change coin. Whether slowed or not by cultural factors, development and change are coming to Bornu, and they are exerting pressure on values and life styles long at the center of Kanuri culture. This intensifies the identity concerns of many. Again, social research cannot tell people with such concerns what is right and wrong. But by shedding light on the implications for Kanuri culture of development in Nigeria generally and in Bornu particularly, it may help people to anticipate and plan for the future, and to shape their destiny with greater accuracy.

Thus, in sum, the goal of these chapters on the Kanuri of Nigeria is an assessment of the interaction of several key aspects of culture and development. It is an attempt to find out whether and in what ways Kanuri cultural identity is an impediment to development and, conversely, whether and in what ways the general pressure for change and economic growth in Nigeria is modifying Kanuri identity. To that end, we will turn in Chapter 8 to a discussion of the basic context and symbols of Kanuri identity. In Chapter 9, the nature of the superior-subordinate relationship will be explored in a variety of forms and contexts for it is here that pressure on Kanuri identity is greatest. This will provide the background for an analysis in Chapter 10 of survey data on attitudes toward clientship, occupation preference, and individual achievement motivation. These data will serve as a basis for commenting in Chapter 11 on the future of Kanuri identity.

8

The Context and Symbols
of Kanuri Identity

Located in open savannah country in northeastern Nigeria, the flat sandy countryside of Bornu fades, on the northwestern edges, nearly into the fringes of the Sahara. Here, the heat and dust contrast sharply with the cool wetness of Lake Chad, which lies on the northeastern border of this ancient realm. The rains, barely adequate for plant, beast, or man, come between June and September. The remaining eight months of the year are dry and, depending on the season, are either relatively cool or very hot. This is the physical context of Bornu, the homeland of the Kanuri. But of far greater importance for this inquiry into the changing nature of Kanuri identity is an overview of the sociocultural context. In presenting this context, the historic, religious, political, social, and economic bases of Kanuri identity will be discussed.

HISTORY

The present-day Kanuri are the descendants and heirs of one of the several Sudanic kingdoms distributed across time and space from the tenth century kingdom of Ghana in the west to the nineteenth century kingdom of Darfur in the east. From the Kanuri vantage point, Bornu has occupied the chronological and geographical center of this vast region. And indeed, there can be little doubt about the importance of their role in shaping its cultural and historical development. However, the fortunes of the Kanuri state have fluctuated greatly over its lengthy history.[1] The succession of events that have occurred over the past 160 years

[1]As for the length of this history, we have the testimony of Murdock (1959: 136 n.) and the evidence of written and oral Kanuri traditions for suggesting the Kanuri Sef dynasty, with roots extending back to the eighth century and a terminal date of 1846, may be the world's longest recorded reign of a single dynasty.

provides an essential context for understanding the contemporary setting of Kanuri daily life. As a people, they are well informed about their past and take considerable pride in it. Indeed, the past provides fundamental symbols for their collective identity.[2]

At the center of Kanuri history and identity are the kings of Bornu. The names and exploits of the first dynasty kings stretch back in an unbroken line for a millennium. The last kings of this dynasty were involved in a most significant social and political development. Early in the nineteenth century, the neighboring Fulani were in the midst of a *jihad* ("religious war") and, believing the Kanuri to be unfaithful Muslims, carried this war to Bornu. The Fulani destroyed the capital city and sent the king into a hasty retreat. But a very learned *malam* ("Koranic scholar and teacher") named al-Kanemi organized the Kanuri for a counter-offensive that was successful in driving out the Fulani. As a result, al-Kanemi became the *de facto* ruler of Bornu. His sons terminated the royal line of the first and ancient dynasty and consolidated the new dynasty started, in effect, by their father.

The next few decades, however, were marked by internal strife and instability, and the *Shehu* ("king") was defeated again near the end of the century by a Sudanese conqueror—Rabeh. Also, at about this time, British, French, and German colonial interests were converging in Bornu. For several years, it was not certain which of these powers would dominate. At the turn of the century, however, the British incorporated Bornu into their nascent colony. One of the key steps taken by the British in this effort was the reinstating of the Shehu in the new town of Maiduguri. This development was important because then, as now, the Shehu was the focal point of Kanuri loyalty and identity. Traditionally, the king was the source of law, order, and inspiration; he was and still is the leader of the faithful, the arbiter of disputes, the healer of social wounds. The Kanuri are his people; "we are his slaves," they say. The land in Bornu is his; "we are his tenants." Where the king went, both spatially and in terms of loyalty, the people of Bornu would follow. Although the British made many changes (for example, they replaced the system of royal fiefdoms with a

[2]Unfortunately, space limitations prevent giving a detailed review of Kanuri history. The interested reader should examine, in addition to the various nineteenth century accounts of European travelers such as H. Barth (1857), Denham and Clapperton (1826), and Nachtigal (1879), the excellent historical material provided by Boahen (1964), Brenner (1973), and Cohen (1967 and 1971a).

smaller number of political districts), the king has remained a
central figure in Kanuri history, politics, and identity.

RELIGION

Equally important to Kanuri identity is their religion. When one
speaks of Bornu, one must speak of Islam in the same breath.
The history of Bornu is also part of the history of the Islamic
world; the culture of Bornu is, in part, a manifestation of the great
cultural traditions of the Middle East. However, the history of
Bornu is also part of the history of the Sudan and all of West
Africa, for much of the cultural richness of Bornu is derived
from other cultures in this vast region. These facts place a heavy
burden on those who would estimate the balance between the
forces which have shaped the Bornu we see today. It is tempting
to say it is a draw, noting simply that for the past 800 years,
the ebb and flow between these two sources of inspiration has
been dynamic and vital. Nevertheless, one cannot help but notice
the power of Islam in Bornu today.

Emerging for almost 800 years as the dominant ideological
force in the area, its influence is felt in the innermost parts of
Kanuri culture. However, no error could be greater than to see
Islam as a great monolithic cultural force that uniformly stamps
its character on any culture it touches. Nor is Islam without
ideological competitors in Bornu today, for at various times in
the recent history of this kingdom, pan-Africanism, nationalism,
and westernism have been forces of great significance. Because
of this, the goal here will simply be to illustrate some of the ways
Islam, as it is practiced in Bornu, shapes Kanuri identity. First,
some basic sociocultural patterns that have their roots in Islam
and the Middle East will be noted. Second, certain doctrinal
characteristics of Islam in Bornu will be discussed.

Islam is community-centered, and this influence may be seen
in aspects of culture ranging from the organization and physical
layout of towns to the character of the sociopolitical organization
of believers. Von Grunebaum, an astute observer of the Islamic
world, notes that it is the Islamic community which is the "guardian of the road to salvation" (1955:22). Moreover, since the community is essential if one is to fulfill many of the minimum obligations of being a Moslem, political organization is stressed. Elsewhere, von Grunebaum indicates Moslem towns are characterized
by two main focal points—the Friday mosque and the market-

place. Moreover, in cosmopolitan towns, sections distinguishable by the ethnic identity of the inhabitants were typical and important centers of activity, with separate markets, mosques, and other important facilities. While the loyalty of townsmen is to one's family, there long has been an ideal that supported the "substitution of religious affiliation for kinship as the rationale of social organization . . ." (1955:142–148).

These themes are everywhere evident in Bornu. The city of Maiduguri and many of the smaller towns have wards for newcomers (strangers' quarters), and all have at least one marketplace and a Friday mosque. The common link of religion and not simply the genealogical ties of kinship or clanship is a primary basis for Kanuri social life. Truly, in Bornu, the *scope*[3] of Islam is very great. One could list hundreds of cultural details to illustrate this. Dietary restrictions, the seclusion of women, the rules of inheritance and aspects of law in general, art and clothing styles, musical themes, folklore, medicine, cosmology, the calendric cycle, and many other cultural features come to mind. Nevertheless, as was indicated, Bornu is not outside the tradition of non-Islamic Africa, either. Thus, rain-making rituals and ceremonies that were related to the sanctification of a new market in Bornu, though accompanied by Islamic prayers and almsgiving, were primarily the concern of secular leaders who relied for the most part on non-Islamic procedures.

Islam has had an important impact on the economic outlook of people in Bornu. As von Grunebaum has observed about Moslems in general (1955:25), "the peasant . . . is held in low esteem by Islam and never attracts the attention of the learned." Instead, Moslems prefer the sedentary and urban over the nomadic and/or rural life. "It [Islam] accepts the artisan but respects the merchant." In much the same vein, Trimingham (1968:95) goes so far as to suggest that in Africa "the trader is a Muslim and the cultivator is a pagan. . . . The Muslim trader in his cultivation is a pagan, just as the pagan trader is a Muslim." Though extreme, these observations do serve to illustrate the opinions of many regarding the importance of trade and commerce in the Islamic kingdoms of the western Sudan. And indeed, Islam did come to the western and central Sudan on the backs of traders' camels

---

[3]Geertz (1968:112) defines the "scope of a religious belief system" as "the range of social contexts within which religious considerations are regarded as having more or less direct relevance." It is used in that sense here.

and donkeys. Many have repeatedly and correctly stressed the role of trade in the development of the various states in these regions (see Bovill 1933, Trimingham 1959, Lewis 1966, Boahen 1964, among many others).

There are numerous views that depict Islam as a force for economic and social conservatism. This conservatism has commonly been attributed to a fatalistic theme in Islam linked to the ideas of determinism and predestination. Since these chapters are, among other things, to consider whether and to what extent Kanuri culture is an impediment to economic growth, a consideration of contemporary doctrinal themes in Bornu is in order. Insight into the character of this facet of Kanuri identity can be gained by an examination of the doctrines of the Sufi order which is today dominant in Bornu. This order, which is dominant especially among the young and educated, is the Tijaniyya (Trimingham 1959:98). As a Sufi order, emphasis is placed on mysticism and asceticism, with special rituals and prayers inculcated to novices by the leaders of the order. According to Abun-Nasr (1965), who has provided the most detailed analysis of this Moslem order, the dominant doctrinal theme emerges from a claim by its founder, al-Tijani (d. A.D. 1815), that on one of his "meetings" with the Prophet he was ordered "to remain without solitude or isolation from the world, until he should attain the elevated rank predestined for him" (Abun-Nasr 1965:46).

It was this statement that proved to be the basis of the Tijani reinterpretation of the importance of *zuhd* or "asceticism." Perhaps the ultimate Tijani interpretation of asceticism was given by the great Sudanic *malam,* Hajj 'Umar. Quoting him, Abun-Nasr observes (1965:47–48) that asceticism is "the 'emptiness of the heart' from desire for worldly things, rather than the 'emptiness of the hand' which often produces those desires." Deprecating others who are dependent on charity, 'Umar exhorts Moslems to work hard and earn a respectable living because work enables them to become good *zahid's* ("ascetics").

It is not difficult to see how such a view of asceticism could lead to a relatively dynamic approach to material and economic aspects of life. Indeed, from almost the very outset of the order's history many wealthy people joined the Tijaniyya. And, in the context of modern Nigeria, it has been shown that the doctrines of this order were important elements in the orientation and organization of a group of very successful Hausa traders (A. Cohen 1968, 1969). Although similar patterns have not yet been shown for Bornu, it is nevertheless an important potential which bears directly on the issue of the inhibiting nature of Islam. In short, while Islam is a vital and moving force in Bornu, it is essential to be cognizant of the doctrinal variations within the Islamic world. A view of Islam that overly stresses the nature of the "great tradition" without ascertaining the specific character of Islam as it lives in Bornu today would be a serious error. As noted, a most significant variation for the Kanuri on this Islamic theme is the doctrinal character of the Tijaniyya.

SOCIAL ORGANIZATION

For the Kanuri, a basic social unit is the family as it is manifested in the form of households consisting, ideally, of an adult male, his wives, concubines, their unmarried children, and a varying but sometimes large number of other adults and minors who are dependent upon the adult, male, household head. Descent is cognatically reckoned but has a male emphasis. Descent groups rarely hold land or other property in common. These factors plus the common occurrence of client relationships not based on kinship explain why it is more informative to center this brief discussion of Kanuri social organization around the household. For most Kanuri, the daily round of social events, economic pursuits, and political prospects are intimately linked to the household. Relationships within households are, moreover, basic to the development of an appropriate Kanuri worldview. The father-son relationship, for example, is an axis of considerable importance to this social unit. Training in the skills needed for farming, small-scale manufacture, politics, and trade are generally acquired by men from their fathers, at least initially. But more important is the acquisition of ideals and values regarding the character of superior-subordinate relationships. The ideals of respect, honesty, loyalty, shame, and obedience are essential to such relationships and they are learned by sons as they interact with their fathers. Indeed, as will be noted in the next chapter, the father-son relationship provides a basic model for the client relationship, and the household provides a context for the organization of political and economic life which is based on such relationships. In truth, it may well be said that to understand the nature of Kanuri identity is in part at least to understand the household and the role of an individual in it. For the rural farmer or the city sophisticate, this is an inescapable but pleasant fact of life.

POLITICAL ORGANIZATION

Two features of the political system which are vital symbols of Kanuri identity will be noted; The traditional political hierarchy articulates with the contemporary government of Nigeria. These observations provide an overview of one of the most striking aspects of Kanuri culture—striking because this ancient and elaborate political system is once again under pressure to change.

The principal feature of the political structure in Bornu, and the basic character of political processes within that structure, provide two major touchstones of Kanuri identity. First, the apex of the Kanuri political system, especially from the vantage point of older and less western-educated Kanuri, (also the apex of the several symbols of Kanuri identity as a collectivity), is the person and office of Shehu, the king of Bornu. His role has been so important that perspectives of the many ascending levels of the contemporary Nigerian political system have been effectively blocked by the Shehu's continuing symbolic brilliance. The epitome of strategic behavior within the political system is also the epitome of individual identity in everyday behavioral terms. This behavioral style is clientship—the diffuse, personalized relationship between a superior and subordinate, especially within the political system. For many in Bornu, the behavioral norms associated with clientship are so important they effectively block alternative bases for interpersonal relationships.

Although the office of Shehu as an institution in Bornu has been under increasing political pressure, it remains as a key feature of the political system and the sociocultural system as a whole. Clientship is facing an even greater challenge in the form of an expanding civil service, staffed by young and educated Kanuri (and other Nigerians) who are being rewarded for behavior more characteristic of bureaucratic and western social systems.

Before 1900, during the precolonial era in Bornu, the Shehu dominated the political structure because it was through him that individuals received the political titles which were prerequisites for power. These individuals were responsible for the day-to-day governing of sectors of the kingdom: taxes were collected, armies raised, and trade regulated by them in the name of the Shehu. This complex hierarchy forged a vital link between the Kanuri populace and the Shehu.

The British introduced many changes into this essentially feudal political structure. The principal change was the elimination of the land-based fiefs, replaced by a smaller number of political units known as "districts." No longer were district heads to be linked exclusively to the Shehu; they ultimately were to become involved in various political entities, and to be responsible to individuals at several levels of the colonial and subsequently postcolonial political system. These changes gradually reduced the amount of political power controlled directly by the Shehu. Political control of the kingdom has passed into the hands of members of various councils, ministries, and similar governing bodies above and below the Shehu himself.

Nevertheless, it is still the case that individual Kanuri see their place in society in terms of what is essentially an ancient and very basic political hierarchy.[4] An individual Kanuri is a member of and identifies with political entities based on the household. This hierarchy, smallest to the largest, is for the person in rural areas, the hamlet (or, if large enough, a village), the village area (consisting of several hamlets and a principal village), and the district (consisting of numerous village areas). Each of these levels is headed by an individual with a traditional title: *bulama* ("hamlet head"), *lawan* ("village head"), and *ajia* ("district head"). For the person in a city,[5] for example, the same basic hierarchy is relevant, but the *bulama* is the leader of what may best be described as a sub-ward, the *lawan* heads a ward, and the *ajia* heads the entire city.

This basic hierarchy is also reflected in the judicial system in Bornu. For example, a grievance between two neighbors would be brought first to the hamlet head, then to the village head, and the district head. Then the case would be sent to a district court to be presided over by an *alkali,* a judge versed in Moslem law. The case could proceed to the Chief *Alkali's* Court in Maiduguri and, depending upon the case, either to the Shehu or to the system of civil and criminal courts of the Federal Nigerian government.[6]

[4]While the political structure of Bornu is strongly hierarchical, it no longer conforms (if it ever did) to a simple pyramidal structure; a more complex metaphor (such as a tree) would be more appropriate. For a recent and effective demonstration of the importance of this point, see Moris (1972).

[5]Maiduguri, the capital and most populous city in the state, is the center of the traditional kingdom and the contemporary provincial and state levels of government.

[6]Bornu and the other Moslem kingdoms of Nigeria were among the last in West Africa to change their system of religious *shari'a* law courts to a system based on Nigerian civil law. This change was announced shortly before the field-

Nigeria is currently a military federation comprised of 12 states. The Kanuri live in the Northeast State, the largest state in Nigeria (almost one-third of the country). Of the dozens of ethnic groups, the Kanuri are among the largest, numbering well over a million people. There are four provinces (the largest sub-state political unit) in Northeast State, of which one is Bornu Province (see map). This province was created by the British when they grouped together, for administrative purposes, five major precolonial traditional states (along with dozens of smaller, weaker, and politically less autonomous ethnic groups living in the same area). Each of these states was left more or less intact by the British and now, as then, these units are known technically as "divisions." The largest of the five divisions in Bornu Province is Bornu Division.

In 1971 several administrative units at a level between district and division were created. These units, known as "development areas" (clusters of districts), are designed to foster more direct contact between the basic hierarchy of *bulama, lawan,* and *ajia,* and the State and Federal levels of Nigeria's government. Nevertheless, the divisional level retains considerable importance in the scheme of things because it is this unit that is referred to when such phrases as "the kingdom of Bornu" or the "Kanuri kingdom" are used, and it is with this unit that most Kanuri have their strongest identity.

SOCIAL STRATIFICATION

Social differentiation resulting from making an evaluative distinction between individuals is a universal of human social life. The structuring of this social inequality is the essence of social stratification. In Bornu, the formal political structure is the single most important factor bearing on the identification of named, social "strata" ranked in terms of prestige and power. Traditionally, if an individual had a title granted him by the king or some other high-ranking official, he was considered to be a part of the political organization and, consequently, a part of the upper stratum of society. Individuals in this stratum are known as

---

work on which this research is based was terminated. Details of recent changes in local government in this part of Nigeria are summarized in a useful series of local government yearbooks prepared by the Department of Local Government, Institute of Administration, Ahmadu Bello University, Zaria, Nigeria.

kəntuoma ("important people"). The rank of one's title was an important though not the sole indicator of one's social rank.

Though less common in the precolonial period, there are many people in the political system today who do not have a title. There are also people with titles who are not currently holding an office within the political system. With or without a title, those who have a position in the political system are described as having *nyama* ("position" or "office"). Other things being equal, an individual with a position has more prestige than an individual without one. It is important to remember, however, that having *nyama* is neither necessary nor sufficient to be classed as an "important person." Thus, a person with a title who loses his office (as sometimes happens) is still a *kəntuoma.* However, having both a title and a position would place an individual in the topmost social group. Opinion varies, in Bornu, as to the social rank of individuals having only one of the two qualities, although it was universally agreed that having neither was least desirable (though not uncommon).

Individuals who have neither title nor position in the political organization may be grouped into a single (and the largest) class called *talagaa* ("commoners"). Rank within this group is determined by a complex combination of indicators. The three most important of these are occupation, education, and demeanor. Other criteria (e.g., wealth) could be mentioned but most are not independent of these three. Occupation-ranking will be discussed at some length in Chapter 10. Suffice it to note at this point that occupations are generally ranked in an order based on the degree to which one works with his hands and/or gets dirty (e.g., well-digging, butchering, and tanning are ranked very low), and the degree to which the occupation is viewed as moral or legal (e.g., religious specialists rank high; moneylenders rank at the bottom). Otherwise, the key factors in occupation-ranking are power and wealth, the rank corresponding to the public image of the amount of either typically associated with an occupation. Men with exceptionally large amounts of wealth are known variously as "rich men" or "big men" and receive deference and other indications of status in about the same degree as important people.

The second major factor differentiating individuals in the commoner class is education. Traditionally, formal education was restricted to Islamic knowledge. Men who studied the Koran and taught Arabic to children were and are still today known as *malam's*. Recently, this title has been extended informally to include those who have been educated in other traditions—especially secular, Western-style schools. For centuries, formal education was an important social asset; although on a broader front now, it continues to be so.

The third major factor in social rank—demeanor—is so complex we can do little more than touch the surface of it here. People in Bornu, like people everywhere, are very alert to the way in which people perform their roles. They are also sensitive to the manner in which individuals meet general expectations regarding certain key character traits. Among the most important of these are *hima* ("sophistication"), *kanadi* ("patience"), and *nongu* ("shame"); the most important of all aspects of demeanor is *bərzəm* ("respect"). Such character traits have been noted for other Islamic groups in this region (e.g., see Smith 1959, on the Hausa, or Stenning 1959, on the Fulani). These traits are more generalized aspects of behavior than are usually associated with the term "social role" since they can be expected to characterize behavior in many social roles. The importance of these character traits will be noted again when we discuss social mobility in Kanuri society. Suffice it to say at this point that other things equal, the more sophisticated, patient, shame-conscious (i.e., careful in matters that are shameful), and respectful one is, the higher one's social rank.[7]

ECONOMIC ACTIVITY

Economic activity in Bornu is most easily comprehended, even in all its complexity, in the context of the household. Production, distribution of the products, and their consumption all center on this unit. Only recently have non-household-based units of production begun to have significance for the Kanuri, and then almost exclusively in the large urban areas such as Maiduguri. These are usually organized trading companies, although a few manufacturing companies are beginning to be established. These produce essential goods, including tanned leather, smoked meat, and the "basic B's"—bread, boots, and bricks. The range of craft

[7]Numerous other details of the system of structured social inequality could be discussed here, but as with the summary of the Kanuri political system, this would only deflect us from the main objective. Moreover, detailed information on Kanuri stratification, as well as of similar neighboring groups, is available elsewhere (see R. Cohen 1970a, Smith 1959, and Vaughan 1970).

and artisan roles is great, but the most common and important economic activity is farming.

At some time in his life, virtually every man in Bornu engages in farming, either for himself or as a laborer for someone else. Farmland is generally the common property of the household that works it, although its control and disposition rest with the head of the household. Such land can be inherited, but unused land may be farmed by asking the owner for permission, who, if he grants it, will expect to receive a portion of the harvest. New land is available, but, as might be expected, it is located at more distant points from villages and towns. Permission to use this land is obtained, in a routine way, from the Village Head. If this land is used more or less continuously over a period of years and the user dies, it is expected the plot may be inherited by the man's sons. Land is still plentiful in Bornu, so there are few serious disputes over land rights.

Men provide the heavy physical labor needed for farming. They clear the fields and do most of the sowing, weeding, and harvesting. Women assist in these activities, especially in the actual collection of the crop, which, depending on what it is, the men will have either cut, uprooted, or picked. Though less common, women also assist in the other steps in the agricultural cycle, including clearing and weeding. In any case, the role of women in the economic activities of a household is extensive and essential.

By means of these agricultural activities, Kanuri produce several varieties of millet, some maize, peanuts (including many tons for export), and rice. Orchards, carefully tended by wealthier farmers, produce oranges, lemons, limes, mangoes, and papaya. Vegetables, including okra, beans, yams, cassava, and onions, are usually plentiful. Numerous varieties of roots, small shrubs, and wild fruits are used as spices and for making soups and sauces.

Cattle are kept in fairly large numbers. They are grazed in herds comprised of the animals from entire hamlets or, in the case of villages, from each of its wards. Such herding patterns provide safety and convenience. Herdboys, skilled at recognizing the cattle belonging to a particular household, make sure they return to it each evening. Goats, sheep, chickens, ducks, and rabbits are also kept, with emphasis on the first three. Fishing is an important activity, especially in and around Lake Chad. During the rainy season, many villages have access to streams and ponds with enough fish to justify the effort expended in trying to catch them, and consequently fish are a regular part of most people's diet.

Besides farming and animal husbandry, the main production activity in Bornu is small-scale manufacturing. In the remote rural areas, most of the nonagricultural necessities of life can be obtained from nearby households. Artisans in these areas are farmers during the rainy season who engage in their craft occupations during the dry season. Shoemaking, general leatherworking, smithing, the making of calabashes, knives, cloth, jewelry, mats, saddles, gowns (and tailoring in general), as well as the various building trades (bricklaying, carpentry, etc.) are among the more common dry-season activities. A number of service occupations such as barbering, medicine-selling, and hunting are also important supplements to farming. In the rural areas, the income from these activities is used for paying taxes, and/or for purchasing manufactured items which a household does not produce itself.

Closely linked to both agriculture and manufacturing is the ubiquitous activity of trading. Kanuri find trading very attractive; given the chance, most men would discontinue farming to take up trading.[8] It is carried out on the smallest to the largest of scales. In the villages and on city streets, not only small boys but mature men as well can be found selling single cigarettes and small bunches of matches. Almost anything that can be subdivided into smaller units which are still of some use will be divided and sold. This becomes more common the farther the village is from the main source of supply. This interest in trade, coupled with improvements in communication and transportation, has resulted in products from literally the entire world being sold in Kanuri marketplaces—everything from Polish water buckets to Dutch portable radios and decks of playing cards from mainland China. Many men who today are wealthy, large-scale traders, driving Mercedes-Benz automobiles, and who live in fancy concrete houses, began as little boys, trading kola nuts in the village marketplace. Even as the scale of the trading increases, however,

[8]Indeed, many do just that, and this causes problems for the Agriculture Department, for example, since it is encouraging improved farming methods and the involvement of students in farming. With the increased income from improved farming and with some degree of literacy and skills in record-keeping, there is a tendency for individuals to think about taking up trading. Nowadays, there is a real possibility they will act on what they are thinking.

a significant portion remains centered around the household. Initially, a trader may accept offers from people outside his household who wish to trade for him. But as these outsiders demonstrate their skills and begin to realize a steady profit, these men will be encouraged to become more closely linked to the household by establishing themselves as clients of the household head. In Maiduguri, there are many households organized in this fashion in which large-scale trading is conducted, often in specialized products such as fish, hides and skins, meat, or dry goods of various types. The competitive spirit and drive of these entrepreneurs is well known in Nigeria (see A. Cohen 1969, for an account of this type of trading organization).

In Bornu, trading and related commercial enterprises of various kinds far outnumber manufacturing companies. In Maiduguri, for example, the largest industrial activity is the production of peanut oil, but this industry was not developed by individual Kanuri entrepreneurs. There are, however, a few small, individually owned bakeries, lumber mills, and brickworks. Of even greater importance are the many opportunities for educated, skilled workers, primarily in commercial firms—banks, retail stores, foreign-owned trading companies, transport companies, and the like. Maiduguri is also the center of many government administrative agencies and departments for both the Northeast State and the Bornu Emirate. Consequently, much of the available local manpower has become involved with the commercial and administrative sectors of the economy, rather than the industrial sector. In all of Bornu, there is only one indigenous, privately owned industry that utilizes modern machines and skilled wage-labor. It is a shoe factory, and it and its products are the pride of Maiduguri, the city where it is located. Virtually all other skilled labor is employed either in the government agencies needing such skills (e.g., the Public Work Department or the Printing Department), or by firms owned and managed by European expatriots.

CHANGING BORNU

In addition to the previously noted political and administrative changes that have occurred in Bornu since the arrival of the British at the outset of this century, a number of important technical, demographic, and social changes have occurred which may be briefly noted. First, while the tradition of large towns serving as the center of social, political, and economic life has continued to the present, there also has been a slow but steady growth in the number and size of truly "urban places." Maiduguri, with a population of about 140,000, is easily the largest of these in Bornu Division. The towns in Bornu, and most importantly, their marketplaces, are connected by an ever-improving system of roads, with excellent paved highways connecting the largest towns to the city of Maiduguri. The Nigerian railway system was extended to Maiduguri in 1964, and there is a very large airfield on the edge of the city which, although built during World War II, is capable of handling large, modern jets. Telephone and telegraph service has been in the area for decades, and electricity is so common as to be noticed only when it fails because of some mechanical difficulty. Gasoline stations do a thriving business serving the large number of cars and trucks. There is even a parking problem at the cinema most evenings.

The physical appearance of towns is beginning to change in many ways. In Maiduguri, while many houses are made with thick walls of mud—a style that is both esthetically pleasing and affords some relief from the heat of the afternoon, an increasing number are made of concrete blocks with corrugated metal roofs.[9] Almost all of the streets in Maiduguri, though often narrow and winding, have been paved and are drained by a modern and complex system of open ditches—a system conceived and financially supported by the Bornu Local Authority. The main streets of the city are lined with row upon row of shady trees, giving the city a character that is at once urban and sylvan.

There has been rapid growth in public-service institutions and in specialized economic-development projects. Medical facilities in Maiduguri, for example, are diverse and reasonably modern, with several hospitals and many local dispensaries and public-health clinics. There are two cinemas, a radio station, and a large number of specialty shops that cater to the needs of a growing urban population. There have been several US-AID projects (for cattle breeding and range management, for example) in the area. Other organizations (including the World Health Organization,

[9]These metal roofs, although more watertight, radiate heat like an oven. They are safer, however, than the more traditional roofing materials because they do not soak up water during the rainy season. Mud roofs, for example, while ordinarily well drained and coated with a hard outer layer that resists water, still often soak up more water than they can support. Under such circumstances they can collapse, and every year during the period of heaviest rains, there are several deaths from falling roofs.

the Food and Agriculture Organization, and various Nigerian Federal Government agencies) have sponsored pilot and research projects aimed at expanding the fishing industry, increasing wheat and rice production, and eradicating various major diseases.

But perhaps the single most important development or impetus to change in Bornu has been the rapid and recent expansion of the school system. This expansion has been numerical, geographical, and conceptual. Today, primary schools can be found in the most remote corners of the Division, although there still is room in these schools for only a small portion of the children of Bornu. There are four postprimary schools in Maiduguri, each with no more than about 125 students in five grades. Two other such schools are located elsewhere in the Province, and there are plans for additional schools. Conceptually, the schools have been transformed in recent years from institutions that were seen as alien intrusions to their current status as the core of the development effort in Bornu.[10]

In sum, while there have been many social and economic changes in Bornu in recent decades, most Kanuri are not facing an intense, across-the-board period of doubt about the major symbols of their identity. There are factories in Maiduguri, but industrialism, in the usual sense of that word, has not really been established. Education, while expanding rapidly, still reaches only a small portion of the population. Urbanism, an old and respected way of life in Bornu, is growing, but the rates are still not great. In short, their homeland, language, religion, major political symbols, and basic social units are virtually unchallenged. To be sure, Bornu, and these symbols and institutions, are changing, but only in comparatively minor ways and, as yet, with relatively minor social dislocations.

Most Kanuri still live in Bornu; land pressures are not yet so great that people are forced to look outside Bornu for a place to farm or a market in which to trade. Many people do leave Bornu for other Nigerian and West African cities, but these movements do not appear to be the result of widespread, division-wide pressures of the sort faced by the young men of Pare. Similarly, the Kanuri language, while not a major one in West Africa, is spoken

[10]For an excellent account of the life of primary school students in contemporary Bornu, see Peshkin 1972. For a discussion of the role of education and nation-building in Nigeria in general and Bornu in particular, see Peshkin 1970 and 1971.

by over one million people and will continue to be an important tongue in multilingual Nigeria for some time to come. There are many Kanuri who speak Hausa or Arabic, French or English, and there are a few who wonder about the possibility that Hausa may become the language of all élites in the northern part of Nigeria in the future. But this is neither a widespread nor an immediate concern.

Islam is the established religion of Bornu; it has been for centuries, and will continue to be so for the foreseeable future. Moreover, there are no signs, as yet, that major doctrinal splits are developing of the sort noted for Tunisia regarding the fate of the Ramadan fast (see Chapters 1 and 12). It is possible that with time the major Sufi sect in Bornu, the Tijaniyya, will exert subtle influences on the Kanuri religious worldview, but again, this change (if it comes) can be expected to be relatively gradual, and will not pose a major threat to religious symbols of Kanuri identity.

Major political symbols, and especially the kingship, are immersed in a much wider and more pervasive context than in the distant past, but the continuity of the ancient system is still visible and vital in the lives of Kanuri. This was made dramatically evident in December, 1967, when the old Shehu, after reigning for thirty years as the monarch of Bornu, died. Falling back on traditional wisdom, many people feared that his death would bring a period of strife and lawlessness, for after all, he was traditionally the source of law and order in Bornu. From the viewpoint of many, this was a time of grave crisis; for others, especially those in government outside of Bornu, it was an opportunity for change. But a new Shehu was picked from among the traditional royal eligibles and, while the new Shehu will in all probability offer a style that is different from his predecessor, the geneaological line and symbolic potential of the kingship were preserved. To be sure, there had been an adjustment, but not a basic alteration in this major symbol of political identity in Bornu.[11]

Economic life has centered on agriculture and commerce for centuries, and these are to be the mainstays of economic development in Bornu for many years to come. And, finally, the Kanuri household, that multifaceted fundament of Kanuri social identity, continues to serve as a basis of political, economic, and social

[11]For further details on this most important development in recent Kanuri history, see R. Cohen 1970b and 1971c.

life for the vast majority of people in Bornu. It is a cornerstone of individual identity. When meeting a person for the first time, people ask: *"Ndu sunəm?"* or literally, "Who is your name?" In a very real sense, it is a way of asking, "Who are your people, your household?"

In the midst of these signs of stability, there is, however, a significant area of change. This change, moreover, concerns a basic feature of Kanuri identity—the norms of interpersonal relationships. In particular, attitudes and beliefs about superior-subordinate relationships and about clientship are being subjected to increasing criticism, especially by the young and educated. Diffuse, unquestioned, and exaggerated forms of respect, obedience, and patience, as the principal bases for establishing social, marital, working, or political relationships with superiors, are under mounting pressure. In the next chapter, therefore, the basic structure of interpersonal relationships in contemporary Bornu will be examined.

9

Superiors and Subordinates
in Contemporary Bornu

The context and symbols of Kanuri identity, as described in the previous chapter, are a prelude to the examination, in this chapter, of a most fundamental but changing aspect of Kanuri culture and identity. This aspect concerns the basic character of interpersonal relationships in general, and of the superior-subordinate relationship in particular. In a strict analytical sense, the superior-subordinate relationship may well be a universal aspect of human interaction. But its form and elaboration in Bornu, while not unique in the world, is striking in its cultural importance. Indeed, its most elaborate form—the client relationship—is a focal point of Kanuri identity, both individually and collectively.

It is in the context of the client relationship—a relationship between a patron and his client that is founded on a premise of inequality tempered by mutual trust and diffuse obligation—that most individual Kanuri envision and evaluate their chances for advancement through the status hierarchy in their social system. Basically, "achievement in Bornu is . . . a function of profitable social relations . . ." (R. Cohen 1960:276). The client relationship is the interpersonal bond with the greatest "growth potential" in this regard and, as a consequence, is seen as the normal means for achievement and advancement in the culture. Much of Kanuri social life is bound up with the process of "investing" in interpersonal, superior-subordinate relationships. In addition, clientship is recognized by many outsiders (for example, other Nigerians) as a key aspect of what it means to be Kanuri. If you are a Kanuri, you will very likely be involved in client relationships.

This analysis will be continued, then, by examining the scope and force of superior-subordinate relationships, and especially the client relationship, in Kanuri culture and identity. Initially, this will be done by examining the character of interpersonal relationships associated with three major social events common to the lives of almost all individuals in Bornu. These three are the naming day, marriage, and divorce. They are included here for two reasons: first, they illustrate in diverse ways the scope and force of the superior-subordinate relationship in the lives of individuals in Bornu; second, they provide further insight into the role of superior-subordinate relationships for Kanuri identity. As a means to this dual end, extended case material will be used to describe these events.[1] After reviewing these general instances of superior-subordinate relationships in the lives of individuals in Bornu, the nature of the client relationship will be examined and its role in social mobility will be considered.

THE NAMING DAY

The naming day is a joyous occasion for Kanuri, not only for the members of the infant's family but for all who know or are acquainted with them. But more importantly for this analysis, the naming day illustrates that aspects of superiority and subordinance enter the lives of Kanuri even at this early stage of life. We can see this in the events that followed the birth of Ibrahim's child.

A few days after the child was born, Ibrahim sent Musa, one of his several clients, to the market to buy a large bag of kola nuts. In making the plans for the naming day, Ibrahim was unusually optimistic because when the child was born, part of the placenta was still attached to it—a particularly good sign. Such babies are destined to be fortunate in life. Indeed, at that very moment, one of Ibrahim's most trusted friends—an old *malam* wise in the ways of medicines and charms—was enclosing a bit of this good omen in a small leather-covered amulet. Ibrahim's child would wear it for many years.

On Musa's return from the market, Ibrahim inspects the kola nuts to be sure they are all clean and free from imperfections of any kind. Then, giving the usual instructions on such an occasion, he sends Musa on his way. Though the news was beginning to trickle out to a few intimate friends, it was essential for all to be formally notified of the impending naming day. Musa was to take

---

[1]These three events will be presented here by means of composite descriptions. They are based on notes made in the field while attending several naming ceremonies and weddings. The divorce described here was not one that I observed directly. It was, however, one that was described in vivid terms by a reliable informant and is, in its broad outlines, a well-known pattern in Bornu.

a few of these bittersweet nuts to the heads of all the neighboring households, all the households of distant relatives and friends, to a few households in neighboring hamlets, and to the compounds of local political leaders. Gentle hints would be given, though in fact few would be needed, that on the coming Tuesday, there would be a naming ceremony at Ibrahim's compound. Thus, the rumors of a few days before are confirmed; a birth has indeed occurred. If the "little kitten" or "little stranger" can but survive the rigors of the first seven days of life, the naming will be done.

Not long after Musa finishes his journey, the thump of pestle against mortar can be heard coming from the compound of the new child's family. Female friends and relatives of the mother have begun to prepare the food that will be distributed after the naming. Quiet laughter from the excited younger girls blends with the rhythmic pounding of the pestles.

Early in the predawn light of the eighth day after the birth—the Tuesday of which Musa had spoken—the village comes to life. After the men have seated themselves on mats in front of Ibrahim's house, the women, walking silently except for the sensuous rustle of their long, tight-fitting gowns, enter the compound. They carry large bowls of food which they balance deftly in their hands as they dip slightly on passing through the low doorway of the entrance room to the compound. They are careful to avert their eyes away from the men, who themselves are looking away. The long, single file of women begins to fade into a trickle as all arrive.

The men, seated in tight clusters against the chill of the hour, sit quietly talking with their nearby friends. All are waiting for the appearance of the Village Head; no one has missed noticing the large empty mat in the center of the group, placed in expectation of Abubakar's arrival. Barely using the cane that has become one of his trademarks, the Village Head rounds a corner, followed closely by several of his clients and two of his sons. Rushing forward, one of Ibrahim's sons spreads a thick, white goatskin on the waiting mat and the old village leader takes his place. Much laughter accompanies the flurry of friendly greetings that are exchanged with the old man. A special greeting is extended to Ibrahim—a distant relative of Abubakar's.

The idle chatting diminishes as the aged fingers of the most learned malam present begin reverently to untie the bindings of the leather box in which is kept an ancient, hand-written Koran. Section by section, the well-worn pages are distributed to the other malams sitting nearby. In a tangle of voices, rising and falling in timbre as suits the readers, the sacred texts are read simultaneously. The voices diminish as each finishes the portion he has been given. Then the old teacher, Mustafa, calls for the sections in just the proper order so the great book will be whole once again.

Inside the compound, the women sit talking quietly, hearing the voices of the men in the distance, but concentrating on the preparation of the child. Barbers are in the midst of shaving the baby's head. On finishing, the most experienced barber takes a small, sharp instrument from his leather pouch and prepares to cut tiny marks on the infant's forehead and cheeks. With swift strokes the minute marks are made, the child barely noticing what has happened. Several of the women sitting near the infant look closely to see if they can tell whether it is a boy or girl since this important piece of information has been revealed to only the closest friends and relatives. A clue will be whether or not the barbers make other cuts around the baby's navel—a pattern more common for girls. The barbers clean their instruments and pack them away without making any more marks. It could be a boy. How lucky for Fatima if this should be so! She had so wanted this child—her third—to be a boy. As yet she had none but each of her two cowives had two. This would be a great boost to her morale as well as to her status in the household.

While these women are speculating and hoping, two of the older men in the group outside also sat wondering aloud to each other about whether the child was a boy or a girl. Their thoughts were more than idle curiosity, however. The moon had just entered the second quarter a few days before and the first half of the month is associated with "femaleness."

"If Ibrahim's child is a boy," muttered one of the men, "it will be a good sign because men born under the star of women are certain to be lucky."

"Yes," responded the other, "people will love him like a woman; his popularity will be great."

"If it is a girl, it will be a pity she was not born in a few weeks —in the male half of the month. Then she would be blessed with the character of a man. She would have a strong heart, be generous, honest, and would surely be a leader."[2]

---

[2]These characteristics emphasize a number of the personality attributes thought to be vital if a man would be successful. Several of these, if not all of them, are essential in the context of client relationships. Being "popular" is desired because it is the basis for acquiring clients. Generosity is important

Meanwhile, the malams had reassembled the Koran and were sitting patiently while Musa and two other men began to distribute gifts from Ibrahim to the malams who had done the reading. These little gifts, consisting of a large handful of kola nuts, candy, and a few pennies, are given out of respect for the learning of the malams and for their having come to officiate at the naming.

There is much pleasant chatter as Musa and the others walk among the men, reaching first into the pile of gifts on a tray and then depositing them deep into the cavernous pockets in the men's gowns. At the same time, Muktar, the youngest son of the Village Head, carries a cup of pungent perfume to the guests. Each dips his index finger and his prayer beads into the cup. The scent is rubbed onto the gowns and the back of the neck. Some of the men sniff it and discover it is a very expensive variety popular with the big men in the city. Does this mean Ibrahim is especially proud of something? Could it be his newest child is a son? Such wonderings are short lived as Ibrahim is heard quietly saying to the Village Head, "We have named him Abubakar Lawan."

Names are chosen primarily by the father, who must review and consider his social relationships carefully before making the final selection. Namesakes often have an important relationship to the new child. If there is no genealogical link between the namesake and the child, it is expected that in time an important social relationship will develop, especially in the villages where there is greater chance for such a relationship to grow and prosper. The name also signals publicly the feelings of the father for the man whose name has been adopted. As a kinsman and respected leader the old Village Head is doubly rewarded to have been chosen as the namesake for a child who is surely destined to grow into a fine, respectful man. His father, Ibrahim, sits quietly as the men comment among themselves on the fine name that has been announced. The women have heard it, too, and are also pleased. A few of them break into excited chatter and others ululate with joy.

For a few minutes, the guests remain to chat with friends. Shortly, however, the women who are less well acquainted with

---

because it is the means, par excellence, for continuing client relationships once they have been established. Honesty and steadfastness (i.e., a strong heart) are essential attributes for a good client. A subordinate should be honest in his dealings with his patron and loyal to him.

Fatima or who are kept in strict seclusion will rise and begin the walk home, their steps lightened by having left the food they brought as gifts and by the knowledge that one of their sisters has had a healthy boy-child. Most of the men leave at about the same time. The sun is well up now and since it is Tuesday, it is time to go to the weekly market held in their village. For the others who are closely related by ties of kinship or friendship, there will be longer visits. Some may remain to enjoy the entire day with the family. It is truly a happy day—a day set aside for welcoming a new member of the household and the village. He has survived the first days of life and it is hoped by all that he will continue to thrive. New relationships have been established; potential bonds have been initiated. It is a time for happiness and optimism.

MARRIAGE

The second social context to be considered that illustrates the importance of superior-subordinate relationships for Kanuri is marriage. In most cultures, marriage is among the most complex of the rites of passage. Within a single culture, but depending upon many different variables, such as the social status of the principals, whether it is a first marriage, the time of the year, and the myriad other individual and social nuances of personality and situation, a marriage may consist of several different combinations of events. Consequently it is difficult to describe "marriage." One can, however, describe *a* marriage and hope to indicate something about its typicality as well as its uniqueness.

R. Cohen (1971b) and Imam (1969), in their analyses of Kanuri marriage, emphasize the symbolic aspects of this rite. Cohen spotlights the single most important symbolic feature of Kanuri marriage—*dominance.* Describing Kanuri marriage rituals as "dramas of dominance," he is stressing the fact that, in Bornu, these rituals portray in public, symbolic form, the collective understanding regarding the social relationships being established in a marriage. In point of fact, the marriage relationship is only a special form of the superior-subordinate relationship, but the "dramas of dominance" bring to center stage a most important element in such relationships. This is the tension growing out of the dominance of the superior over the subordinate (in this case, the dominance of the husband over the wife).

There are several essential steps for all Kanuri marriages.[3] These involve the payment of a number of fees that are negotiated between the representatives of the bride and groom. Metaphorically, such fees (i.e., the bridewealth) may be understood as the seal on the social contract that is being established between the kinsmen of the couple about to be married.

A young man who is about to marry for the first time consults his father or another appropriate senior male about the basic arrangements. Of particular concern is selecting the most suitable bride—a topic that will entail some discussion. Ultimately, discrete inquiries will be made to the family of the girl. Such inquiries are made through trusted intermediaries who will present gifts representing payment of the "asking the question" fee. This is paid by these intermediaries on behalf of the groom once it seems clear the chances for the marriage are nearly certain.

If these inquiries are successful, negotiations begin as to the date of the wedding, the amount of the bridewealth, and other details. Prior to the actual wedding day, the bridewealth is paid to the guardian of the bride who will distribute the cash and gifts normally given for this purpose to the relatives of the bride. Accompanied by his male friends, the groom's representative goes from the groom's house (where the groom sits waiting for their return) to the home of the bride early in the morning of the wedding day. When the two groups reach agreement as to the appropriate amount for the final marriage fee, the money is exchanged and the marriage is considered binding. The groom's friends return and spend the remainder of the day conversing, playing cards, and entertaining the groom.

The bride meanwhile is preparing for the short journey she will be making that evening. As dusk approaches, the girl is brought to the house of the groom, his friends (except for the most intimate ones) having earlier bid him farewell. The bride, struggling and crying in mock resistance, is carried inside to the waiting groom. Later that night, and again after the payment of some small fees, the marriage is consummated.

[3]Interestingly, those aspects of the marriage ceremony most heavily laden with symbolism are also the most optional, especially in subsequent marriages. The significance of this is a complex issue that need not detain us at the moment (and moreover, it is discussed at some length in Cohen's analysis). However, we may note that if the first marriage ends in divorce and subsequent remarriage, the realities of married life render such symbolic activities more or less superfluous.

This, then, is an outline of a Kanuri marriage. Few would take place which are simpler; many would occur which are more elaborate. It is these additional steps that contain much of the symbolism and drama to which we have alluded. Of these "dramas" four are relatively common and all illustrate the same theme. The first of these events takes place about a day or two before the wedding. At this time the women related to either the bride or groom will have begun to arrive for the wedding. The mood is festive, but the work of preparing the food, gifts, and other details of the wedding is difficult and tiring. Periodically these women pause in their activity and sit to rest and sing. Selecting a few dried corn stalks from the supply kept on hand as fuel for cooking, the women begin to tap them rhythmically on a small calabash floating upside down in a large tub of water. The resonating thump accompanies them as they sing about the monkey, and his clumsiness and inexperience. Though the song is about a monkey, in fact they are singing about the bride and groom. At the bride's house, they sing about the importance of the young girl being properly respectful and obedient. The female kinsmen of the groom, in complementary fashion, sing about the need for the groom to establish his authority over his bride, admonishing him that if he does not, he will suffer as though he had a monkey on his back.

The second optional feature in the marriage process is more entertainment than ceremony, per se. In many aspects of Kanuri life, the role of praise-singing is vital. Whenever a major public official appears on important holidays, or other public occasions, his coming and going is marked by the playing of music. The songs relate all the glories of his family, friends, and, of course, himself. The praise singers are supported and retained by these high ranking individuals. There are, however, many praise singers who perform for public occasions of lesser note, such as in the market, at minor political rallies, and at ceremonial events such as weddings. At virtually all of these, they sing about the past and present glory (whether real or fictitious) of the individual being praised. At weddings, however, a different theme is stressed. Here they will sing about married life. Though their songs parody the trials and tribulations the bride and groom may expect, they are recognized by all as sources of insight into the nature of the marriage relationship. Much of the singing advises the groom to maintain his position as the head of the household and to be dominant over his wife. The bride is reminded of the importance of being properly submissive and respectful. Typical episodes in the life of a married couple may also be enacted. For all, it is a time of merriment as well as for recollecting their own experiences. There are few who are unable to find something in the singing that does not strike a tender nerve or a familiar situation.

After the bride has been brought to the groom's house, another event may take place before she goes to his room. The groom, with his close male friends, will sit together in a small room in the house. After a few minutes a young girl enters and without saying anything, kneels before them very respectfully. One of the young men will ask, pointing to the covered tray she has placed beside her on the ground, "What have you brought?" Almost in a whisper, and in a most respectful manner, she may reply, "I have peanuts for sale." Then follows a series of exchanges in which the girl, usually a very close friend of the bride, attempts to sell the "peanuts" to the men. The men know the tray probably contains nothing but stones but they also know they must buy them from her before the groom can go to his bride. The asking price will be great—often several pounds. After much banter and yet serious bargaining, the girl will collect her money and leave the "peanuts." This may be repeated several times, each girl selling a different thing. Among other things, this little drama symbolizes (as has been noted by R. Cohen 1971b) the importance of paying and/or rewarding subordinates for services rendered— or in this case, about to be rendered. This aspect of the superior-subordinate relationship is stressed in Bornu and is fundamental to it. The superior in a relationship must, though judiciously perhaps, use his wealth to maintain the loyalty and support of his subordinates—whether it be his wife, servant, or client. Only in this way can he continue the relationships that are so important if he is to achieve his goals. Using one's wealth in this way is an essential, and at times stressful, part of adult life in Bornu.

During the day following the consummation of the marriage, another ceremony takes place which may be translated as "to be matured." In separate parts of the compound, the bride and groom will be offered food three times; each time, they will spit or throw the food into a bowl with as much force as possible. The belief is expressed, though not too seriously, that the one who throws the food hardest will be dominant in the marriage. For the bride, the removal of the food from her mouth symbolizes, that "although husbands are dominant, authority rests on consent;

. . . it can never be total [and] it can be abrogated if the wife subordinate decides she does not wish to continue her subordination" (R. Cohen 1971b:86). Here the emphasis is on the importance of protecting one's rights within a relationship. This is true, as well, for all such relationships in Bornu, whether they involve marriage or not.

DIVORCE

The third event to be considered which illustrates the character and role of superior-subordinate relationships is divorce. In Bornu, divorce is almost as common as marriage. Divorce is frequent primarily because it is easy, although fertility, rural-urban experience, and socio-economic status are also important factors (see R. Cohen 1971b:*passim*). The reasons given for divorce by informants cover almost every possible category, as might be expected given the large number of divorces for which reasons may be given. The experience of Muktar is somewhat unusual but not extreme for a person in his circumstances. The details of his situation, moreover, illustrate several important characteristics of the superior-subordinate relationship in Bornu; prominent among these is the role of respect.

Muktar, a busy and successful trader, lives in a poorer section of town, unlike most of his fellow fish dealers. People in his neighborhood wondered about the poor condition of his house since everyone "knew" his income was very large. With mud walls in a bad state of repair, no electricity and no water tap in the house, he was living in a fashion unsuited to a man who in most other respects was "up-and-coming."

There were many signs Muktar was destined to be a very successful man someday, if it could be said he wasn't already. Besides fine clothes, a car and servants, Muktar had two wives. Nana, his senior wife, was not particularly beautiful but she worked hard and had produced two children who were almost grown to manhood. His second wife, Bintu, was more comely but she had a zest for life that included work, too. His business depended on the goodwill he maintained with both the traders who took the fish in trucks to Kano and Lagos as well as with those who made the trip to Lake Chad where the huge lakefish were caught, dried, and salted. All the people in his household, and especially his wives, were essential to his goal of providing appropriate Kanuri hospitality to his customers. His wives were virtually in full charge of these important activities and they were well known for their skill. Muktar's energy, knowledge of trading, numerous friends, and his capable household were an excellent combination for success.

Muktar was anxious to expand his business. He was also very much an admirer of the beauty of the daughter of Alhaji Ganama, one of the biggest fish dealers in Maiduguri. His relationship with Alhaji was one of long-standing friendship and respect. Almost daily, Muktar would drive his car to his friend and advisor's house for a visit. Alhaji's cream-colored Mercedes looked gigantic next to Muktar's Opel Kadet, but this didn't bother him since he knew he was among the closest of Alhaji's many friends and followers. Almost before the car had stopped, several of Alhaji's servants came forward with a large, contoured cloth and began to cover Muktar's car to protect it from the sun and dust; their work was done almost before the first speck had settled on the hood.

Muktar, meanwhile, was on his way into the entrance room of Alhaji's fine, blue, concrete-block house. Deftly, he slipped his shoes from his feet and waited to be announced. Alhaji was studying the Koran when Muktar entered. They exchanged friendly greetings and sat down on a thick rug Alhaji had purchased years ago in Mecca. As usual, the old man waited for Muktar to begin the conversation but he registered a little surprise at Muktar's seeming disinterest in the latest news of the fishing at Lake Chad. Instead, Muktar began inquiring at greater than usual length about Alhaji's family. Among those mentioned was Alhaji's 13-year-old daughter, Jalo. Warming to the topic of conversation, Alhaji boasted of her excellent record in primary school and of her skill as a cook. "I have given special attention," he added with a serious tone, "to her training in household skills. We have all heard so much about the declining abilities of schoolgirls who neglect these important matters. It is said some of the girls can barely pound grain any more, so weak have they become from so much study. Why can't they do both?"

Muktar seemed to miss the question and instead discretely asked of her plans. With an attentive smile, Alhaji indicated she had none as yet. He only knew she would not be going to the secondary school and so would probably begin to prepare for marriage. Muktar said little after that. After a short while, he finished the bowl of gruel Alhaji's wife had brought, and he rose to leave, promising to return again the next day, as always.

The next day, however, Muktar's trusted and closest friends, Ali and Yahiya, paid a visit to Alhaji. They discussed the possibility of a marriage between Alhaji's daughter Jalo, and Muktar. Alhaji's response seemed favorable. If anything, Ali and Yahiya were a little surprised that Alhaji seemed to have been expecting them. At any rate, their gifts on behalf of Muktar were acceptable, for not long after they left they received word that Jalo and Alhaji were in agreement about Muktar's proposal.

Many preparations were necessary and Muktar and his friends began them with relish. Although it would cost Muktar a considerable sum of money in gifts, fees, and miscellaneous expenses, the alliance that would be forged would be good for all concerned. He was also confident he could keep his other wives happy. After all, Jalo and Bintu were slightly acquainted through a friend they had in common, and Nana, with so important a position in the household, would certainly not want to leave such favorable circumstances. She did not have to work hard—Bintu and the servants did most of the truly hard labor; and she had a great deal of authority for a woman. Besides, in calculating his wedding expenses, an amount equal to what was being spent for Jalo's gifts had been included for gifts to be divided between Nana and Bintu. Of course, he had noticed an unpleasant expression on the politely half-hidden face of Nana when he told her of his plans, but most women felt this way at first. By expression at least, Bintu had not indicated any particular feelings, though she had reaffirmed she knew Jalo.

The wedding took place as planned and Muktar was justifiably proud of the large number of important people who came to his house that day. The first several months after the wedding were going well, too. He had been a little surprised, however, by a request from his senior wife, Nana. It had been her turn to visit him in his room, and they were sitting on a mat talking softly to one another. Abruptly, Nana asked in rather sharp tones why he hadn't put electricity into the house. And, for that matter, she wondered why he still had mud walls and mud roofs, and no water tap. The rainy season was about to come and she did not want to have to worry about leaks in the roof or the poor service of the water carriers. In response, he tried to explain the problems of having to keep cash reserves ready for the purchase of fish from the dealers from Lake Chad who often came at unpredictable times. He also tried to tell her of the problems he was having trying to collect the money owed him from his customers in

Kano and Lagos. He, too, wanted these things for the house but they would have to wait until his financial circumstances were better. The conversation ended there and Nana silently began to rub her husband's back as she had done so many times, only that night her mind seemed to wander to other things.

She had welcomed Jalo after the marriage. There was much to do in the household and another woman to help would be a good thing for everyone. She had noticed Jalo's eagerness to help, too, and appreciated it. Jalo and Bintu seemed to get along very well. In fact, Bintu had taken on the responsibility of instructing her in the many new duties she would have. Bintu seemed to enjoy this very much, and so did Jalo, or at least so it seemed. Many times Nana had noticed the two of them talking and laughing together. And many times, as she approached to join in the chatter, the two of them would stop their merrymaking and begin discussing the special needs of the next few day's guests. What were they laughing about? . . . She knew such thoughts were not good but neither were they easy to put out of one's head. Her husband's slow, measured breathing told her she could sleep, too, although uncharacteristically, she could not. The bed must be in need of repair—why else should she not be able to sleep where she had slept so many times before?

All that week, little things began to bother Nana. First, she noticed Jalo was spending an inordinate amount of time with the hairdresser. She seemed excessively proud of her thick, beautifully braided, black hair; the way she sat with her head so erect was entirely too disrespectful for a girl so young and newly married. And Bintu seemed to be acquiring a new interest in her appearance, all of which seemed unnecessary since she was already more attractive than either of her cowives. And on top of all that, the water carriers had been late in coming again, and there was no water for doing the pans and dishes from the night before, even though the sun was well up. Now the chore would have to be done in the sweltering heat of the afternoon. Moreover, although she didn't have enough water in the big, moss covered water storage pots, she had too much in the larder. The old roof had begun to leak in a new place and had soaked a week's supply of millet flour.

She noticed old Muktar in his sitting room, seemingly in deep thought—about what, she wondered? Respectfully, but not without a tinge of anger in her voice, Nana greeted her husband and requested a private word with him. Again, she asked for the badly needed improvements in the house. And again, this time with greater seriousness, Muktar explained the difficult financial burdens he faced. Almost without thinking, he added that the wedding expenses had been even greater than he had planned. He could see no other way than asking for all to be patient. "Well, then, can you at least tell Jalo to clean the larder?" queried Nana. Muktar's negative answer was bolstered only by his authority and a reference to Jalo's youth and education, and something about this sort of work being unsuited to such a girl. The anger mounting in her stomach, Nana managed to control her voice as she protested such a thing, but she was overruled and told to oversee while one of the servants did the job.

Muktar was miffed at her behavior. At first he suspected jealousy but then this seemed out of the question. Had he not been so very careful to give each wife the necessary gifts, and was he not especially attentive to them when they visited him in their turn at night? Had not both Nana and Bintu said it was easier to see to the needs of his many guests now that there was an extra person to help with the women's work, and had he not increased their weekly expense money? What more could they expect him to do! With three of his most important business contacts from Kano expected any minute, he had to relax and put such domestic troubles out of his mind. His first concern was showing these Hausa visitors to Bornu just what genuine hospitality was meant to be.

The excited shouting of the children playing in the street told Muktar his friends had arrived; he waited less than a minute or two before they were announced. When they had exchanged greetings several times and after polite inquiries had been made about the difficulty of the journey, Muktar called to Nana to bring food and gruel. The men sat waiting. They began discussing the magnificent new stretch of highway between Beni Sheik and Maiduguri. The tooth-jarring old road had been replaced, at long last, with a double—almost triple—lane highway. Minutes passed and still the food had not come. Muktar called again, this time in firm tones, but not without some embarrassment as his guests sat looking around the moderately furnished sitting room. They haltingly began again to discuss the new road, noting the advantages of such a highway for trade. One of them commented that the smooth road would not destroy trucks as had the old bumpy one. Another countered with the observation that the speed the drivers made now that the road was smooth would destroy them even faster than had been the case before. All nodded in agreement and leaned back waiting for the next topic—or Nana—to emerge. They sat in silence for a long minute when suddenly Muktar rose and was through the door in one swift movement. He shouted for Nana. Bintu and Jalo were pounding grain and singing a slightly bawdy song in the far corner of the compound, but when they saw Muktar striding so swiftly in their direction, they fell silent. Almost hissing, Muktar demanded the whereabouts of Nana. On hearing their answer, he whirled around and went directly to her room where, as they had said, he found the hairdresser braiding Nana's thinning hair. In a loud but controlled voice, he demanded that she bring food and gruel. "It is on the table in the kitchen," she blurted; "have one of your wives get it!" She rose and looked him directly in the eye as he stepped forward speaking in angry tones. "You are my wife and you have been asked to bring food. You have a final chance to get it; if you do not, you must leave this house." In a flash, Nana grabbed his shirt in her hand and shouted for all to hear, "You have spent your money on a wife and have embarrassed us all by waiting so long without putting even a zinc roof on the larder or a water tap in the kitchen. Other women prepare themselves for their nightly visits to their husbands by sitting in front of mirrors in rooms lit by electric lamps while I must struggle with a flickering kerosene lantern. I say again; have one of your wives get the food for I am no longer one of them!" Muktar, so angry he could but whisper, said, "I divorce you. Leave my house!"

As the "case" of Muktar and Nana illustrates, a common reason for termination of marriage, other than failure to live up to primary role expectations (i.e., for women, childbirth; for men, providing food), is disobedience and disrespect on the part of the woman (no matter the reasons for such behavior). More generally, any superior-subordinate relationship in Bornu is predicated on the maintenance of the proper degree of respect by the subordinate for the superior. From this is derived the equally important necessity of being obedient, since disobedience is taken as a sign of disrespect, not disagreement. Failure to live up to these expectations will usually be sufficient to jeopardize such a relationship altogether. For a woman in Bornu, marriage is classically a matter of obedience and respect for her husband. She will gain favor and admiration in the eyes of her husband and others to the degree she is able to live up to these ideals.

The husband is not without obligations, however. In addition to providing money for the basics of life for his wife, he should, within reasonable financial limits, reward obedience and respect by giving gifts and, in general, showing due appreciation for his wife's good behavior. A failure on his part will ordinarily result in a breakdown in the woman's commitment to her role. Insubordination and divorce are likely to follow, and as we have seen, this sequence of events may be set in motion by the woman. While all of this is obvious to Kanuri, not to mention most readers in all cultures, it also dramatizes the importance of the superior-subordinate relationship to Kanuri. Other evidence from relationships outside of marriage reinforces the view that Kanuri divorce is, among other things, an expression of a general concern for seeking satisfactory social relationships. Moreover, it illustrates that such relationships are often founded on a premise of inequality.

Indeed, the events and character of the naming day, marriage, and divorce merely illustrate this concern in contexts that are fundamental to the lives of all Kanuri. A more diffuse and basic setting for this search for profitable and satisfying interpersonal relationships is clientship. In such a context, the concern for seeking adequate relationships (i.e., those where one receives appropriate rewards) emerges as the key to understanding the dynamics of social mobility in Kanuri society. Hence, we will turn now to a consideration of social mobility and clientship in Bornu.

CLIENTSHIP AND SOCIAL MOBILITY

Kanuri explain differences in individual success by reference to a single, fundamental concept—*arzegi,* or "good fortune." "Like Calvinistic predetermination, *arziyi* [sic] is hoped for before the fact, and is indicated and substantiated after the fact—of success" (R. Cohen 1966:134). Kanuri stress that the extent or potential of an individual's "good fortune" cannot be manipulated, it cannot be inherited, and it is not limited to people of particular social standing (e.g., to royalty). The amount of one's *arzegi* is fixed at birth. With such a view, all of life can be seen as a process in which one's predetermined fortune is played out. Some of these aspects of *arzegi* are illustrated in the case of Bukar Waziri.

Bukar Waziri was an old man who, over the years, had become quite wealthy. He had a son, also named Bukar, and a client-servant named Mohammud. As the years went by, it became clear to those who knew Bukar's household that it would be better if Mohammud, rather than Bukar's son, were to inherit the old man's fortune. However, when the old man died, the son did inherit his father's property. And, as people had predicted, this son soon spent all of the money and sold all the property. Mohammud, who had also received some of his master's property, though much less than the son had received, became wealthy—so wealthy that people called him "Alhaji," even though he had not been to Mecca. The son, in fact, now lives in the house of the servant. The servant has *arzegi;* the son does not.

While emphasizing *arzegi,* however, Kanuri are also well aware that success is the result of considerable personal effort; it does not just materialize. It takes work to demonstrate that one has *arzegi* just as it did for a Calvinist to prove he was one of the "elect." Indeed, from the point of view of most Kanuri, people work to achieve their success in life in one of two general kinds of relationships: by becoming involved in client relationships, or by embarking upon a kind of individualized self-reliant role. The first of these is by far the most common and admired context for social mobility; the second is uncommon and generally repudiated by Kanuri. Each of these will be discussed in turn.

CLIENTSHIP IN BORNU

The term clientship refers to the diffuse relationship between two individuals (adult males), one of whom is considered the superior or patron and the other the subordinate or client. It is a diffuse relationship because the patron may demand a wide range of services from the client, while the client may expect a wide range of considerations from his patron. The relationship is unequal in that the superior has virtually all of the material wealth and/or power in the relationship since any wealth or power the client has stems directly from his patron as a reward for services rendered.

In Bornu, the basic client relationship is centered around the dyad of *abba njima* and *tata njima,* or literally, the dyad of "father of the house" and "son of the house." As the words indicate, the basic relationship of these two people is patterned after the father-son relationship. In spite of the numerous distinctions in the various client relationships formed, the father-son relationship serves as an implicit model for all. However, a client generally does not have a kinship link with his patron.

These relationships are established explicitly to foster the immediate and long-term ambitions of both individuals involved. This is especially true of client relationships established in the political sector of Kanuri society where success, other things equal, is closely linked to the number of subordinates (clients) a man has. The advantage for the subordinate comes with the success of the superior, for it is in this way that his own position in the political hierarchy is advanced. It is true, for all intents and purposes, that in the political sector, having clients and being the client of someone else are, respectively, necessary and sufficient conditions for social mobility and political success.

Theoretically, each person in Bornu is the client of someone else. It is said, for example, that "all people in Bornu are the 'slaves' of the *Shehu*." The ideology behind this view is not far from being a reality. Everyone depends to some degree on another person to teach him the skills of a particular craft, including farming, and everyone with a position in the political structure (excluding some modern elective and civil service offices) has been appointed by someone higher in the hierarchy. Thus, if asked, people would agree they have a superior to whom they feel some degree of allegiance, the degree varying according to the extent of the favors granted. However, in the common day-to-day perceptions of Kanuri, some people are simply not thought of as *being* clients; rather they are seen as *having* clients. Such a view is more than a semantic subtlety. It is a view which grows out of important though subtle distinctions in the varieties of client relationships.

In general, two types of client relationships may be distinguished: the apprentice-master relationship, and the "simple" dependence relationship. For both, the relationship is entered into on a voluntary basis after initiation by the subordinate and with the agreement of the superior. To emphasize this, informants said it would be just as meaningful to speak of the "son of the house" (the *tata njima*) as being a *tata ardigama* or "son by agreement." That is, the prospective client agrees to be the subordinate of the *abba njima* and the *abba njima* agrees to have him; they both "agree with" or are satisfied with the *behavior* of the other. The stress on behavior in such agreements reflects their mutual trust in the willingness and ability of each to meet the role expectations of the other.

They each believe they know how the other will respond to the obligations of the relationship. Implicit in such an agreement is the client's expectation about the rewards he will receive for being trustworthy and respectful. If these rewards are insufficient and if negotiations on this point fail, then the client is free to break the relationship.

The apprentice form of the client relationship is common among those involved in occupations requiring extended training and/or considerable capital before one can be either proficient or self-sufficient at it. Such skills include blacksmithing, barbering, and leather-working, though there are many others. An apprentice client will be taught a craft while being provided with food and shelter. Depending on the circumstances, money and other forms of assistance may be provided in order to satisfy many other kinds of needs, including money for a marriage or other special expenses (including taxes). The client's superior, the master craftsman, receives a number of benefits. In the first place, the products and/or income from the apprentice are turned over to him. Though this practice will be discontinued after the apprentice establishes his own business, the master can expect other benefits of the relationship to continue. The most important of these concerns the obligation of the client to perform general services for the patron, which can range from delivering messages to assisting on his farm. Moreover, a former apprentice who has grown to maturity will, if he is properly concerned with the correctness of his social relationships, continue to consider himself the client of his *abba njima,* even though he himself may have clients of his own. A favorite Kanuri example illustrates this.

Two men, Ali and Illia, live in a large city. Ali is the *tata njima* ("client") of Illia. When Ali established the relationship, Illia was famous and wealthy. In due course, however, Ali became even more famous and wealthy than Illia. Their houses were across the street from each other, and one day, someone asked Ali what his address should be for purposes of mailing and shipping things to him. Ali responded by saying, "Ali of Illia."

As time went on, Ali became still richer while Illia's wealth began to decline. Illia began to sell his property to cover his debts, and was finally faced with the prospect of having to sell his own house. Ali bought the house at public auction and Illia paid his creditors. Nevertheless, Ali continued as Illia's client. And, as had been the case before Illia's financial ruin, Ali continued to bring kola nuts and porridge to Illia each morning as a sign of respect.

The second type of client relationship has aspects which are similar to the first type just described, but is different in one important respect. In this relationship, the subordinate recognizes he lacks sufficient capital to work at his craft (typically trading) independently. In such a situation, he will, through a careful building of trust, be given greater and greater responsibilities by the patron. There is only a very indistinct apprentice-master character to this relationship. Ordinarily, the parties to this type of client relationship are mature men who are skilled at their work, but where one of the two is dependent in some way on the other for support—either materially or morally.

Within this general, nonapprentice form of clientship, there are several kinds of clients, differentiated in terms of the work they do and/or other aspects of their relationship to the patron. For example, a household servant who may be assigned menial tasks is a *walidi*. Ordinarily, he does not have his own house or even a special place to sleep within the *abba njima's* house. In many cases, he will not have a family of his own. In such circumstances, he is completely dependent upon the abba njima for everything he has or the satisfaction of any need that may arise. Another type of *tata njima* may serve as a highly skilled assistant to the head of a household. In such cases, he may serve as the abba njima's representative, carry out extensive trade in his name, and otherwise serve as the patron's assistant or manager. This type of client is known as *wakil*.

This does not mean clients are typically menials. District Heads give service as clients of the *Shehu* by performing their duties as administrators of large portions of the kingdom. At this level of analysis, their role is no different than that of the servant of the District Head. There is a difference in the type of duty, but not in the relationship in which the duties are carried out.

One of the most common and unstructured forms of the "simple" client relationship is that established between an individual outside the political hierarchy and someone within it. Depending upon the duration of the relationship and the extent of the subordinate's involvement in the relationship, he may expect to receive advice, useful information, loans, and hopefully, a position of some kind within the political structure. Such men will, from day to day, perform few if any specific tasks for their patron. A most important aspect of such a relationship, however, is frequent visiting and gift-giving by the client. In so doing, he indicates his awareness of past obligations as well as future intentions. The relationship endures because of the potential for an eventual promotion of both parties to the relationship. This possibility exists by virtue of the higher position held by the patron and the moral and financial support given by the client.

The promotion of those in the relationship (but most importantly, of course, the client) can come about in two ways. First, the patron may be promoted, thus opening the way for him to appoint his loyal followers (i.e., his tata njima or clients) to more important positions. The second way, and one that is frequently neglected in the analysis of clientship, is for a client to demonstrate, by his actions, that he has superior ability in performing the duties of his position. In most instances, a patron will have several clients who can be considered for a newly vacant position. Though the selection may be limited to those who have been loyal followers, the decision will be based on the superior's perception of the relative abilities of these candidates, the most capable being the most likely to succeed. To be sure, many characteristics are important in assessing capability in its broadest sense. Thus, in addition to specific skills, certain key aspects of personality and demeanor are also vital to an individual client's chances for success. It is important, for example, for a client to demonstrate to his patron that he is sufficiently patient, respectful, and "shameful," as these are essential aspects of Kanuri behavior, especially for clients who are seeking to rise in status. And as previously noted, gift-giving is an indirect indicator of individual ability since the frequency and amount of the gift are always carefully noted by the person receiving it. In short, any view of social mobility within a system resting on the clientship principle would be seriously in error if it did not recognize the importance of the combined talents of ability in a specific role, individual initiative, the use of wealth in gift-giving, and the cultivation of certain aspects of personality and character.

In summary, the client relationship forms the basic setting within which individuals in Bornu seek to advance in the status hierarchy. As such, the relationship forms a major component of Kanuri identity. In Bornu, one's demeanor in close interpersonal relationships is the essence of being Kanuri, and the most exemplary behavior is clientlike behavior. Thus, success striving and identity are closely linked in Bornu because the heart of the latter is the key to the former. Although often subtle and elusive, these facts of life are widely known to and highly valued by Kanuri.

SELF-RELIANCE IN BORNU

The second way of achieving success in Bornu—through one's own self-reliant, independent efforts—is, as we noted previously, an unpopular method. The reasons for the negative evaluation of this approach to mobility may best be understood through an analysis of the Kanuri word, *yamga.*

The word "yamga" has several meanings reflecting subtle though important differences. These are noted in speech by the context and/or by the use of modifying adjectives or descriptive metaphors. Depending on these variations, the word covers a range of meanings, from a simple "desire," to "need," "ambition," or "greed." Accordingly, when used to refer to an individual or character type, the term can denote either a desirous, needy, ambitious, or greedy person. In its most common use, "yamga" is best translated as "ambition."

Kanuri believe all people have their yamga; "Yamga is clotted in the heart of every man like butter, and it melts when it gets the chance." However, while all people may have their yamga, everyone is not a *yamgama,* or "ambitious person." Consequently, it is necessary to ascertain what it is that is distinctive about a yamgama. According to Kanuri viewpoints, there are two major and interrelated characteristics that differentiate the yamgama from others (i.e., from those who have a yamga but are not thought of as being a yamgama): failing to conceal ambitions "in your heart," and having diffuse and/or unrealistic ambitions.

Being open about one's ambitions, in addition to being perceived as poor judgment and a breach of etiquitte, is seen as an implicit rejection of client relationships. Such a view is linked to the semiprivate character of the client relationship in Bornu; indeed, modesty and discretion are important aspects of all Kanuri interpersonal relationships. In the context of the client relationship, such behavior will enable both parties to be appropriately circumspect about their ambitions. The importance of this aspect of clientship is such that one may question whether those who are open about their ambitions are involved in clientship; the best that can be concluded is that if they are, they are behaving poorly.

Some men have rather unrealistic and/or diffuse goals. As is the case in any society, there are men in Bornu who are constantly involved in new ventures, forever trying to make deals, always trying to add to their wealth—but often in ways that are destined for almost certain failure. However, it is difficult to behave in such a manner and still live up to the ideals of discretion. Consequently, having such diffuse or unrealistic goals is taken as evidence that such an individual is a yamgama. Even so, this flurry of activity is not necessarily unheard of among people who are involved in long-standing client relationships. And indeed, many people who are thought of as yamgama's are involved in such relationships, though the goals they are seeking (whether diffuse, unrealistic, or publicly known) will generally be ones unrelated to the potentials of their particular client relationships.

One example of this sort of yamgama is provided by the case of an official in the local government bureaucracy who was widely known because of his desire to be a District Head. Given his circumstances, this was a remote but not altogether unreal or unacceptable goal for him. However, it was asserted by informants, including the man himself, that he was a yamgama. His willingness to admit this was in itself an indication of the acceptability of his yamga. Moreover, his general behavior and character had always been exemplary, especially vis-à-vis his superiors. In this case, the man's yamga was not diffuse or outside the realm of possibility since he was already in the political structure. His only "failing" was his lack of discretion about his ambition.

There is, however, one kind of yamgama for which the matter of clientship is fundamental. A yamgama who seeks his goals through the use of guile, cunning, and most importantly, through independent, nonclient relationships, is described as a *yamgama bultu gai,* or "one who is ambitious like a hyena." Although informants estimated only 10 percent of all Kanuri were hyena-like in their behavior, even this was thought to be "too many." This behavior is, quite simply, uncharacteristic of being a "good Kanuri man." And while it was admitted many such men had become wealthy, it was still a role model to be repudiated.

Both the use of the hyena as a metaphor, and the negative view of such behavior are consistent with the role of hyena in Kanuri folktales and proverbs. He plays the role of the trickster, and is often involved in ambitious, singlehanded projects involving deceit, bending of social norms, cheating, and putting obstacles in the paths of others. And yet, while the hyena may be scorned for his deviant behavior, his success is still admired. Nevertheless, self-reliance outside the context of the client relationship is condemned with the pejorative label *yamgama bultu gai*.[4] And indeed, throughout much of the northern part of Nigeria, clientship—a role that is the opposite of "hyena-like" self-reliance—is held up as the role model for those who would be successful.

SUMMARY

As with the major symbols of Kanuri identity discussed in Chapter 8, most facets of Kanuri life-cycle rituals remain steadfast in the midst of many other more technological and demographic changes. It is true that many parents are choosing not to have their children marked with the facial scars that signify their Kanuri ancestry, but this trend is not a new one. Moreover, these scars, which for the child are relatively superficial wounds, are for the adult rather superficial symbols of identity. More basic are land, language, and loyalty to the Kanuri political system. Other life-cycle events—marriage, for example—are well established in their details, but the details also vary greatly with social class and individual circumstance, so that changes for the most part do not seem beyond acceptable ranges. And most importantly, there is, within the context of these social events, a pronounced orientation to the nuances of the superior-subordinate relationship, an orientation that appears likely to continue for some time to come. At the same time, however, there are tensions and strains in such relationships (as the divorce case illustrated) and these must be dealt with effectively if such relationships are to endure for long. Moreover, there are other role models in Bornu besides that of clientship. The hyena represents an extreme, but it also serves as a signal, especially to the young and educated. Additional, more quantified data will be examined

---

[4]The Kanuri concept of *yamgama*, and especially that of the *yamgama bultu gai*, would seem to fit M. G. Smith's description (1960:245) of the Hausa man who does not have a patron. In Hausaland, "a commoner without a patron is not merely a deviant but also a rebel . . . ." Lacking personal ties with others superior to him, "such an individual occupies a disadvantageous position in his society." Moreover, Hausa view the avoidance of client relationships as "an indication of *overambition,* disloyalty, and of social disorganization through change" [italics added].

in the next chapter in order to further consider the implications of this cultural development. This will be attempted by looking at two aspects of social mobility and social change. First, evidence for the changing role of clientship as a facet of Kanuri identity will be probed, and second, the implications of this change will be considered in terms of factors influencing occupation preference and economic development.

10

Clientship, Achievement Motivation, and Change

The institution of clientship discussed in the preceding chapters is important not only because it is a major axis of Kanuri identity, but also because it may relate directly to the potential of Kanuri society to develop economically. The hypothesized relationship between economic development and clientship is based on two related considerations: (1) to some, it appears that clientship directs people away from economically productive roles, and (2) it appears that achievement oriented individuals who generally fill entrepreneurial roles tend to exhibit self-reliant rather than clientlike attitudes and behavior. In this chapter, accordingly, we shall first consider whether and to what extent clientship, as a key element of Kanuri identity, may be changing. Then we will consider the implications of these findings for economic-growth potentials in Bornu. This will be done primarily by an analysis of achievement motivation in relation to clientship and business occupation preference. Throughout, the overall concern will be the dual character of change, first as it affects Kanuri identity, and second in terms of the implications of any changes that may be observed for economic growth and subsequent change.

THE SAMPLES

The individuals whose responses constitute the data source for this portion of the analysis were selected for interviewing using quota-sampling procedures (see R. Cohen 1973, for a discussion of procedures similar to these). Of the total number in this analysis (N = 148), 125 are adult males who were living in Maiduguri in 1967, at the time this study was being conducted. These men represent a wide range of social, occupational, and chronological backgrounds. The remaining 23 individuals were, in 1967, students in the Boys' Teacher Training College in Maiduguri. These students were in the last year of a five-year post-primary school program that prepared them to teach in primary schools in Nigeria. Respectively, these will be termed the *Townsmen* and *Teacher College* samples.

CLIENTSHIP IN CHANGING BORNU

Some indication of the changing significance of clientship in Bornu can be discerned simply by talking to Kanuri about this important aspect of their culture. When among their peers, students were often very negative in their views of clientship. The official change in policy concerning the removal of shoes on entering public government offices represented, for most students, a significant shift in policy—a shift seen by many as long overdue. But not all students felt this way and, moreover, there was some variation in opinion among other segments of the population on this and similar issues.

In order to more systematically assess the range of opinions about clientship, a standardized measure of this concept was developed. This measure consisted of 41 different items selected from a questionnaire used in this research in Bornu (see Appendix A, p. 189). These were all the items in the questionnaire which, on the basis of the manifest content of the item, fit our operational definition of clientship or, more precisely, of attitudes favorable to clientship. Clientship was defined, for this purpose, as any response which indicated that an individual (1) positively evaluated playing a subordinate role, (2) wished or preferred others to take such a role, (3) would make decisions about other issues because of the positive effect such a decision would have on the maintenance of a client relationship, and (4) negatively evaluated independent and/or self-reliant behavior. In using this measure, all responses falling within this definition were counted equally. The total number of such responses for an individual then produced a score, the Clientship Score, with a high value indicating strong, positive attitudes about clientship. For the sample as a whole, the Clientship Scores ranged from a low of 7 to a high of 33.

An assessment of the extent to which attitudes about clientship are changing in Bornu may be made by comparing the attitudes of people who differ in age. Here the hypothesis is that those who are younger will have more negative attitudes about clientship if in fact clientship as an institution in Bornu is declining in importance. The general comments of students and townsmen alike give us some basis for expecting that such a change is occurring. The Townsmen sample is the only one in which there is adequate variation in age to permit testing this hypothesis. On examining the relevant data,[1] it was found there was no relationship between age and clientship among the townsmen ($\chi^2 = 1.71$; df = 3; P < .50).

Further consideration of changing attitudes about clientship can be made, however, by comparing the attitudes of individuals who have participated differently in institutions most often associated with changing attitudes and opinions. In this regard, few institutions can compare to the Western-type public school. In Bornu, this is unquestionably true. Moreover, in the context of a discussion of clientship in Zambia (Colson 1967) written before the research reported here had been completed, R. Cohen suggests that in Bornu "clientship ... can only be challenged by an expanding educational system which will ... change the criteria for mobility and recruitment in valued roles ..." (R. Cohen 1967: 105). Since the results of the previous hypothesis minimize the importance of age differences, we may usefully compare the Clientship Scores of those who differ in amount of education, regardless of their ages. Of the Townsmen sample, 32 have had some amount of Western education; the remaining 93 individuals have had none. With the Teacher College sample, these provide us with three samples defined in terms of educational experience: (1) those with no Western education, (2) those who have had some Western education in the past (the average is five years of school), and (3) those who are currently in school (their twelfth year of education). It was found (see Table 10.1) that the average Clientship Scores for these samples do differ greatly. The townsmen with no education have the highest average Clientship Scores ($\overline{X} = 22.37$), the townsmen with some education in the past have the second highest average score ($\overline{X} = 18.69$), and the Teacher College students have the lowest score ($\overline{X} = 14.09$).

These three groups of scores can be compared simultaneously to determine whether the differences observed are simply due

[1]The data for this analysis may be summarized as follows (with high and low Clientship Scores being those above and below the median, respectively):

| | | AGE | | | |
		11–25	26–40	41–55	56–71
CLIENTSHIP	HIGH	9	31	19	5
	LOW	5	34	19	3

Table 10.1 Clientship Scores and the Effect of Educational Experience in Bornu

Group	$\overline{X}$ Clientship Score		One-way Analysis of Variance Results[a]		
		Variance Source	Sum of Squares	df[b]	Mean Square
Townsmen, uneducated	22.37	Between Groups	1367.815	2	683.908
Townsmen, educated	18.69	Within Groups	3176.265	145	21.905
Teacher College Students	14.09				

[a]$F = 31.22$ (F at the 1 percent point with 2 and 150 df $= 3.06$; thus P $<$ .01). A test for the homogeneity of variance indicated the variance was acceptably homogeneous for this analysis ($F_{max} = 1.709$).
[b]"df" $=$ degrees of freedom.

to chance. The statistical method to be used is the one-way analysis of variance since there are more than two groups and there is only one factor involved (type of educational experience). The results of this test are also in Table 10.1 and show that average scores differing as much as these do would occur by chance alone far less than one time in a hundred. We can be confident then that chance factors do not explain these results.

These results are informative because it seems almost certain that as time goes on, more and more of the young people of Bornu will attend school, and they will be attending for longer and longer periods. This will result in greater exposure of increasing proportions of the population of Bornu to views that will contribute to a generally reduced commitment to clientship.[2] What this may mean for the future of Kanuri identity, at least insofar as it is involved with clientship, will be considered in the next chapter. The implications of these findings for economic development in Bornu will be explored further in succeeding sections of this chapter.

CLIENTSHIP AND ECONOMIC DEVELOPMENT IN BORNU

The significance of the finding that attitudes toward clientship in Bornu appear to be changing with exposure to Western-type schools can be assessed from several directions. Here the discussion will be limited to a consideration of its implications for economic-growth potentials in Bornu.[3] A central question in this

[2]It is possible, however, that these results also indicate that the effect of exposure to Western-type schools may "wear off," so to speak, at least as far as attitudes toward clientship are concerned. This may be due to the lack of exposure of men no longer in school (i.e., the educated townsmen) to the attitudes expressed in schools in Bornu that undermine clientship. This decline might also be due to the exposure these men receive to the views of many of their colleagues and coworkers who have not been to school, or to the pressures and characteristics of the clientship-dominated social system of Bornu. If this is the case, then, it would also be true that even though attitudes toward clientship are changing, the changes will be modified (for the time being, at least) by those who have not been to school and/or by the effect of other institutions besides schools that influence the formation of attitudes.

[3]As noted, this discussion will review only the impact of changing attitudes about clientship, as it relates to achievement motivation and occupation preference. This should *not* be taken to mean, however, that no other factors are thought to have a bearing on the economic growth potential of Bornu. Numerous other factors certainly will need to be considered in order to gain a complete picture. At this point, however, the data for such an analysis are not available.

discussion will be whether or not there is evidence that relatively negative attitudes among students about this key facet of Kanuri identity provide a basis for expecting a shift in the involvement of individuals in entrepreneurial business roles.

Only a few studies have considered the link between clientship and economic growth. Of the research in Africa which makes such an inquiry, one of the most interesting is LeVine's (1966a); it too was conducted in Nigeria. His research focuses on the relationship between types of "status-mobility systems" and variations in a particular psychological motive—the need to achieve.[4] LeVine's data indicate that social systems emphasizing clientship as the means for being socially mobile have low levels of achievement motivation. This in turn leads him to suggest that economic growth rates in such societies will continue to be relatively slow. LeVine makes such a suggestion because there has been extensive research on the relationship between achievement motivation and economic growth rates. Most of this research has either been carried out or stimulated by the psychologist David C. McClelland (1961; and 1969 with Winter).[5]

Specifically, McClelland suggests that achievement motivation leads to a preference for business occupations which in turn assures that roles vital for economic development are filled. Thus, the causal chain that emerges from the work of McClelland and LeVine suggests that (1) status-mobility systems influence (2) levels of achievement motivation that in turn influence (3) the numbers of businessmen and entrepreneurs in a society that influence (4) the rate of economic development. And, more specifically, clientship-oriented status-mobility systems lead to low levels of achievement that in turn reduce tendencies toward entrepreneurship and, ultimately, retard economic growth. The

---

[4]The need to achieve is sometimes expressed as "*n* Achievement" (the *n* standing for "need for"); another term which is often used interchangeably with the need to achieve is "achievement motivation." These terms will be used virtually interchangeably in this discussion.

[5]Some of the more significant studies of this motive include those by Atkinson (1958), Atkinson and Feather (1966), Botha (1971), Burnstein (1963), Cansever (1968), Caudill and DeVos (1956), Crockett (1962), DeVos (1960), Finney (1971), Heckhausen (1967), Kahl (1964), Kemper (1968), Lazarus et al. (1969), McClelland (1963, 1965a, and 1965b, among many others), McClelland and Friedman (1952), J. N. Morgan (1964), Mukherjee and Verma (1966), Ostheimer (1969), Rogers and Neill (1966), Rosen (1959a, 1959b, 1961, 1962, and 1964), Shrable and Stewart (1967), Singh (1969), Strodtbeck (1958), Tedeschi and Kian (1962), Williams (1960), and Zajonc and Wahi (1961).

implications of this complex hypothesis for Bornu are important: there would seem to be a conflict between the desire for accelerating growth rates and one of the major facets of Kanuri identity, the clientship system.

However, these postulated relationships have been challenged, especially by people in Bornu and other parts of Nigeria with such social systems. More important, these relationships have not been examined in Bornu. This must be done before statements about the implications of Kanuri attitudes toward clientship can be advanced, or before the consequences of attitudinal changes can be assessed. Therefore, we now turn our attention to an examination of the two variables linking clientship to economic growth–achievement motivation and business-occupation preferences. First we shall briefly define these two variables and review the postulated relationship between them. Then we shall consider the way this relationship may be affected by clientship. These findings, coupled with those already noted about the relationship between education and clientship, will provide an empirical base for the discussion in Chapter 11 of the future of Kanuri identity in Bornu. We will begin by reviewing the relationship between achievement motivation and occupation preferences.

ACHIEVEMENT MOTIVATION AND BUSINESS-OCCUPATION PREFERENCE

Achievement motivation is a concept that refers to a need some people have to perform tasks at a level equal to or better than some culturally defined standard of excellence. It has been found that individuals vary greatly in their need to compete with such standards; i.e., people vary in their need to achieve. Much of McClelland's research has been directed to the development of procedures for measuring this variation precisely (e.g., see McClelland et al., 1953). McClelland has also been interested in assessing the theoretical and practical significance of such variation.

Of the many conclusions reached by McClelland in investigating the need to achieve, one of the most important was that *rates* of economic development vary with changes in societal levels of the need to achieve. These results, moreover, indicated that changes in levels of *n* Achievement came *prior* to changes in rates of economic growth. Achievement motivation was not related to a society's previous rate of economic growth. For example, it was found that the level of *n* Achievement in a sample of societies in 1925 was an excellent predictor of subsequent rates of growth up to 1950, but the level of *n* Achievement in these societies in 1950 was not related to their previous rates of growth (McClelland 1961:92). As McClelland observes, these findings are important because together they "bear on the issue of economic determinism. It is difficult to argue from these data that material advance came first and created a higher need for achievement. Rather the reverse appears to be true . . ." (1961:93). Although rather controversial, such findings are important also because they are linked to hypotheses about the role of business entrepreneurs in stimulating economic growth.

It is McClelland's contention that persons with a strong need or disposition to achieve (i.e., persons with high *n* Achievement) will tend to seek roles in society that provide good opportunities to fulfill their achievement needs. Thus, such individuals will tend to seek roles where there is a good chance to excell or compete with some standard of excellence. However, he also suggested that not just any role would do. Rather, a person with high *n* Achievement would be expected to seek roles where there was good indication that what he was doing was indeed an achievement. Three kinds of information appear to be important to the individual with high *n* Achievement if he is to make this assessment.

First, there needs to be some information that will indicate in advance that the task is neither extremely difficult nor extremely easy; rather, roles are preferred in which a moderate risk must be taken in order to be successful. The reasoning here is that if the task is seen as being very difficult (and hence there is little chance for success), a person high in *n* Achievement would view success (should it occur) as being unrelated to any skills he possessed. Similarly, if the task is very easy (and hence there is every chance for success), then success would still be seen as unrelated to any skills an individual possessed (i.e., "anybody could do that!"). Both of these problems are avoided by seeking a moderate risk. The second kind of information needed has to do with estimating how well one is doing. With failure and success so indeterminant at the outset of some moderately risky task, it becomes useful to have a regular flow of information about how well one is doing. The third aspect of the information requirement suggests that it is important that the information be unambiguous. That is, the information should be relatively easy to recognize and assimilate in the process of making an assessment of the achievement character of the task.

It is McClelland's view, a view supported by extensive research, that the social role best fitted to these three conditions is that of the businessman-entrepreneur. This is a role, first, in which an individual may be fairly certain his own efforts and abilities will influence his chances for success. That is, it offers moderate risks where success is neither assured nor impossible. Second, in such a role it is not difficult to obtain information in reasonably steady amounts about how well one is doing. Typically, there are many decisions an entrepreneur will have to make and the results of such decisions will not be long in coming. Third, one of the most unambiguous kinds of information—money—is one of the principal elements of the entrepreneurial world. For the person high in *n* Achievement, money is not the goal. Rather, the goal is information about how well one is doing and money serves well for this purpose. How much money an individual entrepreneur gains is a widely recognized and unambiguous standard of how well he is doing.

Reasoning in this way, McClelland undertook research to determine whether or not people high in *n* Achievement would prefer business occupations. He was generally (but not uniformly) successful in this effort, showing that, for numerous and diverse cultures, people high in *n* Achievement did prefer business occupations and entrepreneurial roles (1961: *passim*).

Another important aspect of McClelland's overall formulation concerns the behavioral style of the achievement-oriented entrepreneur. In analyzing the behavioral tendencies of individuals high in *n* Achievement, McClelland argues (1961: chap. 8) that the entrepreneurial spirit is best exemplified by the mythical figure of Hermes—a deity in the Greek pantheon. Hermes' character traits included such tendencies as being a brazen liar, a cunning schemer, a trickster-hero, and an innovator. He took real pleasure in developing schemes for getting ahead and he selfishly pursued any career so long as there was money in it for him. He was virtually the "patron-saint" of the *nouveaux riches* of ancient Greece, and was seen by the landed and wealthy aristocrats as being exemplary only of the aggressive and hence disliked merchant class.

McClelland's research has been the center of considerable debate and skepticism. A major concern has been expressed by those who view his concept of achievement motivation as a

Western, ethnocentric, capitalistic idea simply not applicable to non-Western, precapitalistic cultures (e.g., see the views in Field 1967:91–107, and of Lloyd 1967:46–47). There is a wealth of data to contradict many (if not all) of these criticisms, but these views are still attractive to many. And, more importantly, those having these negative views have often suggested hypotheses that are interesting and testable alternatives to those based on Mc-Clelland's theory.

An example is provided by Barrett (1968), who presents his views as an alternative to the research in Nigeria by LeVine (1966a) which, as noted above, had generally supported Mc-Clelland's findings. LeVine's study consisted of a comparative assessment of the variation in achievement motivation in the three largest ethnic groups in Nigeria—the Yoruba, Igbo, and Hausa. On the basis of the results of his study, LeVine concluded that the Igbo had significantly higher achievement motivation than did the Hausa, while the Yoruba scores fell in between these two groups. These results, it may be noted, had been predicted in advance on the basis of differences in the "status-mobility systems" of the three groups. In particular, LeVine hypothesized that individuals from societies with status-mobility systems based on clientship would have the lowest levels of achievement motivation, and in fact they did. These results were seen not only as consistent with previous economic history in Nigeria but also as a basis for making tentative predictions about future economic trends.

Barrett's alternative suggestions bear directly on the predictions about future growth trends anticipated by LeVine. Noting LeVine's suggestion that the low achievement motivation scores of the Hausa may be partly understood as being the result of their client-centered political system, Barrett suggests this may not tell us much about future economic growth rates. Moreover, he suggests that clientship and a political orientation may not mean a people will have low achievement needs. Rather, he suggests, political office and not business roles will be the focus of individual aspirations, with the need to achieve being channeled into the political sector. Thus, he reasons, "an increase in *n* Achievement at the personality level would not result in rapid economic development, but would simply intensify the populace's obedience to the political élite in order to gain their favour, *given the continuation of the Hausa value system*" (1968:71, italics added).

Prior to Barrett's published views, McClelland (1961:239–258) considered a more general form of the alternative hypothesis just noted. He suggests such an alternative is unlikely to be supported primarily because of the excellent fit between the information needs of a person high in *n* Achievement and the information characteristics of the entrepreneurial role (see above, p. 160). However, McClelland's argument may well beg the original question. Using McClelland's principles of the information needs of the achievement-oriented individual, it is possible individuals with high achievement motivation might prefer political or other non-entrepreneurial occupations *if* these are seen as of moderate risk and/or provide good feedback about how well one is doing. As Barrett suggests, political positions in societies with social systems such as that of the Hausa (and, we would add, Bornu) may provide individuals high in *n* Achievement with just such information. Indeed, as others have suggested (e.g., Brown 1965:466), the crucial question may not be whether a society has a particular level of achievement motivation and thus a certain hypothesized number of entrepreneurs, but rather, whether those with entrepreneurial personality characteristics (e.g., high *n* Achievement) are recruited to entrepreneurial roles. For less-developed societies, and especially for those with clientship-based status mobility systems, making a comparative assessment of these divergent views is a vital matter. We are, after all, concerned with an issue that bears not only on economic growth but also on the fate of individual and collective identities.

The Key Issues in Summary
This review of McClelland's research and theory was presented in light of suggestions by some (e.g., LeVine) that clientship is related to slow rates of economic growth because social systems emphasizing clientship tend to produce individuals with relatively low levels of the need to achieve (*n* Achievement or achievement motivation). Bornu is such a social system, but, as was shown above, clientship is not universally admired by people in Bornu. Indeed, there is evidence that with an increase in education, clientship tends to be less strongly supported. Thus, although clientship *may* have inhibited economic growth and achievement motivation in Bornu in the past, it probably will not have this effect in the future; certainly, at least, not to the same extent.

Others (e.g., Barrett) have suggested, however, that achievement needs, should they increase in societies where clientship is important, will not produce more interest in economic roles (nor, consequently, a more rapid rate of economic growth). Rather, people will attempt to achieve in whatever sector of the society is deemed culturally most appropriate. McClelland would presumably counter this view with extensive empirical data suggesting that universally there is a positive relationship between individual achievement needs, a preference for business occupations, and rates of economic growth. He might also note that there is a tendency for individuals high in *n* Achievement to behave in entrepreneurial roles in a Hermes-like fashion rather than in clientlike ways.

Thus, in addition to providing a basis for probing further our original question about the implication of changing attitudes toward clientship for economic growth in Bornu, the data to be analyzed below can be used to clarify the conflicting views just cited. After noting how achievement motivation was measured in Bornu, the relationship between achievement motivation and occupation preference will be explored. Then the combined impact of *n* Achievement and clientship on business-occupation preference will be considered.

TESTING THE RELATIONSHIP BETWEEN ACHIEVEMENT MOTIVATION AND OCCUPATION PREFERENCE IN BORNU

Achievement motivation is ordinarily measured through the use of projective tests designed especially for this purpose. Projective tests, such as the pictorial Thematic Apperception Test (TAT), are used because they permit the person being interviewed to express freely his own ideas about the stimulus picture. Such a test, with eight photographs taken in Bornu especially for this purpose, was used to collect projective data. Analysis of the achievement themes in this material indicates that this measuring device produced reliable and valid data (Spain 1973). Individual scores were determined on the basis of a system for scoring achievement themes in projective material. This system, which has been used throughout the world, was developed by McClelland and his coworkers (1953). For the projective material from Bornu, the interrater scoring reliability was .804, which is acceptably high.

In his discussion of the aims of his study of achievement motivation and its relationship to rates of economic growth, McClelland places considerable emphasis on the link between high *n* Achievement and a tendency for individuals to prefer business occupations and business success (1961:55). Using procedures similar to McClelland's, the individuals in the two samples presently under consideration were asked to rank-order 24 occupations according to their prestige (*daraja*). These occupations covered a wide range from traditional political positions to modern business and professional occupations. From the data on the ordinal ranks assigned these occupations (see Table 10.2) it was found that agreement on the rank-ordering was very high. When comparing students and townsmen, the Spearman-Brown rank-order correlation coefficient (r_s) was .44 (P < .05); when comparing those high and low in *n* Achievement in the Townsmen Sample, r_s = .83 (P < .001); and when comparing those high and low in *n* Achievement in the Teacher College Sample, r_s = .81 (P < .001). This suggests that regardless of differences in age, education, and achievement motivation, there is in Bornu high agreement as to the overall prestige rank-ordering of these occupations.

Even though the agreement in the overall rank-ordering of the 24 occupations was high (far higher than chance alone could account for), there was not perfect agreement. Indeed, the relatively low value of r_s observed in the comparison of townsmen and student rankings (.44) indicates there was a fair amount of disagreement. It is possible to examine these points of disagreement as a means of shedding light on at least two important questions. First, we may examine the differences between students and adults to determine what divergent trends there are, if any, in the occupation rankings of these two very different groups. Second, we may determine whether or not there is a tendency— a tendency predicted by McClelland's theory—for individuals high in *n* Achievement to prefer entrepreneurial business occupations more than do those low in *n* Achievement.

One way of making these assessments is to use the *t* test to determine whether group differences in the average rank assigned an occupation are greater than would be expected by chance alone. With 24 occupations and three basic pairs of comparisons (those high and low in achievement within each of the two samples and a direct comparison of the two samples) we will be looking at the results of 72 *t* tests. Using the common "significance level" of P ≤ .05, we can expect approximately four of these tests to show significant differences simply by chance (5 percent of 72 = 3.6). A standard method for handling this problem (see Fisher 1942) is to raise the minimum significance level; in so doing, fewer of the results which are still "significant"

Table 10.2 The Ordinal Ranks for 24 Occupations, as Ranked by Townsmen and Students Generally, and by Townsmen and Students High and Low in n Achievement

Job #[a]	Description	Townsmen n Achievement High N = 62	Low N = 63	$d*$	Townsmen and Students N = 125	N = 23	$d*$	Students n Achievement High N = 12	Low N = 11	$d*$
1	Big kola and groundnut trader	6	9	−3	8	20	−12	18	29	−2
2	Army officer	4	3	1	4	2	2	7	1	6
3	Engineer	12	7	5	9	6	3	5	4	1
4	Bank clerk	20	16	4	18	14	4	14	15	−1
5	Radio announcer	22	18	4	21	19	2	21	13	8
6	Local Authority Council member	7	6	1	6	4	2	4	2	2
7	*Imam* (major religious leader)	1	1	0	1	16.5	−15.5	19	10.5	8.5
8	Truck owner and driver	16	23	−7	19	22	−3	20	22	−2
9	Tailor with own machine	18	12	6	16	24	−8	24	23	1
10	Primary school headmaster	15	10	5	12	18	−6	15	18	−3
11	District Head	9	11	−2	10	7	3	9	6	3
12	Large shop owner	10	14	−4	13	16.5	−2.5	16	17	−1
13	Goldsmith	24	20	4	23	23	0	23	24	−1
14	*Alkali* (judge)	11	4	7	7	9	−2	11	8	3
15	Doctor	3	2	1	2	3	−1	1	5	−4
16	Manager of a large business	8	13	−5	11	5	6	3	7	−4
17	Machine operator in a new factory	21	19	2	20	12	8	12	12	0

Job	Occupation								
18	Big contractor	17	15	2	15	8	7	7	9	-2
19	Provincial Agricultural Officer	5	8	-3	5	1	4	2	3	-1
20	Owner of a transport company	14	21	-7	17	10	7	7	16	-9
21	Big farmer	2	5	-3	3	15	-12	13	19	-6
22	Village Area Head	23	24	-1	24	21	3	22	21	1
23	Secondary school teacher	13	17	-4	14	11	3	10	14	-4
24	Gasoline station manager	19	22	-3	22	13	9	17	10.5	6.5

ªThe job number is the same as the serial position of the item in the questionnaire.
*"d" may be understood as a measure of disagreement or difference in ordinal rank; it can be positive or negative. In this table, d has been calculated by subtracting ranks listed in the right half of each pair of ranks; in effect, the ranks of those low in achievement are being subtracted from those high, and the ranks of the students are being subtracted from the townsmen. Consequently, the occupations preferred *more* by those *high* in *n* Achievement or by the townsmen will have negative *d*'s.

at this higher level can be attributed to chance. Fisher suggests setting the significance level at 1 time in (20) (n) times rather than the usual 1 time in 20 (or, P = .05). For our data, with n = 24, the significance level would be P ≤ .002 (or, 1 time in 480).

Even when using this stringent value, we still find a number of statistically significant differences between the students and townsmen (see Table 10.3). The occupations of "manager of a large business" (#16) and "big contractor" (#18) are preferred much more by the students than the townsmen (P < .001). Similarly, the office of "Imam" (#7) and the fundamental Kanuri occupation of "big farmer" (#21), along with other traditional occupations such as "tailor with own machine" (#9) and "big kola and ground nut trader" (#1) are preferred much more by the townsmen (P < .0001). In short, in the student sample there are statistically significant differences in their preferences for occupations which, taken together, indicate a trend toward less traditional occupations.

However, when making similar comparisons of those high and low in *n* Achievement in the two samples, there were *no* occupations with differences which were statistically significant at the stringent .002 level. To be sure, there were a number with differences greater than chance at the .05 probability level, and some of these were business occupations which were ranked higher by those high in achievement motivation. Nevertheless, these data do not, when examined in this way, lend strong support to McClelland's hypothesis.

A second means of assessing the nature and extent of the differences in the rankings of these occupations is to compare the differences in the ordinal ranks of particular occupations. Using the data in Table 10.2, and considering only one of the many comparisons of this sort that might be made, we may note that the students, who are training to be teachers in primary schools, rank the position of "primary school headmaster" (#10) quite low (ordinal rank = 18th); this is considerably lower than the ordinal rank assigned this occupation by the townsmen (rank = 12th).[6] There is, then, a difference of opinion when com-

[6]Although this pattern might seem surprising, it in fact is consistent with a trend, widely observed in Third-World countries, for students to show less interest in jobs that will place them in rural and relatively less developed parts of their countries. The moderately high rank (11th) assigned by these students to the position of "secondary school teacher"—a position associated with schools in cities—gives further support to this observation.

paring these two groups such that the ordinal ranks differed by six positions ($18 - 12 = 6$); such differences will be identified as *d* and are calculated for each occupation (see Table 10.2).

Using this method of assessing the points of disagreement in the rank-ordering, we may again consider whether business occupations will be given a higher ranking by those high in *n* Achievement. By examining the column headed *d* in Table 10.2, it can be seen that of the 12 occupations ranked higher[7] by those high in *n* Achievement in the Teacher College sample, eight are business occupations. Of the 11 occupations ranked higher by those high in *n* Achievement in the Townsmen sample, seven are business occupations. Although not in perfect agreement with the expectations of McClelland's hypothesis, since there are a few nonbusiness occupations preferred by those high in *n* Achievement (and notably in the Teacher College sample), the general trend is strikingly in line with expectations.

To further analyze these trends, trends which are also reflected in the values of *t* in Table 10.3, a consolidated score measuring business occupation preference will be utilized. It is a score designed to assess an individual's interest in entrepreneurial business occupations, and was constructed by calculating the average of the sum of the ranks an individual assigned the most entrepreneurial business occupations in the list of 24. Using a broad definition, there are 12 business occupations in the list of 24 ranked by the respondents in Bornu (occupations numbered 1, 4, 8, 9, 12, 13, 16, 17, 18, 20, 21, and 24). Some of these 12 are not, however, entrepreneurial in character because they seldom if ever require individual decision making, especially with regard to the use of relatively large amounts of capital in the process of seeking a profit in a "risky" business venture. Occupations such as "bank clerk" (#4) and "machine operator in a new factory" (#17) are examples of essentially nonentrepreneurial business occupations. Others of these "business" occupations (e.g., "gasoline station manager," #24) are less entrepreneurial in Bornu than they sometimes are elsewhere. In Bornu, managers of gas stations have very limited responsibility and are usually under the close supervision of an owner who makes the essentially entrepreneurial decisions. Similarly, the occupations of "tailor with

---

[7] For these data, a higher rank is indicated by a lower ordinal number. Therefore, when subtracting the ranks assigned by those low in *n* Achievement from the ranks assigned by those high in this motive, a negative *d* will be obtained when an occupation is preferred more by those high in *n* Achievement.

Table 10.3 The Average Ranks for 24 Occupations, as Ranked by Townsmen and Students Generally, and by Townsmen and Students High and Low in n Achievement

Job #	Description	Townsmen				Townsmen and Students				Students			
		n Achievement								n Achievement			
		High N=62	Low N=63	t	P*	N=125	N=23	t	P*	High N=12	Low N=11	t	P*
1	Big kola and groundnut trader	10.56	11.62	.95	.345	11.10	16.30	3.73	.0001	15.08	17.63	1.12	.274
2	Army officer	8.42	8.73	.25	.801	8.58	6.47	1.37	.174	9.25	3.45	2.39	.026
3	Engineer	12.73	11.03	1.61	.109	11.88	9.13	2.07	.040	9.33	8.90	.18	.861
4	Bank clerk	15.46	14.00	1.33	.187	14.72	12.69	1.48	.141	12.41	13.00	.27	.791
5	Radio announcer	16.05	14.38	1.64	.053	15.21	14.91	.23	.817	16.83	12.81	1.95	.064
6	Local Authority Council member	11.46	9.80	1.55	.125	10.63	7.60	2.21	.028	9.58	5.45	1.73	.099
7	Imam	4.89	5.02	.14	.889	4.95	13.00	6.20	.0001	14.83	11.00	1.17	.255
8	Truck owner and driver	13.72	16.06	2.37	.019	14.89	17.73	2.30	.023	16.66	18.90	1.23	.232
9	Tailor with own machine	14.69	13.15	1.28	.203	13.91	19.47	3.82	.0001	19.33	19.63	.18	.861
10	Primary school headmaster	13.37	12.26	1.06	.293	12.81	13.73	.69	.490	12.83	14.72	.79	.439
11	District Head	11.93	12.87	.88	.378	12.40	10.56	1.33	.185	11.75	9.27	.84	.413
12	Large shop owner	12.13	13.65	1.30	.195	12.90	13.56	.45	.652	13.50	13.63	.05	.958

#	Occupation											
13	Goldsmith	17.63	15.19	2.22	.028	16.39	20.09	2.67	.008	19.33	21.00	.91	.375
14	Alkali (judge)	12.45	9.39	2.92	.004	10.91	11.13	.16	.876	12.25	9.90	.81	.428
15	Doctor	7.45	8.10	.68	.497	7.78	7.04	.61	.544	5.08	9.18	1.94	.066
16	Manager of a large business	11.63	13.38	1.66	.100	12.51	7.95	3.42	.001	6.50	9.54	1.33	.198
17	Machine operator in a new factory	15.64	14.76	.87	.386	15.20	12.32	2.14	.034	12.41	12.30	.04	.967
18	Big contractor	13.93	13.76	.17	.863	13.84	9.60	3.37	.001	8.91	10.36	.63	.536
19	Provincial Agricultural Officer	9.15	11.43	2.15	.034	10.29	6.60	2.81	.006	6.83	6.36	.25	.804
20	Owner of a transport company	13.25	15.57	1.11	.682	14.43	11.52	2.38	.019	9.91	13.27	1.38	.181
21	Big farmer	6.07	9.23	2.69	.008	7.66	14.34	4.37	.0001	13.41	15.36	.67	.509
22	Village Area Head	16.99	15.87	1.19	.236	16.42	18.17	1.47	.144	18.41	17.90	.23	.819
23	Secondary school teacher	12.80	13.97	1.24	.219	13.39	10.86	2.10	.038	9.00	12.90	1.84	.080
24	Gasoline station manager	15.43	15.47	.04	.967	15.45	12.86	2.04	.043	14.58	11.00	1.36	.188

*P is two-tailed.

own machine" (#9) and "goldsmith" (#13) are occupations which are more artisan-like than entrepreneurial, involving cooperative relationships with coworkers in guild-like associations rather than entrepreneurial behavior.

If such occupations are eliminated, seven remain as the most entrepreneurial business occupations ranked by respondents in this study. These are:

big kola and groundnut trader	(# 1)
truck owner and driver	(# 8)
large shop owner	(#12)
manager of a large business	(#16)
big contractor	(#18)
owner of a transport company	(#20)
big farmer	(#21)

The measure of business occupation preference was based on these occupations; for convenience it will be referred to as the BOP Score (business occupation preference score).

With this score, we can again assess McClelland's hypothesis for the samples in Bornu. Our expectations are that those high in achievement motivation will have a stronger interest in business occupations and this will be reflected in their having a lower BOP Score than those low in achievement motivation have.[8] And, as expected, it was found that in the Teacher College sample, those high in achievement motivation had an average BOP Score of 11.94, while those low in achievement motivation had an average BOP Score of 14.10 ($n = 23$; $t = 1.95$; $P < .032$, one-tailed). Similarly, for the Townsmen sample, those high in n Achievement had an average BOP Score of 11.56, while those low in n Achievement had an average BOP Score of 13.29 ($n = 125$; $t = 3.25$; $P < .001$, one-tailed). Thus, we may conclude that the differences in business occupation preferences (as measured by the BOP Score)—differences which were in a direction consistent with McClelland's theory—were not due simply to chance. Rather, they probably represent a true positive association between achievement motivation and a preference for entrepreneurial business occupations.

On the basis of these results, Barrett's hypothesis that an increase in achievement motivation in a clientship-oriented society will only foster an intensified political orientation would seem to

[8]A high preference is indicated by a low number and so it follows that the lower a BOP Score, the higher the prestige of business occupations for that individual or group.

be weakened considerably. However, he offered this hypothesis on the assumption that the value system of such a society would be stable. As we noted (see Table 10.1), one of the key values in Bornu—clientship—is changing in importance and it is possible this value will have an impact on BOP Scores. Therefore, we will turn to an assessment of the combined impact of achievement motivation and clientship on business occupation preferences in Bornu. This is done with a view toward considering further Barrett's alternative hypothesis and McClelland's view of the nature of the entrepreneur, and as a basis for assessing the impact of social change and development goals on clientship as a facet of Kanuri identity.

To assess the combined impact of achievement motivation and clientship on BOP Scores, a method will be used which is similar to that employed in assessing the effect of educational experience on Clientship Scores (Table 10.1). However, since there are two independent variables which may be affecting the dependent variable, instead of one as in the earlier analysis, the method is known as a two-way analysis of variance. This analysis revealed that clientship has no statistically significant effect on BOP Scores, either alone or in interaction with achievement motivation. Achievement motivation is the factor which has the most impact on the score (for the townsmen, $F = 31.38$; $P < .001$; and for the students, $F = 4.41$, $P < .05$). However, the effect of clientship is not the same for the two samples. For the Teacher College sample, clientship is totally unrelated to BOP Scores ($F = .001$) while for the Townsmen sample, clientship has a noticeable but still statistically nonsignificant impact on these scores ($F = 2.20$; $P < .20$). These trends are, from the viewpoints of both Barrett and McClelland's hypotheses, somewhat surprising and will be explored further, below.

UNIVERSAL VS. CULTURE-SPECIFIC VIEWS OF ACHIEVEMENT

McClelland's view of the nature of achievement motivation leads him to suggest that the archetype of the achievement motivated entrepreneur is represented by the mythical Greek figure of Hermes. As noted before, this deity in the ancient Greek pantheon exhibited extreme amounts of such character traits as trickery, intense concern with success, and self-reliance. In a word, Hermes is strikingly similar to a role-model held in low esteem in Bornu— that of the *yamgama bultu gai* ("one who is ambitious like a hyena"). Hermes also stands in marked contrast to the most esteemed role-model in Bornu—that of the obedient, shame-conscious, respectful client. As noted previously, many people have criticized McClelland's theory on the grounds that it is ethnocentric and Western; as such, it is thought not to apply in non-Western cultures. In particular, it is often suggested that the Hermes role-model for the achievement-motivated individual does not apply universally.

The utility of the Hermes model for Bornu may be considered by comparing the business occupation preferences of individuals in light of two points of view: McClelland's versus one based on the specific cultural characteristics of Bornu. In this analysis, we will be considering the BOP Scores of individuals defined in terms of their clientship and achievement-motivation scores. Dichotomizing these into high and low scores (i.e., those above and below the median) produces individuals of four "types": (A) those high in both achievement motivation and clientship, (B) those high in achievement motivation and low in clientship, (C) those low in achievement and high in clientship, and (D) those low in both achievement motivation and clientship.

The logic of McClelland's theory suggests that business occupation preferences will be strongest for group B, followed in descending order by groups A, D, and C. A hypothesis incorporating clientship as a factor related to success suggests a different order, with the strongest preference expected in group A, followed by groups B, C, and D. The data for this analysis are summarized in Table 10.4, and they reveal an interesting pattern (recall that a lower BOP Score indicates a stronger business occupation preference, so BOP Score values should increase in the sequences predicted if the hypotheses are correct).

Table 10.4 Average Business-Occupation Preference Scores (BOP Scores) for Groups Varying in Achievement Motivation and Clientship in the Townsmen and Teacher College Samples[a]

| Sample | High *n* Achievement | | Low *n* Achievement | |
	High Clientship	Low Clientship	High Clientship	Low Clientship
Townsmen	11.36	11.73	12.87	13.76
Teacher College	12.23	11.65	14.12	14.10
Group Labels:	A	B	C	D

[a]The sequence of scores (from low value to high) predicted by McClelland's theory is B, A, D, C; for the culture-specific viewpoint it is A, B, C, D.

In the Teacher College sample, the average BOP Scores increase in the order predicted by McClelland's theory, while in the Townsmen sample, these scores increase in an order predicted on the basis of assumptions about the importance of clientship for success in Bornu.

These are admittedly only trends and differences in degree, but they are striking, both in their clarity and in their implications. They are consistent with what we know about Kanuri culture and they provide interesting new perspectives on the theories and hypotheses at issue here. Clientship is an important factor in social mobility, especially for older Kanuri men not educated in Western-style schools. Moreover, and contrary to Barrett's expectation, clientship tends to increase slightly an older person's interest in business occupations if he is high in *n* Achievement. More important, however, it would appear the values associated with the highly achievement-motivated, business-oriented person in Kanuri society are changing. For the adults, clientship, if anything, has a positive influence on business-occupation preference; among the students, it is just the reverse. In effect, these students are rejecting the values of the traditional status-mobility system— values at the heart of Kanuri identity.

Finally, the finding for the Townsmen Sample is a basis for considering anew some of the criticisms of McClelland's use of Hermes as the archetype of the achievement-motivated entrepreneur. Hermes may illustrate the characteristics of the archetype, but for specific individuals in specific cultures, it may fall far short of the mark. The finding for the Teacher College sample is a basis for considering not only the fate of clientship as an axis of Kanuri identity but also for the whole process of economic development and social change in Bornu. These and related issues will be considered in greater detail in the next chapter.

11

Interpersonal Relationships and the Future of Kanuri Identity

In this chapter the implications of the data presented thus far will be considered. Initially, the broader context in which this research was conceived will be noted in order to provide an adequate perspective from which to evaluate the plan of the research, the shape of the analysis, and the tone of the interpretations made in these conclusions. A number of theoretical issues related to economic development and social change will be considered but of primary importance will be linking these findings to several recent social and political issues relevant to Nigeria in general and Bornu in particular. These will be expressed largely in terms of issues of interpersonal relationships and identity in Bornu.

A FUNDAMENTAL QUESTION

An old and fundamental question in the social sciences asks why societies differ from time to time and place to place in their influence on the world (however less than global that world in some contexts). The answers to this question that have been put forward over the years have unleashed everything from debates and "schools of thought" to religions and wars. At the most basic level, however, the question has been "answered" by the theory of sociocultural evolution. A central idea in this view is that societal complexity is the direct result of long-term developments in the capacity of a given sociocultural system to obtain the material necessities of life. Moreover, the capacity to organize and control the production of these necessities is directly related to the extent to which a given sociocultural system is, vis-à-vis the rest of "its" world, preeminent.[1]

This "answer" quickly led, of course, to another question

[1]For examples of these views, see the works of Marx (1936, 1957), Engels (1942), Childe (1946, 1951), White (1959), and M. Harris (1968).

closely related to the first one. It asks what factors lead to differences in the level of economic productivity of a given sociocultural system. Many who have examined this issue emphasized the role of individual choice and action as these affect the course of development.[2] Depending upon the investigator, his discipline, and "his" people, individuals who effect social change and economic development have been described as innovators, opinion leaders, early adopters (of innovations), high need achievers, Protestants, and entrepreneurs. Though these terms can hardly be used interchangeably, all of them direct our attention to individuals who initiate changes which lead to significant increments in economic productivity. A significant development in the context of this general issue has been the recognition that individuals vary greatly in their interest and capacity to perform these innovative roles and in their willingness to change their way of doing other things in order to achieve greater levels of economic productivity. But in spite of their supposed importance, the available literature on such innovative, entrepreneurial individuals remains scanty. The relationships between particular syndromes of cultural characteristics, symbols of individual and collective identity, and aspects of personality are even less well documented.[3] Consequently, this research was stimulated by age-old questions concerning differences in societal patterns of economic growth, by more recent questions concerning the characteristics of individuals who will implement this growth, and by the seldom explored relationship between these issues and changes in individual and collective identities.

THE DATA FROM BORNU

With these issues in mind, then, data were presented that bear on four basic substantive and theoretical issues. These were (1) the nature of Kanuri identity, (2) the characteristics and ramifications of the superior-subordinate relationship in Bornu, (3) the changing nature of clientship in this social system, and (4) the

[2]Of the recent literature, that of Weber (1930), Schumpeter (1934), Barnett (1953), Lerner (1958), Mead (1956, 1964), Rogers (1962, 1969), Hagen (1962), McClelland (1961, and 1969 with Winter), and Barth (1967) have been prominent.

[3]A recent insightful discussion of these issues has been provided by Spicer (1971). His concern is the characteristics of "identity systems" that are able to persist over time. For an excellent earlier anthropological study related to identity and social change, see Goodenough (1963).

implication of this change for achievement motivation, occupation preference, and economic development.

Kanuri Identity

Kanuri set themselves apart from others on the basis of a variety of symbols and behavioral patterns. These range from hair styles, facial markings, and clothes to the cultivation of an especially dignified style of walking. But these are relatively minor indications of one's status as a Kanuri or what it means to be a Kanuri. For centuries, centuries that are recorded in chronicles studded with names, dates, battles, and heroes, the key elements in Kanuri identity have been kingship, Islam, and hierarchy. All of the other characteristics of Kanuri sociocultural life, characteristics that also serve to round out Kanuri identity, can be linked to these. The Shehu or king of Bornu stands at the apex of a complex hierarchy. This hierarchy is characterized by significant social distinctions and is based on the organization of thousands of individual households. Each person knows his place in this hierarchy, but more importantly, he works to improve that place through a complex pattern of interpersonal relationships. Economic, social, and political life is organized around households but is made active by the interplay of relationships between superiors and subordinates. One of the most elaborate and important types of these relationships is the client relationship. Clientship, the term used to refer to the dynamics of the relationtion between a client and his patron, is a key element in Kanuri identity.

Islam is pervasive in Bornu. It provides major elements of the law, social organization, commercial orientation, and, of course, spiritual life. Life-cycle rituals have important Islamic elements, villages and towns are shaped in part by traditions with roots in the Middle East, and the basic social groups are communities of believers, not clans or lineages. Trading, including a long tradition of large-scale, trans-Saharan commerce, has been fostered by Bornu's relationship to the Islamic world.

The Kanuri world has undergone dramatic changes over the centuries. They have moved in and around the Lake Chad Basin, have seen in recent times the change of an ancient dynasty, and have been defeated and victorious in seemingly endless cycles. But the changes of the past few decades would seem to be among the most important of all. Since the close of World War II, Bornu has experienced a rapid growth in population, a dramatic increase in the influx of Western-style schools and, for at least some of its people, there has been a marked shift in views about the fundaments of interpersonal, superior-subordinate relationships.

And yet, there is stability in the midst of this change, as well. The kingship has survived what was a potentially serious blow (namely, the death in 1967, of the Shehu who had reigned for 30 years), Islam has remained the cornerstone of spiritual life, and the importance of hierarchy in the lives of many individuals has increased by virtue of the incorporation of new levels of government in Bornu. There are few signs, moreover, that the Kanuri language will decline in importance in the near future, nor is their any indication that large numbers of Kanuri will be forced to migrate to new areas outside of Bornu in search of a place to farm. Neither is industrialism coming to Bornu with great rapidity, although commercial interests are growing. And urbanization in Bornu only parallels the trends which can be observed elsewhere in West Africa in that urban life is hardly a new development for the Kanuri. In short, the Kanuri are responding flexibly to the changes that are occurring, they are creating many of the changes themselves, and they are preserving many of the key elements of their identity in the process. The significant exception to this general trend, however, is clientship, both as a model for social relationships and as a basis for social mobility.

Superior-Subordinate Relationships in Bornu

The extended discussion of Kanuri superior-subordinate relationships (Chapter 9) reflected both the central role these play in shaping Kanuri identity and their changing nature in Bornu today. In the naming ceremony, marriage, and divorce, a number of themes predominate. From the onset of life, there is a concern for success, well-being, and for profitable ties with superiors. In the midst of the process of forming a new household, itself a key element in Kanuri identity, there is a pronounced symbolic recognition of the importance of superior-subordinate relationships. And in the dissolution of this household, the pervasive tension of such relationships is dramatically evident.

The most elaborate development of the superior-subordinate relationship is the client relationship. Diffuse obligations on the part of the subordinate (the client) are balanced over the long run through infrequent but significant rewards by the superior (the patron). Continuation of the relationship is dependent upon each party to it feeling he is receiving appropriate benefits from the other. The major benefit the patron receives is "support." This can be in the form of a flow of goods, money, and other valued things from a number of clients, or it can be in the form of political loyalty and moral support. The client may receive training in an occupational role, financial support, and the provisioning of numerous, practical, everyday needs. Social mobility is the aim of both individuals, the patron by means of his numerous supporters, and the client by means of appointment to office on the promotion of his patron. This system approximates rather closely the ideal-type authority structure which Weber (1947) terms "patrimonial." It is a system that emphasizes mobility through a system of patron-client relationships, and it is one in which personal loyalty, respect, and obedience are key elements for success. Most importantly, however, such systems appear to be giving way to more "modern" bureaucratic authority systems. Evidence for this trend in Bornu comes from a variety of sources, much of it relatively informal but no less persuasive. In Chapter 10, however, it was shown that with increased exposure to Western-type schools, clientship attitudes become weaker. This was not, it should be emphasized, an unqualified result. Adults who have had some education, for example, have also entered the mainstream of Kanuri society. It is possible, therefore, that the effects of schooling, while powerful, may be modified by later experiences. Moreover, this suggests that clientship, while under significant pressures, is still a very powerful idiom in Kanuri culture, and it may be expected to remain so for some time to come. What this will mean for the future of Kanuri identity in this regard can only be guessed at, but at least it may be suggested that whatever changes in clientship are to be seen in the future will be relatively slow.

Achievement Motivation in Patrimonial Systems

In Chapter 10, the views of LeVine (1966a) and Barrett (1968) were cited regarding the role of achievement motivation in the strongly hierarchical, patrimonial social systems of the Hausa, an ethnic group in Nigeria culturally similar to the Kanuri. LeVine's analysis and his empirical data supported the notion that achievement motivation would be low in such systems because mobility was not based on individualized competition with a standard of excellence to the same degree it appeared to be in nonpatrimonial social systems (e.g., in Igbo society). Barrett, on the other hand, suggested achievement motivation would be directed to political rather than economic activity in patrimonial systems such as that of the Hausa, and that as a result it would not be very useful to attempt to predict rates of growth on the basis of this motive.

These issues and views have not been commented upon extensively in the previous chapter. We will do so now by considering first the findings of research undertaken by George DeVos in Japan.[4] His findings offer several theoretical insights which apply directly to the data from Bornu.

In criticizing McClelland's theory, DeVos states flatly: ". . . the model presented by McClelland and others does not seem to work for Japan" (1968:358–359). It was DeVos's impression (p. 361) that "human psychology as it influences history cannot be so engagingly reduced to a single paramount motivation." Rather, a complex configuration of values seemed to impel individuals to act the way they did in Japan. In particular, DeVos was struck by the fact that while achievement themes were found in a large number of the fantasy stories Japanese respondents told about TAT pictures, the stories and themes were in contexts that differed markedly from similar stories told by Americans. Rather than strongly individualized settings for achievement, he found the Japanese oriented to groups, and especially to the family. Achievement in Japan, according to DeVos, is for the family unit; *"success for oneself only was considered a sign of excessive immoral egoism"* (DeVos 1968:359, italics added). The parallel in this to the Kanuri view of the behavior of the *yamgama bultu gai* ("one who is ambitious like a hyena") is striking and significant. It is in light of the views of the Japanese regarding individualized success striving that DeVos joins others in questioning the use of Hermes as the universal model for the individual with high need achievement. For DeVos (1968:360), such a notion is "rather a curious concept," at least from the standpoint of the Japanese orientation to achievement as an act of social dedication.

DeVos's work in Japan has been reviewed to this extent because our research in Bornu, like his, asked whether or not an achievement-motivated person would have to behave in an aggressive, Hermes-like manner, as McClelland's theory suggests. The question is appropriate for at least two reasons. In the first place,

[4]DeVos's work has been presented in a number of places, including the following: DeVos (1960, 1965); DeVos and Wagatsuma (1961); and Caudill and DeVos (1956). The comments cited in this section are from DeVos (1968).

many critics are skeptical of McClelland's universal theory.[5] In the second place, in Bornu clientship and not individualized self-reliance is at the center of Kanuri identity. Thus, the setting was appropriate for putting McClelland's ideas to a further test.

Achievement Motivation and Clientship

Several aspects of McClelland's theory and data on achievement motivation were considered in Chapter 10. A principal concern was the impact of clientship and levels of achievement motivation on occupation preference and, ultimately, potential for economic growth in Bornu. When prestige ratings of occupations were examined, it was found that overall, there was high agreement in the ranking, even when comparing those high and low in *n* Achievement. Within this general agreement, however, it was found that individuals high in *n* Achievement did tend to rank business occupations higher than did those who were low in *n* Achievement. Those low in *n* Achievement tended to rank non-business occupations higher. This was found coinsistently in both samples, regardless of age or education. These results lend support to McClelland's theory and to LeVine's research in Nigeria; they tend to undermine the position taken by Barrett. That is, it would appear that an increase in achievement motivation, even in patrimonial, clientship-oriented societies, will stimulate interest in business occupations rather than simply intensifying political concerns as Barrett had predicted. These results also serve to balance a common misconception about the nature of LeVine's findings. That is, our data (as well as LeVine's) do not indicate that achievement motivation and an interest in clientship are totally incompatible.

Barrett's position, as we noted, was predicated on the assumption that the main values of the social system would not change. There is evidence, however, that one of the principal value orientations in Bornu—clientship—is undergoing significant change. Hence, the impact of clientship on occupation preference was examined. In so doing, we were able to reconsider Barrett's hypothesis as well as comment on McClelland's use of Hermes as the archetype of the achievement-oriented entrepreneur. It was found that while clientship had no effect on business-occupa-

[5]It may be added that while the views of these critics have bolstered this inquiry, marshaling evidence to support their doubts is far more difficult than just asserting such a view (as so many have done).

tion preference for the students in the Teacher Training College, it did have a noticeable effect among the townsmen. That is, it was found that preferences for business occupations were stronger when clientship increased in the Townsmen sample; among students, the reverse is true. These findings further undermine Barrett's hypothesis because they indicate that not only will achievement motivation foster an interest in business occupations in a clientship-oriented society but also that clientship can even enhance such an interest for some parts of the population. These results also serve, once again, to balance a common overextension of the implications of LeVine's research. That is, it may well be that the inhibiting nature of clientship for achievement motivation and economic growth may be limited to younger and more educated segments of the population, and these were, after all, the segments of the Nigerian people LeVine studied. Generalizing from these students to the whole of Nigeria may not be a recommended inference to make on the basis of LeVine's research.

The results of this study in Bornu also cast McClelland's view of Hermes in an interesting light. McClelland's model does not seem to apply to the townsmen but does fit the students rather well. Not only are students less oriented to clientship, they are also, if they are strongly oriented to business and have high achievement motivation, becoming more Hermes-like in their attitudes. It must be emphasized, however, that not all students are rejecting clientship and many of these have strong achievement motivation. However, those in this latter category do tend to have weaker orientations to business occupations and it is this that the logic of McClelland's view would lead us to expect.

But then, what is the answer to the question raised much earlier concerning the necessity, if that is what it might be, for entrepreneurs everywhere to be individualistic, self-reliant, Hermes-like and/or hyena-like in their behavior? To comment on this, let us consider some additional views of McClelland. In his discussion of the characteristics of entrepreneurs (1961:chap. 7), McClelland does note the important contrasts in the motives of foreign and American managers (pp. 287–292). Among other things, he discusses the *need for affiliation,* or the need for (p. 160) "establishing, maintaining, or restoring a positive affective relationship with another person. . . ." He indicates this relationship "is most adequately described by the word friendship" (p. 160). He found that the need for affiliation was low among American managers who were high in *n* Achievement. Just the opposite patterns were found among managers in countries such as Mexico, parts of Italy, and Turkey. There, those high in *n* Achievement also tended to be high in affiliation needs. As McClelland notes (p. 287), such results parallel "nicely" the observations made by others (e.g., Fayerweather 1959, 1960) to the effect that "foreign executives in [such] countries . . . often seem more concerned with adjusting relationships among people than with solving a problem more efficiently, whatever the cost in personal relationships." These observations also fit "nicely" with the observations of DeVos for Japan. Moreover, our measure of clientship touches on themes broadly similar to McClelland's measure of affiliation needs in the sense that clientship reflects in culture-specific terms the concern Kanuri individuals have for utilizing particularistic, affect-laden interpersonal relationships in the course of their efforts to be upwardly mobile.

It is on the basis of such data as that in the analysis of clientship in Bornu as well as the data about the relationship between the need for affiliation and achievement motivation in Japan, Mexico, Italy, and Turkey that the universality of McClelland's model of the achievement-oriented individual has been questioned, if not rejected outright. However, since much of this data is presented by McClelland, we must examine carefully just what claims are (or can be) made for his universal, Hermes model.

In fact, McClelland is somewhat ambiguous about the limits (if any) on this model. He does claim (1961:chap. 8) that Hermes is the spirit of the achievement-oriented person. He also shows, as we have noted, that managers high in *n* Achievement in various countries differ from their American counterparts. And we have noted that many, including DeVos, for example, use such findings to question the universality of Hermes-like self-reliance, ambition, and trickery as the model for all achievement-motivated persons. However, if we consider this model to represent the *pure* or *ideal-type n* Achievement personality, then the observation of cultural variability makes more sense (and, of course, so does McClelland's use of Hermes as a universal model). This pure type can, as we have seen, be modified greatly by a fairly large number of specific, culturally based attitudes and motives, including quite commonly (or so it would seem) a need for affiliation and/or the positive evaluation of clientship.

Thus, surprisingly, we can accept McClelland's use of Hermes as the universal model, but *only* if it is seen as a pure personality characteristic, *unmodified by any other kind of attitude, motive, or cultural factor.* Although such a model is indeed universal, it is also one that (like Weber's ideal type) does not exist in fact because it always is modified to some degree by the cultural context in which it occurs. The effect of these cultural and motivational factors on *n* Achievement is, of course, of considerable interest because it bears on the specific syndrome of behavior that we may expect entrepreneurs to exhibit—behavior that will be shaped by and will in turn shape local conceptions of right behavior as well as individual and collective bases for identity. Moreover, different combinations of motives appear to have important implications for the course of economic development. Thus, McClelland has shown, for example, that under certain conditions, high needs for affiliation tend to be related to slower rates of economic growth (1961:164). However, since our data indicate that clientship (which is similar to the need for affiliation) may be on the wane in Bornu, we might predict that in the not-too-distant future, achievement needs and, perhaps, economic growth, will be enhanced as a result of this shift in the character and identity of the Kanuri entrepreneur. Although our data suggest we can expect this shift, they also indicate it almost certainly will be slow, difficult, uneven, and subject to modification by other as yet unassessed factors. The trend does, however, seem to be established.

KANURI IDENTITY AND THE NIGERIAN CIVIL WAR

At the outset (in Chapter 7), a number of dominant themes in Kanuri culture were noted. An incident at the cinema in Maiduguri one evening illustrated in vivid terms the meaning and importance of political power and the dangers of insubordination in a society where clientship is a principal form of interpersonal relationships. In the world of stereotypes, such incidents can reinforce weakening images, giving them great staying power. In a flash, they cancel a hundred incidents that contradict the image. But even knowing all of this, it was (and is) impossible not to notice the consistency of this theme with an image long associated with the peoples who have been politically dominant in the northern part of Nigeria for centuries. Tragically, while those incidents were happening, young men elsewhere in Nigeria were dying in a bitter civil war. In such a context, the actions of those in the theater that night in Maiduguri were doubly important. And, most importantly, this analysis of Kanuri identity can provide a useful vantage point from which to examine this incident and its relationship to issues and tension points central to that strife-ridden and war-torn period in Nigeria's history.

First, we must recall the distinction made in previous chapters, and in our concluding remarks above, between achievement motivation accompanied by clientship behavior and that associated with hyena-like self-reliance. Though discussed most specifically in terms of occupation preference, it is clear that general issues of social mobility in a hierarchical structure are at issue here. That is, in the context of Kanuri culture, there is concern about the rude and unacceptable behavior of the "man who is ambitious like a hyena." Similarly, there is, especially among those who are older and less educated, a strong emphasis on the importance of the client relationship. Indeed, we have indicated that such a relationship is at the heart of Kanuri identity.

But, in this era of African social change, identities such as this are often being forced into the cold light of introspection and doubt. For many in Bornu, this process involves the search for an identity that will best fit the world of the future into which they are moving at an ever-accelerating rate. And most want to know how a given identity—whether old or new or something in between—will suit those who possess it. Will it help or hinder?

In this context, the theoretical distinction between *favored* and *exemplary* identities (cf. Crockett 1966) becomes a very practical matter. An exemplary identity is one held up as a model to be emulated, while a favored identity is that configuration of values, attitudes, and motives that actually pays off, for example, in terms of success in the social system (i.e., social mobility). Clearly, in Bornu, the exemplary identity is that of the client. But one wonders whether, in fact, the favored identity might not be something closer to the hyena-like individual. Most older Kanuri would insist such an identity is neither exemplary nor favored, though increasing numbers of younger, more educated Kanuri indicate their conviction on this point is changing. Only the future will give us the answer to this question.

Nevertheless, as an indication of future trends, we may note here a pejorative term used in the Nigerian press in the 1960s (and cited in Kirk-Green 1968:258) that refers to the clientship-based model for social mobility. This term, *Ranky-Daddyism,* is a play on the words of a formal Hausa greeting between people of different social ranks.[6] The lower ranking of the two greets the superior by saying, *"ranka ya dade"* ("may your life be prolonged"). In the view of many, the long-standing emphasis (some would say, over-emphasis) on respect and obedience is summarized symbolically by this greeting. The pejorative label "Ranky-Daddyism" was prompted by feelings similar to those that resulted in the official banning of the practice of removing one's shoes as a sign of respect when entering public offices.

The evaluative connotations of Ranky-Daddyism and hyena-ism provide an important contrast. Clientship is the exemplary model and basis for Kanuri identity. But for some people, and especially young students and non-Kanuri Nigerians, such behavior becomes mere Ranky-Daddyism. On the other hand, hyena-ism is clearly not admired by most people in Bornu, and yet self-reliant, ambitious, performance-oriented behavior is admired by some, and as Kirk-Green demonstrates (1968), was officially encouraged in civil-service training programs in the northern part of Nigeria.

Experience seems to indicate that if these two identities are found in the same hierarchical setting, a number of possibilities emerge. If it is a patrimonial authority structure (the type that best describes the structure for Kanuri and Hausa societies), then Ranky-Daddyism is likely to be rewarded with success, while hyena-like people will tend to be seen as "pushy," if not immoral. If the authority structure is of the bureaucratic type, then the pattern of success may well be reversed. Here, it is performance and merit that are admired, and hyena types may well be rewarded with social mobility. Similarly, Ranky-Daddyism in a universalistic, bureaucratic, achievement-oriented authority structure may in fact be a liability.

In this context, it is useful to view social mobility as in part a phenomenon that involves the utilization of assets or resources that have value in one's society (where value is related to the extent to which a resource is useful in enhancing one's status). Moreover, the character of the game being played (i.e., the status-seeking game) appears to be influenced by the nature of the resources available to the players (and/or that are recognized by others as being resources or assets). Such differences in re-

---

[6]In Bornu, a greeting with essentially the same meaning is in everyday use. For further commentary on the significance of the distinction between "Ranky-Daddy" and "Hyena," see Spain (1971).

sources are fundamental issues in and of themselves, but when they become virtually synonymous with an individual's identity, then the demands in the context of a rapidly changing situation are likely to be difficult to handle and may well lead to both inter- and intra-personal conflict.

Though the contrasting identities we have described here are couched in terms most directly related to Kanuri culture, the tensions and potential conflicts generated by these conflicting role models are not limited to Bornu. Neither are they limited to the small-scale, but no-less-serious, conflicts surrounding disputes over matters of personal style or the appropriateness of one's behavior. Rather, such conflicts were at the heart of much of the recent political crisis in Nigeria. During the early phases of that crisis, for example, a group of Nigerian "leaders of thought"[7] suggested that among the root causes of the political crisis were a number of character traits that were common, they felt, throughout the nation. These included the traits of "sycophancy, deference support, and [a] pathological craving for praise" (cited in Kirk-Green 1968:269). These views, though often stated in less carefully chosen words, were widely held throughout Nigeria, especially in reference to the Islamic peoples of the northern part of the country. Thus, although many believed the Igbo were pushy, overly aggressive in business, uncooperative (i.e., overly independent), and "clannish," the Hausa were seen by others as being lazy, corrupt, and politically motivated aristocrats.

It is easy and probably wise to dismiss out-of-hand such obviously crude stereotypes, especially if total acceptance or rejection of them is the only choice.[8] And yet, such images parallel the contrasting Kanuri roles of the independent, self-reliant hyena,

[7]The initial military coup in Nigeria resulted in the removal of all high-ranking civilian politicians from positions of official power. However, and not unexpectedly, many of these men were able to continue to influence public opinion. Indeed, the leaders of the military government often sought their opinions. As these men met from time to time, their views were reported to the people of Nigeria through the press and radio. Collectively, these people were identified as "leaders of thought."

[8]LeVine (1966b) and R. Brown (1965) offer a number of insightful and theoretically important observations about the nature and role—both social and scientific—of stereotypes. Among other things, we may note that stereotypes are not always negative, inaccurate, or useless concepts. In any case, it is clear that great care must be used when examining stereotypic statements about any group.

on the one hand, and the more highly regarded obedient and respectful client, on the other. Thus, although we would join with McClelland and LeVine in noting the importance of societal differences in levels of *n* Achievement, we would also note the equally important issue of ascertaining other attitudes and motives that can be associated with this universal achievement drive. In the case of the Kanuri, a central but changing aspect of their identity—clientship—will in all probability temper this motive, but in varying ways for different groups as Bornu moves into the future.

Appendix A   Content Summary of Items in the Clientship Score[a]

Part I, Section 1:

When given a job to do, do it as you were told.
Having an important father is a key to success.
Take a job where there is someone to help with decisions.
Success gained through power in getting others to do things is desirable.
To improve life, we need more strong leaders.
I would prefer reading a book about government jobs.
It is better to work for a friendly headman.
The advantage of wealth is that it leads to power.
Important people are successful because of their relatives.
Do not dismiss a kinsman from a job, even if he does poor work.
It is not good to openly disagree with the opinions of others.
Take a secure job where you will not be blamed for failure.
With many children, you can succeed because of their help.
Take a job with prestige over one with money.
Friends are more important for success than self-reliance.
A good son should live and work near his parents.
Respect is due elders, no matter what. (B)
A child should do as he is told; no reasons are necessary. (B)
Luck, not self-reliant hard work, is the key element in success. (B)
It is better to have secure, safe goals. (G)
Only if he is raised in a wealthy family can a wealthy man behave properly. (G)
The amount of success one will have in life is determined at birth. (G)
One should let his parents make important decisions for him.
Hire the friendly, well-known person over the expert.
Choose a government career (over a religious one).
No good comes from continually trying to earn more money.

Appendix A   *(Continued)*

Part I, Section 2:

   Disagree: the advice of old people has little value today.

   Agree: relatives are more important than friends.

   Agree: a good son should live and work near his parents.

   Agree: leaders are more important than followers.

   Disagree: I set difficult goals for myself which I attempt to achieve. (B)

   Agree: only if raised in a wealthy family can a wealthy man behave properly. (B)

   Agree: a man's success in life is determined at birth. (B)

   Agree: respect is due elders, no matter what. (G)

   Agree: a child should do as he is told; no reasons are necessary. (G)

   Disagree: there is no such thing as luck; people who are successful did things for themselves. (G)

   Agree: people need strong discipline and should work hard for their family and country.

   Agree: people do not admire the self-reliant man.

   Agree: a leader should always be obeyed.

Part II, Section 4:

   Take a job that is the same every day.

   Take a dull job lasting several years.

   Take a job where someone else helps make decisions and solve problems.

   Take a job requiring few decisions.

   Take a job where a superior person takes credit for success and blame for failure.

Part II, Section 7:

   A son should obey his father and work near home.

   A man should accept the opinion of his District Head.

   Children should be guided a lot by their parents.

   ªIndividuals were given a total of 41 of the 47 items summarized here. In addition to the 35 unmarked items, respondents were randomly given either the 6-item set labeled "B" or "G". These sets differed in format only. All items in Part I, Section 1 and Part II, Section 7 were complex stories which involved a dilemma. Respondents solved the dilemma by making a choice between two or sometimes three choices. The choice which is part of the Clientship Score is summarized here. The items in Part I, Section 2 were Likert style, agree-disagree questions. Part II, Section 4 contained a series of questions in which pairs of occupations were described, each member of the pair more or less the opposite of the other. The respondent was asked to indicate which he would choose for himself.

PART FOUR

The Tunisians

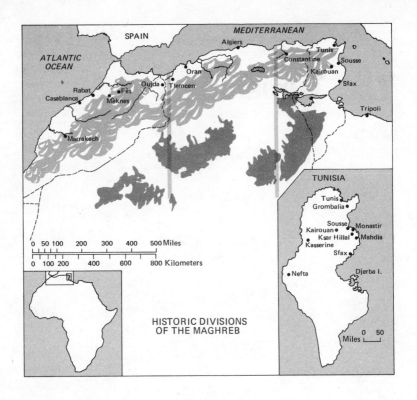

SPAIN

MEDITERRANEAN

ATLANTIC
OCEAN

Algiers

Tunis

Constantine

Sousse

Oran

Kairouan

Rabat

Fès

Oujda

Tlemcen

Sfax

Casablanca

Meknes

Tripoli

Marrakech

0 50 100   200   300   400   500 Miles

0   100 200   400   600   800 Kilometers

TUNISIA

Tunis

Grombalia

Sousse

Monastir

Kairouan

Ksar Hillal

Mahdia

Kasserine

Sfax

Nefta

Djerba I.

HISTORIC DIVISIONS
OF THE MAGHREB

0   50

Miles

12

Four Young Tunisians

The ambiguous interplay of competing cultures leads to in-
congruous scenes in contemporary Tunisia. Scribbled on the
whitewashed wall of a narrow alley in the oldest quarter of Tunis
are the words *"Vive Johny Haliday, le roi du rock et du twist."*
In suburban *Ras Tabia,* by a dormitory of the new university, a
similar wall has been decorated with the chalk drawing of a
woman. Underneath, in Arabic, is her name. It is Oum Khalthoum,
the famous Egyptian *chanteuse.* Perhaps it should be no surprise
that someone in the *medina* likes Western rock and roll and a
student at the French-speaking university enjoys classical oriental
music. But such observations challenge the facile generalization
that in societies like Tunisia social change involves a straight-
line progression from old to new, traditional to modern, Arab to
European. Mahmoud, Samia, Ahmed, and Ali are four young
Tunisians who live in a world where such a view is contradicted
as well as confirmed at every turn.

MAHMOUD

I was glad Mahmoud remembered me when we met again in
Djerba. Certainly I had not forgotten our pleasant conversation
in Tunis several months earlier. Mahmoud had impressed me
almost immediately. Although twenty-eight, he has an appealing
boyish charm, maybe because he smiles a lot. He is tall by
Tunisian standards and solid without being stout. On the day I
met him in the travel agency where he works, Mahmoud was
wearing a dark Western business suit of obvious quality. The excellence of his French was apparent too, although he does have
a slight accent revealing that French is not his native language.
As we talked, I learned that Mahmoud speaks and reads English
with no difficulty and can also converse in Spanish. "But," he
assured me with modesty, "it is because of my work that I have
learned these languages." He said he enjoys his work as a travel
agent and reported with special pride that a supervisor had

nominated him for an *Air France* prize, a tour of the Far East. If awarded, it would be Mahmoud's first trip outside Tunisia. Also, because of his good work, Mahmoud earns an excellent salary. He receives the equivalent of $165 a month. But, then, Mahmoud's expectations are not low. He has completed all but one year of high school which, though not exceptional, makes him better educated than most Tunisians. He says he has had much good luck during his short lifetime and, indeed, he is still young and doing well. When we met, he was planning to be married within a month.

I was rather surprised to learn Mahmoud is a practicing Moslem. In fact, he smiled shyly when he told me, perhaps knowing I would not expect this. But, he said, he prays regularly, five times a day, and goes to the mosque every Friday. Naturally he fasts during Ramadan, the Moslem holy month, and he never drinks alcohol of any sort—not even locally produced wine. Of course, my surprise was justified. Only a few of the Tunisians with whom I talked are this devout. Yet Mahmoud is not rigidly orthodox in his religious views. He believes a Moslem should not fast during Ramadan if to do so will impair his work. He acknowledges a certain incompatibility between religion and modern life which, he says, is not entirely resolved in his own case. "Perhaps Islam has to evolve," he told me; "certainly Tunisian Moslems ought not to practice the religion in the same way as their fathers and grandfathers." In all, Mahmoud is open and easygoing. He enjoys meeting people and makes friends easily. But he has a quiet side too. He says that he would rather listen than talk when he is with a group of people. Reading and music are his hobbies.

In spite of everything, there is something dogmatic about Mahmoud. Perhaps that is putting it too strongly. But there is something I had felt and it was recalled when we met again in Djerba. Mahmoud is one of the few Tunisians I met who claimed to want a traditional wedding. Far more typical is the quip of a Tunisian student who, it turns out, lives near Mahmoud. "Who needs all that 'tra la la'?" was the way she put it. But this is what Mahmoud wants. Mahmoud also feels Tunisian women should not wear make-up. And he does not believe women should have the same right as men to marry non-Moslems. Similarly, a married woman should never go with friends to a coffee house. And, at home, a man should have more authority than his wife. Mahmoud's view of a father's role is like his view of a husband's. A father should not play with his children too frequently. The mother should display affection toward children but it is up to the father to punish youngsters when they are naughty. A father must command the respect of his offspring. Mahmoud believes respect takes precedence even over love.

My wife and I arrived on the island of Djerba after three weeks in the dusty oasis of Nefta. We were glad to be back by the sea and were looking forward to several days of relaxation. Mahmoud arrived the next day. He was on his honeymoon. By a happy coincidence, Mahmoud and his bride checked into our hotel and, in fact, were put in the room next to ours. When we saw them in the hotel restaurant that evening, it was apparent they had had the traditional wedding Mahmoud desired. Still on the hands of his wife was the traditional sign of happiness and celebration, finely painted tracings in henna dye. Mahmoud did not introduce us to his wife. But he did accept my invitation to bring her for a ride the next day. We decided to tour the island.

During our ride, I wondered whether Mahmoud's wife was ill at ease. She was very quiet. When she did speak, however, I was surprised at the excellent quality of her French. She told me she had gone to French schools and it was obvious she had received more education than most Tunisian women, more possibly than even Mahmoud. Certainly she speaks better French than he. In fact, as she told me later, her vocabulary in Arabic is quite limited and she can read the language only with difficulty. Mahmoud is concerned about the future of his country. He hopes Tunisia will become a bicultural society and feels Tunisian schools should teach both French and Arabic. He also wants Tunisian pupils to study the history of France, believing it to be as important as the study of Islam and the history of the Arabs. But Mahmoud has married an educated girl and given her a traditional "henna wedding." She is not to wear make-up and she will be discouraged, perhaps prevented, from going out socially with friends. After all, the man is the final source of authority within a family. Despite her education, she will probably live a life similar to that of her mother and grandmother, for this is as Mahmoud wishes it.

SAMIA

Perhaps Mahmoud's wife prefers the life that appears to await her. But, if she is like Samia, there will be a conflict. Samia is a very attractive young woman of twenty-five who has recently gone into business for herself. Slender and with delicate features, she speaks quietly, and gives the appearance of being shy. But, if that be the case, it is a warm and appealing shyness, not at all nervous or even retiring. In all, she has a soft quality about her.

Born in Nabeul, a coastal village renowned for its pottery, Samia moved to Tunis with her family at the age of seven. Her father, a baker, had received no education whatsoever—either in traditional Koranic schools or in French-run *Franco-Arabe* schools. But he wanted an education for his eldest daughter and so Samia enrolled in school. However, like most girls, her education was limited. After six years, she left school without even receiving the standard certificate of graduation. Today Samia can read both French and Arabic, but she does not enjoy reading. She says she never reads a newspaper and only occasionally glances through a French magazine. She keeps her business records in French but claims to be more comfortable speaking Arabic. On the other hand, she usually listens to French-language broadcasts on the radio. She prefers the Western music they play and the programs are also more to her liking.

Several years ago Samia married a successful commercial manager. Her husband is the director of a government-run cooperative and earns about $265 a month, an excellent salary by Tunisian standards. After her marriage Samia moved away from her family and, something less common, her husband moved away from his. This, for example, is not the case with Mahmoud. Mahmoud's two married brothers and their families reside in the house of their father. Mahmoud and his wife will live there as well. Fortunately, everyone is steadily employed and they have been able to purchase a large house. But Samia and her husband prefer to live differently. They have taken a four-room apartment which, because of his job, her husband is able to rent at a good price. Although Samia's aging grandmother has come to live with them, they clearly have their own home.

Samia has three children; but she was bored being home all day. She does not want the kind of life traditionally reserved for women. Samia feels strongly that marriage is a partnership. She does not believe a husband should have more authority than his wife. She also feels it is acceptable for a woman to work at any job for which she is qualified. Samia is one of the relatively few Tunisians I met, male or female, who is not opposed to women having authority over men in the professional world. Furthermore, she sees no reason why a woman should be discouraged from going out with friends, to a café or elsewhere. This is not to say Samia is a crusader; she is not. She does not belong to the National Union of Tunisian Women nor to any other organized group. When asked what she hopes to do with her life, she simply replied, "to bring up my children." But, in her quiet way, Samia knows what she believes. She feels a father should play with his children often and, like their mother, display affection for them. "Children," she added, "must be taught the importance of thinking for themselves, even if they occasionally disobey their parents." And, when a child deserves to be punished, either parent may perform the task.

Samia's newly founded business is prospering. Her husband has established her in a small but rather chic clothing shop in a good Tunis location. She feels, however, that she deserves credit for the success of the store. Although sales vary, she claims to average about $175 a month in profits. Samia was particularly happy to tell me she has just made her first trip to Europe—to Paris. It was not so much that she likes Paris; indeed she is not sure she likes it at all. But by going alone on a business trip to buy merchandise for her shop, she has proved, in case anyone needs proof, that she, Samia, the daughter of an illiterate baker from a small Tunisian village, is making her way in the world and building the kind of life that only a few Tunisian women succeed in achieving in today's world.

AHMED

Ahmed, the successful director of a Tunis-based commercial society, is in some ways a bit like Samia's husband. For one thing, Ahmed earns about the same salary. Moreover, like Samia and her husband, he lives alone with his wife and children in a four-room Tunis apartment. They pay about $35 a month in rent and live in comparative, if hardly excessive, comfort. They have a car, a television set, a refrigerator, a hot-water heater, and a full-time maid. They do not have a telephone, nor is their home heated.

Ahmed's wife does not work but he is not opposed to women working. He sees no reason why women should not be doctors, lawyers, or even court justices. He does, however, question the desirability of having a man work under the direction of a woman. Nevertheless, Ahmed hardly subscribes to traditional notions about the place of women. Though he takes his religion seriously, he agrees women ought to have the same freedom as men to marry outside the faith. He has no quarrel with women wearing make-up and feels it is acceptable for a wife to go out socially without her husband.

As a parent Ahmed assumes the same liberal posture. "Of course children can play in the house when their father is home. Indeed, a father should play with them whenever he can." Ahmed agrees a father should be respected by his children, but considers it more important that he be loved. Like Samia, he believes children should think for themselves. And, when a child is ready to marry, the choice of a spouse is entirely his own. This is a good deal more than many parents are willing to accept. Moreover, for Ahmed, this applies to daughters as well as to sons.

Ahmed was raised in Sfax, the second capital of Tunisia and the metropolitan center of the southern part of the country. But, although he is from an urban area, Ahmed's origins are modest. His grandfather was an illiterate agricultural worker and his father, who still lives in Sfax, a mason. The latter had four years of education at a local Koranic school. Ahmed, however, went to school under the French. He began at the Franco-Arab school, learning both French and Arabic, and then went to the *lycée.* At the age of twenty he left for Paris to continue his studies. He stayed two years.

Upon his return Ahmed settled in Tunis. That was eleven years ago, making Ahmed thirty-three today. He said he likes France and looks forward to those occasions when his work takes him back to Europe. He has returned three times in the last two years on a variety of business and training missions, and the only trip he did not enjoy was a business session in Poland. Ahmed's schooling and visits abroad have influenced his tastes. Unlike many of his friends, he never wears the traditional *djebba* robe in summer. Although literate in both Arabic and French, he usually prefers to use the latter. Reading is one of Ahmed's favorite pastimes. He said he learns a great deal from his books and he likes to think of reading as "research." Moreover, he reads a newspaper every day, purchasing always the French-language *La Presse.* But Ahmed is not a "Frenchified" Tunisian. He does not read the journals of France that many of his colleagues regularly buy. He likes French cooking and Western music, but in both cases the Tunisian variety remains his favorite. He does not care much for movies of any kind.

In contrast to his views on child-rearing and women, Ahmed is conservative with respect to religion. He disagrees with the government's effort to "modernize" Islam. First of all, he does not feel Islam is incompatible with the modern world. "The religion was meant for all ages and those who think it is not relevant for the world of today do not understand it properly." No matter what the government says, Ahmed believes a Moslem ought to keep the fast of *Ramadan*—whether it interferes with his work or not. Moreover, he does not agree with the government's attempt to discourage, as economically harmful, the traditional slaughter of a lamb for *al-Aïd,* the holiday commemorating the sacrifice of Abraham. Ahmed also thinks it important for Moslems to observe the dietary laws and the religious interdiction of alcohol. He himself observes them strictly.

Ahmed sees the youth of Tunisia turning away from religion and this disturbs him very much. Like many of his countrymen, Ahmed believes Tunisian children should be taught the Koran. But he goes much further. He wants Tunisian schools to provide solid instruction in the history and development of the Moslem faith. He considers this instruction to be more important than the study of either European or Arab political history. Ahmed goes to pray at the mosque every Friday and he will continue to do so. But he does not find many of his friends there. Mostly he sees old men. This causes him to wonder a good deal about the future of the faith and always on Friday such thoughts are uppermost in his mind. Ahmed usually leaves work alone and walks to a small mosque on the fringe of the central city. Wrapped in thought, he moves along the bustling sun-drenched avenues, past the fashionable downtown cafés filled with young Tunisians sipping their afternoon *apéritifs.*

ALI

Ali is thirty-seven and has lived in Mahdia all his life. An important coastal village about 130 miles to the south of Tunis, Mahdia is not a town without a history. The present city was founded in 912 by the Fatimid Caliph, Obaid Allah El Mahdi, for whom it was named. Until the capture of Cairo in 973, Mahdia was, together with Kairouan, the capital of the Fatimids. Today Mahdia is an important center for the traditional production of silks and wools and it is rapidly becoming one of the principal fishing ports of the nation. Its natural fine-sand beaches suggest it is also likely to become a major recreation and tourist center. In less than eight years, Mahdia's population has grown from under 10,000 to over 15,000 inhabitants.

Ali is thin enough to give the appearance of being taller than he really is. In fact his looks border on gaunt. He has a long thin face topped by a shock of black curly hair. When he puts on his glasses he has an intellectual air, not thoughtful but rather zealous and intense, almost hostile. Ali looks as if he belongs in politics but, actually, he is not very active in the nation's political life. He is a member of Tunisia's only political party but does not participate in any of its activities. When I asked him, he could not identify the party's national director. In fact, he could not even name the date on which Tunisia had obtained independence. But Ali is not politically alienated. He believes that political leaders care about the average citizen and that people like himself have a voice in government. Most important, he believes the government is making a great effort to develop the nation and this is as it should be. He does not agree with the bourgeois argument that if too much is done for the people, they will become lazy and no longer help themselves.

The issue about which Ali feels most strongly is the nation's economic progress. Unlike Ahmed, he agrees with government efforts to modify religious practices that are judged economically harmful. He does not feel a Moslem should fast during *Ramadan* if to do so affects the quality of his work, and he is opposed to the traditional manner of celebrating *al-Aïd*. It is not that Ali is against the religion; he is not. He claims to believe in an afterlife and he wants Tunisian children to study both the Koran and the history of Islam. But he wants a reasoned and intelligent approach to Islam. Tunisians must not continue to practice the Moslem religion in the same way their fathers and grandfathers did.

Professional practices, as well as religious ones, are the object of Ali's attention. I asked him whether, because of new social and economic needs, traditional methods of production ought to be modified. While most people agree that some change is needed, Ali favors a complete transformation. While many state that the craftsmen of traditional handiwork industries continue to play a vital role in society, Ali believes they are of little contemporary significance. I told him the true story of a master craftsman who turned down a chance to significantly increase his income by refusing work in a textile factory. The craftsman considered a factory job beneath his dignity; Ali thought he was foolish.

Ali himself has been only moderately successful in the professional world. As an accountant, he earns about $105 a month—

more than most people in Mahdia do, but not a great deal to support his wife, his parents, and his seven children. He lives with them all in a three-room, one-story Arab-style house, which his family owns. Ali has three older brothers, all of whom are married. One of these, along with his own wife and children, lives with Ali and his family. Because the brother earns about the same salary as Ali, the family manages fairly well. They have bought a refrigerator and a second-hand car.

Although Ali has been to school for only eight years and has never been outside of the country, or even to Tunis for more than a day or two, he considers himself fairly Westernized. "But," he told me, "this does not mean I no longer appreciate things Arab or Tunisian." Ali said he usually skims through two newspapers daily. One is *La Presse* and the other is *al-Amal,* the Arabic language daily of the Destourian Socialist Party. He likes to listen to the radio every day and enjoys programs in both French and Arabic. He also claims to appreciate European music and Arabic music about equally. In fact, Ali believes he is at home in either culture and that this is the way Tunisians ought to be. He says the study of Arab history (as distinguished from Tunisian history) has about the same importance for Tunisian school children as the history of France. He does not believe Tunisian schools ought to devote more time to the study of Arabic than to the study of French. On the other hand, he does not want the French language to become more important than Arabic in Tunisia. Each language is important and each should be learned and appreciated.

For the most part, Ali is satisfied with the progress the nation is making. He thinks his own circumstances are improving and that the world in general is getting better. The most noble thing he hopes to do during his lifetime is to somehow help the government in its attempt to build a better society.

The views of Mahmoud, Samia, Ahmed, and Ali reveal a profound ambivalence toward the possibility of radical cultural change. An eagerness to be liberated from traditional constraints is widespread, but so too is a fear of losing the sense of identity afforded by time-honored and sometimes sacred traditions. Expressions of this ambivalence abound in contemporary Tunisia. When a local women's magazine sponsored a roundtable discussion on "Love and the Young Tunisian Male" (*Faïza,* May–June, 1967), for example, participants both asserted and denied that young Tunisians wish to behave as do the youth of Europe. Ahmed, a married bureaucrat who was the oldest participant, noted that Tunisians with a *"mentalité européene"* are forced to reside in traditional surroundings. "This," he said, "is the problem of our generation. We live with European thoughts in a Tunisian environment." Rafik, a twenty-one-year-old student, argued that problems are the result of growing up too fast; but Moncef, another student, replied that Tunisian children cannot be blamed for their precocious maturity. "Boys and girls," he insisted, "grow up normally in Tunisia. It is the society, our parents and their taboos, whose evolution has not paralleled our own." It was Rafik, however, who had the last word. No one denies the older generation has something less than a European outlook. But are young Tunisians really so different? Rafik doubted that even one of his companions on the panel "would be willing to marry a girl whom he had seen five or six times in the arms of another boy, friend or otherwise." He was not challenged.

The problems and choices confronting the people of Tunisia are not very different than those reviewed by Daniel Lerner in his classic study of the Middle East:

The underlying tensions are everywhere much the same—village *versus* town, land *versus* cash, illiteracy *versus* enlightenment, resignation *versus* ambition, piety *versus* excitement. But the process reaches people in different settings and induces different dilemmas of personal choice. In Turkey, the grocer exhilarated by the sight of the city must live out his life in a traditional village; in Iran, a newly entrepreneurial peasant proudly owns his first store-bought suit in his walled hamlet but rarely dares to wear it among his envious fellows; in Jordan, an illiterate Bedouin chieftain professes the tribal law of the desert but plans to send his son abroad to school; in Lebanon, an educated Muslim girl loves the movies but fears her orthodox parents; in Syria, an undereducated overambitious clerk dreams of being a Tito; in Egypt, a young engineer has eaten pork in the West and seeks atonement in the Muslim Brotherhood (1958:7–8).

Lerner's remarks capture the drama of social change from the perspective of the individual. Both the excitement and the agony of modernization are called to mind. But Lerner does more than establish the range of alternatives between which individuals must choose. He strongly implies these choices will be made, these tensions resolved, in favor of that which is new and Western. Such a view seems plausible; but examples to the contrary can easily be found, suggesting that a harder look is in order. The principal goal of these chapters on Tunisia is to determine whether and how traditional cultural values are being modified by changing conditions. The next chapter reviews selected aspects of Tunisian history in order to introduce more fully the context of contemporary social and cultural change. Chapter 14 then examines the confrontation between traditional and nonindigenous models for thought and action in five important areas—language, religion, women's rights, child-rearing, and professional practices. Chapter 15 will be devoted to an analysis of changing individual attitudes toward these cultural foci. Findings from two public opinion studies recently carried out in Tunisia will be presented. Finally, in Chapter 16, the future of the country's traditional cultural system and the changing nature of its people's collective identity will be assessed.

13

Recurring Themes in
Tunisian History

Three recurring themes in Tunisian history are particularly worthy of note. First, throughout the ages, Tunisia has been repeatedly conquered and occupied by foreign powers. Second, despite its constant incorporation into larger spheres of influence, Tunisia has consistently reasserted its identity as a stable geopolitical entity. And finally, from the earliest days of recorded history, Tunisia has had urban centers of considerable size and importance. Continuous exposure to the broader currents of the Mediterranean world, the possession of a seemingly indestructable unity, and an unbroken tradition of urban life—these qualities tell of Tunisia's dynamic and cosmopolitan past.[1] An elaboration of each will not only introduce the setting of this study, it will explicate and clarify some of the major forces that gave rise to the cultural system now being buffeted by social change in Tunisia.

CONQUEST AND OCCUPATION

In a certain sense, change and growth are themselves traditions in Tunisia. The French Protectorate which lasted from 1881 to 1956, was only the most recent colonial movement to establish itself on Tunisian soil. It was preceded by a rush of invasions so dizzying that the hero of a novel set in Tunis experienced vertigo whenever he thought of the nation's history: "Phoenicians, Romans, Vandals, Byzantines, Arabs, Spaniards, Turks, Italians, French, I forget them all and get confused. Five hundred steps and one finds another civilization" (Memmi 1966). Thus, there has been a recurring cycle of cultural change: invasion brought

[1]This chapter deliberately emphasizes the history of urban Tunisia for it was primarily there that the nation's traditional normative order was molded and it is in the cities that the confrontation upon which subsequent chapters will focus is today most intense.

contact with foreign elements; occupation resulted in a deeper penetration of new ideas; and political incorporation meant the ultimate assimilation of many previously alien cultural patterns. Tunisia's President, Habib Bourguiba, explained this national legacy in the following terms:

Providence established Tunisia in a privileged location at the center of a sea which is the mother of civilization . . . the Latin and Germanic West and the Punic and Moslem East first confronted each other and later intermingled there. And, in a world in search of comprehension, Tunisia offers itself as a land of reconciliation among men, religions and nations (reprinted in LeLong 1957:284).

The earliest known inhabitants of North Africa were Berbers. They are mentioned in Egyptian scriptures as early as 1300 B.C. However, by the twelfth century B.C., the Phoenicians of Sidon and Tyre were building trading settlements in Tunisia and, in 874 B.C., they founded their capital along the sandy northern flank of the Bay of Tunis. The metropole was called *quart hadasht,* meaning "new city" or Carthage, as it is known today in the West. The Phoenicians were not principally concerned with colonizing the interior of the country. Rather, ruled by a wealthy and aggressive commercial aristocracy, they looked to the sea from which they had come and made their capital the center of a growing Mediterranean empire. At the height of their power, in the sixth and fifth centuries B.C., they secured control of the entire western Mediterranean and fought the Greeks in Sicily. Their merchants traded in the Far East and their explorers charted the coast of Africa as far south as what is today Camerouns. Although the Carthaginians left the hinterland relatively unchanged, and brought a new civilization only to the coastal regions of the eastern and northern parts of the country, they built on Tunisian shores one of the most important civilizations of the ancient world, laying the foundation for that part of Tunisia's personality that has always been oriented toward the Mediterranean.

Between 262 B.C. and 146 B.C., Carthage fought three wars with Rome. During the second of these Punic Wars, Hannibal took his troops across the Alps to launch a surprise attack against the Romans; but, after an initial victory, the army of Carthage was defeated and the city itself subsequently destroyed. Tunisia was brought within the Roman Empire and designated as the province of Africa. At first, the *Pax Romana* was extended only to the coastal cities, the hinterland being left to Berbers who had helped in the fight against Carthage. Slowly, however, the country was unified. Roman cities, connected by Roman roads and watered by aqueducts that still stand, sprouted throughout the region. In the countryside, grain was produced for export and the local merchants, who managed the trade, developed into Africa's first indigenous middle class. By the third century A.D., this bourgeoisie had adopted Latin as its language, fashioned an art copied from Rome, and converted to Christianity. Most of the unassimilated Berber peasantry also soon embraced Christianity.

Roman control of Tunisia faltered during the fifth century. In 430 the Vandals began their push from Spain and, by 439, Carthage was under their control. They held *Provinca Africa* until routed by the Byzantine armies of Justinian in 533. However, since the Vandals had provided little formal administration, their hegemony permitted the revival of a Berber nationalism that was to hamper greatly the rebuilding of Roman civilization in North Africa. But, by the seventh century, a far more formidable enemy was arising in the East. Mohammed died in 632 and within a decade the warriors of Islam were sweeping into the Maghreb.

Tunisia possesses a kind of openness, or even vulnerability, that has enabled alien civilizations to plant their seeds in her soil. And since the tangible fruit of this recurring experience is a synthetic and cumulative Tunisian culture, the arrival of the Arabs with their new faith only contributed to and enlarged upon an already familiar pattern of change. But the Arab invasions were also different. Despite initial resistance, the Arabs introduced their ways into North Africa more completely than has any invader before or since. As Bourguiba himself has written, Tunisia became totally integrated with its conquerors only once, when the Arabs occupied the country (1962:16). Today the Tunisians *are* Arabs; yet, as the President states elsewhere, they are Arabs by adoption (1966a). Thus the historical meaning of Arabization is a paradox. On the one hand, with the nation intensely and definitively Arabized, the future of culture was, in a few critical centuries, settled for all time. On the other hand, the assimilation of Arabism and Islam was a staggering act of acculturation, magnificently reaffirming the propensity for change and growth that has consistently characterized Tunisian history.

Most resistance to the Arab invasions came not from the tottering Byzantines but from Berber separatists, led by Kahina, among others, a judaized Berber princess from the Aures. Nevertheless, the Arabs soon took control of Tunisia's major cities and, with remarkable speed, converted the Berbers to Islam. Kairouan, the first capital of the Arab West, was founded in 670. Carthage was taken in 697 and, shortly thereafter, Morocco and Spain fell to the advancing Arab armies.

Tunisia, the old Roman province of Africa, was called *Ifriqiya* by the Arabs; and after the ninth century, was ruled by a succession of Arab dynasties owing little allegiance to the Caliph of Baghdad. First the Aghlabides ruled from Kairouan in medieval splendor. Theirs was an era of peace and prosperity. Then, in the tenth century, Tunisia was taken over by the Fatimids, a Moslem group that rejected orthodox Islam. The Fatimids had come to Tunisia to reestablish the true Caliphate and, in their efforts, were aided by those Berber groups that had resisted Aghlabite domination. In fact, however, the Fatimids ruled as had their predecessors, though magnifying both abuses and bounties. Their hegemony was marked by political tyranny, but the Fatimids also brought economic prosperity and a flourishing of the arts and sciences. Indeed, if only for a brief period, they made Tunisia the center of a vast and powerful Arab empire. Yet, in the end, it was the Fatimids who wrought upon Tunisia a destruction that was to affect the nation's development radically.

The Fatimids shifted their capital to Cairo in 973, leaving their agents to administer Tunisia. However, ben Ziri, the Fatimid governor in Kairouan, soon declared his independence and established his own ruling dynasty. He also denounced the doctrines of the Fatimids and named the Caliph of Baghdad in his official prayers. In 1049 the Fatimids sent their response. Two hundred thousand nomadic warriors, the beni Hillal and the beni Sulaim, poured into Ifriqiya, felling trees and destroying wells, laying waste to Kairouan, and causing the country to dissolve into a number of minor principalities. Against this destruction, however, must be balanced the cultural contribution of the new invaders. Now, for the first time, the language and customs of the Arabs penetrated the countryside and the region assimilated Arab culture rather than simply the religion of alien Arab rulers. Moreover, the Arabization of the Maghreb rekindled the religious fever of the Berbers, to the point in fact where they in turn were able to instill in the invading Arabs, who were rarely devout, a respect for Islamic prescriptions. Thus, in a century of turbulence and upheaval, the interaction of language and religion and the contact between Arab and Berber forged the pillars upon which Tunisia's identity continues to rest. This is why the noted French historian, Charles-André Julien, calls the Hillalian invasion the most important event of the Middle Ages in the Maghreb (1961:74).

The inevitable theme of conquest and occupation resumes in the middle of the twelfth century. Partially in response to the Arabization of the eastern Maghreb and partially as a consequence of intensified religious sentiment, Berber nationalism had been growing in the West. During the second half of the eleventh century, the Almoravid Berbers made Morocco the center of an empire stretching from Spain to Senegal. Now their successors, the Almohades, were sweeping into Ifriqiya to found another Berber kingdom. The resistance of the Hillalis was broken; the autonomous principalities were reunited; and the Normans, who during this period had established themselves in the coastal towns, were quickly driven out. The invading Berbers united the Maghreb and ruled their domains from Marrakech. In 1228, however, the governors of Tunisia broke away and founded the independent Hafsid dynasty which was to rule for the next three centuries.

The Hafsids provided stability, but their reign did not produce the brilliant advances that had characterized the early Islamic empires. As Ibn Khaldoun who was writing during this period tried to tell his contemporaries, the age of medieval splendor was ending. Nevertheless, some important new strands were woven into the fabric of Tunisian civilization during this period. First, the thirteenth and fourteenth centuries marked the arrival of Moslems fleeing the reconquest of Spain. The influence of these Andalousians may still be noted in Tunisian architecture and Tunisian *malouf* music. Tunisia's population was also augmented by Jewish refugees from Spain and the Balearic Islands. Second, a flourishing overseas commerce brought European merchants to Tunisia's cities. Residing for the most part in separate neighborhoods known as *fondouks,* they were protected by treaties which the Hafsid Sultan negotiated with various European states. Finally, to these cosmopolitan influences must be added the emergence of Islamic mysticism. Many Moslem saints established maraboutic orders in the thirteenth and fourteenth centuries and, today, places like Sidi Bou Saïd and Saida Manoubiyya, are still called after them.

By 1574 undisputed control of Tunisia had passed to the Ottoman Turks. As usual, the change followed a period of decline and instability. For more than a century, Hafsid rulers had been plagued by rebellious Arab tribesmen. Then, in the sixteenth century, Tunisia was besieged by both Turkey and Spain, who engaged the Hafsids in a three-way struggle for power. Both nations established garrisons on the Tunisian mainland, but eventually the Turks prevailed and a veritable army of Turkish administrators descended upon the country. As the disorder of the sixteenth century came to an end, Tunisia was left to draw what it might from yet another set of governors and another alien civilization.

Initially Tunisia was administered as a province of the Ottoman Empire, authority being invested in a military governor, or *dey.* But the control that Constantinople exercised over the province soon diminished. In 1631 effective rule passed from the *dey* to the *bey*—until that time an appointed functionary charged with controlling local tribes. This suggests, as one scholar notes, that the Turkish military caste had become dependent upon indigenous support to maintain its position (Moore 1970:24). Then in 1705 the Hussainid dynasty of Tunisian beys came to power, establishing itself as an hereditary monarchy, doing away with the office of dey altogether, and offering only token allegiance to the Sublime Porte.

Ottoman and Hussainid Tunisia was characterized by immigration, piracy, commerce, and a mixture of political repression and enlightened reform. Early in the seventeenth century, between 60,000 and 80,000 additional Andalousian immigrants settled in the northern part of the country. Also arriving during this period were thousands of Italian Jews. They entered the nation's commercial life and founded the important *Souk el Grana,* the market of the Livornese. This was also the golden age of Tunisian piracy and the bazaars were filled with treasures seized upon the high seas. But within a few decades, piracy declined and legitimate trade with Europe increased. Especially during the second half of the eighteenth century Tunisia enjoyed an era of peace and stability. Arabic was gradually replacing Turkish as the principal language of political life and, after many generations in Tunisia, the ruling Turkish élite was becoming just another part of the local mix of races and nationalities. In the nineteenth century, however, European colonialism emerged to threaten the independence of Hussainid Tunisia and raise once again the prospect of conquest and occupation. By 1850 France was in undisputed control of Algeria.[2] France and Britain were actively contending for supremacy in Egypt, and a struggle between Italy and France over Tunisia was taking shape. Partly to prepare for the confrontation with Europe, Tunisia's rulers enacted important reforms. Slavery was abolished, the administration was reorganized, development projects were initiated, and schools for the first time began to teach European languages and modern science. Nevertheless, the French had little difficulty when they invaded Tunisia in the spring of 1881. The Bey of Tunis was forced to sign a treaty accepting a French protectorate; and while the indigenous monarchy was permitted to remain, the colonial administration became the power behind the throne.

With the advent of French colonialism, yet another set of acculturative forces entered Tunisia. France set out to remake Tunisia in her own image and, for a while at least, many Tunisians took this policy of "assimilation" seriously. One local official, for example, expressed the hope that his countrymen would acquire a "French mentality" and be considered as much a part of France as the people of Normandy, Brittany, or Corsica (quoted in L. Brown 1964:26). Education was expanded by the colonial government but the language and curricula of the metropole were usually used. French also became the language of politics, causing one student of Tunisia to complain that it was impossible to get any official business done in Arabic, except in the Moslem religious courts (Ziadeh 1957:32). By 1956, French language newspapers were outselling Arabic editions among Tunisians (LeLong 1957:255) and some young Tunisians were even affecting the styles of the metropole. Thus, interpreting similar trends throughout the postwar Arab world, the first Arab Cultural Conference noted unhappily in 1946 that "most students who have 'taken up' with a foreign culture have been seduced by it, reading its books with ardor and 'going away' from Arabic works and Arabic letters which they tend to regard with a certain scorn and without much interest, even though Arabic is their national tongue" (Monteil 1960:98).

In addition to expanding education, the French added to Tunis-

---

[2]French colonial rule in Algeria began in 1830. The "pacification" of the country is usually said to have been completed in 1847, with the defeat of the forces of Emir Abdelkader.

ia's industrial base, enabling Tunisians to play new occupational roles and to acquire the technology and economic orientations of Europe. The presence of a large European community was an equally important agent of acculturation. In addition to French settlers, thousands of Italians came to Tunisia, driven in part by demographic pressure in Sicily and southern Italy. By 1921, there were 150,000 Europeans living among 1.9 million Tunisians. By 1946, the number of Moslems had increased by another million while the number of permanent non-Moslem residents, including Jews, had more than doubled. In a remarkable if somewhat implausible statement, Bourguiba later testified to the impact of French colonialization: "If Tunisians had been given exactly the same treatment as the French, the history of Tunisia, or even the whole of North Africa, would certainly have been quite different. Perhaps the policy of Frenchification would really have succeeded. If the French had . . . freed themselves from racial prejudice, integration might perhaps have been successful with time" (1962:15-16). In any event, European influences penetrated Tunisia during the Protectorate and most have remained to mingle with Arab and Berber traditions.

This brief account of Tunisian history reveals a recurring pattern: invasion, occupation, prosperity, decadence, disorder, and invasion again. This repeating cycle has made her truly a crossroads of civilizations. Her national patrimony is open-ended; she has continually incorporated new elements into her mainstream.

UNITY

An important geographic constant seems to be at work in Tunisia, giving the nation a tradition of physical and social unity that is somewhat unique among African states. Throughout the centuries, every period of disorder and confusion was followed not only by an era of stability and prosperity but also by the apparently inevitable reemergence of a certain geographic unity. To be sure, the boundaries of the Maghreb in general and Tunisia in particular have not been without some variation; but the whole of North Africa from Tripoli to the Atlantic Ocean was never united for longer than a few years. Invariably the region divided into the same three segments: Tunisia or Ifriqiya, Morocco or the West, and Algeria—the great indeterminate space in between. To quickly visualize this recurring trifurcation, one need only consult and compare maps of North Africa in the eleventh, thirteenth, and eighteenth centuries. Two vertical north-south axes are always in evidence, one running from the sea down to the Aures Mountains in eastern Algeria, passing slightly to either the right or the left of Constantine, and the other running never far from Tlemcen in western Algeria. The division of the Maghreb we know today reflects a tradition of diversity in unity legitimated over the centuries.

The geographical basis of modern Tunisia appeared in its rough outlines with the Roman creation of *Provinca Africa*. Not only did this province distinguish itself as a natural unit with an affinity for independence within a larger North African and Mediterranean sphere, it also manifested from an early date a noticeable amount of internal cohesion. As one author notes, it would be erroneous to conclude that "Tunisia, having been successively Punic, Roman, Arab, Turkish, and French, has never been 'Tunisian.' This would be to forget that in the midst of these vast political edifices, Tunisia constantly rediscovered, within its natural geographical framework, its own character and its individuality" (Raymond 1961:16). By the Middle Ages this character and individuality were very much in evidence. The Aghlabides were in theory responsible to the Caliph of Baghdad. But in fact they were a largely independent Tunisian dynasty. The same was true of the Zirids under Fatimid rule, the Hafsids under the Almohades, and finally a series of dynasties, most notably the Hussainids, under the Turks. Each of these dynasties ruled an area roughly equivalent to modern Tunisia; each became politically autonomous and self-sufficient in a fairly short time; and each possessed a unified and cohesive administrative network which futher solidified the Tunisian national entity. Finally, in the course of several generations, each came to think of itself, in the idiom of the age, as the legitimate ruler of the Tunisian people rather than the heir of an occupying power.

A brief examination of Tunisia under the Hafsids will reveal more concretely the integration of Ifriqiya during the Middle Ages. There was a flourishing commerical life, manifest not only in the volume of maritime trade but also in the variety of goods transported from the interior to the capital for sale. There were olives and citrus from the orchards of the Sahel, dates from the sprawling oasis of the south, wool from the flocks that graze on the interior steppelands, and handloomed rugs from Kairouan. In other words, nearly the whole of the nation was tied to Tunis by strong and stable economic links. Moreover, trade with the Levant was often carried on by caravans passing south from Tunis and traversing the length of the nation. Finally, European trading communities established themselves in major towns, testifying to the ability of the Sultan in Tunis to assure their protection beyond the capital. Sfax, Gabes, and Djerba, located at regular intervals along the coastal road between Tunis and Tripoli, all had large Christian *fondouks.* Thus, Tunisia during the fourteenth and fifteenth centuries was a highly cohesive geopolitical unit.

Tunisia's legacy of solidarity is defined and interpreted differently by various scholars. Indeed there are some differences of opinion about the degree of political unity that existed prior to the period of French colonialism. Some take the position that Tunisia was a unitary state from the fourteenth to the nineteenth century (Raymond 1961:20) and that, by the Hussainid period at least, the political authority of the capital extended to most individuals in all parts of the country (Saumagne and Cardoso 1950: 227). Thus, writes historian Leon Carl Brown, "When the French occupation started in 1881, Tunisia had long been a unified country, possessing all the institutions of a viable society. It did not have to discover that it was a state; thus it could concentrate on the task of becoming a modern state" (1964:6). Other scholars believe the case for unity predating the period of French colonialism should not be overstated. In a series of lectures at the University of Tunis in 1965, Jean Duvignaud argued that groups at different social strata and in differing geopolitical locations did not interact enough to constitute a "global Tunisian society." In the same vein, Clement Moore writes that "nineteenth century [Tunisian] society was segmented into tribes, clans, villages, and urban castes . . . the sum of the parts incapable of articulating a political community or defining a public interest" (1970:23). Despite these differing interpretations, however, all agree that there was a legacy of geographic continuity, religious and linguistic homogeneity, and comparative social solidarity in Tunisia on the eve of the French invasion.

French colonialism stimulated greatly Tunisia's development as a nation. Its significance from a nation-building point of view is twofold. First, the French consolidated the economic and administrative linkages that had traditionally unified Ifriqiya. Second, their presence generated among Tunisians a sentiment of opposition that solidified their sense of common destiny and ultimately carried the nation to independence. Supporters of French colonialism point with understandable enthusiasm to the creation of a modern and comprehensive infrastructure in Tunisia. A port facility at Tunis–La Goulette was built from 1888–1893 and upgraded on several occasions. A major shipping and naval yard was installed at Bizerte in the northwest and the ancient ports of Sousse and Sfax were completely revamped in order to handle modern ocean-going vessels. A comprehensive railroad system linking the nation's major urban and extractive centers was also completed in the early years of the Protectorate and the story of highway construction is much the same. In 1880 there was only one strip of paved road, that linking Tunis with the Bey's palace in suburban Bardo. By 1939, Tunisia had approximately 5000 miles of surfaced highway. Nevertheless, as the Tunisian professor Paul Sebag pointed out over twenty years ago, the balance sheet of colonialism is favorable only in the eyes of those who are content to measure progress in terms of roads, harbors, post offices, and the provision of electricity and water (Sebag 1950). To many, French colonialism was a highly dubious blessing. However, despite its obvious shortcomings—and in fact partly because of them—the French created a cadre of nationalist leaders who gave expression to their "Tunisianness" and who helped to fashion from the nation's legacy of solidarity the ideological consensus necessary for a modern state.

URBANISM

Though not a country of skyscrapers and freeways, Tunisia is an urban nation by African standards. For one thing, while less than 10 percent of all Africans live in cities, about one half of Tunisia's population is urban. More important, however, is the fact that most of Tunisia's major cities have been in existence for hundreds and often thousands of years. Tunisia's rulers were, for the most part, urban peoples who directed their domains from flourishing capitals[3] and who left upon the evolving Tunisian patrimony the unmistakable imprint of urban social and political institutions. Three interrelated strands of this urban tradition may be dis-

[3]Urbanism in Tunisia is a cause as well as an effect of the historic cycle of conquest and occupation. Moore (1970) notes that Tunisia's population was "easily exploited like the fellahs of the Nile and hence a stable support for any government" (p. 23). He reminds us that Ibn Khaldoun once remarked, "it is much easier . . . to govern a passive, relatively homogeneous population than a heterogeneous assortment of highly spirited tribes" (p. 23).

tinguished: that of Tunis and Carthage, that of Kairouan, and that of the cities of the Sahel.

Tunis was the site of a Phoenician trading station as early as the thirteenth century B.C. However, after the building of Carthage only ten miles away, the separate identity of the city was obscured until the first Islamic invasions. Nevertheless, a sprawling urban complex swept up the entire region to the north and east of the Bay of Tunis and 200,000–300,000 inhabitants resided in Carthage alone. Moreover, though oriented primarily toward the sea, Carthage reached out to the surrounding countryside. Tens of thousands of local Berbers came to do the city's work and to fight in its armies. Many more came to sell the goods upon which the town depended.

The Romans destroyed Carthage in 146 B.C. along with its smaller neighbor, Tunis. However, both cities were later rebuilt and the region was soon more prosperous than ever. The Romans united the country surrounding their towns in a way the Carthaginians never had and *Provinca Africa* was ruled from Carthage by a proconsul responsible to the Roman Senate. Advisors of the proconsul and a supporting military legion resided in Carthage. The city became a center of commerce, the arts, and religion as well as politics. A Latinized middle class applied itself to the study of Greek and Roman culture, adorning the city with the art of these civilizations. Christianity flourished too, finding ready converts among the Berbers. St. Cyprian was born in Carthage early in the third century and became its bishop in 249. St. Augustine lived in Carthage during the latter part of the fourth century.

The decline of Carthage and the extension of Tunis began late in the seventh century. Under the Arab and Berber dynasties that ruled Ifriqiya during the Middle Ages, Tunis prospered and was, at intermittent periods, the administrative capital of the region. In the thirteenth century al-Mostansin Billah, the Hafsid Caliph, established Tunis as the definitive center of the area and expanded the city. He rebuilt the Kasbah and laid magnificent watered gardens throughout the town. After that the Hafsid capital grew rapidly, soon reaching 100,000 in population and including among its residents luminaries like Ibn Khaldoun and ambassadors from as far away as Norway and the Sudanic kingdoms of Kanem and its successor state, Bornu. Thus, following a visit early in the sixteenth century, Leo Africanus was moved to describe Tunis as one of the most singular and magnificent cities of Africa.

Under the Turks and the French, Tunis remained the center of the country. A regular port of call for European, and especially Italian, vessels, the commercial importance of Tunis increased and many Europeans came to live there. The Turks, for their part, built new markets, increased the number of schools and encouraged the development of important craft industries. The production of *chechias,* a local variety of fez, was centered in Tunis. The craftsmen who made them were organized in a prestigious guild and, even today, are viewed as an artisanal élite. Weavers, dyers, tanners, and many others also had their professional organizations and their special market areas. Further, the Turks built monuments and fine homes around the city and refurbished many old ones as well. The Beylical residence was established at Bardo, a suburb on the western periphery of the city, in a huge renovated Hafsid palace. Thus, with important new industries and markets, with mosques, schools, and a religious and intellectual aristocracy, with a municipal council and a royal court to rule over the growing metropolitan area, as well as the interior, Ottoman, and later Hussainid, Tunis contributed enormously to the cosmopolitan character of traditional Tunisia.

If Carthage and Tunis reflect the Punic, Roman, and Turkish— in short the Mediterranean side of Tunisian urbanism—Kairouan symbolizes the great competing urban tradition: the classical grandeur of the medieval Arabo-Moslem city. During the Middle Ages, Kairouan rose to splendid height and sustained a life reminiscent of Damascus, Baghdad, or, later, Cairo. In 670, when the town was founded on the interior steppe, Kairouan was the campsite of an Arab army bent on conquest. Its very name means "place of arms." By 711, the invading Arabs had passed into Spain and were in control of the Iberian Peninsula. By 730, they had penetrated western France and were knocking at the gates of Charles Martel. All of these domains were ruled from Kairouan although, after 750, Spain broke away as eventually did the western Maghreb. Nevertheless, for about 200 years the emirs of Kairouan controlled an area ranging from central Algeria in the west to Tripoli in the east.

Kairouan was not only an administrative capital, it was a spiritual center of major proportions. The Moslem sciences flourished in institutions of higher learning and special attention was given to questions of religious law. According to Julien, a traveller returning to Iraq was asked, "Of what do the people of Kairouan talk today?" His reply: "Of the names and attributes of God."

Religious architecture was also a major preoccupation. The great mosque of Kairouan, the oldest Moslem monument on the African continent, was demolished and rebuilt in 695, 774, and 836, and restored, enlarged, or embellished on repeated occasions from the nineth to the thirteenth centuries. Kairouan was also known for the refined existence led by its upper classes. Palace life had all the attributes of a medieval oriental court: musicians, poets, concubines, jesters. The nobility amused themselves with strolls through the town's gardens and with races and displays of horsemanship. In short, Kairouan burned with a medieval brilliance which even today, in the city's decline, has not been forgotten.

Kairouan prospered until the middle of the eleventh century. But the Beni Hillal sacked the city shortly after their arrival in Ifriqiya, turning out the reigning Zirid dynasty and dealing the city a blow from which it was never to recover. From the glory of the Middle Ages, Kairouan steadily withered in both population and spirit. The Hafsids and the Turks made their respective capitals in Tunis, leaving Kairouan to become, on the eve of French colonization, a decaying town of barely 20,000 with only the memory of a glorious past (Ganiage 1959:146). Nevertheless, even then, the city remained true to its heritage and access was denied to non-Moslems. Today, though Kairouan numbers less than 50,-000, it is considered a holy place and efforts to modernize and redecorate the city continue to be resisted.

Sfax and Sousse are today the second and third largest cities in Tunisia. They are located about seventy-five miles apart along the eastern seaboard and between them lies a string of over 50 villages which collectively constitute the third center of urbanism in Tunisia. The region is known as the Sahel, or coast.[4]

Many cities in the Sahel date from the Carthaginian period. Sousse, originally known as Hadrumetum, was founded in the eleventh century B.C. and was an important Phoenician trading station. In fact, it served as a base of operations for Hannibal during the second Punic War. Nearby Monastir, which originally bore the Punic name Ruspina, was used by Caesar in his African campaign less than 200 years later. Mahdia was also an important center during this period. However, it was not until the Middle Ages that the present character of the Sahel was fixed. Most of the important structures in the area were erected at that time. In

---

[4]Actually, the Sahel does not usually refer to Sfax. But this major urban center is part of the complex of coastal cities we are considering here.

the eighth and ninth centuries, the emirs of Kairouan built a series of fortresses, or ribats, to repel the Christians trying to retake Ifriqiya. The ribat of Monastir, of which it is said a three-day visit suffices to open the gates of paradise, dates from 796, and the ribat of Sousse was built in 821. The walls of Sfax, though later enlarged, were also built during this period and the great mosques of Mahdia, Monastir, and Sfax came only a few years later. During the tenth century, Mahdia was intermittently the capital of the entire region.

With their backs to the sea, the cities of the Sahel have historically been a battleground for forces seeking to control Ifriqiya. In the twelfth century, the Christians again tried to retake Tunisia and the Normans, under George of Antioch, held Mahdia, Sfax, and Sousse for five years. In the sixteenth century the Sahel in general and Sousse in particular figured prominently in the Spanish effort to take Tunisia and forestall the installation of the Turks. However, when the Turkish forces triumphed, the cities of the Sahel prospered under an administration oriented toward the Mediterranean. By the end of the nineteenth century, the population of Sfax was equal to that of Kairouan and, in 1881, the city actively resisted the French invasion. Sousse, Mahdia, and Monastir were also thriving centers and the region as a whole was known for its production of olives and olive oil. Thus, in 1865, a consular officer in Sousse estimated that the Sahel had a settled population of 140,000, over a tenth of the nation's total population and about a fifth of the nation's sedentary population.

Tunis and other cities are, as it were, visual symbols of the progression of history. An ancient mosque, built when the Arabs first arrived, stands at the center of the medina and fanning out from it in all directions is a complex of crooked streets and covered bazaars that tells of medieval prosperity. Climbing higher, in Tunis, one soon approaches the *kasbah,* the old administrative center refurbished by the Turks. *Dar el Bey,* the palace of the Hussainid Bey, Hamouda, occupies the uppermost point of the medina just below the kasbah; and elsewhere on the periphery of the old city are the fine homes of a more contemporary upper class, many of whom are of Turkish descent. Traditional in style, two stories with inner courts, artesian wells, and white, windowless walls facing the street, these homes are located at the city's point of transition and are expressions of the dialogue and tension between an inner and an outer world. Following the sloping arch of the medina's perimeter in either direction brings one slowly around and down to the quarter of the first Europeans in the lower reaches of the old city. Sainte Croix Church and the stately British Embassy remain to tell of a precolonial Christian presence within the medina. Then, descending still further, one is suddenly beyond the Arab quarter altogether, out in the brilliant sunlight of the more exposed European city. In an earlier day, one passed beneath the watchful eye of a statue of Charles Lavigerie, the nineteenth-century French cardinal who founded the order of the White Fathers. Today, however, though the "Gate of France" remains at the base of the medina, the statue is gone and the place renamed. And, finally, if one continues, there is always the sea, giver of life and, so often, civilization. A descent through the town is, as Berque says, a journey through the generations. Each new step confirms again, with symbols that assault the senses, the continuing and simultaneous Tunisian traditions of an urban heritage and a *débat avec l'autre.*

This is the Tunisia of the *Mahzan,* the land of law and government. It does not embrace the totality of Tunisian society, for it excludes the important world of peasants and bedouins. But it is nonetheless the historic center of growth and dislocation and, in contemporary Tunisia, the site of an intense confrontation between traditional and nonindigenous normative orders. Urban Tunisia is the home of ambivalent Tunisians like Mahmoud, Samia, Ahmed, and Ali; and it is the possessor of a traditional system of values whose future these men and women are struggling to define. In the next chapter we shall explore the components of this cultural system in more detail and return to the dilemmas of the young Tunisians.

14

A Panorama of Social
and Cultural Issues

The cultural objectives of a developing nation often conflict with one another. On the one hand, there is a call for the repudiation of traditional norms in the name of progress and increased growth. Longstanding attitudes and beliefs are reexamined, and those that appear to retard economic, political, or social development are denounced. Similarly, customs judged to be backward and inhibiting are discouraged; they are to be replaced with more productive modes of behavior. On the other hand, there is a determination to preserve traditional culture in order to provide identity and continuity. The collectivity desires to be viewed as heir to a noble civilization, one whose force and wisdom are as relevant today as they were in the past. Many individuals also desire to maintain time-honored traditions in order to minimize dislocations associated with rapid social change. Therefore, with respect to many aspects of traditional culture, the same awesome question appears: how to admit change without sacrificing continuity, how to pursue development without losing identity.

This question does not always pose a cultural dilemma. Traditional values that threaten to retard development can be readily disavowed if they are not firmly tied to the society's quest for identity and continuity. Similarly, traditions that provide an important measure of continuity or that are an integral part of the national patrimony can be supported and even given a place of honor if they are not incompatible with developmental objectives.[1] But some sets of traditional values are centrally linked to the struggle for both development and identity. They cannot be preserved without limiting the former; they cannot be repudiated without impairing the latter. In these instances, a society is indeed faced with a cultural dilemma, and ambivalence and tension are the

[1]The compatibility between many aspects of traditional culture and the pursuit of development is discussed in Chapter 17 (pp. 322–324).

inevitable results. Tunisia is confronted with cultural dilemmas in a number of areas, the most important of which concern traditional values pertaining to language, religion, the status of women, child-rearing, and professional life. This chapter will examine the pressures upon contemporary Tunisia for both continuity and change in each of these areas.

CULTURAL DILEMMAS IN HISTORICAL PERSPECTIVE

Excellent histories reviewing the intellectual accomplishments and classical traditions of the Arab world abound in today's literature. According to Jacques Berque, the Arab is a Greek of the underworld. "His theology, his grammar, his law, nourished by Aristotelian rationalism, distinguish between subject and object, between good and bad, between precise and imprecise" (1960:24). H. A. R. Gibb recalls the golden age of Islamic civilization. "Industry, commerce, architecture, and the minor arts flourished with immense vitality as Persia, Mesopotamia, Syria, and Egypt brought their contribution to the common stock" (1953:7). And Philip K. Hitti tells us that when the crusaders entered the Middle East they had "little to impart and much to learn. Though by that time Islam the culture had lost its creative character, it still stood on a higher level than European culture" (1962:81). Yet leaders of Tunisia and other Arab nations recognize that much of their classical heritage is today outmoded. Tunisia's President, Habib Bourguiba, speaks for many when he contends that certain traditional Arabo-Moslem values are inconsistent with the needs of a developing society. Bourguiba believes that Tunisia must effect a "psychological revolution," as the following excerpts from his speeches show:

Faith and spiritual values are only effective to the extent that they are based on reason . . . (1965).

A large majority of our people . . . are still entangled in a mass of prejudices and so-called religious beliefs . . . (1963a).

In the final analysis . . . underdevelopment stems from intellectual causes. It is man's mind which is the driving force and the agent in improving the human condition . . . (1963b).

A true psychological revolution is necessary in order to assure the success of the [National Development] Plan . . . (1961a).

Bourguiba's call for a psychological revolution is by no means new. Concern for coordinated cultural reform in the Arab world is usually considered to date from 1798, the year in which Napoleon invaded Egypt. Bonaparte's invasion took the Arabs by surprise. By the end of the twelfth century, the last of the great Arab dynasties, the Fatimids, lay in ruins and, under the Mongols and later the Turks, the Arab world entered a period of political decay and intellectual stagnation. But, ruled by Moslems during a period of Islamic expansion, the basic assumptions of Arab civilization and the Moslem sciences were never called into question. The result was therefore one of shock and confusion when the French occupied Egypt with ease and revealed a sophisticated and powerful West to the pious Moslems. The Egyptian campaign was the first confrontation between East and West since the Crusades and, in the words of Gibb, it "tore aside the veil of apathy which had cut off the Arabs from the new life of Europe and gave the death blow to medievalism" (1926:159). According to Bourguiba, who traces reformist efforts in Tunisia to the Egyptian experience, Napoleon's forces "caught the country submerged in centuries old lethargy. The people believed their country belonged to the 'Commander of Believers' and was consequently inviolable" (1962:9). After Napoleon's departure in 1801, there emerged in Egypt and other Arab countries reformist movements dedicated to making their societies as strong and prosperous as the nations of Europe.

In Tunisia, the first important reforms of this period were undertaken during the reign of Ahmed Bey (1837-1855). The system of taxation was revised, slavery was abolished, military installations were established, and the production of armaments was begun. Most important, an effort was made to acquaint Tunisians with the ways of Europe. In 1850 Ahmed Bey opened the Polytechnical School of Bardo in order to teach European languages and the secular sciences. In the 1870s, on the eve of the French invasion, Kheireddine Pasha, Premier of Tunisia under Ahmed's successor, expanded reformist activities, emphasizing again the need to give Tunisians the knowledge possessed by the nations of Europe. Kheireddine considered his expansion of Western-style education, and especially the establishment of Sadiki College, the most important of his many accomplishments. He wrote in his memoirs:

I repaired and enlarged the primary schools which I [also] reorganized. Sadiki College was founded (by a decree of January 13, 1875) according to the model of European *lycées;* 150 students were enrolled at government expense and received solid instruction in, aside from the Arabic language and Moslem sciences, the study of diverse modern sciences and the Turkish, French, and Italian languages. Instruction at the Great Mosque of "Jimaa Zitouna" was carefully regulated (Khairallah n.d.: 193).

Under the French social reformers grew more numerous, expanded their efforts and, at the Congress of North Africa in Paris in 1908, offered a permanent record of their concerns. Education remained an issue. Mohammed Lasram introduced a plan for reforming the Zitouna Mosque University and Khairallah Ben Mustapha presented the case against the *kouttab's*, the Koranic primary schools. They were physically decrepit, intellectually stagnant, and pedagogically outrageous. Almost all of the other cultural issues which concern Tunisia today were also discussed in Paris in 1908 (Congrès de l'Afrique du Nord 1909, and Khairallah n.d.). Ali Bach Hamba pronounced himself on the matter of language. He urged that Tunisians be educated entirely in French because secular subjects could not be properly taught in Arabic and because a person could not be prepared for the modern world without the knowledge of a European language. Aspects of traditional Islam were criticized. Mohammed Bel Khodja urged reform of religious courts which he believed were incompatible with contemporary needs. More generally, Mohammed Lasram blamed stagnation in the Moslem world on the fact that intellectual inquiry had been discouraged since the Middle Ages when Islamic doctrine came to be considered complete. Sadok Zmerli discussed problems of women. He pointed out that North Africa seriously lagged behind Egypt and Turkey, which already had many women of letters. Finally there was a lively discussion of economic concerns. Bechir Sfar asked the French to teach modern agricultural practices to Tunisian farmers. After reviewing professional life in urban areas, Abdeljelil Zaouche called for the creation of technical courses to familiarize Tunisians with "the progress realized in the economic order of the Western world."

While acknowledging that desired economic and social objectives required a modification of traditional values, few of these early social reformers advocated a wholesale rejection of Tunisia's Arabo-Moslem culture. On the contrary, they pointed with pride to the classical heritage of Tunisia and the rest of the Arab world. In the nineteenth century, most who sought reform were motivated by desires to revitalize their own civilization and to fortify their nation against the growing spector of European imperialism. The introduction of European ways was merely the instrument by which they hoped to accomplish these objectives. They were eager to borrow technical skills and normative patterns which they believed accounted for the strength of Europe; but they did not wish to see their society develop along purely Western lines. The larger goal of their revolution remained the restoration to society of its original grandeur and dynamism. Kheireddine, for example, ordered his new schools not to teach that which was contrary to Islam. He called on the professors to "inculcate in the students a love of the faith by showing them its beauties and excellence, by telling them the deeds of the Prophet, the miracle accomplished by Him, the virtues of holy men" (quoted in L. Brown 1964:10). But the difficulty of balancing concerns of development and concerns of identity soon became apparent. Economic and technological progress could not be made unless the society was willing to modify sacred traditions. Foreign languages had to be learned and traditional modes of education revised. Many religious prescriptions also had to be modified. Yet, if the goal of the reformers was to defend and enrich their classical Arabo-Moslem legacy, how could the alteration of such basic tenets be admitted? This is the same dilemma that confronts Tunisia and other developing societies today. It took shape early in the nineteenth century and ever since, as von Grunebaum notes of the Middle East in general, Tunisia and other Arab nations have been "wavering between assimilation and rejection of European culture—both equally impossible as total objectives—and groping toward a redefinition of religious and social traditions" (1961:121).

Cultural dilemmas intensified under colonialism as Tunisians and other Arabs attempted to sort out fact from fiction in imperialist doctrines. Europe had devised an elaborate philosophy that divided the world into civilized and savage and spoke of the rights and obligations of the former with respect to the latter. The "white man's burden" and the *"mission civilatrice"* proclaimed the moral duty of Europe to carry her civilization to those endowed with inferior cultures; and cultural interaction became irrevocaby cast in the form of a discourse between superior and inferior. There may indeed have been a noble and generous streak in many advocates of colonialism, but it was inevitable that the cultural racism implicit in their views would sensitize and complicate the dilemmas of colonized peoples.

The prevailing European view of Arab culture is perhaps best illustrated by the work of Ernest Renan, the French Islamicist and historian. Renan advanced the thesis that the Moslem religion constitutes a system of values which is hostile to innovation and the spirit of science. In a lecture at the Sorbonne and later in *L'Islamism et la Science,* he argued that Islam breeds fatalism and intellectual myopia and is therefore a primary cause of stagnation in the Arab world. Similar views were put forth concerning the Arab language. Specifically, it was argued that Arabic was not a fit instrument for conducting the business of a modern society. As one Frenchman wrote in 1926, Arabic "is of that disorganized richness that is more of an encumbrance or a confusion than an aid to the mind. It is absolutely devoid of precision, unsuited for analysis. It is a floating veil thrown upon the thought more than it is an expression of it" (Bertrand 1926:53–54). With the development of this kind of thinking the context surrounding cultural questions changed dramatically. The tension between tradition and change became infused with a new emotional charge.

There was no single Arab response to the colonial doctrines of Europe. Some prominent Moslems accepted the validity of the European charges while many others branded them as totally false. In between, however, was a growing school of Arab intellectuals who insisted that the criticisms of Arabo-Moslem culture were totally out of proportion but who did admit that some traditions the Arabs had diligently preserved were in fact contributing to their decline. The case of the Egyptian sheikh, Mohammed Abduh, is instructive. Acknowledging the stagnation of the Arab world, Abduh argued that this was a "passing illness," caused by certain political and social currents rather than the fundamental principles of Arabo-Moslem culture (Haim 1962:18). Nonetheless, he believed many reforms were long overdue, including the reorganization of al-Azhar, the ancient and venerable mosque university of Cairo.[2] Criticized by conservatives, the famous sheikh

---

[2]It may be noted that Abduh's influence in Tunisia was considerable. Abduh was at the height of his prominence during the early years of the French protectorate and spent part of this period in Paris where he collaborated with al-Afghani in publishing a bi-monthly journal, *al-urwat al-wirthqa,* which reached Tunisia in fairly large numbers. In 1884–1885, Mohammed Abduh visited Tunis and the appearance there within a few years of an organized group of reformers and modernizers seems to be closely connected with his visit (Ziadeh 1962:62–65).

was once sarcastically asked, "But didn't you study in al-Azhar . . . and find [your] matchless wisdom there." Abduh's reply was scathing: "If I have had the good fortune to remember any worthwhile knowledge, I acquired it only after I had spent ten years sweeping the filth of Azhar out of my mind. And even today I have not yet finished cleaning up" (Amin 1953:85).

A passionate defense of Moslem civilization coupled with a fierce attack upon conservatism and narrowmindedness, this was what the times brought forth from Arab intellectuals like Mohammed Abduh. Yet such dilemmas were not unknown to earlier Arab thinkers. The new element was a dialogue with Europe about these intimate concerns. It was profoundly degrading to debate the validity of one's own civilization and especially to acknowledge that the Europeans were partly correct in their criticisms— even if forward-looking indigenous scholars had come to this conclusion independently decades before. Right or wrong, exaggerated or not, the doctrines of Europe pierced to the root of Arab self-awareness and planted a doubt that was impossible to expunge completely. To prove the Europeans wrong, both to themselves and the world at large, nationalists in Tunisia and other Arab countries turned to the task of cultural reform with increased determination. Yet, lest they prove the Europeans correct by affecting too great a transformation, they redoubled their commitment to historic traditions. It was the dilemma of old with a new poignancy and a new urgency. Nothing describes the troubled spirit of the Arabs better than the brilliant insight of Jacques Berque: "Colonialism and expanding capitalism played in the Arab world, and in the Oriental world in general, the role played for us [in Europe] by the doctrine of original sin" (1960:27).

While the preoccupation with cultural questions in Tunisia is not new, the scope and intensity of that preoccupation have increased dramatically in recent years. In the decade and a half since independence, the literacy rate has climbed from 15 percent to over 40 percent, and students today pour out of the schools by the hundreds of thousands. These men and women reside in a world that exposes them regularly to new ideas and new dilemmas. Their newspapers and radios bring to them daily the events of the world. Their jobs constantly demand of them the ability to function in an automated factory, a modern office, or a complex bureaucracy. And the rapid expansion of urbanization, education, communication, and employment—the classic agents of cultural diffusion that are everywhere eroding traditional life—are not alone responsible for increased attention to cultural questions. The Destourian Socialist Party is spearheading a vigorous program of mass-mobilization and resocialization; and though the Kheireddines and the Bach Hambas are their intellectual precursors, the party's leaders have unprecedented resources to devote to the task of shaping the country's cultural character. Thus, for the first time, it is possible to talk about the effective management of culture on a national scale.[3] Nevertheless, despite this expanded and intensified concern, the balance between development and change on the one hand and identity and continuity on the other remains precarious. With respect to language, religion, the status of women, child-rearing, and professional practices, Tunisians at all levels face a crisis of culture. They are struggling to define the parameters of a normative system that will be, in the words of Bourguiba (1965), dynamic and open, yet faithful to permanent moral and spiritual values.

LANGUAGE

Morocco's short-lived attempt to Arabize education after independence (see Gordon 1962:66 ff.) illustrates the linguistic dilemma confronting all the North African states. The Fundamental Law of Morocco stipulates that the state must provide education which has an Arab and Islamic national orientation. As Ahmed al-Ahdar, director of the Institute for Arabization, explained, "Arabization is absolutely necessary if Morocco is to rediscover her Arabic and Islamic personality." However, because most teachers had been educated in French and were consequently unprepared to offer instruction in Arabic, the country was forced to limit school enrollments severely after it disallowed education in French. By 1958, two years after independence, enrollment figures had declined alarmingly. There were simply too few qualified instructors. In the end, the Arabization program had to be quietly shelved with al-Ahdar explaining, "We are not fanatics;

[3]Despite some disorganization during the past few years, the Party has been an effective instrument of political recruitment and political socialization in independent Tunisia. As recently as 1971, a prominent student of Tunisian affairs wrote that Tunisia, more than any other Arab state, has developed a durable political organization that articulates and implements its ideology (Moore 1971).

we want to enter the modern world." It had not been possible to pursue simultaneously the identity goal of Arabization and the development goal of putting children in school.

Tunisia has never attempted to Arabize education totally. Since its creation in 1958, the nation's educational system has been bilingual. At first, Arabic was used exclusively in grades one and two. After that, French was introduced in ever-increasing quantities until, in high school, most work was done in that language. In 1968, however, procedures were revised and pupils began to use French in the first year of school. This change was made because many primary-school graduates were not sufficiently fluent in French to do high-school work successfully. Nevertheless, despite the weight given to French, Tunisian leaders hope it will some day be possible to Arabize the educational system to a significant degree. When introducing the educational program in 1958, Bourguiba declared that special attention would be given to the training of teachers in Arabic in order to establish eventually a school system "able to reinforce the national character of Tunisia which is rooted in Arab culture, the Moslem religion and a past of glory" (quoted in Gordon 1962:69). In the meantime, Arabic has been made the principal language of a number of government ministries, making an ability to read and write the language fluently an essential requirement for many jobs.

Three distinct factors contribute to a desire for Arabization in Tunisia and other Arab lands. One derives from the special bond between the Arabic language and the Islamic religion; another derives from the importance of Arabic as a political symbol; the third consideration involves the difficulties language-related issues pose for many individuals.

According to orthodox Moslem doctrine, Arabic is the language of the angels, the holy tongue in which the Koran was dictated. Indeed, since Mohammed is considered to have been illiterate, the language is itself part of God's gift and, as such, the only suitable form for the expression of His word. For this reason the Koran is held to be incapable of translation. It may be rendered in another language, but the result is not the Koran (see Hitti 1962:14, and Schuon 1963:49). Marmaduke Pickthall, the most recent translator of the Koran into English, warned that he offered his readers not the Glorious Koran, only a kind of imitation (1930:vii).

It is not only for reasons of religious orthodoxy that the Koran is said to be untranslatable. The Koran is not only a message;

it is an inspiring work of art wrought through the medium of the Arabic language and this artistic quality is lost in translation. While Thomas Carlyle found a translation to be "as toilsome reading as I ever undertook" (1897:64), Pickhall assures his readers that the real Koran is an "inimitable symphony, the very sounds of which move men to tears and ecstasy" (vii). The language of the Arabs is thus an object of considerable veneration, possessing both religious and artistic properties. Grammar lessons at traditional Moslem universities, such as al-Azhar in Cairo, often begin, "Praise to God who has made the Arabic language the most beautiful of languages" (Monteil 1960:92).

The bond which makes the Arabs a people, and indeed a nation in all but the most narrow political sense, is primarily cultural and above all linguistic (see, for example, Monteil 1960, and von Grunebaum 1961). Even in Tunisia, with its Mediterranean heritage, the official *La Tunisie au Travail* proclaims that "the mother tongue of Arabic has poured into our nation all the resources of the Islamic civilization and has been the means of its expression" (p. 28). And since the Arab polity is above all a collection of those who speak the Arabic tongue and share the values it transmits, political consciousness and cohesion are made meaningful in countries like Tunisia only by a permanent commitment to the primacy of the Arabic language.

Colonialism greatly reinforced the importance of Arabic as a political symbol. Though supporters of European colonialism sometimes suggested the Arabs were less than civilized, the beautiful Arabic language unmistakably affirmed the classical heritage of the Arabs. It stood in contradistinction to the doctrines of the imperialists and, for this reason, colonialism was often criticized particularly bitterly for its educational and linguistic policies. In the 1920s Tunisian nationalists published a sensational pamphlet entitled *La Tunisie Martyre*. It demanded Arabization and asserted that French culture was superfluous in Tunisia. In 1961, when colonialism was still alive in his country, an Algerian writer described the result of French policy as "cultural asphyxia" (Haddad quoted in Gordon 1962:36). To these men and others, Arabic offered tangible evidence of the noble spiritual, political, and esthetic tradition of the Arabs, becoming, along with Islam, a symbol of identity and resistance. And in the postcolonial era of the present, moreover, the importance of Arabic as a political symbol is growing. The language offers the developing Arab nations a continuing tie with their proud past. It provides dignity in a world where economically and technologically advanced nations dominate. It holds out the possibility of international unity and a realignment of power relationships. And it gives continuity at a time when economic development and social change are increasingly modifying the structure of Arab society (Laroui 1967:93).

The binding up with language of questions of identity exists for individuals as well as for nations. When Arabic is not the language of intellectual and professional life in an Arab country, there is enjoined upon many individuals an obvious pressure to master the language of the former colonial power. It is easy to see the strains this can produce. For one thing, the already formidable educational difficulties confronting children of im- poverished and illiterate parents may be exacerbated if studies are conducted in a foreign language. Yet many who receive only a few years of schooling fail to overcome these obstacles[4] and hence are limited in their career possibilities. Equally important, emotional problems can sometimes result from the inferiority they feel when they compare themselves to persons with a better command of the European language (Abou 1962). Then there are those who do not clearly fail in their efforts to learn the European language but who do not wholly succeed either. Among persons with only intermediate levels of schooling, the result of studying both Arabic and a European language is all too often a functional bilingualism where neither language can be used with total facility. In Tunisia, for example, it is widely acknowl- edged that the level of French in many lycées is unsatisfactory.[5] Yet many students have an inadequate command of Arabic too, and in one recent study, 76 percent of the highschool students sampled reported that they sometimes had trouble expressing their thoughts in Arabic (Riguet 1972:47; see also L'Enseignement du Français 1972:22, and, more specifically, Elayeb 1968). Under such conditions, personal instability as well as educational difficulty can result. Functional bilinguals are often

[4]It is generally agreed that bilingualism *by itself* is not a cause of educational difficulties but that it significantly intensifies the problems of students whose educational circumstances are already unfavorable (see Garmadi 1968:17–18, 28; more generally see *Development and Education in Africa* 1961:118, and Tabouret-Keller 1961, and 1968:137–138).

[5]A review of difficulties associated with the teaching of French in Tunisia may be found in a special double issue of *An-Nachra At-Tarbaya* (1972: Nos. 5–6) devoted to "L'Enseignement du Français." See also Riahi (1968:*passim*, and 211).

partially at home in two radically different cultural systems but fully at ease with neither. This, along with the difficulty they sometimes have in expressing themselves, may lead to loss of identity and depersonalization (see Blondel and Décorsière 1962).

At the upper levels of the bilingual educational system, there are few who have not mastered the European language. But even this does not assure the absence of problems. There is a saying that "if an Arab grasps his pen, he shall not know his mother." This generally refers to the difference between spoken and written Arabic. But the touching self-portrait of Kateb Yacine, the famous Algerian essayist, shows that it also applies to his own struggle to learn French (1962). Yacine recalls his father's sudden decision to throw him into the "face of the wolf," the French school. Solemnly his father tells him, "You will not go far with Arabic ... The French language dominates, so you must dominate it. You must leave behind all we have taught you in tender childhood." Yacine also recalls sitting alone with his books, growing further and further away from his family. Later he is to say, "I have never ceased to resent to my innermost depths that second rupture of the umbilical tie, that inner exile, which would never again bring a schoolboy and his mother together except to separate them a little more." And what of the mother? Her quiet desperation was expressed the day she came to her son and said, "Since I may not distract you from your other world, teach me then French."

Despite Tunisia's understandable desire to be faithful to its Arab heritage and to minimize personal tensions associated with a forced bilingualism, serious obstacles to Arabization exist. The first is that most of the nation's élite are unable to do their best work in Arabic. A brief review of educational development in Tunisia shows why. At the time of independence, approximately one Tunisian child in four was attending primary school. This gave Tunisia the highest literacy rate in the Maghreb. However, about 25 percent of these pupils were attending traditional Koranic schools (kouttabs) where students spent most of their time learning to recite the Koran from memory, rarely acquiring in the process an ability to write or even to read secular works. Another 15 percent attended the modern Koranic schools founded after the turn of the century. These schools were superior to the old kouttabs but were still a far cry from modern institutions of learning. Consequently, they provided almost none of the leaders of the Tunisian nationalist movement. Most Tunisians attended Franco-Arab schools, the first one of which was built in 1896. Here young Tunisians, after having learned French, would study the subjects usually taught in that language. They also learned classical Arabic under the direction of Tunisian instructors. The Franco-Arab schools had standards generally comparable to those of the purely French-run schools and yet were notable for being able to offer Tunisians some training in Arabic. Nevertheless, graduates were far more proficient in French than in Arabic. Finally, a small proportion of the Tunisians enrolled in school, about 7 percent, attended totally French schools along with the children of the colonists.

In secondary schools, a preponderant use of French was also in evidence. The Zitouna Mosque University formed the capstone of the traditional educational system; but its graduates, though trained in Arabic, were prepared almost exclusively for work in traditional Moslem professions. As late as 1961, some 5000 Zitouna graduates were unable to find employment in a country seeking cadres of all sorts (Gordon, 1962:74–75). A Zitouna student accepted for study at the *École Normale Supérieure* found that in spite of great efforts he could not pass into the second year (Monteil 1960:99). Sadiki College was the pinnacle of the bilingual Franco-Arab system and here a small number of students did do serious work in Arabic. However, despite its reputation as a producer of prominent Tunisians, Sadiki never graduated more than a small number of students. And, equally important, most modern subjects were taught in French. Quite typical is the young journalist who told an American interviewer, "Our generation thinks in French and it is very difficult for me, for example, even though I am a Sadiki graduate, to adjust myself to thinking in Arabic" (Gordon 1962:60). In any event, most Tunisians who attended high school during the Protectorate were enrolled in French *lycées* and received no training at all in classical Arabic. The situation has been only partially modified since independence. Most high schools are patterned after the Sadiki model, but the preponderant use of French remains.

University training is also almost entirely in French. Traditionally, students pursued their studies overseas and many still study abroad, usually in France. For the rest, the University of Tunis was founded after independence but it offers few courses in Arabic, except in the department of Arab letters. In fact, when a course in the Faculty of Law was experimentally given in Arabic, it was necessary to print a resumé of the lectures in French for students who did not understand the classical language (A. Attia 1966:136). In sum, though Tunisians are reading and writing Arabic more than ever before, many and probably most educated Tunisians are still able to do their best work only through the medium of the French language. Arabization would thus reduce the ability of many educated Tunisians to contribute maximally to the development of the nation, and in some cases it would undoubtedly deny their services to the country altogether.

A second consideration militating against rapid and widespread Arabization is the importance many Tunisians attach to the French language and culture. Some persons educated in French undoubtedly favor bilingualism because it assures their professional future;[6] but many also support the continuing widespread usage of French because they sincerely believe it offers the country intellectual enrichment and a means of communication with the outside world (see Deuxième Seminaire de Linguistique 1968: *passim,* and, more specifically, Riguet 1972:43–45). At present, books, magazines, and movies in the French language enjoy wide distribution in Tunisia's major cities, making the cultural currents of the West available not only to the intellectual élite but also to many persons with relatively little schooling. Increased Arabization would greatly reduce this direct popular access to European civilization, and to many this would be a serious loss. Some also fear more Arabization would make it harder for the nation to borrow and/or adapt the ever-changing technology of the West and its continuing innovations in the natural and social sciences. In sum, social benefits derived from bilingualism are considered by many to be significant. As a result, these persons are either ambivalent about Arabization or inclined to believe its objective should not be the dominance of Arabic but rather its parity with French in public life.

A third obstacle confronts those who desire to make Arabic the primary vehicle of political, commercial, and, above all, intellectual life in Tunisia and elsewhere. Classical Arabic is an eminently rich language, but it is in many ways poorly suited to the needs of societies seeking development (Pellat 1956:iii). Three

---

[6]With the Arabization of a number of important government ministries, some lycée and university students have in fact begun to take private tutors in an attempt to improve their Arabic and thereby increase their chances of finding a job after graduation.

interrelated aspects of this problem may be briefly noted. First, Arabic is charged with a failure to make a sufficient distinction between the real and the symbolic. Second, there is the relative paucity of Arabic's technical vocabularly. Finally, there is the wide gap between the classical language of the Koran and the various and often mutually unintelligible spoken dialects of Arabic.

Several scholars have taken a hard look at the symbolic and affective nature of expression in a language considered by those who speak it to be the most beautiful of tongues, a language that takes pleasure in creating the effect of which it is so proud. Monteil explains that the liturgical language of Islam is not a precise instrument. Form almost always takes precedence over content (1960:356). For Berque, the problem is that the content of any communication is "surrounded, dominated and sometimes contradicted by that which emerges from the signals, first religious then social, that the community requires in order to recognize itself" (1960:187). The dilemma of course is that should Arab scholars try to purge the language of its emotionalism and its classical symbolism in order to render the language better suited to modern society, they will be accused of trying to undermine the very qualities which make the language so precious.

The lack of a modern vocabulary in Arabic is partly the result of a reluctance to borrow words from foreign sources. In classical times, borrowing was common and some new words even found their way into the Koran. Indeed, in the view of some scholars, this borrowing was an important part of the process by which Arab culture assimilated foreign ideas and produced the brilliant synthetic Islamic civilization of the early Middle Ages. But as religious doctrines hardened, linguistic innovations, like other new interpretations, came increasingly to be regarded as anti-Islamic. The assimilation of foreign words was discouraged and the vocabulary of Arabic became more and more petrified. Thus, by the beginning of the twentieth century, a renowned Egyptian scholar could write that Arabic is "inadequate not only to express the concepts of modern science but also to describe the subtle movements of the heart" (al-Sayyid quoted in Ahmed 1960:104). Today the problem is more serious than ever, partly as a result of the fact that technical terms are being created in the West at an ever-increasing rate (Gallagher 1966:86–87). Yet many still oppose the borrowing of foreign words in the name of linguistic purity. As a result, Arabic is a language whose technical vocabulary remains largely inadequate for the needs of a modern society.

The gap between the spoken and the written word means that classical Arabic is almost as foreign to most Arabs as are the languages of Europe. Arab children entering primary school are frequently surprised to learn that classical Arabic is quite different from the language they are accustomed to speaking. Yet their educational experiences are of only limited value in enabling them to master the classical tongue. Even in the Middle East where school systems are more fully Arabized than Tunisia and other North African countries, local dialects are the principal media of instruction. In the teaching of most subjects the language of the Koran is not even heard, let alone spoken (Hussein 1954:86). Thus classical Arabic is rarely a living language. There is little stimulus to its natural growth and evolution, and it is a language that even many educated Arabs do not have the opportunity to master completely. It is for this reason that some orientalists, like Jacques Berque, believe many modern texts in classical Arabic were first thought out in French or English, then transcribed into the writer's native dialect, and finally polished and completed in classical Arabic (quoted in Monteil 1960:358).

The gap between spoken and literary Arabic raises difficult questions about the focus of Arabization and the scope of linguistic reforms aimed at solving problems associated with affect and vocabulary. If classical Arabic is allowed to remain a language of religion and ceremony, so that the various local dialects are used to fashion a reformed Arabic suited to the needs of modern life, then each nation will be required to work largely unaided. Furthermore, each nation will have to build on the base of a language which is rarely written, into which little has been translated, and which possesses a comparatively imprecise grammatical structure. In addition, problems of translation will be aggravated considerably; each country will require different translations. And finally, the bonds that continue to give the various Arab states an important measure of solidarity will diminish and the language of a rich classical literature will fall into disuse (Gal 1955). However, if literary language is made the object of reformist efforts, problems of affect and borrowing will increase, opposition to reform will intensify and, potentially most important, problems of communication and coordination will be exacerbated. Further, the language of written communication will still not be the language spoken by most people or even a language that most can use with total facility. Thus one of the principal objections to the use of foreign languages will continue to exist.

Scholars in North Africa and the Middle East are, of course, concerned with these problems and some have worked to produce a "third language," a language which, in the words of Egyptian author Tawfiq al-Hakim, "can be read and pronounced, in turn, in a dialect accessible to Cairo porters and in a language satisfactory from a grammarian's point of view" (quoted in Berque 1960:183). In Tunisia, the language used in Bourguiba's speeches has been described as such a language. A "Seminar on Language" held in Tunis in 1965 noted that Bourguiba has broken with the practice of addressing the people in literary Arabic and has begun to speak to them in an idiom they understand. He has established a "third register" and made it a lively and precise means of communication, capable of assuring the comprehension by illiterate listeners of complex notions (Attia 1966). However, as the animated discussion at the seminar revealed, there are some who do not consider Bourguiba's third register—or any of the other intermediate languages—an authentic linguistic form. Others believe that only the language of the mass media has any chance of becoming a widely used third language and that it will be a long time before even that develops into a vibrant language capable of competing with the tongues of Europe (see Garmadi 1968:14–15).

Because of the problems associated with classical Arabic, because the widespread use of French is believed to offer important social benefits, and because many educated Tunisians are unable to do their best work in Arabic, even if they wish to do so, those who would Arabize for the sake of identity will have to pay a price for their actions. Whether the price is worth paying is a debatable matter and the opinions of various classes of Tunisians will be examined in the next chapter.

RELIGION

In 1932, colonial officials attempted to bury in a Moslem cemetery a deceased Tunisian who had accepted French citizenship. However, when a religious leader in Bizerte declared this a violation of Islamic law, an angry crowd assembled to prevent the interment and the deceased had to be buried under guard. Protests continued with each new burial until French officials finally bowed to public pressure and established special cemeteries for the *naturalisés*.

The naturalization issue not only produced a victory for the Tunisians over the French, it also led to the rise of Habib Bourguiba and the formation of the Neo-Destour Party. The prestige of many religious leaders was compromised severely when some of their number gave in to French pressure. One official suggested, for example, that *naturalisés* be seen as repenting French citizenship and admitted to Moslem cemeteries for burial. Further, Tunisia's traditional political caucus, the Destour Party, censored Bourguiba and his young French-educated comrades for their active role in the confrontation with the colonists. Thus, a new group emerged as the staunchest defenders of the faith. Bourguiba and other fiery young militants founded the Neo-Destour Party in 1934, identifying themselves fully with the institutions and symbols of Islam. They held meetings in mosques, urged people to pray five times a day for national martyrs, and Bourguiba himself was soon being called the "Supreme Combatant," the greatest of fighters in the holy war. In brief, anticolonial nationalism in Tunisia turned on the axis of Islam and Bourguiba's defense of religious values brought him widespread support. His mandate was to work for the establishment of an independent nation committed to a Moslem identity, and in 1956 the constitution of the new state made Islam the official religion (see Moore 1965:32–34, and L. Brown 1964:61–62).

The defense of Islam was an important goal of nationalists in Tunisia and other Arab countries during the colonial period. When Europeans denounced the religion, Arab intellectuals issued vehement rejoinders. When colonial policy was detrimental to Islam, nationalists attempted to arouse the populace in opposition. But Arab intellectuals and political leaders also recognized that some modification of traditional religious values was necessary. After all, by its prohibition of speculation, usury, and commerce in precious metals, the religion had long discouraged such economic necessities as trading in stocks and bonds, banking, insurance, and the use of paper money. Reformers and nationalists were thus on the horns of a familiar dilemma. To reject religious traditions would be to accept the premise of European colonialism. To oppose religious reform would be to turn one's back on the modern world.

None of this, of course, is to revive the proposition that Islam is inherently incompatible with change and development (see page 225 of this chapter). For centuries Islam was a force for progress. The decline of Arabo-Moslem grandeur after the twelfth century was the result of a variety of factors, many of which had nothing to do with the religion. Nevertheless, Arab intellectuals from

Ibn Khaldoun to Mohammed Abduh to the leaders of contemporary Tunisia have contended that the conservatism associated with Islam since the later Middle Ages is indeed a barrier to needed innovation. They may agree or even insist that this conservatism is a corruption of the true Islam and that, moreover, it is a deformation that has not prevailed uniformly throughout the Moslem world. But they also point out that, in the Arab world at least, it is central to the religion as it has long been understood by many of its followers and most of its traditional leadership (see, for example, Bouhdiba 1966:218). To such intellectuals the need for reform is indisputable; and in postindependence Tunisia, despite the fact that their policies were very different under colonialism, nationalist leaders have accordingly argued that the battle for progress and development requires a modification of many traditional Islamic codes. Yet a desire to maintain traditional religious values for purposes of identity and continuity is also strong in contemporary Tunisia, and the duality of these concerns continues to produce ambivalence and tension. Bourguiba's now largely defunct campaign to discourage the observance of Ramadan illustrates particularly well the difficulty of pursuing religious reform in the name of development while at the same time attempting to preserve Islamic values.

In 1960, shortly before the beginning of the month-long fast, Bourguiba made a speech in which he urged his Moslem countrymen to break the fast so that they might be stronger to meet their great enemies of misery and underdevelopment. Observing that the productive capacity of most who fast is greatly reduced, he urged Tunisians not to permit Islam to become an obstacle to development and progress. The President ordered government offices and public schools to remain on regular schedules and instructed state-run restaurants to serve meals as usual. Bourguiba argued that his proposal was not inconsistent with the teachings of Islam. Calling Tunisia's quest for development a type of *jihad* ("holy war"), he reminded his audience that warriors of Islam are exempt from fasting during periods of battle. Thus, Bourguiba concluded, Tunisians should suspend the observance of Ramadan until their poverty is routed (see L. Brown 1966:116, and Moore 1965:56–59).

Despite the President's persuasive appeal, the Ramadan campaign had little success. Religious leaders frequently defied Bourguiba and expressed disapproval of his campaign. In 1960, for example, protesters began and ended the fast one day late, rejecting Bourguiba's scientific determination of the lunar month in favor of the Cairo calendar. And popular disapproval appeared as well. When the government transferred a Kairouan *imam* in 1961 for preaching against its religious policies, thousands took to the street, burning cars and damaging the residence of the district governor. The opposition of most Tunisians has not been this dramatic, but it has been sufficiently widespread to cause the government to abandon its campaign almost completely. A 1964 *New York Times* dispatch estimated that 90 percent of the population were keeping the fast (L. Brown 1966:116).

Each side in the Ramadan controversy was able to offer valid arguments in support of its position; and that, of course, is the problem. The economic consequences of the fast are acknowledged by many. As Tahar El-Arbi, a Tunisian psychologist, convincingly writes, people "cannot stoicly observe a month of fasting without there being an appreciable diminution in their individual outputs." Moreover, El-Arbi continues, this diminution adds to their poverty because "gains registered during eleven months of superhuman effort and privation will be wiped out in one month" (1966:11–12). But opponents of reform are also correct when they point out that the fast cannot be suspended in a country that sincerely intends to maintain an Islamic identity. The observance of Ramadan is not an obscure or minor custom; it is one of the basic pillars of Islam.

There have been other confrontations between reformers and religious conservatives. In the domains of law, education, and land tenure, similar struggles emerged after independence. Reformers, led by Bourguiba, argued that changes were necessary for the sake of development. Conservatives countered that proposed reforms would destroy Tunisia's Islamic legacy more effectively than the French could ever have hoped to do.

Less than six months after independence, the government replaced Koranic law with a Personal Status Code which it considered more appropriate to modern life. The incentive for the new code came from two main sources. First, there was a desire to give Tunisian youth and Tunisian women an opportunity to lead more meaningful and productive lives. Second, there was a desire to institutionalize a normative order more conducive to economic and social development. The code specifically forbade polygamy and made marriage and divorce civil matters. Unilateral repudiation on the part of the husband was outlawed and religious prohibitions against women marrying outside the faith were repealed. Thus the reforms removed the legal basis for the traditionally inferior status of women. The Personal Status Code also modified relations between parents and children. The establishment of a minimum age for marriage—fifteen for girls and eighteen for boys—discourages the practice whereby families arrange the marriage of a very young child. It also gives children, once they attain the legal age for marriage, a voice in the selection of their spouses largely denied them in traditional society.

The Personal Status Code was opposed from the very beginning. In 1956 a group of justices from the religious courts sponsored a petition against it. And even judges on government courts sometimes oppose the code so adamantly that they are unwilling to apply it in the intended fashion. In 1966 Bourguiba acknowledged the problem and intervened in a divorce case where he felt a woman had been judged unjustly. Discussing the matter later before an assembly of jurists, he stated emphatically: "In this country, we intend to behave like civilized men. As a citizen, a wife and a mother, a woman has rights which no one is going to take away from her. Our judges are here to see that she is treated fairly" (1966c).

Religious reforms have not only been directed toward Islamic codes that regulate individual behavior. The state has also besieged some of the organizational bastions of traditional Islam, charging that these powerful institutions are a threat to the proposed new order. For example, Tunisia has disbanded the wealthy Moslem landed estates known as *habous.* Critics charged that *habous* property was stagnating and unproductive, controlled by those who were unwilling to see it exploited rationally (Ardant 1961:61). Yet, at the time of independence, about one fourth of all arable land was under the control of these pious trusts (Micaud 1964:160). In 1956 and 1957, *habous* lands were taken over by the state. They have since been redistributed, taking account of the rights of both traditional beneficiaries and nonowning tenants.

Since education has historically been the preserve of Islamic institutions, reforms in this area further weaken traditional Islam. They undermine the position of the conservative and traditionally important class of religious educators and they virtually eliminate a major vehicle for the perpetuation of religious values. Koranic schools that continued to function more or less normally under the French have all but disappeared in contemporary Tunisia and the Zitouna Mosque University has been reformed and incorporated into the French-inspired Université de Tunis. While religious instruction is provided in public schools, it is hardly enough to suggest that the government has made a serious effort to inculcate the faith among the nation's young. During primary school years, only one hour a week is set aside for instruction in religion and morals while three hours are devoted to the study of Western philosophy (Micaud 1964:153).

Even while pursuing change, political leaders and other social reformers have affirmed vigorously their attachment to Islam. They have repeatedly proclaimed that their efforts are inspired by a desire to recapture the original dynamism of the religion. As Bourguiba stated in a 1966 speech, "Our concern is to revitalize religious truths, to return to the religion its dynamic quality and to adapt it to reality. We will accomplish our mission in accordance with the teachings of the Holy Book and transmit the divine message. It is this desire for revitalization that has constantly inspired our actions since independence" (1966b). But conservatives charge that the reformers are not revitalizing Islam as they claim; they are destroying it. They have removed from society institutions upon which the religion depends and, more significantly, they have embodied the manmade and extraneous into a code more binding than even divinely revealed laws. To do this is to commit the error of association, or *shirk,* the exaltation of the mortal to the status of the divine. Again the arguments put forth by both conservatives and reformers have substantial validity. An identity with Islam cannot be maintained by simply declaring that radical programs are inspired by fundamental religious truths. Yet social and economic development do require a modification of many specific practices that for centuries have been considered an essential part of the religion, and Islam itself will be weakened unless it can demonstrate its relevance to present needs (Cragg 1956:16–17).

Tunisia has formally rejected Western secularism as a model for nation-building. Islam is the state religion. The government devotes resources to religious endeavors such as the building of mosques and cemeteries and the provision of religious education. Religious festivals are national holidays. Even many conservatives recognize that advocates of reform remain Moslem in culture and outlook (L. Brown 1966:114–115). The issue then is not whether supporters of religious reform reject the religion. Clearly they do not. The issue is whether or not, over the long haul, men of reason and good will can make necessary changes without destroying the very Islam they desire to preserve. Without change, the Moslem religion will find itself consistently in opposition to modern life, becoming for many believers an obstacle and an embarrassment. With changes, however, the structures by which Islam socializes adherents and makes of itself a temporal as well as a spiritual force are unlikely to survive. Innovations in the fields of law, land-tenure, and education, as well as worship, pierce the very heart of the Moslem corpus and the revolutionary character of these reforms must be recognized. Thus, in conclusion, we return to the point of departure: the Arabo-Moslem world cannot strengthen itself and develop without fundamental change; yet if a major reason for seeking development is to assure the defense of Islamic values, how can the centrality of change be admitted?

FEMININE EMANCIPATION

A government publication describes the traditional lot of Tunisian women: "In the past, the condition of the Tunisian woman was that of a hidden slave. Married by the authority of her family to a husband she did not know, subject to the tyranny of the latter who could repudiate her at will and keep her children, shut in and veiled, she was cut off from society" (*La Tunisie au Travail* 1960:70).

Attempts to change this situation predate independence. The need to emancipate women was proclaimed at the Congress on North Africa in 1908 and Tahar Haddad caused a sensation in 1930 when his book, *Our Women in Religion and Society,* suggested women lay down their veils and enter modern life. As a result of these and other forces for change, the roles and status of a few women were transformed. By 1947, André Demeerseman, a French sociologist with many years of residence in Tunisia, could distinguish three types of Tunisian women. In addition to the "archaic" type of woman "who give the impression of rejecting with neither difficulty nor remorse the progress of wordly evolution," there were "modern" women, those who model themselves after European women and imitate both their good and bad qualities, and an "intermediary" type, cultivated women of bourgeois origin who are neither ignorant and unconcerned nor eager to uncritically embrace the world of Europe. Nevertheless, calls for reform and natural evolutionary processes had produced only a small cadre of women who resembled the latter two models identified by Demeerseman. In 1948, the year following the publication of Demeerseman's analysis, only 186 of the approximately 3000 Tunisian Moslems attending secondary school were women (Sebag 1950:182).

Today the place of women in Tunisia is changing more rapidly, but with uncertainty and doubt on the part of some and determined opposition on the part of others. For an illuminating and often touching panorama, it is enough to leaf through pages of *Faïza*, a Tunisian women's magazine. A. M., a young man from Gafsa, responds to the question: Should a woman be given her freedom? While not in favor of traditional constraints (few of *Faïza's* correspondents are), A. M. feels compelled to point out that "if a young woman possesses complete freedom, she will be like a tiger freed from its chains. So, be careful. Danger!" F. Z., a *lycée* student in Algiers, writes to complain she is harassed for talking to boys on the way to school. Her brother was furious one day when a boy walked her home. "My friends," he said, "what will they think seeing you this way?" Sihem, a student at the University of Tunis, tells *Faïza,* "I firmly believe that what handicaps the Tunisian woman is her own hesitation and hypocrisy, not only toward others but also toward herself. Why should she be afraid to have it known she has gone out? Does only a man have this right? No! A girl also has the right to date and to know boys. She should not have to feel guilty" (November–December, 1966:66–67).

Si Bechir, a merchant *Faïza* interviewed about styles and dress, states that European clothes are acceptable for Tunisian women— and in some ways very practical. But they are strictly for the home. Outside, the veil must still be worn. "After all!" Asked about girls in slacks and other Western fashions, Si Bechir replied, "It's disgraceful. Don't forget we are Moslems." Thus, it is difficult to practice the openness prescribed by Sihem. There is great pressure to conform. At a bus stop stand two apparent strangers—a boy and a girl who sit together in class as simple friends but who now pretend not to know each other for fear of "being seen." In a café sits a man accompanied by two women. Then another man enters, slaps one of the women and drags her out. Everyone knows a wife should not be in a café without her husband. Fadela M'Rabet, an Algerian journalist, reports that Westernized women in Moslem North Africa are constantly abused and frequently despised. Veritable herds of males lie in wait as these girls leave work or school. Men of all ages mill endlessly in department stores to stare at the clerks. But these girls—the clerk, the postal worker, the secretary, the journalist and even the student—are not admired. "A 'proper' girl does not show herself; she is discreet, effacing, lowers her eyes, wraps herself in veils; these girls exhibit themselves; they are public women. Is a prostitute to be respected?" (1962:39–40).

In addition to the general inertia by which values of many origins[7] are transformed into binding societal codes, two forces of special significance explain the position of women in the Arabo-Moslem world. These are Islam and colonialism. By sanctioning polygyny and unilateral repudiation and by prohibiting women but not men from marrying outside the faith, the Koran offers a moral and legal base for the second-class status of women. Defenders of the religion point out that the Koran improved the position of women at the time of its revelation. For example, a man might take more than one wife only if he could treat all of them equally—a requirement some Islamicists contend actually prohibits polygyny. Also, the Prophet reportedly urged that women be educated (see, for example, Kechrid 1971:69–80). Nevertheless, Koranic law has historically legitimated the inferior position of women and, if the letter rather than the spirit of that law has sometimes prevailed, the result is no less Islamic. It has been traditionally understood that the religion requires a denial to women of the status of men.

Many believe that colonialism increased Arab opposition to feminine emancipation. Analyzing the case of Algeria, Fanon asserts that the French defined a precise political doctrine to destroy the Algerian capacity to resist (1959). Under the guise of benevolent liberalism, they urged a feminist revolution in order to destroy the ultimate repository of Algerian dignity and manhood. "Every veil that fell, every body that became liberated from the traditional embrace of the *haïk,* every face that offered itself to the bold and impatient glance of the occupier, was a negative expression of the fact that Algeria was beginning to deny herself and was accepting the rape of the colonizer" (1959:42). Whether or not the French program was as deliberate as Fanon contends, women were crucial objects in the moral and psychological confrontation with colonialism. As Berque states, "The colonized man retreated into the home. His wife represented for him the last

[7]Tillon (1966) contends that the inferior status of women must be seen as a Mediterranean phenomenon. For a good discussion of the origins of attitudes toward women in North Africa, see Gordon (1968:6–18).

opportunity for an exercise of his freedom, the only person over whom he exercised authority" (*Faïza,* May–June, 1967).

The notion that women must be fettered in order for Tunisia to maintain its dignity is now under ruthless attack. Many Tunisian political leaders consider it intolerable that women should have anything less than full civil rights and think it ridiculous that according these rights somehow compromises Tunisian identity. Many, of course, still disagree; but Bourguiba and others have not been dissuaded. And their forceful statements have been matched by action. First, school enrollments have increased at staggering rates and classes are filled with girls as well boys, even in the smaller villages. Second, the legal reforms outlined previously reflect an unswerving determination to liberate women. Tunisia is the only Moslem country to have formally outlawed polygyny. Third, Tunisia has created several institutions, most notably the *Union Nationale des Femmes Tunisiennes* (UNFT), to stimulate feminine participation in national life. The Union's president, Radhia Haddad, was elected to the National Assembly in 1959. In 1966, 44 women were elected as councilors in eleven different urban centers. Finally, a series of programs run through the Ministry of Social Affairs attempt to ease women into modern life. The government maintains regional centers that teach reading and writing to illiterate women and offer training in home economics. Another program helps unskilled women to acquire professional training. A national center in Tunis prepares girls for work in hotels, offices, and medical establishments.

Two factors have stimulated efforts to liberate women in Tunisia. First, there is a determination to accord women a greater measure of dignity and self-respect. Expressing the very personal nature of this commitment, Bourguiba admitted in a 1965 speech that "my love for my mother has been the keystone of all the efforts I have made to promote women." In another speech, he promised severe punishments for "fanatics" who annoy and abuse women (1966c). Second, there is a belief that feminine emancipation is necessary for national development. In 1961 Bourguiba told a meeting of the National Union of Tunisian Women that progress lagged because "nearly half of the nation's people was practically paralyzed, incapable not only of earning a living but also of assuming national responsibilities" (1961b). Abdulwahab Bouhdiba, a leading Tunisian sociologist at the University of Tunis, comments further on the need for feminine participation in public life and suggests a deeper, less obvious dimension of the problem.

Noting opposition to the Personal Status Code of 1956, Bouhdiba states that many people mistakenly believe the reforms are intended to emancipate the woman alone, failing to understand that the goal is to free both men and women (1966). Bouhdiba is pointing out what other sociologists and psychologists have also suggested: that development is enhanced by the presence in society of certain attitudes and orientations but that these attitudes are rarely well developed in authoritarian, male-dominated cultures (see, for example, Shils 1958, and Berque 1960:chap. 9). David Reisman summarizes this thesis in the introduction to Daniel Lerner's study of the Middle East. He states that it is difficult for men to work together for the betterment of their society if they view one another primarily as sexual rivals. As long as they reject the advice and assistance of those who know more because this threatens their masculinity, their ability to cooperate and to make the changes necessary for development will remain limited (1958: 7–8).

Despite a growing recognition that the battle against underdevelopment requires effective feminine participation in national life, many of both sexes fear that a change in the status of women will injure their dignity and their identity. A number of opinion surveys, for example, reveal continuing opposition to feminine employment (see, for example, Hochschild 1966, and *Faïza,* November–December, 1966). Even Bourguiba apparently believes there must be limits to the rate and extent of feminine emancipation if it is not to produce a "loosening of our morals." "Freedom," he warned in a 1969 speech, "must be coupled with religious and moral education in order to produce the respect for virtue that was formerly assured by long robes and heavy veils" (1969). Thus, there remains for many the nagging *malaise* to which Demeerseman gave expression a quarter century ago. Demeerseman noted three potential dangers in an uncritical imitation of Western norms—the nation might lose its personality, women might lose their traditional prudence, family life might be disrupted—and he therefore urged that feminine emancipation be neither opposed nor blindly followed. Rather it should be directed in order to permit the development of a Tunisian woman who would harmoniously blend the best qualities of East and West. What he wrote in 1947 expresses a view that is still widely held.

To slavishly copy the European would be to deny the traditions of the Orient and to no longer be a good Moslem. . . . Certainly it is necessary to modernize; but the best way to become modern is to return to the true sources of Islam. . . . It is necessary to reconcile religious principles and modern necessities but not at the expense of the former alone. . . . The ideal Tunisian woman should be a vibrant synthesis of East and West (1947:14–15).

To some reformers these perpetual statements about harmony, balance, and synthesis are claptrap and they do not hesitate to say so. Yet such phrases express the fundamental dilemma with which social change confronts Tunisia and tell of a continuing national ambivalence in the face of the ways of the West.

CHILD-REARING

"In the traditional family, the role of the father is preponderant, the respect that is due him appearing in the form of a religious duty. The mother, in her secondary role, while self-effacing before the father, retains some prerogative with respect to household affairs, has much influence on the children and constitutes a moderating element in the family. Nevertheless, important decisions are made by the father, and nothing must challenge his authority. The children in this autocratic society lead a rather marginal existence that imposes upon them certain duties, including among other things every kind of submissiveness. Their behavior is dictated by both respect and fear" (*Éducation Intégrale,* April, 1967:15). This portrait is provided by a publication of the Tunisian Association of Parents and Educators. It describes what is still the most widespread model of family life in Tunisia.

The concern for family organization in general and child-rearing in particular involves the same three elements observed in relation to problems of women. First, there are young people who are frustrated and bitter. Chafing under a medieval system of authority, many educated young Tunisians are desperately seeking to partake of the world revealed to them by their studies. Second, there is the resentful older generation. To these Tunisians, the rate of an unnatural and an unwise evolution is staggering. They are the lost generation, those who feel themselves sacrificed to the cult of youth. Finally, there are the nation's leaders with their official commitment to progress and their tireless attempt to eradicate outmoded beliefs and odious mentalities. They believe that development requires a lessening of the authoritarian family structure.

Among young and old alike, the need for ego strength is great. Consider first the humiliation of Leila, a fourth-year student at the University of Tunis. Every day her father insists on driving her home. He will not permit his 22-year-old daughter to see her classmates outside of school. The situation is extreme, but it is indicative of a general problem. Mohammed Trabelsi, President of the Tunisian Psychological Society, interviewed boys and girls between the ages of 16 and 18 and found that most experienced parental opposition to social activities outside of school (1966:20). In another study, sociologist Carmel Camilleri found 35 percent of the high school seniors he interviewed to be ill at ease with their families (1966). It is small wonder, then, that the new generation is frequently rebellious in its orientation, rejecting the attitudes and behavior patterns of older Tunisians (Demeerseman 1957:208; more generally and more recently see Demeerseman 1967: especially chap. 7, and Camilleri 1973). The problem of parents is also striking. Victimized by the traditional family system in their youth, they have silently suffered, knowing that they would eventually rise in the hierarchy. Trembling before their own fathers who insisted that discipline be based on fear rather than love or even respect, meeting for the first time on their wedding night the spouse selected by their own parents, this generation now finds it has endured these rigors only to have its anticipated compensation threatened by pressures for change within the society (Camilleri 1966). If the old ways are worthless, many parents ask, why were they themselves not liberated?

The confrontation of the generations has important consequences for Tunisian development. Social research has consistently demonstrated that the presence in a society of many individuals with strong entrepreneurial tendencies and high levels of achievement motivation aids in economic development. As McClelland concludes from his comparative studies, "achievement motivation is a precursor of economic growth—and not only in the Western style of capitalism based on the small entrepreneur, but also in economies controlled and fostered by the state" (1966). However, studies by Winterbottom (1958), McClelland (1961), and LeVine (1966a), to name just a few, show that the family structure most productive of the need to achieve is characterized by a somewhat domineering mother emphasizing self-reliance and mastery and a father who does not govern the lives of his children too strictly. Cultures which maintain authoritarian, father-dominated family patterns and which discourage independence and self-reliance among children would thus seem to be limiting their capacity for economic growth.

Tunisian leaders rarely relate concerns of child-rearing and youth to economic development as directly as do students of achievement motivation. Nevertheless they do believe that a weakening of traditional authoritarian family patterns is needed if the society is to be composed of individuals capable of dealing effectively with a changing world. At several conferences and in a number of publications, Tunisian professors, psychologists, and educators have pondered the problem of youth and charted the relationship between social development and family patterns.

The need to teach individuals an open and adaptable approach to life has been stressed often. The child must be prepared to function effectively in a rapidly changing world and to fulfill his social duty upon reaching maturity (see, for example, Trabelsi 1967b:56). But many of these educators and social scientists also point out that the family is not contributing to the social education of the child. Mohammed Trabelsi contends that the "archaic organization" of the Tunisian family frequently prevents it from carrying out its educational duties (1967a:15). The same point is made by the Tunisian Association of Parents and Educators. "The family is losing its qualifications to be an educational milieu. Its social and cultural norms are no longer appropriate for the contingencies of a new life" (*Éducation Intégrale,* April, 1967:16). Accordingly, Abdelmajid Attia, a Tunisian professor, states that parents must display more comprehension, take an interest in the activities of their children, and create a relaxed atmosphere within the home (1967:21–22).

Calls for the modification of traditional family structures continue; but many changes are already visible, brought about in part by the enactment of reforms like the Personal Status Code and in part by increases in education and urbanization. A conference on authority patterns in the Maghrebian family noted in 1966 that the Tunisian family is beginning to abandon its authoritarian character and that father-child relationships are becoming warmer (*Éducation Intégrale,* January, 1967). In a survey carried out by Tahar El-Arbi in the same year, 81 percent of those interviewed expressed the belief that a young man and not his parents should select his spouse, and 80 percent said that it is not desirable for children to fear their fathers (1966).

Children are acquiring more independence; they have greater freedom outside the home and increasingly important roles to play within it. Their relationships with their fathers are becoming less superficial and distant. Yet traditional family patterns remain intact among much of the populace and even many who favor change will go only so far. In the El-Arbi study, only a handful of the respondents rejecting fear in father-child relationships agreed that it is desirable for children to discuss things freely with their parents. Even more opposition to warmth and openness in relations between parents and children was revealed in a survey conducted by Camilleri among young parents of low socioeconomic status. Views about child-rearing were distributed according to the following proportions: 17 percent desire friendship and open discussion with their children; 27 percent desire respect in their relations with them, 57 percent wish to rely on fear and submission (1966:35). Changes are taking place and the trend toward liberalization is cheered by many. But the dogged and determined survival of much that is traditional also continues.

The problem of children is again the problem of old and new, familiar and foreign, and the well-known contradictory currents are at work as ever. Reform is needed if the society is to maximize development and it is therefore supported by many intellectuals and political leaders. Further, a loosening of traditional constraints will improve the lot of certain classes of individuals and they too advocate change. But others feel threatened by blind modernization and notions of progress that have developed outside their experience. And even many who understand the need for change and acknowledge that reformist activities are inspired by high ideals find the proposed new order somehow disquieting.

PROFESSIONAL LIFE

Shortly after independence, intellectuals and political leaders began to insist upon the need to modify traditional codes governing professional life. One problem they noted concerns inefficient and unreliable work habits. In an address to workers at a new paper factory in Kasserine, Bourguiba elaborated this problem (1963b). He said the government had built the factory for several reasons. First, it permitted the domestic transformation of raw materials formerly sent abroad for processing. Second, it created employment where there had been none before. Finally, it integrated the barren and underpopulated central plateau into the national economic circuit. But Bourguiba went on to say that the negligence of many of the workers threatened the success of the venture. The director of the factory had told him, for example, that the men sometimes forget to turn off the machines when they leave work. Bourguiba urged the men to be more responsible and to develop a professional conscience. "Only conscience," he said, "can lead you to do your best work. Each one of you should behave as an artist who only signs a work of art with which he is fully satisfied."

The efficacy of Bourguiba's appeal is debatable. It is by no means self-evident that traditional man can be induced to view the performance of a menial chore as his own personal artistic effort. But the point to be noted is the importance placed upon individual attitudes in the quest for development. Only the human spirit can make the difference and Bourguiba has repeated this message hundreds of times. Efforts to build a new Tunisia will fail unless individuals comprehend the relationship between their own values and the struggle for economic prosperity (1961a). A true psychological revolution is necessary.

The inability to attract workers to certain industries is another unwanted consequence of traditional attitudes toward work. An illustration of the problem may be found in the town of Ksar Hillal where for a time it was difficult to recruit workers, particularly skilled workers, for a textile complex built by the government after independence. In spite of the fact that their incomes would rise and additional benefits would be available, many local artisans and craftsmen preferred not to work in the complex. Yet it would be an oversimplification to conclude that the artisans were not interested in making more money. Traditional wisdom does assert that wealth has nothing to do with a man's intrinsic value; but it does not in any sense either minimize or depreciate the advantages of being rich (Demeerseman 1957). A more plausible explanation is that traditional notions of professional status discouraged the men from accepting employment in the factory. Craft occupations have long enjoyed high esteem in Tunisia, some of them counting members of the bourgeoisie and even sheikhs among their number. Therefore, in all probability, artisans and craftsmen have refused to work in the factory at Ksar Hillal mainly because the traditional status hierarchy was still operative and to change jobs would have meant a loss of prestige.[8]

[8]The tension between artisan and worker values is described at length by Stambouli (1964) in his thesis on Ksar Hillal. However, Stambouli notes that by 1964 the economic advantages of the factory had largely "conquered" the artisan ethic and that work in the factory was not only generally accepted, it was in most cases eagerly sought. The economic difficulties of the last few years have made the stable and well-paying factory jobs more desirable than ever and weakened even further the traditional status hierarchy.

Similar problems affect an important aspect of Tunisia's rural-development program: the provision of trained agricultural workers to upgrade production levels in the countryside, especially in the private sector. Government training centers produce an insufficient number of these skilled workers, but an even greater problem involves the utilization of the graduates of the centers. Many display a reluctance and an inability to perform the jobs for which they have been trained because there exists a fundamental contradiction between the social promotion they expect to result from their formal training and the traditional status of workers, even when skilled, in the private agricultural sector (Zghal 1966:146). A landless agricultural worker is traditionally the lowest of occupations and is still regarded as such in much of the countryside. Therefore, young trainees are able neither to command the authority needed to do their jobs effectively nor to obtain the personal satisfaction necessary to keep them on the job.[9]

The unfortunate consequences for national development are matched by the personal trials of many graduates of the centers. Here is a group of young men trained to do a particular job, to bring needed know-how to the agricultural sectors that remain most backward. Trained in the modern sphere, they are taught that they now possess skills their countrymen desperately need. Proud of the ability to make a contribution, they leave the city with high expectations and a new-found sense of personal worth. On location, however, the reality is quite different. Whereas the newcomer identifies himself as one of the educated, one of the élite, the locals never forget he is a landless agricultural worker. Far from being one of the élite, they all know there are few men in the countryside more lowly than those who work the land of others. A laborer is a laborer and a few years of school cannot change that. If he were really qualified he would have a better job.

Tunisia has had difficulty recruiting enough nurses and this has also been attributed to traditional attitudes toward work. The problem results in part from a large demand for nurses and in part from high professional standards which some candidates cannot meet. But it is aggravated considerably by the common conviction that, for women at least, nursing is not a suitable

---

[9]A broader and more recent study by Zamiti (1971) reveals that there have also been difficulties in the absorption of graduates from industrially oriented training programs.

career (Magnin 1961:344). Despite efforts to attract more young women to the profession, a newspaper study published in 1967 reported that the shortage was at that time as critical as ever, in part because "the unfavorable judgment of the paramedical profession remains" (*La Presse,* May 14, 1967).

It must be stressed that the shortage of cadres in general and technicians in particular is not wholly the result of traditional attitudes toward work. The increased demand for highly skilled workers has grown enormously as the country industrializes and as the government expands services to hitherto isolated regions. Furthermore, reluctance to enter some professions historically developed because of competition from European workers in those fields. And perhaps most important, the post-independence school system has too often failed to give young Tunisians the educational skills they need to work at technologically demanding jobs. Nevertheless, the nursing shortage, the problems of graduates from agricultural training centers, and the hesitation of artisans in Ksar Hillal to do factory work confirm that the traditional status hierarchy continues to be relevant in one way or another for many whom the state would like to see participate in modern economic ventures. As Demeerseman puts the matter, "the exorbitant pressure of human respect has, in practice, for a long time prevented the development of many useful enterprises. It was considered dishonorable to undertake certain kinds of human activity" (1957:189).

In spite of the problems they continue to pose, traditional attitudes toward work are giving way, even in outlying areas. The extension of the cash economy, an acquired taste for manufactured products, and the advent of the transistor radio have all had a devastating effect upon traditional norms. Many social scientists have studied the Tunisian countryside and all report a revolution underway. André Louis (1965) visited Troglodytes in the south and observed that traditional rhythms have been broken by so simple a thing as the availability of canned goods. Women now have more leisure time and men must somehow earn money to purchase what was previously made at home. Pierre Bardin (1965) examined a village in the northwest part of the country and found that the mechanization of agriculture has not only changed the economic life of the community, it has placed ancient social and spiritual values in doubt as well. Mustapha Filali (1966) noted similar disequilibria among recently sedentarized nomadic populations. And Jean Duvignaud (1970), working with sociology students from the University of Tunis, studied the impact of the school and the radio at Shebika, one of the most remote of the Tunisian oases. He discovered that, for the young at least, life is no longer oriented exclusively to local affairs. "Their personal center of gravity is shifted from the village to Tunis, the bright center of national life" (1970:233).

Government activities and programs have intensified greatly the attack upon traditional economic and professional norms. There are efforts to build factories in nonindustrialized parts of the country and programs designed to train cadres who will upgrade agricultural and professional standards. Public-works camps have also been established in many areas. They provide regular employment for those unable to find work and they produce certain needed civic improvements. But, most important, they help to institutionalize new attitudes, precipitating crises of traditional values. A Tunisian sociologist who studied camps in the central part of the country reports that they have contributed to a change in the outlook of the people of the steppe. Men and women "no longer find themselves in a *tete-à-tete* with God" (Attia 1966:31).

There are also urban programs designed to teach professional skills and reshape traditional attitudes toward work. There are, for example, many public-works camps in the cities. Another major government effort involves the operation of centers of professional and preprofessional training. There are twelve national centers of the former type and approximately eighty preprofessional centers. Students who graduate from middle school (three years plus primary school) are eligible for entrance into one of the centers of professional training, each of which specializes in a particular trade. Students who have received less middle-school education may apply to one of the preprofessional training establishments for special remedial work. Rather than emphasizing the acquisition of a particular set of technical skills, however, the stress at these institutions is on learning appropriate attitudes and values. As one of the directors of the program stated when asked about the preprofessional centers for women that were under his jurisdiction, "Our goal is to prepare a woman for work [by helping her] to acquire adequate mental attitudes. The trade she can acquire later" (*Faïza,* November-December, 1966).

Traditional notions about work are under ruthless attack. New conceptions of productivity, new criteria of wealth, and a new hierarchy of professional status are slowly working their way into the Tunisian national consciousness. But the rate of change is relative to the observer and the ability of traditional values to survive is sometimes phenomenal. Bardin expresses this almost poetically when he describes the inertia of tradition in the Tunisian countryside.

Attacked from all sides, rural society is putting up an extraordinary resistance to all invading forces, malevolent or benign, selfish and damaging or disinterested and constructive. . . . It loses a portion of its members who leave to swell the ranks of the urban proletariat; but it continues to survive with its way of life just about unchanged. The strength of this society is in its inexhaustible capacity for retreat and humility, for patience and self-resignation. An ancient alliance among men, soil and climate, a collection of beliefs, traditions and humble procedures, while tenacious and simple yet proven, have perpetuated a way of life that has its own originality and wisdom (1965:136).

Even the most hard-headed advocate of the new order must somewhere nurture a secret hope that this glorious harmony can be preserved. Of course, at the level of daily living, there is nothing poetic about poverty, illiteracy, and disease; and efforts to preserve ancient values that perpetuate these indignities are clearly intolerable. But those who labor in search of change also desire the survival of Tunisia's own originality and wisdom and, as we have seen, they are struggling to define the parameters of a moral order that will retain the best elements of a proud legacy while contributing to progress and prosperity. As always, then, the question is whether men of sincerity and dedication can find a way to preserve continuity in the midst of change, to pursue development without a loss of identity.

15

Cultural Attitudes in Changing Tunisia

This chapter presents findings from two public opinion surveys recently carried out in Tunisia. In 1965 a survey was conducted at the University of Tunis in order to determine student attitudes toward many of the cultural issues discussed in the preceding chapter. In 1967, a larger and more broadly based survey explored these same concerns. Respondents from Tunis and several smaller towns were asked their opinions about the appropriate balance of development concerns and identity concerns in the areas of language, religion, women's rights, child-rearing, and professional practices. In presenting these survey data, our principal concern is to compare the attitudes of Tunisians high in exposure to forces producing social change to those of Tunisians low in exposure to agents of change. The analysis will be based primarily upon data from the more heterogeneous 1967 survey. Later in the chapter, however, the views of the students will also be considered.

The forces producing change in developing societies are well known. Prominent among them are education, urbanization, industrialization, expanded opportunities for employment, the growth of transportation and communications facilities, and the elaboration by national political leaders of programs for development. The characteristics of individuals who are highly exposed to these and other agents of social change are similarly well known. These persons tend to be well-educated, to hold high-paying, high-status jobs, to be heavy consumers of information distributed through the mass media, to be active members of political organizations, in sum, to have high ratings on many indices of acculturation, social status, and involvement in public life.[1] By examining the

---

[1]The principal forces producing social change in developing nations are summarized in Chapters 1 and 17. Chapter 17 also describes in more detail the ways in which changing conditions affect individual life styles and psychological orientations.

attitudes of such individuals and by comparing their views to those of persons who are not highly exposed to agents of change —persons who have low ratings on these same indices of acculturation, social status, and involvement in public life—this chapter seeks to accomplish three specific objectives.

Most important in the present context is informing speculation about how cultural dilemmas may be ultimately resolved in Tunisia and about whether and how traditional values will be modified by changing conditions. In many areas, the country is caught between a desire to preserve its proud heritage and a desire for new models of thought and action. What kind of a cultural system can be expected to emerge? By contrasting the attitudes of men and women who participate extensively in the sectors of society experiencing rapid transformation with those of men and women who do not, it is possible to identify cultural correlates of social change. This in turn provides information with which to predict whether variations in the scope and intensity of development are likely to lead to expanded or reduced support for various normative orientations, information which will be used in the next chapter as a baseline for forecasting the future of Tunisia's traditional cultural system.

A second objective is to examine the homogeneity of the process by which attitudes and values change in a society like Tunisia. More specifically, the question is whether orientations toward a wide range of social and cultural issues are affected by changing conditions in the same manner, and as a result tend to change together, or whether various cultural attitudes respond in dissimilar ways to social and economic development. The answer to this question is of theoretical concern because it will indicate whether or not individuals in a developing society tend to develop an ideological framework that guides their response to a large number of issues and dilemmas. Findings from Tunisia in this regard may offer generalizable insights about the process of attitudinal change at the individual level. This area of inquiry is also of interest to those more directly concerned with Tunisia's cultural future. Information about the presence or absence of mechanisms integrating diverse cultural orientations will help to determine whether normative change in one area reinforces normative change in other areas. To ascertain whether cultural orientations appear as syndromes of values, or belief systems, intercorrelations among attitudes toward the cultural issues discussed in the preceding chapter will be examined. Then, to relate any syndromes that have been observed to changing conditions, the orientations of persons variously exposed to agents of social change will again be compared.

Survey data revealing the cultural attitudes of individuals high and low in exposure to agents of social change may also be used to accomplish a third objective, to expose to view the lines of consensus and cleavage surrounding questions of identity in Tunisia. This is important because it reveals something of the social and political dynamic process governing attempts to resolve cultural dilemmas. Knowledge of the attitudes of persons high and low in exposure to forces producing change, accompanied by knowledge of the relative status and influence of persons in each category, will indicate the locus and extent of present support for competing normative options. It will also shed light on patterns of alliance and confrontation that may emerge in future battles over cultural issues. In addition to reviewing attitudinal differences *between* persons high and low in exposure to agents of change, patterns of consensus and cleavage will be highlighted by considering in greater detail the substance of the attitudes of each category of individuals and by examining *within* each category the variation among individual attitudes.

MEASURING EXPOSURE TO AGENTS OF SOCIAL CHANGE

The 1967 survey collected data which may be used to pursue the objectives set forth above. To assure a heterogeneous and broadly based sample, education, income, and place of residence were employed as criteria of respondent selection. These variables, chosen because of their widely demonstrated importance in social change,[2] were crosstabulated in the manner shown in Table 15.1 and a minimum quota of 15 respondents was set for every combination having empirical referents. The table shows that 283 persons were actually sampled and presents their distribution across the categories of combined sample selection variables. In a few cases that do not concern us here, it was impossible to fill the quota. The Middle East War of June, 1967

[2]Social-science research has consistently identified these variables as indicators of modernization and social change, thus affirming their utility for selecting samples that seek to build in variance with respect to exposure to new social currents. Studies of social change by Lerner (1958), Doob (1960), Prothero (1961) and LeVine, Klein, and Owen (1967), to mention just a few, have used some or all of these variables as a basis for selecting respondents.

Table 15.1 Distribution of Respondents Along
Dimensions of Sample Stratification (N = 283)

Years of Education	Residents of Tunis				Residents of Smaller Towns[a]			
	16	12	9	6	16	12	9	6
Monthly income								
over $235	23	18	13					
$234–120	15	24	16	14		10	6	2
$119–70		17	30	17		6	10	7
under $70			13	17			10	15

[a]Residents of smaller towns include comparable samples from Grombalia, Mahdia, and Nefta. Each town has 10,000–20,000 inhabitants. Each is in a different part of the country.

forced cancellation of a number of projected interviews. In most cases, however, the minimum quota was easily surpassed. Thus, though all respondents are literate and regularly employed, similarity among them ends at this point. The sample includes persons of all ages and many occupations from Tunis and three towns in different parts of the country. Respondents range from university-trained executives of large corporations to agricultural workers in a Saharan oasis, representing most and possibly all of the diversity of the middle class and the working class.[3] Despite the fact that respondents have not been randomly selected,[4] the opinions of these persons should provide a satisfactory base for discerning trends that prevail generally in the sectors of society

[3]Most respondents were interviewed by the principal investigator in French. A few were sampled by means of a questionnaire (also in French) in order to test for interviewer-biasing effects. A comparison of matched subsets of the two groups showed no data distortion. For a fuller account see Tessler (1971a) and (1973b).

[4]Although the use of random-sampling procedures would enable us to generalize with greater confidence, this approach was rejected for a number of reasons. There are major obstacles to the use of random-sampling techniques in developing nations which it is often impossible to overcome, insufficient census data and the difficulty of locating and/or gaining access to respondents being among the most important. An additional consideration in the case of the Tunisian study was the fact that a random sample would have included far too many illiterate and rural respondents, such persons being neither sufficiently familiar with some of the issues under investigation nor sufficiently varied in level of exposure to agents of social change to permit the comparisons necessary for this analysis.

Table 15.2 Distribution of Respondents According to Levels of Exposure to Agents of Social Change

Years of Education	16	12	9	6
Monthly income	High in exposure			
over $235	23	18		
$234–120	15	34	N = 90	
			Low in exposure	
$119–70			40	24
under $70			23	32	N = 119

experiencing most of the growth and dislocation associated with social change.

To identify individuals who are high and low in exposure to agents of social change, respondents have been classified on the basis of education and income as shown in Table 15.2. Persons who have completed high school and who earn at least $120 a month are considered to be highly exposed to agents of social change.[5] Persons who have not completed high school and who earn less than $120 a month are considered to be low in exposure.[6] Education and income have been used to classify respondents not only because they are themselves indicative of levels of exposure to new social currents, but also because re-

[5] Dollar amounts are based on dollar-dinar exchange rates in the spring of 1973. At the time the survey was conducted, the value of the Tunisian dinar relative to the dollar was about 20 percent less.

[6] These ratings, of course, are not absolute. Respondents are classified as high in exposure to agents of social change and low in exposure to agents of social change in relation to other respondents in the sample. However, the groups may be viewed as roughly equivalent to the moderns and transitionals identified by Lerner (1958) and examined in many subsequent studies of social change. It should be noted that persons with high educational levels and low salaries and persons with low educational levels and high salaries have not been classified as either high or low in exposure to agents of social change. It was originally thought that these persons might be treated as an intermediate category for the purposes of the present analysis. However, subsequent analysis revealed that this would be inappropriate. For one thing, the two groups of respondents in this category differ substantially among themselves. Furthermore, rather than being moderately exposed to most agents of social change, each of these groups was high in exposure to some agents and low in exposure to others. It therefore seemed most appropriate to view persons with significantly different levels of education and income as having inconsistent rather

search in Africa and the Middle East has shown they covary with many other relevant indicators. In Nigeria, for example, an "inevitable correlation" was found between education, income, and many other criteria, with acculturation and social status (LeVine et al. 1967:224). Similarly, Doob concluded from a study of three African societies that there is a strong interrelationship among education, occupational status, place of residence, the claim of having a European friend, and much more (1960:49). Lerner identified the same "unified whole" in his study of the Middle East, discovering that political participation is also a part of the syndrome (1958:50–51). Levels of education and income thus covary with one another and with ratings on many other indices of acculturation, social status, and involvement in public life. As a result, respondents who have different levels of education and income may be presumed to vary in exposure to many different agents of social change.[7]

Before proceeding to a comparison of attitudes held by persons rated high and low in exposure to agents of social change, a brief digression is necessary to assure that classifications based on education and income do reflect accurately varying levels of exposure. The assumption that this is the case is based on findings from many studies carried out in many developing nations. However, by demonstrating that these findings are replicated in the Tunisian sample, rather than merely assuming that they are,

---

than intermediate status with respect to levels of exposure to new social currents and to exclude them from that part of the analysis dealing directly with correlates of social change. It should also be pointed out that persons with divergent levels of education and income were deliberately overrepresented in the sample in order to permit future research on the independent effects of acculturation and social status (see LeVine et al. 1967:224). Actually, societies like Tunisia possess relatively few such individuals since education and income tend to correlate strongly in developing nations.

[7]Had not the number of persons with divergent levels of education and income been overrepresented in the sample, it would probably have been sufficient to rate respondents on the basis of education alone, or income alone. This has been done in many studies, the rationale being that education and income correlate so strongly in developing nations that either one is a satisfactory indicator of the various personal attributes associated with differing levels of exposure to agents of social change (see Doob 1960, and more particularly LeVine et al. 1967). Indeed place of residence, the third variable used in the construction of the sample, was not included in the rating system because residents of Tunis were found to differ little from persons living in smaller towns when education and income were held constant (see Tessler 1969).

the suitability of the rating system can be demonstrated more conclusively. If classifications based on education and income do accurately reflect differing levels of exposure to agents of social change, the groups identified in Table 15.2 as high and low in exposure should differ with respect to a wide range of personal attributes. Because social change involves contact with other peoples and cultures, they should have different ratings on many indicators of acculturation. Because the professional and white-collar middle class is more buffeted by change than is the proletariat, they should also differ on various indicators of social class and social status. Finally, because official efforts to manage culture and promote development are important parts of the change process, agents of change being planned as well as unplanned, the political experiences of respondents classified on the basis of education and income should also be different. In all three cases, the groups do differ as expected.[8] Respondents classified as high in exposure to agents of change are more likely than those classified as low in exposure to agents of change to read a newspaper regularly, to have foreign friends, to have spent time abroad, to know English, to reside in apartments or villas rather than traditional Arab-style houses, to have professional or managerial occupations, to be active in political organizations, and to have high levels of political trust and political efficacy. Thus it is clear that groups formed on the basis of education and income do indeed differ in level of exposure to many social, economic, and political forces transforming Tunisia and other similar societies.

Variations in level of exposure to agents of social change are associated not only with degrees of acculturation, social status, and involvement in public life, but also with differences in personality and psychological orientation. Research in developing societies has shown that increased exposure to forces producing change is associated with higher levels of such qualities as self-esteem, intimacy with change, the ability to plan ahead, trust, other-directedness, and sociability (see, for example, Apter 1965; Inkeles 1962; Lerner 1958; Pye 1962; Sherrill 1969). The precise meaning of these terms varies according to the author, but the central thrust of a certain psychological style is clear. Social change is associated with rising levels of social and personal

[8]The data and analysis on which this discussion is based appear in Tessler (1971b). Some of the other findings reported in this chapter appear in the same article.

efficacy. These differences are also replicated in the Tunisian study. Respondents identified as high and low respectively in level of exposure to agents of social change have been compared on multi-indicator attitudinal scales measuring social efficacy and personal efficacy and have been found to differ to a statistically significant degree in both instances. This observation is of interest in part because it provides further evidence that respondents in the Tunisian sample have been appropriately classified. They differ in yet another of the ways that persons with varying levels of exposure to new social currents are known to differ. This observation is also of interest because it testifies to the increasingly self-conscious nature of social change. Although rising levels of urbanization, education, employment, and information consumption still involve a certain unplanned diffusion of what loosely passes for "Western" culture, the self-consciousness of the intellectual and the politician is beginning to characterize the man in the street. Growing numbers of individuals are acquiring an intimacy with change and a realization that nature can be controlled; and they are asking themselves, without official prodding, some hard questions about the future of ancient traditions. Thus, cultural management is no longer the concern of government alone and cultural change no longer takes place in an ideological vacuum.

In sum, using a combination of dichotomized education and income measures, it has been possible to identify groups of respondents that differ consistently and significantly with respect to a number of indices of acculturation, social status, involvement in public life, and efficacy. This confirms that the rating system accurately classifies respondents with respect to level of exposure to agents of social change. By comparing the attitudes and values of respondents in the two groups that have been formed, it will be possible to shed light on the substance, the process, and the cultural and political consequences of the attitudinal modifications produced by Tunisia's social revolution.

CULTURAL CORRELATES OF SOCIAL CHANGE

Tunisia faces essentially the same dilemma in the areas of language, religion, feminine equality, child-rearing, and professional practices. On the one hand, there is a need to modify traditional values in order to remove obstacles to growth and development. On the other hand, there is a need to retain traditional values in order to provide a meaningful basis for national and personal identification. By comparing the attitudes toward these cultural foci of individuals highly exposed to agents of social change and individuals with lower levels of exposure, it will be possible to determine whether and how traditional cultural values are being transformed by changing conditions. This information will shed light on the ways that Tunisia's cultural dilemmas may eventually be resolved and on the ways that the nation's collective socio-cultural identity may be affected by social change.

To measure individual preferences with respect to language, religion, feminine equality, child-rearing, and professional practices, items from the interview schedule have been formed into multi-indicator attitudinal scales.[9] The precise meaning of each scale is best conveyed by its constituent items, given in Appendix B (p. 299). Briefly, however, the five scales measure ordinal dimensions ranging respectively from Arabism to Francophonism in linguistic orientation, from conservatism to radicalism in religious orientation, from male dominance to feminine equality in views about women, from authoritarianism to permissiveness in views about child-rearing, and from low esteem to high esteem for the professional practices of a technologically oriented economic system.

Table 15.3 compares the ratings of Tunisians who are high and low in exposure to agents of social change on each of the five scaled distributions. Each distribution has been trichotomized to show attitudes more clearly and respondents have been classified as either inclined toward one of the poles of the scale or centrally located on the scale distribution. In Table 15.3, persons with different levels of exposure to agents of social change are shown to vary significantly in their attitudes and values with respect to four of the five cultural foci. Highly exposed respondents are more favorably inclined toward religious liberalism, feminine equality, permissiveness in child-rearing, and modern professional standards than are Tunisians with low levels of exposure. Only with

---

[9]All of the attitudinal scales were formed in the same way and assessed by means of a scalogram analysis. Coefficients of reproducibility are given along with scale items in Appendix B. In all cases, coefficients surpass the generally accepted .900 minimum level of confidence. For a discussion of the procedures used to minimize measurement error when constructing scale items, and for further evidence in support of the reliability and validity of scales ultimately generated, see Tessler (1973a).

Table 15.3 Levels of Exposure to Agents of Social Change and Attitudes Toward Selected Cultural Foci

Cultural Focus	High in Exposure (percent)	Low in Exposure (percent)	N	χ^2	P<
Linguistic-Cultural Orientation			200	.48	N.S.
(1) inclined toward Arabism (scale score 0–1)	28	24			
(2) centrally located on the scale (scale score 2–3)	50	53			
(3) inclined toward Francophonism (scale score 4–6)	22	23			
Religious Orientation			199	63.1	.001
(1) inclined toward religious conservatism (scale score 0–1)	7	47			
(2) centrally located on the scale (scale score 2–3)	33	42			
(3) inclined toward religious liberalism (scale score 4–6)	60	11			
Feminine Equality			193	10.5	.01
(1) inclined toward male dominance (scale score 0–1)	26	32			
(2) centrally located on the scale (scale score 2–3)	46	57			
(3) inclined toward feminine equality (scale score 4–6)	28	11			
Child-Rearing			204	47.7	.001
(1) inclined toward authoritarianism (scale score 0–2)	7	43			
(2) centrally located on the scale (scale score 3–4)	52	49			
(3) inclined toward permissiveness (scale score 5–6)	41	8			

Table 15.3 (*Continued*)

Cultural Focus	High in Exposure (percent)	Low in Exposure (percent)	N	χ^2	P<
Professional Life			196	7.7	.05
(1) inclined toward professional traditionalism (scale score 0–1)	7	20			
(2) centrally located on the scale (scale score 2–3)	66	63			
(3) disinclined toward professional traditionalism (scale score 4–6)	27	17			

respect to Arabism do the two groups display similar preferences. The findings about Arabism will be discussed presently, but the conclusion to be drawn from these findings generally is that Tunisians who differ in level of exposure to agents of social change have very different cultural preferences. In four important areas, they disagree about what is good and bad, right and wrong, desirable and undesirable. Thus, in Tunisia at least, there are indeed important cultural correlates of social change.

THE HOMOGENEITY OF THE PROCESS OF ATTITUDINAL CHANGE

Those who study developing societies seek to understand the process as well as the substance of attitudinal changes accompanying social transformation; and an examination of the interrelationship among cultural correlates of social change in Tunisia can add to knowledge in this area. In a very broad way, these attitudes vary together since individuals who are highly exposed to agents of social change reject tradition on each cultural question more fully than do Tunisians with low levels of exposure. However, it is possible, for example, that the respondents most inclined toward religious reform are centrally located on the feminine-equality scale or that those most inclined toward authoritarianism in child-rearing are centrally located or even inclined toward change on the professional-practice scale. In short, it is known only that attitudes and values vary together in a general fashion. To assess more completely the consistency of the process of attitudinal change, it is necessary to determine whether an individual's score on one scale can be used to predict his score on any or all of the remaining scales.

If all the scales strongly intercorrelate, it will be clear that most individuals possess a preference style involving a consistently favorable or unfavorable orientation toward a wide range of cultural traditions. This is what Tunisians would describe as an individual's *mentalité,* the mental set that guides his acquisition of social attitudes and behavior patterns. If the scales subdivide into identifiable and strongly interrelated clusters, we will know that some but not all attitudes vary together, individuals being consistently oriented toward either continuity or change in areas that are reasonably broad but which bear no relationship to views about the future of culture in other areas. Finally, if there is no significant interrelationship between any of the scales, it will be apparent that cultural attitudes develop on a piecemeal basis and are largely the product of idiosyncratic interests and needs.

Each of these possibilities has a certain plausibility and it is likely that there are some individuals who conform to each model.

Table 15.4 Spearman Rank-Order Correlation Coefficients and Associated z Ratios[a] for Five Cultural Attitude Scales

	Language Scale	Religion Scale	Feminine-Equality Scale	Child-Rearing Scale	Professional Practices Scale
Language Scale					
Religion Scale	.118 (1.94)				
Feminine-Equality Scale	.119 (1.90)	.333 (5.56)			
Child-Rearing Scale	.049 (.80)	.393 (6.89)	.377 (6.51)		
Professional Practices Scale	−.006 (−.09)	.260 (4.31)	.308 (5.23)	.261 (4.24)	

[a]The z ratios, given in parentheses, are used to assess the statistical significance of the coefficients (r_s); $z = r_s \sqrt{(N-2)/(1-r_s)^2}$. N varies from 248 to 266, depending upon the amount of missing data for each scale. Critical values of z for an N of this size are 1.96 at the .05 level, 2.57 at the .01 level, and 3.29 at the .001 level.

However, correlation analysis reveals a strong association between the measures of all four cultural foci significantly related to levels of exposure to new social currents. With respect to religion, child-rearing, women's rights, and professional practices, the rank-order correlation between every combination of scales taken two at a time is statistically significant well beyond the .001 level. This is shown in Table 15.4. Since respondents who have the least respect for traditional religious prescriptions tend to be the very same individuals who most strongly favor permissiveness in child-rearing, emancipation for women, and deviation from traditional professional standards, and since those who are opposed to one of these viewpoints tend to be opposed to each of the others, it appears that most individuals do possess a cohesive "outlook" or belief system. Attitudes form a kind of syndrome, suggesting that there is an intellectual unity underlying a person's approach to issues of continuity and change, identity and development.[10]

A somewhat different arrangement of the data may further illustrate these observations. This arrangement will also permit us to show that belief systems differ significantly as a function of exposure to agents of social change. On each of the four significantly interrelated scales—religion, child-rearing, feminine equality, and professional practices—respondents were categorized as either high or low depending on whether they were in the upper or the lower half of the scale distribution. Classifying respondents in this manner creates five quantitatively distinct and mutually exclusive categories. A respondent may be high on all four scales; he may be high on three of them and low on the remaining one; he may be high on two and low on two; he may be high on one and low on the remaining three; or he may be low on all four scales.

Not all of these five quantitatively different distributions are equally likely to occur. For example, on the basis of chance alone, few respondents are likely to be either high or low on all four scales. The frequency of each combination that is expected on the basis of chance alone is given by the formula:

---

[10]Intercorrelation matrices computed using only persons high in exposure to agents of social change and persons low in exposure to agents of social change reveal, for each subgroup, the same pattern of statistically significant relationships. Thus the existence of a cohesive belief system does not appear to vary as a function of exposure to changing conditions.

$$p(e = r) = \frac{N}{r}\, p^r\, (1 - p)^{N - r}$$

where $p =$ the probability of event e,
 $r =$ the number of times that event e is predicted to occur,
 $N =$ the number of cases or trials,
 $\frac{N}{r} =$ the number of possible combinations of N cases taken r at a time.

A comparison of the actual and expected frequency of each combination confirms the findings of Table 15.4. Two and one half times as many persons as expected are either high or low on all four scales. Less than half the number expected is high on two scales and low on two scales. The difference between the actual and the expected distribution is more systematically expressed by a chi square value of 93.2 (df $= 4$, P $< .001$), and this confirms again that there is a strong tendency for scores on these attitude scales to covary.

Since each of the four significantly interrelated attitude dimensions is associated with levels of exposure to agents of social change, it is to be expected that the belief system or attitude cluster they define also covaries with exposure levels. Table 15.5 shows this is indeed the case. Respondents who are high on all four attitude scales are almost always highly exposed to agents of social change. Respondents who are low on all four attitude scales, by contrast, almost all have low levels of exposure to agents of change. The differences between Tunisians high and low in exposure is only slightly less striking in other categories. Thus Table 15.5 summarizes the conclusion toward which the

Table 15.5 Levels of Exposure to Agents of Social Change and Clusters of Social Attitudes

Cluster of Scale Rankings	High in Exposure (percent)	Low in Exposure (percent)	N	χ^2	P<
High on all four scales	27	6			
High on three scales and low on one scale	32	17			
High on two scales and low on two scales	18	19			
High on one scale and low on three scales	22	33			
Low on all four scales	1	25	175	35.6	.001

data have consistently pointed. Normative orientations appear as a syndrome of attitudes, the content of which differs as a function of exposure to agents of social change. There is one outlook that is particularly characteristic of persons with high levels of exposure and another that is strongly associated with low levels of exposure. These attitudinal syndromes are important cultural correlates of social change, and, as the next chapter will attempt to show, they portend a significant transformation of Tunisia's traditional normative order during the next few decades.

CONSENSUS AND COLLECTIVE AMBIVALENCE

Tunisians with high levels of exposure to agents of social change are found primarily in the professional and white-collar urban middle class. These individuals are on the forefront of social change in all relevant respects, being the most participant elements of the nation in political, economic, and informational terms. Indeed they are sometimes considered prototypes of a new Tunisian citizen. Tunisians with low levels of exposure to agents of social change are members of the working class, the mass of literate and regularly employed individuals so often referred to as transitionals. These persons are not totally unaffected by changing conditions, but they are far less buffeted by them than are members of the nation's middle class. The discovery that these two segments of the population have different belief systems suggests a gradual redefinition of Tunisia's normative inner order as social and economic development continue. It also points to tension in the more immediate future as persons and classes with differing orientations confront one another. But the values of individuals who are high and low in exposure to agents of social change converge in some of the areas examined. Furthermore, in some of these areas there are important differences of opinion among persons with similar levels of exposure to new social currents. These patterns of consensus and collective ambivalence, as well as the cultural differences associated with exposure levels, must be examined in order to lay a foundation for the discussion in Chapter 16 of the future of Tunisia's traditional cultural system.

Views about Arabism and Francophonism most noticeably counterbalance tendencies thus far observed. For one thing, as shown in Table 15.3, the distribution of attitudes toward language is almost identical among respondents who differ in level of exposure to agents of social change. The highly exposed middle class neither rejects nor embraces Arabism more than the less-exposed working class. Furthermore, there is a marked preference for bilingualism among both groups of respondents. Two additional items from the interview schedule show this even more clearly. One asks whether high government officials should be expected to know French and the other asks whether they should be expected to read and write Arabic. Taken together, the two items show the linguistic standards set for national leaders and reveal again a preference for bilingualism. Nearly two-thirds of those queried consider French and Arabic to be equally important, some believing a knowledge of either language to be sufficient (evidenced by the fact that neither language is rated as essential) and others believing both languages should be known by aspirants for high political office. Moreover, there are only minor differences between the opinions of persons high and low in exposure to agents of social change.[11] Among each group, respondents who place importance on Arabic alone or on French alone are few in number compared to those who favor bilingualism.

Another opportunity to examine attitudes toward language is provided by the student survey conducted in 1965.[12] Ninety-six students at the University of Tunis were asked to rate the contemporary value of various cultural patterns on a scale from 0 through 10, and their ratings of languages indicate that support for bilingualism does not diminish appreciably as one moves from the broader middle class to the more élite sectors of society. The students were asked whether it is important "that every Arab be able to read classical Arabic" and whether it is important "that every Arab know a foreign language." Their responses indicate overwhelming agreement concerning the need to know both languages. Approximately 90 percent rate classical Arabic and a European language as equally important, and over four-fifths of these consider a knowledge of both languages to be essential.

[11]Though not statistically significant, there is some tendency for persons high in exposure to agents of social change to be more critical of bilingualism than other Tunisians. This is perhaps because of their greater awareness of the practical difficulties of an ambitious policy that aspires to teach children, many of whom have monolingual and illiterate parents, to read and write with ease in two languages. Nevertheless, these middle-class respondents still prefer linguistic parity much more frequently than either the dominance of French or the dominance of Arabic.

[12]For an account of this sample see Tessler (1969).

All of these fragments point to the same conclusion. There is widespread popular support for a cultural perspective that assigns an important place to both Arabism and Francophonism. The less exposed working class agrees that French should retain a significant place in Tunisia, though many of its members have only a limited command of that language. The more exposed middle class desires that Arabic also play a major role in public life, although many of its members work most productively in French. And university students, the nation's future élite, favor both increased Arabization and a maintenance of the importance of French. At all levels, then, preferences are overwhelmingly for a bilingual solution to the country's linguistic problems.

Attitudes toward language are not distributed in the same fashion as attitudes toward religion, the status of women, child-rearing, and professional life. But they indicate a concern for both development and identity among Tunisians high and low alike in exposure to changing conditions, and we must note that the juxtaposition of these concerns is not confined to the area of language. For example, with respect to each of the other cultural foci explored in these chapters, working-class Tunisians, who are low in exposure to agents of social change, are neither overwhelmingly nor unanimously opposed to cultural change. They favor retaining more traditional normative patterns than do their more exposed middle-class countrymen, but they are nonetheless opposed to many traditions and cognizant that some cultural change is in their interest. Table 15.6 identifies traditional norms that the great majority of Tunisians low in exposure to agents of social change find inappropriate. The table shows that almost 90 percent think it very important for a girl to go to high school, that about the same proportion believe a young man, rather than his parents, should choose his wife, that 83 percent consider the once-important profession of *meddab,* or Koranic school teacher, to be of little contemporary social value, and so forth. Table 15.7 identifies issues that pose the most difficult choices for Tunisians who are low in exposure to agents of social change. It presents responses to items about which these individuals are almost evenly divided in their views, reminding us that social change produces a *crise de conscience* at many levels of society and indicating that a large proportion of the working class actually desires to modify a rather substantial number of specific traditional codes. For example, 58 percent consider the profession of *mufti* to be relatively unimportant today, 42 percent disagree; 60

Table 15.6 Responses of Tunisians Low in Exposure to Agents of Social Change Indicating Widespread Opposition to Traditional Values

Item	Response Indicating Opposition to Traditional Values	Percent Opposing Traditional Values
(1.) Do you think it would be better if Tunisian children did not learn the French language at school?	No	95.8
(2.) Religion and modern life are not compatible.	Disagree	68.4
(3.) Do you think it is very important for Tunisian girls to go to high school?	Very important, as opposed to somewhat or a little	89.1
(4.) Do you think that it is acceptable for a Tunisian woman to work if she wishes to do so? Indicate which of the following occupations you feel it would be acceptable for her to have.	Woman may work as doctors	94.0
(5.) Children should not speak to their father unless he addresses them first.	Disagree	66.0
(6.) When Tunisian children choose their spouse, what do you think is the best way to make the choice? Indicate your opinion according to the following classification first for women and then for men.	A young man, rather than his parents, should select his spouse	89.0
(7.) Rank the following 10 professions according to their importance in the society.	The profession of *chouechi* (maker of traditional *chechia* caps) ranked sixth or below	94.8
(8.) Rank the following 10 professions according to their importance in the society.	The profession of *meddab* (Koranic school teacher) ranked sixth or below	82.8
(9.) A factory offered a job to a master craftsman. The craftsman would have made more money, but he refused the job, saying that work in a factory was not worthy of a master craftsman like himself. In your opinion, was he correct?	No	74.8

Table 15.7 Responses of Tunisians Low in Exposure
to Agents of Social Change Indicating Collective Ambivalence

Item	Response Indicating Opposition to Traditional Values	Percent Opposing Traditional Values
(1.) Do you think that it is regrettable that many Tunisians know the French language better than the Arabic language?	No	55.5
(2.) Do you think it is important today that wine be forbidden to Moslems?	No	39.8
(3.) Rank the following 10 professions according to their importance in the society.	The profession of *mufti* ranked sixth or below	58.6
(4.) Do you think that it is more important for a boy to go to school than it is for a girl?	No	43.5
(5.) Would you prefer that Tunisian boys and girls not be put in the same classes at school?	No	60.5
(6.) Do you think that it is acceptable for a Tunisian woman to work if she wishes to do so? Indicate which of the following occupations you feel it would be acceptable for her to have.	Women may take jobs involving authority over men	44.8
(7.) In general, it is the father of the family, rather than the mother, who should punish the children when they are naughty.	Disagree	47.1
(8.) In general, it is preferable that children do not play when their father is in the house.	Disagree	53.9
(9.) Rank the following 10 professions according to their importance in the society.	The profession of mechanic ranked fifth or above	51.7

percent believe that boys and girls should attend school together,
40 percent disagree; 54 percent consider it acceptable for children to play when their father is home, 46 percent feel children should be still when their father is in the house. Tables 15.6 and 15.7 leave no doubt that many and probably most working-class

Tunisians reject some outmoded beliefs and are in agreement with at least part of the nation's developmental effort.

Parallel findings emerge from a closer look at the attitudes of Tunisians who are high in exposure to agents of social change. These individuals are sensitive to concerns of identity—and not only in the area of language—just as their less-exposed countrymen are sensitive to concerns of development. Table 15.8 lists items these middle-class individuals almost always answer with statements supporting traditional values. Almost 80 percent, for example, deem it important that Tunisian children be taught the Koran; over 70 percent say it is unacceptable for a married woman to go out socially unless accompanied by her husband; and about two-thirds feel that traditional modes of production should not be completely revised, despite changing social and economic conditions. Though much more inclined to favor the modification of traditional values than Tunisians who are low in exposure to agents of social change, it is clear that there are identifiable limits to the psychological revolution currently underway. Highly exposed middle-class Tunisians articulate cultural preferences that leave room for time-honored traditions. They do not appear to favor the institutionalization of a normative system constructed entirely of new or nonindigenous values.

It is important to note the concern for identity and the desire to preserve time-honored traditions expressed by respondents highly exposed to agents of social change. But these observations are appropriate only if employed to place in perspective the statements about change already made. Tunisia is rapidly moving away from its traditional cultural base. The erosion of traditional beliefs is distinguishable among literate and regularly employed urban Tunisians at all levels and a profound psychological revolution is taking place among the middle class. Even if all of the old order is not to be swept away, Tunisia is rapidly departing from the normative system by which it was characterized as recently as 1956. Table 15.9 presents selected responses of persons highly exposed to agents of social change in order to show more clearly—and in a fashion less relative than Table 15.3—the dramatic rejection of much of traditional culture by the middle class. Eighty-six percent believe Tunisians should no longer practice the religion as did their fathers and grandfathers and, more specifically, almost three-fourths think a Moslem should not fast during Ramadan if to do so impairs the quality of his work. The call for change is equally pronounced in the areas of

Table 15.8 Responses of Tunisians High in Exposure to Agents of Social Change Indicating Widespread Support for Traditional Values

Item	Response Indicating Support for Traditional Values	Percent Supporting Traditional Values
(1.) Do you think it is acceptable that French become a more important language in Tunisia today than Arabic?	No	82.2
(2.) It is important Tunisian children study the Koran today.	Agree	78.7
(3.) Rank each of the following eight subjects according to their importance for Tunisian school children.	The history of the Moslem religion ranked fourth or above	63.1
(4.) Is it acceptable, in your opinion, for a married woman to go to a café with friends if her husband is not there?	No	71.6
(5.) Within a family, the father should have more authority than the mother.	Agree	65.6
(6.) Within a family, the mother should be more affectionate toward the children than the father.	Agree	63.1
(7.) When Tunisian children choose their spouse, what do you think is the best way to make the choice? Indicate your opinion according to the following classification first for women and then for men.	Parental consent required for a young man	70.0
(8.) Because of new social and economic needs, traditional methods of production should be transformed.	Less than completely	65.9
(9.) Rank the following 10 professions according to their importance in the society.	The profession of *moualam* (master craftsman) ranked fifth or above	68.3

Table 15.9 Responses of Tunisians High in Exposure to Agents of Social Change Indicating Widespread Opposition to Traditional Values

Item	Response Indicating Opposition to Traditional Values	Percent Opposing Traditional Values
(1.) Do you think that it would be better if Tunisian children did not learn the French language at school?	No	98.9
(2.) Do you think a Moslem should observe Ramadan even if this means that he will be less productive in his work?	No	74.4
(3.) Tunisian Moslems ought to practice their religion today in the same fashion that their fathers and grandfathers practiced it.	Disagree	86.5
(4.) Would you prefer that Tunisian boys and girls not be put in the same classes at school?	No	93.3
(5.) Do you think that it is acceptable for a Tunisian woman to work if she wishes to do so? Indicate which of the following occupations you feel it would be acceptable for her to have.	Women may work as doctors	94.4
(6.) Children should be encouraged to think for themselves even if this means that they occasionally disobey their parents.	Agree	80.0
(7.) Children should not speak to their father unless he addresses them first.	Disagree	94.4
(8.) Rank the following 10 professions according to their importance in the society.	The profession of *chouechi* (maker of traditional *chechia* caps) ranked sixth or below	92.1
(9.) A factory offered a job to a master craftsman. The craftsman would have made more money, but he refused the job saying that work in a factory was not worthy of a master craftsman like himself. In your opinion, was he correct?	No	83.1

women's rights, child-rearing and professional practices. Ninety-three percent believe boys and girls should go to school together; 80 percent believe children should be encouraged to think for themselves even if they sometimes disobey their parents; only 8 percent think the traditionally prestigious maker of *chechias* (a type of fez) is important today; and other examples are given in the table. This pervasive discontent with traditional beliefs of course characterizes university students, and their iconoclasm emerges particularly clearly in view of the scaled items to which they responded. Table 15.10 presents a selection of attitude distributions heavily skewed toward the change or nontraditional end of the scale. It shows that in each of the cultural areas examined, many long-standing traditions are widely felt to be inappropriate to modern life. University students, like highly exposed middle-class Tunisians more generally, ruthlessly denounce many of the values that have long defined the individual and the collective identity of most Tunisians.

Table 15.8 and Table 15.9 reveal the areas of consensus among Tunisians who are high in exposure to agents of social change. There is widespread criticism of traditional culture and overwhelming acceptance of the need for reform. Yet there is also general agreement that some ancient values must be preserved. There is, in short, a desire for a cultural system that will promote both development and identity. These joint and somewhat incompatible desires represent the familiar dilemma with which Tunisia and other Arab nations have long wrestled and, in view of its poignancy and intractable nature, it is to be expected that a collective ambivalence should characterize attitudes toward particularly difficult cultural issues. It is no easy task to translate a concern for both continuity and change into unambiguous views about the future of one's culture. Table 15.11 presents a list of items to which about half of the highly exposed middle-class Tunisians answer in one fashion and about half answer in the opposite fashion, suggesting the difficulty of articulating policy preferences when an intense desire for change must accommodate itself to an acknowledged need for continuity. In all four areas where cultural orientations are significantly related to levels of exposure to changing conditions, as well as in the area of language, there is much disagreement about which values should be part of the nation's normative future. For example, 45 percent of the highly exposed middle-class respondents feel that children should study more Arabic than French at school, 55 percent dis-

Table 15.10 Responses of University Students Indicating Widespread Opposition to Traditional Values

Is it necessary for contemporary Islam to take steps to modernize further?

	Not at all				Completely	
	0–1	2–3	4–6	7–8	9–10	
	11%	6%	19%	15%	49%	N = 96

Are the Islamic notions which have discouraged profit and risk-taking compatible with the modern world?

	Completely				Not at all	
	0–1	2–3	4–6	7–8	9–10	
	14%	10%	20%	14%	42%	N = 88

Education is as important for a girl as it is for a boy. Do you agree?

	Not at all				Completely	
	0–1	2–3	4–6	7–8	9–10	
	2%	3%	0%	4%	91%	N = 96

That boys and girls should have the same type of education is desirable. Do you agree?

	Not at all				Completely	
	0–1	2–3	4–6	7–8	9–10	
	10%	6%	10%	12%	62%	N = 96

In the family, authority should reside

	Completely in the father				In both parents equally	
	0–1	2–3	4–6	7–8	9–10	
	2%	5%	10%	12%	71%	N = 96

That children should play an important role in family affairs and family decisions is desirable. Do you agree?

	Not at all				Completely	
	0–1	2–3	4–6	7–8	9–10	
	8%	7%	25%	18%	42%	N = 94

New economic and social needs will require the transformation of traditional methods of production. Do you agree?

	Not at all				Completely	
	0–1	2–3	4–6	7–8	9–10	
	3%	3%	2%	8%	84%	N = 95

Between a public-school teacher and a *meddab* in a Koranic school, which occupation is more valuable?

	Meddab completely				Teacher completely	
	0–1	2–3	4–6	7–8	9–10	
	1%	0%	5%	13%	81%	N = 95

Table 15.11 Responses of Tunisians High in Exposure to Agents of Social Change Indicating Collective Ambivalence

Item	Response Indicating Opposition to Traditional Values	Percent Opposing Traditional Values
(1.) It would be preferable for Tunisian children to study more Arabic at school than French.	Disagree	55.1
(2.) Rank each of the following eight subjects according to their importance for Tunisian school children.	The history of the great Arab centuries ranked fifth or below	49.3
(3.) Moslems should not kill sheep at the festival of *al-Aïd*.	Agree	47.8
(4.) Religion and modern life are not compatible.	Disagree	55.2
(5.) Moslem women should have the same rights as Moslem men to marry foreigners.	Agree	54.4
(6.) Do you think that it is acceptable for a Tunisian woman to work if she wishes to do so? Indicate which of the following occupations you feel it would be acceptable for her to have.	Women may work as judges	58.4
(7.) The money that Tunisian women spend for make-up and for the hairdresser is wasted.	Disagree	56.6
(8.) A father should be both respected and loved by his children, but it is more important that he be respected.	Disagree	44.4
(9.) Do you think a child of twelve or thirteen should participate in important family discussions?	Yes	49.4

agree; 48 percent favor the traditional slaughter of a sheep during the festival of al-Aïd, 52 percent oppose this custom;[13] 54 percent

[13]An illustration of the unwanted consequences of the traditional observance of al-Aïd is presented in "Tunisie: la vie chere," *Jeune Afrique* (May 25, 1971). The article notes that the ritual slaughter of sheep has contributed greatly to the current domestic shortage of meat. In 1971, 300,000 beasts were killed in a single day, the number otherwise consumed in metropolitan Tunis during one full year.

believe Moslem women should not have the same rights as Moslem men to marry outside the faith, 46 percent do not concur; and other differences of opinion are equally clear.

Collective ambivalence is also striking among the students, as striking indeed as the desire for change revealed in Table 15.10. Table 15.12 lists items to which responses of the students form a bimodal and, in most cases, a polarized distribution. Attitudes on the much-debated Ramadan issue, for example, are quite divided and views about the importance of prayer and the significance of dietary laws are almost completely polarized. Similarly, there is no agreement about whether women should have the same rights as men to marry non-Moslems, about whether a married women should be able to go out socially unaccompanied by her husband, about whether fear should remain an important element in father-child relationships, about whether the director of a modern factory plays a more important social role than his traditional counterpart, the master craftsman or *moualam,* and so forth. In addition to these polarized distributions, some heavily skewed distributions indicating a nearly unanimous concern for continuity among the students are included in Table 15.12.

Differences of opinion among students and within the group of Tunisians high in exposure to agents of social change are particularly significant. They characterize groups of well-educated individuals who are in the forefront of the nation's effort to resolve pressing cultural issues. These persons are heavily exposed to official efforts to manage culture and thus are thoroughly familiar with the world beyond the traditional nexus. They are also high in efficacy and the desire to plan ahead. Therefore, it is a measure of the intensity of Tunisia's cultural dilemma that they have not evolved a common response to so many important questions. Though most agree that neither development nor identity is tenable as a total objective, they are unable to agree on an appropriate cultural mix. Though most believe the nation's normative future must be both receptive to change and consistent with values that define Tunisia's place in history, they disagree about the content of a value system that will meet these noble goals.

In conclusion, the trends indicated by the data are clear. A comparison of the belief systems of Tunisians high and low in exposure to agents of social change reveals the former to be consistently and significantly more favorably disposed toward Islamic reform, feminine equality, liberalism in child-rearing, and

Table 15.12 Responses of University Students
Indicating Collective Ambivalence

That a Moslem pray five times each day is important. Do you agree?

Completely				Not at all	
0–1	2–3	4–6	7–8	9–10	
29%	6%	20%	9%	36%	N = 94

Ramadan is compatible with the modern world. Do you agree?

Completely				Not at all	
0–1	2–3	4–6	7–8	9–10	
23%	10%	18%	12%	37%	N = 96

That a Moslem observe the dietary laws is important. Do you agree?

Completely				Not at all	
0–1	2–3	4–6	7–8	9–10	
25%	11%	27%	10%	27%	N = 94

Are the bases for the future evolution of Islam to be found in the Koran?

Completely				Not at all	
0–1	2–3	4–6	7–8	9–10	
44%	16%	27%	3%	10%	N = 92

Moslem women should have the same rights as Moslem men to marry non-Moslems. Do you agree?

Not at all				Completely	
0–1	2–3	4–6	7–8	9–10	
32%	8%	12%	7%	41%	N = 94

That a married woman go out in public unaccompanied by her husband is admissible. Do you agree?

Not at all				Completely	
0–1	2–3	4–6	7–8	9–10	
27%	7%	21%	20%	25%	N = 94

The father of a family should be both loved and feared, but that he is feared is more important. Do you agree?

Completely				Not at all	
0–1	2–3	4–6	7–8	9–10	
12%	8%	26%	16%	38%	N = 95

The youth of Tunisia today generally have too much freedom. Do you agree?

Completely				Not at all	
0–1	2–3	4–6	7–8	9–10	
6%	6%	39%	22%	27%	N = 95

Between the director of a modern factory and a traditional craftsman who is a master (*moualam*), which occupation is more valuable?

Craftsman completely				Director completely	
0–1	2–3	4–6	7–8	9–10	
7%	4%	38%	10%	41%	N = 95

Table 15.12 (*Continued*)

Between a skilled factory worker and a craftsman in a traditional corporation of artisans, which occupation is more valuable?

Craftsman completely				Worker completely	
0–1	2–3	4–6	7–8	9–10	
4%	2%	26%	19%	49%	N = 95

Is it regrettable that traditional garments are worn less today?

Completely				Not at all	
0–1	2–3	4–6	7–8	9–10	
20%	9%	26%	22%	23%	N = 95

Is traditional Arab cuisine compatible with modern living?

Completely				Not at all	
0–1	2–3	4–6	7–8	9–10	
23%	20%	24%	10%	23%	N = 94

Is it regrettable to spend much money on jewels when one marries?

Not at all				Completely	
0–1	2–3	4–6	7–8	9–10	
71%	7%	6%	4%	12%	N = 95

modern professional norms than the latter. An eagerness to rethink traditional values and to reject outmoded beliefs is thus an important consequence of exposure to social change. But highly exposed middle-class Tunisians couple their calls for change with expressions of a desire to preserve aspects of tradition and an unwillingness to assimilate Western standards completely and indiscriminantly. For these individuals, Tunisia's cultural system should be a carefully constructed balance of that which is old and that which is new, that which is foreign and that which is authentically Tunisian. However, it is one thing to suggest that many Tunisians desire a mix of standards that is hostile neither to development nor to identity; it is quite another to predict the composition of such a mix with respect to given cultural foci. Indeed the striking attitudinal variation within the groups of students and middle-class respondents indicates the nation itself has not yet evolved a broad consensus about the substance of the proposed new order. Nevertheless, Tunisia is struggling to define a cultural system that will reconcile antagonisms and harmonize differences. In a 1965 speech at the University of Tunis, Bourguiba characterized Tunisia's philosophy of modernization as one of "cultural rapprochement." He said that the emergent character of the country's "modern civilization" was faithful, dynamic, and open: "faithful because it respects permanent moral and spiritual values, dynamic because it is capable of evolving on an intellectual and scientific plane . . . , and open to a constructive dialogue among civilizations and cultures" (1965). In the next chapter, we shall consider the process by which Tunisia's "modern civilization" is likely to be forged during the next few decades and offer some tentative suggestions about the content of the cultural system that will probably take shape.

16

The Future of Tunisian Culture

On the one hand, there is intense political opposition to outmoded beliefs accompanied by growing individual exposure to new ideas and cultural patterns. On the other hand, there is official determination to preserve fundamental values coupled with reluctance on the part of many to give up hallowed traditions. What, then, is to be the future of Tunisia's traditional normative order? While this question cannot be answered definitively, data presented in the preceding chapter do enable us to determine the probable distribution of cultural preferences across social categories and thereby offer a baseline for gauging the rate and direction of cultural change. Five conclusions from the data should be kept in mind by those concerned with the future of traditional values in Tunisia.

A Psychological Revolution Is Taking Place

The belief systems of Tunisians who are high and low in exposure to agents of social change differ significantly. The former are more oriented toward religious reform, feminine emancipation, permissiveness in child-rearing, and modern professional practices than are the latter and this suggests that increasing levels of education, employment, and political mobilization are moving the society away from a strict adherence to traditional standards.

The government has devoted 25 to 30 percent of its annual budget to education since 1956. Forty percent of the population is below the age of 14, and 70 to 80 percent of the school-aged children are now in school. The economy is also expanding, as is the proportion of the population residing in urban centers. And most of the more than 1200 territorial and professional cells of the Destourian Socialist Party maintain impressive programs of mass mobilization and resocialization. Thus, there can be little doubt that the character of Tunisia's population is being radically altered. Already a large urban middle class of professional and white-collar workers has emerged and, as we have seen, these teachers, nurses, druggists, bureaucrats, managers, lawyers, and businessmen attach far less importance to traditional cultural patterns than do other Tunisians. These individuals are the most participant citizens in the nation. They are a class that serves as a model for development. Therefore, as their numbers grow, their cultural preferences and social conduct are bound to affect the normative standards of the entire country.

Opposition to Cultural Reform Will Remain for Some Time

Tunisians who are low in exposure to agents of social change tend to be conservative by the standards the government has set for its social revolution and in comparison with better-educated and more prosperous individuals. Our data do not indicate whether these working-class Tunisians are more liberal than the nation's peasants and urban slum dwellers who, for the present, still comprise the majority of the population. We would expect this to be the case, but such a view may overestimate the conservatism and homogeneity of these groups. In any event, working-class Tunisians are significantly more tradition-oriented than middle-class Tunisians who are higher in exposure to new social currents, and their views will be a powerful counterweight to the more liberal tendencies of the latter for some time to come.

The working class is probably the fastest growing sector of the nation. While the country is rapidly moving toward mass literacy, the number of students leaving school at the primary and intermediate levels is substantially higher than the number of students who complete high school and, possibly, go on to the university. Further, the number of high-paying and prestigious jobs is certainly not expanding as rapidly as the total number of jobs. Thus, factory workers, salesmen, secretaries, policemen, postmen, repairmen of radios, watches, and appliances, and clerks in the bureaucracies, banks, and business establishments—these working-class individuals, along with their families, will become an increasingly important element in changing Tunisia. Within a generation, Tunisian society will be less disjointed as the importance of the peasantry and even the élite shrinks with the growth of the proletariat and the middle class. But the first of these latter classes will outnumber the second for some time to come and its relative conservatism on cultural issues will certainly limit the locus and intensity of the psychological revolution that social reformers seek to bring about.

Tunisians Low in Exposure to Agents of Social Change Are Not Totally Opposed to Cultural Reform

Persons low in exposure to agents of social change are in no sense totally opposed to the reformist orientations of political leaders and many middle-class Tunisians. The fact that almost all value the French language indicates that the working class is hardly composed of pure traditionalists. Moreover, with respect to the other cultural foci that have been examined, a substantial number of respondents are located centrally or even inclined toward change on each scale distribution. In the areas of religion and child-rearing, about half of the working-class persons interviewed desire at least moderate reform. In the areas of women's rights and professional practices; the proportion of those who do not favor traditional standards actually exceeds two thirds. Admittedly data are in the form of cumulative scales that offer relative rather than absolute ratings. But responses to many individual items also reveal that persons low in exposure to agents of social change generally oppose at least some traditional values. Whether influenced by the regime's public-information campaigns or by other acculturative experiences, almost all working-class respondents agree that the ways of the past are not a wholly satisfactory normative base for contemporary Tunisia and its future.

There are also important differences of opinion among these Tunisians low in exposure to agents of change. This indicates that ambivalence over cultural questions characterizes subsets of the population as well as the nation as a whole. Even a relatively homogeneous group of working-class Tunisians has no agreed-upon response to the cultural dilemmas confronting the nation and this, in itself, testifies to their poignancy. Further, these disagreements suggest again that working-class Tunisians are not a monolith of opposition to the values that officials seek to institutionalize and that middle-class citizens desire to use as standards for their own conduct. Rather, the diversity of opinion among respondents with low exposure levels indicates that there probably exists in working-class Tunisia an element with whom social reformers and nation-builders can agree on cultural issues.

Tunisians High in Exposure to Agents of Social Change Recognize the Need for Preserving the Nation's Cultural Heritage

The government may desire more of a departure from tradition than some are willing to accept, but it does not want to transform society beyond recognition or to remake the nation in the image of Western societies. Fused always with its call for cultural change in the name of development is a call for continuity in the name of identity. Data presented in the last chapter reveal that most Tunisians who are highly exposed to new social currents, despite their conviction that traditional values are in need of reform, also desire to set limits for the modification of those values. For one thing, most of these individuals believe the Arabic language should play an important role in Tunisia. Most also wish to retain traditional values in other areas. For example, there is little enthusiasm for a total waning of Islamic sentiment. There are also generally accepted limits to feminine emancipation. In short, disagreements between persons high and low in exposure to agents of social change are not about whether Tunisia should remain attached to its Arabo-Moslem legacy, they are only about how strict an adherence to traditional norms the maintenance of that connection requires in view of the need to remove obstacles to progress.

Tunisians High in Exposure to Agents of Social Change Do Not Agree on How to Balance Concerns of Development and Identity

Among middle-class Tunisians, and among university students, there are important areas of normative agreement. Some of these concern the maintenance of traditional values; others involve support for cultural reform. But there are also important differences of opinion within the two groups. On many specific cultural issues, the views of these Tunisians who are high in exposure to agents of social change are almost completely polarized.

The lack of a consensus about the future of traditional culture is particularly striking among university students. Because university students constitute a small and relatively homogeneous upper stratum of the population, their lack of agreement dramatically highlights the difficulty of translating a desire for both development and identity into specific preferences and policies. But there is also an impressive list of cultural questions to which about half of the middle-class Tunisians from the larger sample respond in one fashion and about half respond in the opposite fashion. Thus, the view that persons who are highly exposed to forces producing social change have evolved a consensus about the kind of society they wish to construct, and the concomitant suggestion that the only major check upon their ability to lead the nation to a new cultural destiny is the relative conservatism of the lower classes, are quite unjustified. An equally serious obstacle is the inability of university students, and middle-class Tunisians more generally, to agree on the composition of a cultural system that will neither limit the nation's quest for development nor impair its effort to maintain identity.

THE DYNAMICS OF CULTURAL CONFLICT

The process by which Tunisia forges the normative base of its national character will be of major concern during the next generation and the preceding specific observations suggest two broader tendencies that are likely to shape the dynamics of that process. First, the distribution of attitudes and values across social categories is relatively even, suggesting an absence of the polarization that might have been expected in view of the sensitive nature of cultural issues. Since many persons low in exposure to agents of social change are at least moderately sympathetic to the reform of traditional culture, and since most persons high in exposure to agents of social change desire to maximize identity as well as development, it is clear that differences of opinion between middle-class and working-class Tunisians are differences of degree, not of kind.

The views of working-class Tunisians may act as an ideological counterweight to the more radical orientations of the middle class, but these views will not be lightly dismissed by the latter for they too desire to retain the flavor, if not always the letter, of traditional patterns. At the same time, the belief of middle-class individuals that a flexible approach to tradition is necessary will be taken seriously by much of the working class. Thus, there is reason to believe a constructive dialogue over cultural issues can take place and Tunisians with varying cultural preferences can move toward a reduction of differences in a way that will minimize tension. This is not to ignore the potential for serious conflict that still exists. Neither is it to set aside the determination of those whose self-interest demands either an acceleration or a slowing of the pace of change. It is simply to say that the prospects for orderly change are about as favorable as could be expected in view of the centrality of cultural issues and the abiding differences of opinion.[1]

---

[1]Less-optimistic projections are also possible. Growing economic disparities may strain relations between working-class and middle-class individuals, and in such an event the cultural differences between them could assume increased importance. Furthermore, there is already evidence that cultural differences between persons high and low in exposure to agents of social change are

The second conclusion to be drawn is that we are unable to discern the content of an unambiguous cultural model toward which the nation is likely to gravitate. Middle-class Tunisians—and, for that matter, university students—simply are not in agreement on many important cultural questions. Thus, in addition to asking whether continuing social and economic growth will eventually impose the views of this group upon the nation, we must ask how, if at all, disagreements that continue to characterize the Tunisians most exposed to that growth will be resolved. Certainly there is no clear and painless way to balance the concerns Tunisia must balance. Moreover, the issues at stake are not trivial. They have major ramifications for the nation as a whole, as well as for individuals, and it is significant that a cultural consensus is not evolving among the privileged upper echelons of society.

In the final analysis, the ability to have both continuity and change with respect to given traditional values probably depends on the ability of a people to alter the ideological process by which it understands the significance of its past and, more specifically, to distinguish between that which is traditional and that which is authentic. If identity and continuity must be viewed as requiring adherence to the wisdom of another age, then no matter how glorious the civilization to which that wisdom once gave rise, major reform is in fact precluded. In such a view, cultural dilemmas become zero-sum games; change can be had only at the expense of the traditional values that provide identity and continuity. But if identity can be defined in more dynamic terms, then continuity with the past can grow out of an ability to apply to the needs of the present the creative genius forged by a society's unique and particular history. This is the essence of substituting authenticity for tradition as a basis for continuity in the midst of change. "Cultural rapprochement" and "the harmonization of differences" are a part of the Tunisian vocation. Thus Tunisia can retain its historic posture and be true to its own identity by the very act of seeking development. As the President has said, Tunisia's history has taught her to be capable of evolving on an

---

greater today than they were a generation ago (see Tessler and Keppel n.d.). Nevertheless, for the present at least, cultural attitudes are not extremely polarized; and indeed recent research indicates that Tunisians experiencing cultural cross-pressures develop social and psychological mechanisms for reducing the tension produced by forced interaction with persons of different normative orientations (see Camilleri 1973).

intellectual and scientific plane and to be open to a constructive dialogue among civilizations and cultures.

The distinction between tradition and authenticity is disarmingly simple, as is Bourguiba's call to the nation to find its identity in historic dynamism. But such precepts are not easily translated into concrete policy and, in any event, they mask what is, for all its appeal, quite a radical view. The substance of more than a millennium cannot be disavowed with ease in the name of a larger reading of history. This is not to say that such a view is inappropriate, of course. Not only is it serviceable, it is also grounded in an accurate perception of the nation's past and it represents an ideological readjustment that some Tunisians have already made. But others, including many middle-class individuals and university students, take a more literal view of history; and, in theory at least, their contention that fidelity to the past requires the preservation of attitudes men have carried in their heads and permitted to shape their lives for centuries is probably the more defensible. For these Tunisians, no amount of intellectual gymnastics can change the fact that there will be no continuity without some retention of traditional standards, even if this means making do with a little less change than might be desired.

These competing approaches to the dilemmas of cultural change largely explain the lack of a consensus among middle-class Tunisians and among university students. The more radically oriented of these individuals articulate what may be the only satisfactory solution to a major cultural crisis. But there is a certain lack of realism in their philosophy; and in any event, it is not easily communicated. Those who do not possess the ability to define tradition in a special way cannot have their own thirst for identity and continuity sated by a tightly reasoned ideology. They cannot accept the premises from which it is deduced. For these individuals, compromise will remain the only possible key to solving cultural dilemmas and this will unite them with working-class Tunisians on, at the very least, the rules of the game. What emerges, in conclusion, then, is a three-cornered struggle between conservatives, moderates, and radicals wherein none is likely to prevail. Conservatives will insist upon minimal change, radicals will call for an ideological transformation to permit development to satisfy expressive needs, and moderates will continue to claim that neither orientation can give a reasonable modicum of both development and identity, and that temperance in both directions is the only solution. Out of this dynamic political competition will come Tunisia's new normative order and the resemblance it will bear to the substance of the past can only be guessed. But with views too diverse for any to predominate, and with orientations evenly enough divided to preclude total polarization, the center of gravity will most probably fall toward the kinds of compromises the moderates indicate their willingness to make. This is not a wholly satisfactory prospect for anyone—not even for the moderates who often take this position because they see no other—but it suggests that the coming generation will affect neither a total rejection nor a total preservation of traditional culture and will thus continue to debate many specific normative issues.

THE SHAPE OF THE FUTURE

Emerging trends can be projected in order to draw conclusions about the cultural foci examined in these chapters. The extent to which prognostications ultimately prove correct will of course depend upon the validity of our more general conclusions about the dynamics of cultural conflict.

Despite its distance from the heartland of Arab nationalism, and despite a self-concious awareness of the Mediterranean side of its personality, Tunisia identifies strongly with the interests of Arabism, at the center of which is the Arabic language. Moreover, the renaissance of Arabic desired by most Tunisians is being given a major boost by linguistic reforms and innovations throughout the Arab world. The classical tongue is slowly being forced to shed its sacred trappings and, sometimes almost in spite of itself, to accept its destiny as the linguistic base of modern and industrializing nations. Thus, it is not surprising that the resurgence of Arabic as a literate language is already apparent in Tunisia. Nevertheless, French remains the principal language of education, especially secondary education; and, with monumental increases in school enrollments, it is not only necessary to conclude that French is used more widely than ever, it must also be observed that the mass-élite gap is being bridged by a competent middle class that could not contribute fully to the development of the nation if nationalist desires for Arabization were to prevail. Therefore, the expanded use of Arabic notwithstanding, the nation is at present no less dependent on French than it was in 1956, when it gained independence and made Arabic the language of state.

Ultimately Tunisia will probably reserve for French a more limited role, perhaps akin to that played by English in Scandinavia. French will be an indispensable tool for many professions and a language that students are taught from the earliest grades; but it will no longer be a major vehicle for the conduct of affairs within the nation. It is also possible that the Arabs will eventually develop the intellectual base necessary to make their language as self-sufficient as French, or German, or Japanese. After all, the Arabic-speaking world numbers more than 100 million. But even the more immediate of these prospects will not be realized until literate Tunisians find it easier to work in Arabic than in French and this, even by optimistic assessments, is at least a genera-tion away. In the meantime, few Tunisians appear unhappy about the continuing importance of French. Bilingualism is what most people claim they prefer.

While the future seems to portend the gradual resurgence of the Arabic language, there will probably be a steady transforma-tion if not an outright decline of Tunisian Islam. Islam and Arabic have long been the bastions of civilization in the Arab world, but until recently the language was the servant of the religion. Lines of social and political solidarity were essentially those set down in the Koran and the significance of Arabic lay in its sacred qual-ities and its collection of intellectual and literary treasures ac-cumulated during centuries of Islamic grandeur. However, for the last seventy-five years, the relationship between language and religion has been changing. Modern Arab nationalism is rapidly replacing classical Moslem solidarity; and this nationalism is based primarily on language and has made of Islam a servant.

Islam of course remains important in Tunisia. It is officially enshrined as the religion of state and its centrality in Tunisia's postcolonial cultural renaissance is regularly expressed by public officials. Moreover, as we have seen, not even middle-class Tunisians or university students desire to modify the religion com-pletely. But, again, the role for Islam that is emerging in contem-porary Tunisia is not that envisioned by the Koran or advocated by its traditional guardians. Islam is no longer the fountain-head from which flows the wisdom or the inspiration needed to manage human relations effectively. It is rather a plank in the nationalist platform aimed at combating foreign domination and providing dignity to an emergent people seeking pride in its own accomplishments.

Certainly one should not announce the passing of traditional

Islam in too cavalier a fashion. The stubborn and persistent resistance which met Bourguiba's Ramadan campaign suggests that many oppose the cooptation of Islam by modernists and nationalists. But the controversy over Ramadan should not obscure the other reforms that have been quietly consolidated. And, perhaps more important, literate and regularly employed Tunisians at all levels are predisposed to accept some religious reform, and high-school graduates and university students support most, if not all, official attempts to "revitalize" Moslem values. In short, with the consolidation of political gains and a continuing revolution in education, one can only conclude that traditional Islam will sink into even greater disarray and the modernist's conception of a dynamic and secular Islam will gain support. Nevertheless, it is unlikely that the religion will be transformed beyond total recognition or that Tunisia will embrace a purely secular national ethic. Reformers are not dedicated to an eradication of religion from public life and many who support them believe that Islam will be of little value in the quest for dignity unless it retains at least some of its sacred qualities.

Tunisian leaders are justifiably proud of their efforts to change the traditional status of women. Those familiar with other Arab countries are often surprised to see substantial numbers of well-dressed Arab women on the streets of Tunis and other major cities or to see men and women sitting together in coffee houses and working together in business establishments. In only a few other Arab states do women have the social and professional liberties of their Tunisian sisters. Government reforms cannot, of course, take all the credit. Radio, television, and the cinema familiarize Tunisians with life styles quite different than those they have traditionally known. And education is obviously a crucial variable. But these things too can be controlled, and even a casual visit to one of the more conservative Arab states will indicate that the erosion of ancient values can sometimes be a slow affair. Tunisia is not the only nation in the Arab world where the role of women is changing rapidly, but it is in the forefront of the feminist revolution.

Despite the cosmopolitan appearance of urban Tunisia, and despite impressive statistics about the number of women attending school, a core of resistance to feminine equality lies behind what is sometimes only a façade of liberalism. Relatively few persons favor the complete equality of men and women and even university students have some important reservations about a true feminist revolution. For example, most Tunisians at all levels continue to believe that a married woman should not go out socially unless accompanied by her husband. However, while the ranks of avid women's liberationists are not being rapidly swollen, the ranks of staunch traditionalists appear to be shrinking and here is the importance of Tunisia's experience in the battle for women's rights. Within the modernizing sectors of society, among that great and growing mass of literate and regularly employed Tunisians, almost everyone favors at least a moderate revision of traditional codes governing the status of women. The need for a woman to be well-educated is widely accepted. There is also general agreement that a woman may take a job.

Many Tunisians find traditional patterns of male-dominance out of date. But most also find a total revision of the status of women rather unsavory. Thus, despite the differences between persons with high and low levels of exposure to agents of social change, we must conclude that moderate quantities of change are what most people want. As a result, the coming generation will probably witness a steady diminution of the abuse traditionally heaped upon women and the disappearance of the veil, a major symbol of that abuse. But there will remain some broadly agreed-upon limits for change and those who go beyond them will face, for some time, the scorn of their elders and many of their peers.

The distribution of attitudes toward child-rearing and family organization illustrates particularly clearly the general trends that have been noted. The middle class appears to be divided about evenly between those who completely oppose traditional standards and those who desire moderate reform. The working class is also divided. About half its members prefer little or no change in the area of child-rearing. Most of the rest agree with more moderate middle-class Tunisians. Thus, once again, a cultural dialectic appears to be at work. Radically oriented individuals will attempt to pull the country toward what they view as a necessary revision of traditional codes while conservative elements will try to hold back the tides of change in the name of fidelity to time-honored values. Moreover, each side is in possession of resources and allies. The peasantry, though generally apolitical, provides a reservoir of support for the conservatives by virtue of its traditional life style and normative code. Radicals will be aided by their relatively élite position in society. They are often able to influence resocialization activities of the Party and/or shape the content of information transmitted by the schools and the media.

So, at least in the short run, conservatives and radicals will probably fight one another to a stalemate, leaving the center of gravity to the moderates, whose ranks are already large and can be expected to grow.

It seems safe to predict that customs like parentally arranged marriages and children living in fear of their father will surely pass from the Tunisian scene, although they may remain common in certain sectors for a few more years. Similarly, it is reasonable to assert that the independence enjoyed by youth in the West and the spectacle of fathers cavorting with their children will be rare in Tunisia for the foreseeable future. In short, neither the classical authoritarian patriarchy with its strict hierarchy of age nor the complete egalitarianism advocated by some is likely to secure an unambiguous hold on Tunisia during the next generation. Examples of the former will still be found and, though fewer in number, examples of the latter will also be visible. But this co-existence of old and new will most likely attract others to a more moderate and synthetic orientation. Fifteen years after independence, after the passage of a sweeping new Personal Status Code and after mass literacy has been largely achieved, traditional patterns of child-rearing and family organization are indeed giving way. However, most defectors claim to prefer moderate change to the adoption of highly permissive standards.

It is probably in the area of professional life that traditional standards are passing most dramatically. Almost no middle-class respondents in our sample seriously desire to preserve traditional codes about work and professional status and, more surprisingly, only a handful of working-class individuals are inclined toward traditionalism in this area. These tendencies may be exaggerated a bit by the nature of items used to construct the professional-practices scale. But responses to specific questions indicate that they are generally accurate. Literate and regularly employed Tunisians are virtually unanimous in the belief that new social and economic needs require, at the very least, a moderate transformation of traditional attitudes toward work.

The waning of support for traditional standards does not mean that a radical transformation of professional norms is desired by many. Between a fourth and a third of the Tunisians interviewed do feel that most of the old order must be swept away. They believe traditional modes of production must be completely revised. They have little respect for traditional crafts which, until recently, were highly prestigious. And, moving from production to consumption, they claim to prefer European styles in food and clothing to their traditional Tunisian counterparts. But most middle- and lower-middle-class Tunisians do not share this ruthless iconoclasm. Indeed, even a majority of university students feel that a total revolution in the professional domain is not desirable. Again, however, most Tunisians are willing to modify traditional norms about work and professional status that hinder development. They are simply eager to distinguish between areas where change is essential and areas where traditional practices can be maintained.

In the area of professional practices, as with each of the other cultural foci examined, we have observed a desire to balance continuity and change, to sweep aside obstacles to development and well-being without transforming society beyond recognition. This desire has been consistently articulated by Tunisian leaders and we find from our analysis that it is consistent with the wishes of most of the populace. There are, of course, differences of opinion about the kind of cultural mix that will best serve the needs of the nation. But it appears that only a handful oppose all change and that equally few favor the wholesale rejection of traditional standards. Thus, we are led to conclude that, in a generation or two, Tunisia will possess something quite different than what has traditionally been viewed as Arab culture, but that its normative system will nonetheless be easily distinguishable from social and cultural orders in the Western world.

POSTCOLONIAL NATIONALISM

Few educated individuals oppose change, despite the fact that it necessitates personal adjustments that at least some are unable to make. The possibility of controlling nature and achieving a better life is becoming understood by the masses in nations like Tunisia and it has led to a growing realization that traditional cultural patterns often impede progress. Thus, for reason of both individual gain and national prestige, the citizens of developing nations are being drawn to a rational and pragmatic policy of dismantling prejudices and outmoded beliefs. However, neither personal satisfaction nor national pride is provided by material advances alone, and a romantic nationalism directed toward more expressive needs is also strong in Tunisia and other newly independent nations. A concern for identity and continuity has been articulated by intellectuals and public officials in many lands.

President Leopold Sedar Senghor of Senegal has spoken of the need to assimilate European culture without being assimilated by it. His writings and poetry have given renewed vigor to the concept of *négritude* as an expression of those unique black African qualities that must survive as Africa industrializes. Similarly, a group of intellectuals in the Congo (Zaïre) issued a proclamation shortly before the independence of their country. They asserted their intention to be civilized Congolese, not dark-skinned Europeans. These ideas, examples of which could easily be multiplied, express feelings similar to those at the root of Tunisian nationalism.

This romantic strain of nationalism may partly reflect a lingering desire to disprove, at least to oneself, colonial doctrines about the inferiority of indigenous culture. After all, how can a people tear down the very institutions and moral codes in whose name it rejected colonialism? How can it now admit that the Europeans were right, that the noble tradition in which it took such pride is indeed a cause of stagnation and misery. The desire to limit change may also reflect an attempt to minimize dislocations produced by the uneven penetration into society of agents of change and mobilization. If the cultural gap between classes and generations were to grow too large, might not the fabric of the nation abruptly tear? However, to the extent that these factors explain the presence of a concern for identity, it is probable that the phenomenon will have but a limited course to run. As vivid memories of colonialism have begun to fade with independence, so will the sense of humiliation that once made abstract notions of dignity so important also pass. Similarly, social cleavages that make the nation a tenuous affair are likely to wane as the nation moves from a traditional to a modern political culture. In Tunisia at least, the mass-élite gap is being rapidly plugged and cultural pluralism poses no problems. Thus, after a newly independent nation has had a few decades to grow, the need for a self-image rooted in a proud past may be far less intense. The conditions which lead even the most prosperous and well-educated citizens of nations like Tunisia to a preoccupation with tradition in the 1960s and 1970s may no longer be present in the 1980s and 1990s.

All of the above notwithstanding, the forces that make a people cling to tradition and reject assimilation into a universal culture seem unlikely to prove quite so transient. For one thing, there is a natural and timeless tendency to retain age-old ways simply because they are familiar and comfortable. And if one is, in fact, among the heirs to a high culture of classical brilliance, so much more persistent will be that tendency. It is also possible that contemporary efforts to reshape normative traditions for the dual objectives of development and identity will be successful and that the civilization now being forged will be well suited to the needs of future generations. Should this occur, the possibility of managing culture will no longer pose dilemmas to an ambivalent nation. There will be no price to be paid for concerns of identity. Finally, it is conceivable that the meaning of development may be rethought more generally. The old response of the colonized to his oppressor—that dignity and honor require more than efficiency and growth—may become the watchword of an age that decides some problems cannot be solved by technology. Indeed, should this occur, developed nations might even turn their attention to the non-Western experience in an attempt to learn to satisfy these less-material needs. In any event, a decade and a half after independence in Tunisia, a romantic strain of nationalism remains almost as strong as the desire for social and economic development. Thus, Tunisia continues to grope for a middle ground between the assimilation and the rejection of Western and supposedly universal values, to search for a way to preserve its traditions without limiting its capacity to acquire the personal liberties and material advantages of the twentieth century.

Appendix B Items Used to Form Scales Measuring Attitudes Toward Language, Religion, the Status of Women, Child-Rearing, and Professional Practices

Item	Response Indicating Preference for Cultural Change
Cultural-Linguistic Orientation: Coefficient of Reproducibility = .913	
(1.) Do you think it is regrettable many Tunisians know the French language better than the Arabic language?	No
(2.) It would be preferable for Tunisian children to study more Arabic at school than French.	Disagree
(3.) Do you think it is acceptable that French become a more important language in Tunisia than Arabic?	Yes

Item	Response Indicating Preference for Cultural Change
(4.) Rank the following 8 subjects according to their importance for Tunisian school-children.[a]	Arab history not ranked first or second.
(5.) Rank the following 8 subjects according to their importance for Tunisian school-children.	European history ranked first or second.
(6.) Rank the following 8 subjects according to their importance for Tunisian school-children.	French history ranked first or second.

Religious Orientation: Coefficient of Reproducibility = .915

	Agree
(1.) Moslems should not kill sheep for the festival of *al-Aïd.*	
(2.) Moslem women should have the same rights as Moslem men to marry foreigners.	Agree
(3.) Do you think a Moslem should observe Ramadan even if this means he will be less productive in his work?	No
(4.) It is important Tunisian children study the Koran today.	Disagree
(5.) Tunisian Moslems ought to practice their religion today in the same fashion their fathers and grandfathers practiced it.	Disagree
(6.) Rank the following 8 subjects according to their importance for Tunisian school-children.	The history of the Moslem religion not ranked first.

Views About Women: Coefficient of Reproducibility = .910

(1.) Do you think it is important for Tunisian girls to go to high school?	Very important, as opposed to somewhat or a little important.
(2.) Do you think schooling is more important for a boy than for a girl?	No
(3.) Within a family, the father should have more authority than the mother.	Disagree
(4.) The money that Tunisian women spend for make-up and the hairdresser is wasted.	Disagree
(5.) Is it acceptable, in your opinion, for a married woman to go to a café with friends if her husband is not there?	Yes

Item	Response Indicating Preference for Cultural Change
(6.) When Tunisian children choose their spouses, what do you think is the best way to make the choice? Indicate your opinion first for a young woman and then for a young man.[b]	Boys and girls accorded the same degree of liberty.

Authoritarianism-Permissiveness in Child-Rearing: Coefficient of Reproducibility = .907

(1.) Children should be encouraged to think for themselves, even if this means they occasionally disobey their parents.	Agree
(2.) A father should not play with his children too much.	Disagree
(3.) A father should be both respected and loved by his children, but it is more important that he be respected.	Disagree
(4.) Children should not speak to their fathers unless he addresses them first.	Disagree
(5.) Within a family, the mother should be more affectionate toward the children than the father.	Disagree
(6.) When Tunisian children choose their spouses, what do you think is the best way to make the choice? Indicate your opinion first for a young woman and then for a young man.	A young man, rather than his parents, should select his spouse.

Economic-Professional Orientation: Coefficient of Reproducibility = .906

(1.) Do you think that it is acceptable for a Tunisian woman to work if she wishes to do so?	It is acceptable for women to take jobs involving authority over men.
(2.) Because of new social and economic needs, traditional methods of production should be transformed.	Completely, as opposed to much, moderately, little, or not at all.
(3.) Rank the following 10 professions according to their importance in the society.[c]	The profession of mechanic ranked fifth or above.
(4.) Rank the following 10 professions according to their importance in the society.	The profession of teacher ranked first.
(5.) A factory job is offered to a master craftsman. The craftsman would have made more money there but he refused the job	

Appendix B *(Continued)*

Item	Response Indicating Preference for Cultural Change
saying that factory work was beneath the dignity of a master like himself. In your opinion, was he correct?	No
(6.) If you were to win five hundred dinars in the national lottery, what would you do with the money?	Some or all of the money would be saved.

[a]The 8 subjects are the history of tropical Africa, modern Tunisia, France, the socialist countries, the Arab countries, the Moslem religion, Europe, and the great Arab centuries.

[b]The following 4 choices were offered: the child chooses without parental consent being necessary; the child chooses with parental consent being necessary; the parents choose with the consent of the child being necessary; the parents choose without the consent of the child being necessary.

[c]The 10 professions are judge of a court of appeals, *moualam* (master craftsman in a traditional industry), *mufti,* primary-school teacher, mechanic, *imam,* section head in a factory, *meddab* (Koranic school teacher), *chouechi* (maker of traditional *chechia* caps), and minister in the government.

PART FIVE

Conclusions

17

Tradition and Identity
in Changing Africa

THE CONTEXT OF SOCIAL CHANGE IN AFRICA

The environments in which most Africans live have been under-going radical transformation in recent years. Most Africans con-tinue to reside in rural areas, but the traditional isolation of the African hinterland is becoming a thing of the past. An expanding transportation and communications network carries people and ideas from city to country and country to city in a continual cycle of action and reaction. Out from the urban areas come teachers, development planners, agricultural experts, and political or-ganizers—all of them seeking to integrate the periphery into the main economic and psychological circuits of the nation. The elaborate developmental strategies of nations like Tanzania, Nigeria, and Tunisia illustrate these processes particularly well; but even in countries with more laissez-faire development orienta-tions, new technology and calls for innovation radiate from the cities to the countryside. Yet there is movement from the African countryside to the city as well. To the urban areas come men in search of employment. These labor migrations are, however, usually temporary or seasonal. Many workers maintain house-holds both in the city and in their place of origin, thus operating in a social network that stretches from village to town and back again. Even agriculture itself is changing. Though mechanized farming is still rare, a scientific agricultural revolution stands in the wings waiting to be called on stage.

The social environments of Africa's urban residents are also undergoing rapid change. In numbers alone the magnitude of urban growth is staggering. Lagos, for example, increased its population from 230,000 to 675,000 between 1950 and 1962. During approximately the same period, the population of Dakar, Accra, and Bamako doubled, tripled, and quadrupled respectively. But changes in the quality of urban life are perhaps even more dramatic. Cities predating colonialism are swollen by *sabon gari,* "new towns" for strangers, where Africans of various geographic and ethnic origins have come to live and work. Even more important as focal points of Africa's urban future are new cities such as Lagos, Dakar, and Nairobi. These, along with older urban centers such as Tunis and Ibadan, pulse with the dynamism of a modern and changing Africa. Their vigor derives not only from the mixing of cultures, but also from an accumulation of the technological and financial resource base out of which the instruments of Africa's accelerating and increasingly institutionalized social development are emerging: industry, schools, and communications media.

The response of individuals can be observed in many domains. Traditional life styles are changing, reflecting the exigencies of new social environments. People are more mobile, more tied to clock and calendar, and plans for the future are longer-range. Perhaps the most significant facet of this complex arena of change comes from wage earning capabilities. Often wages are exploitative, but regardless of amount or fairness, their impact is always immediate and deep. Bridewealth payments soar, relationships of dependence are often severed, and manufactured goods replace the hand-crafted products of the home and the local artisan. The individualization of economic decisions increases too. No longer, for example, are there plans for planting and harvesting to be made by extended families. Individual wage earners move in and out of the labor force, and to and from the cities and factories with an independence unknown amongst those who work the land. But even for the farmer, the picture has changed. Now it is "agribusiness" with all this implies for capitalization, futures trading, world markets, producing a crop that is of export quality, and so on. Agricultural workers are now more likely to be wage-earners than kinsmen; land is more likely to be purchased or rented than allocated through kinship or community networks; and plans for crops are more likely to be made in terms of world market conditions, national development plans, and profit margins than in terms of social obligations and perspectives of the local nexus. For the professional and managerial classes emerging in the cities, the range of concerns has increased as much, if not more. Contracts, lawyers, banks, development agencies, international contacts, wage-bargaining, strikes, retirement plans, production quotas, wage incentives, and much more combine to give the daily routine of the African business-man a much different rhythm, a much different style.

Structural changes in the societies of Africa have produced dramatic change in the social as well as the economic life styles of many people. Residence, for example, is geared more and more to the nuclear family, especially in urban settings, with neighbors who share more in terms of social class than gene-alogy. The number and spacing of children, as well as their rela-tionships to their parents, are changing too, due to the advent of new methods of birth control, the viability of long-range planning, and to shifts in the role of women. A key facet of this changing social setting is the increased opportunity for political participa-tion. Nationally oriented political parties seek, and in some cases demand, the active involvement of the individual. So too do labor unions, youth groups, and women's associations. In these and other similar contexts, people are working together on the basis of shared ideas and goals rather than shared village or kinship. It also means they are viewing a wider range of problems as being relevant in personal ways and as demanding of both attention and action.

There are psychological as well as behavioral consequences for individuals caught up in the process of social change. Educa-tion, exposure to urban life, consumption of information trans-mitted through the new communications media, and other ex-periences available only recently are associated with rising levels of self-esteem, intimacy with change, abilities to play alternative roles, desires to plan ahead, and feelings of personal and social efficacy. However, to say that these types of changes in per-sonality and mental state are consequences of social change is incomplete if not inaccurate. As often as not, they are the qualities possessed by men and women who decide to go to school, to leave the village, or to acquire a radio. Thus, they are stimuli as well as responses to changes at the societal level; they are vital components in the cycle of interaction between individuals and their society out of which comes the transformation of both.

The personality of the individual experiencing social change is increasingly adoptive; the individual himself is more and better able to comprehend and identify with previously unfamiliar cir-cumstances; and the range of his concerns is steadily growing. Indeed, though to varying degrees, this is true of persons in-habiting societies differing greatly in levels of complexity. In rural Tanzania, migrant workers are oriented to the urban areas of the nation, not just to the farms and villages of their homeland. Students in Bornu, similarly, think of the future of Nigeria and conceive of their region in the context of the nation as a whole. The middle and working classes in Tunisia's urban centers have equally broad or even broader horizons. Africa, the Middle East, Asia, Europe—all are frames of reference from which these individuals receive intellectual and emotional stimuli. The desire and ability to make long-range plans, to choose among competing alternatives, and to prepare for the future, go hand in hand with expanding horizons. So too does what some call the spirit of science, an incremental trial-and-error approach to life where traditions are judged to be neither immutable nor necessarily desirable. Alternatives are weighed and tested, perhaps to be rejected, perhaps to be accepted in place of familiar and long-standing patterns. All of this leads to new visions of the relationship between people and the rest of nature and an expectation that the future will be shaped as much by men's conscious decisions as by the inevitable continuation of ancient customs.

The psychological integration of the individual into the world at large is almost certainly a positive aspect of social change, but there are also less fortunate psychological consequences of residing in a rapidly changing social environment. New demands sometimes increase more rapidly than do the individual's ability to cope with them. In such cases, when men must adjust to a world they do not fully comprehend, psychological pressures can produce frustration and tension. Urbanization and industrialization can bring about not only greater independence and personal efficacy, but also a sense of anomie, isolation, and social fragmentation. And the range of malevolent forces in an individual's world may well increase with exposure to an unending flow of news about world tensions and disasters.

While changes in life styles and in accompanying psychological orientations introduced by social change are diverse, when taken as a whole, there are striking similarities in some domains between the value patterns emerging in what are otherwise very different kinds of societies. Beliefs about the rights and roles of women, family size, child-rearing, and relationships between superiors and subordinates are all changing in more or less the same way. Women are increasingly accepted as the equals of men. Families are becoming smaller, with decisions about family size being more and more a matter of conscious choice. Children are thought of in new terms too; there is increasing emphasis on warmth in father-child relationships and on the autonomy of the adolescent in choices about career and spouse. In all of these areas, although at obviously varying rates, there is movement toward a general and worldwide set of standards, stimulated by the fact that preferences are no longer formed exclusively on the basis of discussions with relatives and neighbors. The mass media and many official public-information programs disseminate professional advice on all these subjects and tell of practices and innovations in other parts of the world.

The attitudes and values affected by social change assume significance not only as standards of personal conduct, but also as shared norms defining sociocultural identities. So too do the life-style changes introduced by social change. Previous chapters in this book have been concerned particularly with these kinds of changes, exploring their consequences for the people of Pare, Bornu, and Tunisia. In each of these societies, the attitudes and behavioral norms of many individuals are shifting, and traditional foci of ethnicity and nationalism have begun to wane as a result. Social change in Africa is not only challenging traditional world views and rearranging long-standing styles of life, it is accelerating a revolution of culture that is forcing people to reexamine and sometimes redefine the most basic symbols of their collective existence.

THE ISSUE OF TRADITION AND IDENTITY

The basic concern of this book is the fate of ancient and traditional sociocultural identities. In Pare, Bornu, and Tunisia, as well as in other African and Third-World societies, a cultural revolution of major proportions is underway. Research in these three societies reveals that many individuals no longer value all of the ancient traditions nor practice the rituals that institutionalized their identities in the past. As members of a society make new social and psychological commitments, the survival of their traditional identity seems inevitably to be called into question. Thus, many have suggested that historic ethnic and cultural solidarities are unlikely to retain a place of significance in the Africa of tomorrow.

Yet the research reported in previous chapters indicates that traditional cultures and identities may indeed retain a place of significance in Africa for some time to come. For one thing, perhaps ironically, there is much in the process of social change that strengthens long-standing normative patterns. In the three societies examined in this book, changes in the social environments within which people live actually strengthen some aspects of traditional culture. So it is possible, if not indeed probable, that social change in these societies will result in neither the total dissolution of each people's heritage nor the formation of a uniform national or international culture. Even more important for the cultural destinies of these and other developing societies is the increase in psychic mobility at the individual level. Since men and woman comprehend with increasing clarity the revolution of society and culture taking place in their midst, and since they are more and more able to evaluate alternative cultural models and plan for the future, they will, in theory at least, have something to say about their cultural destinies. In Pare, Bornu, and Tunisia, there is growing agreement about the need to embrace a technological and material world culture without destroying the beauty and authenticity of one's own legacy. And the development of political capabilities at the community and especially the national level raises to a high point the ability of societies to manage and control these cultural changes. Community and national leaders deliberately guide their followers toward certain ideologies and value systems and away from others. Their influence on educational curricula and the activities of the communications media, as well as the growing ability of political parties in Africa to perform socialization functions, means that the response of traditional attitude and behavior patterns to social change is far from totally haphazard. Few if any African leaders are attempting to institutionalize normative systems that fail to assign a place of importance to at least some traditionally esteemed attitude and behavior patterns.

In the final analysis, social change holds out the prospect of a radical transformation of traditional sociocultural identities while at the same time providing individuals with the tools and the consciousness necessary for an attempt to accommodate their established and valued norms to the exigencies of the present day. This attempt involves ideological choices and practical problems that can rarely be quickly or easily resolved. But it is an attempt that is underway in Pare, Bornu, and Tunisia, and undoubtedly in countless other societies of varying size and complexity. Indeed, it is the essence of these peoples' responses to changing conditions.

Pare is a stateless society; Bornu is a state society or traditional kingdom; and Tunisia is a nation-state. Despite these differences, however, there are important similarities in the way that each of these peoples has approached the dual quest for continuity and change. These similarities, along with some important differences, will be considered in the comparative analysis of the three cases to be presented shortly. But findings from these societies can also be reviewed in order to shed light on similar societies elsewhere.

Pare and Other Stateless Societies

To understand the responses of stateless societies to the changes of the modern age in Africa, one must first understand something about the nature of such societies. *Stateless* societies constitute a category into which anthropologists and political historians place societies that have not yet developed state-level bureaucracies. It is assumed that states developed from stateless societies, and therefore the latter are of particular interest in understanding the former. The non-Western world that opened up during the age of exploration provided new data for tired speculations about the genesis of states in the West. And now in addition to historians and philosophers, quite a few anthropologists have set out to explain how stateless societies differ from states. Classical theorists concerned themselves with the transition from kin-based societies to those based on contract.[1] More recent theorists have asked questions about how egalitarian societies become ranked and stratified.[2] The processes of transformation continue today, but the circumstances of change are different from those which produced the evolution of the first state-level societies. This transformation is today a secondary development, the result of contact with and stimulation from already existing

[1]Different writers focused on somewhat different aspects of the transformation. Maine (1861), for example, discussed the shift from societies based on status to those based on contract. Morgan (1877) formulated specific evolutionary stages through which he argued European societies have moved. Tönnies (1935) considered the transformation from *gemeinschaft* ("community") to *geselleschaft* ("state"). Durkheim's (1895) consideration focused on the shift from societies integrated through mechanical solidarity to those integrated through organic solidarity.

[2]Steward (1955) provided much of the impetus for neoevolutionary discussions of this process. Service (1962) laid out a more complete typology of stages in the process of sociocultural transformation. Fried's analysis (1967) is in large part an attempt to refine and correct Service's ideas.

state-level societies. Few stateless societies are today left alone.
Only a few are becoming independent states. Much more often,
they are becoming parts of larger states and nations.

In many cases, in order to incorporate stateless societies into
colonial infrastructures, political organization had to be created.
Locally important and influential men were given new roles and
positions of power by colonial authorities. Thus, many stateless
societies found their political structures not just changed slightly
by colonialism but radically altered by it.

Modern anthropology has conceded that many "tribes" were
not important units before colonialism made them relevant. In
Africa, at least, those cases like Tiv and Nuer, which are exceptions to this rule, appear to have existed in sociocultural environments that placed premiums on the ability to mobilize for collective action. Both Tiv and Nuer were expanding at the expense
of adjacent groups and the segmentary political structures capable of mobilizing the societies were useful in opposing their
neighbors (see Sahlins 1961). The changes of the colonial period
thrust many more stateless societies into sociocultural environments that place similar premiums on organization and unity,
causing thereby many stateless societies to develop into "tribes"
with strong collective identities.

Indeed, it was the colonial period that precipitated the development of a tribal identity among the Pare which simply had
not existed in earlier periods of their history. Three primary symbols were employed as badges of this ethnicity: the life-crisis
rituals, the Pare language, and association with the Pare highlands. Colonialism brought about the changes in the sociocultural
environment which fostered the development of the Pare "tribe"
and its cultural symbols from the raw materials which had existed
in the precontact situation.

Changing conditions since the beginning of the colonial period
have resulted in a number of challenges to the symbols of Pare
ethnicity. In ritual, the challenges have been most severe. Individuals have often found themselves compelled to choose between participation in the traditional rituals and the institutions
of Islam and Christianity. As a result of having to choose, the
ritual bases of identity as Pare have been undermined significantly
as many people have tended to choose rather consistently the
demands of church and mosque over those of Pare tradition.

In the areas of language and land, however, there have been
greater possibilities of incorporating various new identities with-

out, at the same time, undermining the older loyalties. With language, for example, the introduction of Swahili and English into the Pare highlands has not resulted in extinction of the traditional language. More typically, Swahili and Pare (Asu), the languages that are used most, have achieved a coexistence that assigns each of them a specific functional context into which the other seldom intrudes.

With respect to land, the Pare people are desirous of maintaining their agrarian identity. The necessity of earning cash (to pay taxes and school fees and to buy goods in the shops) has resulted in many men going to the city to work. This in turn has provided a new base of identification, i.e., that of urban worker. Yet, rather consistently, the outmigrants from Pare, who are for the most part engaged temporarily in cash-earning occupations in the cities, continue to maintain strong ties with the homeland and to retain their identity as rural farmers.

Thus, an examination of the major symbols of Pare ethnicity reveals that the greatest conflict between old and new is in the area of ritual: here, there are only a few points at which indigenous and introduced managed to coexist. Otherwise, changes in the symbols and in the sociocultural environment in which they are expressed has necessitated adjustments (not radical replacements) in the mode of expressing Pare ethnicity. But while ethnic identity is closely tied to the badges that symbolize it, it is not defined by them. The changes of the last several decades have made Pare society a more relevant unit in the East African arena. At the same time, however, its cultural symbols have been subject to a number of changes. Many people have very definite opinions about such changes. Some conservatives seek to preserve the familiar, the known, and the valued; they see alterations in symbols as the demise of the group. Others welcome a modernization of symbols, an updating of what being Pare is all about. But regardless of how people view such changes, what has actually happened is that both ethnic group and cultural symbols have changed and evolved and will doubtlessly continue to do so. The greatest difference between the contemporary situation and the past is that the range of identities is expanding and this inevitably means some divided loyalties. Not infrequently, the various identities conflict with one another as was shown in many of the episodes in Chapter 2. More common, however, accommodation and coexistence have been the case in Pare. In Tanzania, Nyerere's policies of *ujamaa* socialism and national development have aimed specifically at building upon the legacy of indigenous cultures whenever possible, not at denying them in order to develop a new Tanzanian identity. In a few African nations, where some people are more desirous of emulating Europeans, there is a denial of indigenous cultural identities. But in most of the newly independent nations of Black Africa, the goal of developing pride in African identity among the masses represents a significant change with the colonial past—for it is no longer necessary to be ashamed of nor to deny tradition. Instead, traditions become the building blocks of new identities as citizens of the new nations and as Africans—identities often suppressed and sometimes even denied by colonialism.

A number of stateless societies responded during the colonial period to a changing sociocultural environment in a fashion similar to Pare and became important sociopolitical entities. In a recent review of this phenomenon, entitled "The Illusion of Tribe," Southall (1970) points out the generality of this process in Africa. Other especially well-documented cases include the Plateau Tonga of Zambia (Colson 1968) and the Igbo of Nigeria (Smock 1971). Once developed, these societies became important and viable units. Indeed, in the later colonial period in Africa and even today in postindependent Black Africa, such societies are significant forces to be reckoned with—as the well-known nationalistic movements among the Kikuyu of Kenya and the Igbo of Nigeria remind us.

Concerning the genesis of stateless societies in Africa, Colson (1968:201–202) has this to say:

At least in Africa, tribes and tribalism as we know them today are recent creations reflecting the influences of the Colonial era when large-scale political and economic organizations set the scene for the mobilization of ethnic groups based upon linguistic and cultural similarities which formerly had been irrelevant in effecting alliances. Independence gave still further momentum to the process of mobilization, as smaller uncommitted groups found it advisable to identify with one or another of the more powerful alliances.

For anthropology . . . the term [tribe] may well have outlived such usefulness as it has had as an analytic tool. It could be allowed to fall into decent antiquarianism. Even so, we are left with the fact that our fellow social scientists and the public at large believe that both tribes and tribalism exist as distinctive phenomena. Much of the discussion of politics and of political development in the new nations, especially those of Africa, is haunted by both terms. Tribes and tribalism are thus an anthropological problem, if we are interested in applying our subject to current political realities.

What Westerners may see as clinging to identity in stateless societies is hardly describable as resistance to change. Indeed, if it is the case, as suggested here, that many stateless societies developed strong collective identities relatively recently, then what we see are people whose traditional culture is in effect a newfound identity. That they changed so much in the recent past may be taken as some indication that they may continue to do so in the future.

Bornu and Other State Societies

The relative stability of indigenous African states has long been of interest to people concerned with the nature of social change in Africa. In discussing Kanuri identity and social change in Part Three of this volume, the picture painted was of *relative* stability —especially in regard to the key symbols of Kanuri identity. A perspective on this stability can be gained by turning briefly to an examination of the response to European colonial powers by African precolonial states in the nineteenth century.

African states have been known to Europeans for centuries because, in part, they have had leading roles in commercial and political contact with Europe. This has classically been the case with states as diverse as Ashanti in West Africa, Buganda in East Africa, Kongo in Central Africa, and Zulu in South Africa. This contact, moreover, was characterized often by prolonged political and military struggles between the states and the invading colonial powers. Indeed, most African societies resisted colonialism from the start, but by and large this resistance was most evident and successful when attempted by the states. Many factors contributed to their relative success. Indigenous African states had, in the first place, a developed sense of unity, identity, and destiny that bolstered their desire to resist. They also had, in the second place, the organization, manpower, and commercial leverage necessary to make their resistance effective. For these reasons, as well as for reasons of expediency on the part of the colonizers, African precolonial states often emerged from the colonial experience as altered but unbroken sociocultural entities.

The scope of the changes these states did experience, however, has varied considerably. The extent of the changes, moreover, appears to be linked to two closely related variables: the proximity of these states to the coast of Africa and/or the centers of colonial administration; and their proximity to and involvement in trade with the colonial powers. In short, the more involved these states were with the colonial powers, either because they were attempting to utilize the same land or because they were involved with the same economic and commercial endeavors (e.g., slavery), the more they were subject to the forces of change brought by the West. These include, as noted at the outset of this chapter, such forces as Western educational traditions, religions, and political ideologies.

Unlike Ashanti, for example, Bornu was not and is not a state located near the coast of Africa nor was it heavily involved with European powers until recently. Although indirect commerce with Europe via trans-Saharan trade was important prior to the arrival of large numbers of Europeans on the coast of West Africa, such trade later declined. Similarly, and in contrast to Buganda for example, Bornu was not a center of colonial administration although there were a few administrators residing in Maiduguri in order to advise traditional leaders. Indeed, the policy of some of the more prominent early British administrators actually seemed to be to keep Bornu isolated from other segments of the colony of Nigeria as a means of preserving what these colonizers felt was a magnificent culture. To cite but one of many examples, Lord Lugard, the architect of much of the British colonial policy in Nigeria in the early part of this century, stipulated that Kanuri and not the neighboring and more widely spoken Hausa language would be the language of instruction in the schools in Bornu.

Bornu's long history, as we have noted, is studded with contact with Europe and with long-distance, large-scale trade, but the contact does not compare with the extent of involvement experienced by the Ashanti or Baganda. And the scope of contemporary change in Bornu reflects this fact. This is not to say, to repeat for emphasis, that Bornu has not changed in the last 75 to 150 years. It has changed a great deal. But the major elements of Kanuri identity have largely been maintained during a time when many technological, demographic, political, and ideological changes have been introduced—especially in the post-World War II period.

Thus, the kingship, though altered during the recent succession crisis in 1968, is still a mainstay of Kanuri political identity. Land pressures have not been great and will not be for some time;

urbanism is increasing but is not a new way of life for the Kanuri who had cities of great size and importance many years ago. Islam is changing in Bornu, but slowly and not as a result of national-level policy as in Tunisia, for example. The changes, moreover, are within Islam itself and not between an old, indigenous religion and a new one, or between Islam and Christianity, as in Pare. And the Kanuri language, while not the exclusive language of instruction or conversation in Bornu, is still a strong language in a polyglot nation.

The major element of Kanuri identity that does appear to be changing is one that is most central to this ancient kingdom, as it has been for many other indigenous African states; it is clientship. Clientship really can be understood best in the context of the general structure of the political systems of these states. Their structures have been classified according to a variety of systems,[3] and while these have differed in a number of ways, several common themes emerge. The most important of these stresses their centralized authority structure, with so-called "bureaucratic" lines of authority. Recruitment patterns and advancement within these stable and relatively closed structures are based, to varying degrees, on the development of personal ties with individuals having high rank. This contrasts with more egalitarian sociopolitical systems in which recruitment and advancement are based on achievement and performance. The issue of the character of state authority systems is related to a question that has interested many observers of social change in Africa. This question asks whether the existence of large, relatively stable, closed hierarchical authority systems inhibits the transition to more open, merit-based authority systems. This question is also central to the broader issue of changing identity in such African societies since a central aspect of individual identity in state societies is one's position in the hierarchy and/or one's interpersonal relationships with important people in it. Collective identity is intimately linked to these aspects of sociopolitical hierarchy as well because views about proper behavior are couched in terms appropriate to the clientship idiom that often pervades such societies. In short, sensitivity to rank, authority, power, and a concern with mobility

[3]The most famous of such classifications is that of Fortes and Evans-Pritchard (1940). Subsequently, their basic typology was revised in a number of ethnographic analyses (e.g., Smith 1960 and Southall 1956). Several writers have attempted to review and resolve this issue, including Lewis (1959), Lloyd (1965), Murdock (1959), Southall (1965), and Vansina (1962).

via clientship relationships are themes central to the identity of individuals in many state societies in Africa.

Research in Africa on the transformation of such systems has been scattered but there are a number of important studies. In one of these, Fallers (1956) discusses the predicament of individuals in positions of leadership in the Soga state in Uganda. Their state was organized around kinship groups. The traditional leaders of these groups, and hence of the society, were attempting to adjust to the demands of the colonial bureaucracy. However, because the colonial and Soga norms concerning the exercise of authority differed there was often interpersonal conflict and instability. It has often been suggested that institutionalizing an authority system based *exclusively* on principles of performance and achievement is difficult and that such systems may well be inherently unstable. This instability may be no less significant when efforts are made to merge personalized and meritocratic systems. Certainly this appears to have been the case when the Soga attempted to respond to the bureaucratic norms of the colonial power. Leaders tried valiantly to utilize both sets of norms but they were not often successful.

Some but not all of the implications of Fallers' research have been borne out in a later study of a group of young executives and managers in Uganda (Kumalo 1966). Kumalo inquired into the adjustment patterns of several dozen such individuals. He found that a significantly larger proportion of the bureaucrats (as he calls them) had a high "collectivist orientation" (p. 225). He attributes these results to the effect of "socialist thinking" common to contemporary African élites, but he also notes that they managed to balance the collectivist and individualistic values through the "mechanism of segregation" of these two conflicting value systems. The value commitments of these bureaucrats, suggests Kumalo, in reality, seem to have emerged more from the "ethos of the wider African social organization than from that of the bureaucratic organizations for which they worked. They were 'in' but not 'of' these companies" (p. 226). These results, as with Fallers', reflect the likelihood that these two systems cannot be successfully or easily merged, but they also show, unlike the Fallers analysis, that it is possible for an individual to successfully adjust to both normative systems and, indeed, to use them effectively under different circumstances. They also indicate that bringing in bureaucratic authority systems in a more formal sense may not be sufficient grounds for expecting individuals to lose all touch with the value systems of their traditional societies.

Much the same kind of observations were made in concluding the analysis of the changing nature of social mobility in Bornu. There it was suggested that while changes appear to be well on the way to becoming firmly established, there are at the same time indications that the transition will be slow, compartmentalized, and perhaps more form than substance. At the very least, the matter has not yet been decided with finality. It was noted, moreover, that the complete bureaucratization of society and social relationships has not yet been shown to be a necessary prerequisite for the achievement of rapid rates of economic growth (or for fostering high levels of achievement motivation). The case of Japan is the most striking in this regard.

Finally, the contemporary realization in many developed Western countries of some of Weber's more dire predictions regarding the dehumanizing aspects of bureaucratic ideals is in part responsible for the widespread resistance to such norms. In such situations, there is a growing effort to rehumanize personal relationships while at the same time preserving some of the organizational and developmental advantages of the bureaucracy. Some social scientists (e.g., see Foa 1971) are now suggesting that from the standpoint of conflict-reduction alone, some new compromise structure needs to be fostered which will make explicit recognition of the legitimacy of both performance and achievement criteria on the one hand and more affectively based personal ties on the other. It may well be that without such developments, the social life of contemporary man will be conflict-ridden, dehumanized and ineffective in achieving other more instrumental goals. As Apter has noted:

The worth of a man must come to include more than his usefulness. This can be achieved by policy, by the widening of the opportunities of choice to include matters other than productivity and efficiency. The business enterprise is not the prototype organization for modern life. If we act as if it is, our notions of hierarchy, efficiency, and value will become so concentrated on the market mechanism of choice that our humanity will disappear. That, in the last analysis, is what is implied by the notion of the mass society (1965:458).

With such sentiments becoming more and more prominent, it becomes difficult to determine with much confidence the future of clientship and identity in such societies as Bornu. While it is tempting to stress the shift away from the old (clientship) toward the new (self-reliance) in Bornu, there are other relevant movements elsewhere in the world. Indeed, as in all African societies, the target that Bornu is aiming at is not a stationary, unchanging one. And more importantly, it is one that we, from our intensely bureaucratic, Western vantage point, may not be able to see as well as they. As a consequence, their experiences as they work to shift the bases of their identity may well provide vital guidelines for change in our own society, now and in years to come.

Tunisia and Other Nation-States

Most nation-states in contemporary Africa assumed their present form as a result of colonial rule. Their boundaries reflect, to a considerable degree, political divisions imposed by the powers of Europe, and their nationalist movements have most often been led by men whose organizational skills and ideological orientations were at least in part fostered through contact with the West. African leaders are often indignant when told that statehood is not an indigenous African phenomenon. They correctly point out that there were many powerful states in Africa prior to colonial times and they sometimes suggest that these polities could have provided appropriate bases for nation-building in contemporary Africa. Nevertheless, this possibility notwithstanding, few if any of the nation-states of contemporary Africa would exist today had it not been for their colonial experiences. Most of these states came into being when African nationalists seized political and administrative structures created and controlled by Europe. And now that most of the continent is free from colonial rule, these nationalists are turning their attention to the quest for economic development and to the task of defining and institutionalizing appropriate national identities.

Tunisia has been particularly forthright in its attempt to promote development. A decade and a half ago, the nation's President, Habib Bourguiba, stated that many of his countrymen were entangled in a mass of prejudices and outmoded beliefs. Then he went on to say that his country would effect a psychological revolution in order to eradicate the obstacles to progress and in order to assure that each citizen made his contribution to the welfare of the nation. Research reported in Part Four of this volume suggests that Bourguiba's called-for revolution is taking place today. In the area of religion, women's rights, child-rearing, and professional life, long-standing attitudes and values are losing support. Certainly not all of the change that can be discerned in these areas is attributable to the policies and programs of the government. Just as surely, however, the magnitude of changes taking place would be far less impressive had it not been for those policies and programs and the determination that lies behind them.

Not all contemporary nation-states pursue change as ardently as Tunisia does. But neither is the Tunisian case exceptional. It is probably closer to the rule than it is to the exception. Over a decade ago, thinking in particular of the situation in Burma, Lucien Pye characterized the attempts of national leaders to modify the attitudes and behavior patterns of their countrymen as a defining element of what he called the non-Western political process. Pye stated that élites in developing countries feel they must change all aspects of life within their society. They conceive of themselves as representing a prototype of what the entire country will become in time and believe that their opinions on all subjects will become the commonly shared views of the entire population (1962:18). The same point has been made by others, reinforcing the value of the Tunisian example. Apter says that in many new states, social, political, and economic development are pursued with a missionary-like zeal. Reviewing a number of African examples, most notably Guinea and Nkrumah's Ghana, he suggests that these objectives are elevated to a virtually sacred level (1963).

Perhaps the most significant point to be made about sociocultural change from the perspective of the nation-state has to do with the great power to modify traditional normative patterns that national leaders hold in their hands. In most countries, nationalists and intellectuals have discussed and analyzed questions of social and cultural change for decades. The Congress of North Africa discussed in Chapter 14 provides an excellent illustration. So too do the Pan-African Conferences following World War I. Among their objectives was the promotion of Western education in order that Africans might be given knowledge of scientific and industrial techniques. But questions of social and cultural change are no longer merely discussed and analyzed. They are today the policy orientations to which nationalist movements devote substantial resources of manpower and technology in order that the élite visions for remaking society may be realized. Marriott describes cultural politics in the postcolonial nations of the Third

World and makes it clear that sociocultural change has entered a new era so far as nation-states are concerned:

Modern means of communication have gradually been transforming the culture of many nations for more than a century, without having been made the instruments of intentional policy . . . [But] the availability of such means of communication also opens up new potentialities for the manipulation of culture. The possibility of educating citizens to a newly chosen way of life, of mobilizing them in support of deliberately cultivated values, of representing them to the world according to a consciously created image—all of these are open to the élites of the new states, either in actuality or in prospect (1963:29).

Leaders of Tunisia and other new states desire to promote cultural change. Moreover, they have at their disposal unprecedented means with which to pursue this objective. Yet, as they gear up to manage the transformation of their societies, it is apparent that they are unable to sweep away all aspects of their past, nor in fact is this their wish. There are many ironic examples of how would-be modernizers have been unable to induce modifications in traditional attitude and behavior patterns until they incorporated into their appeals the symbols and wisdom of other facets of these very same traditions. Marriot reports a typical debate between a rural development officer in India and a conservative Brahman farmer (1963:33). The officer's aim was to persuade the farmer to adopt the practice of sowing, then plowing under, a green crop in order to enrich the soil for the subsequent planting of grain. All of the officer's arguments failed to convince the Brahman until he finally put himself in the position of the peasant and spoke of the possibility of earning greater spiritual merit by devoting additional wealth to the performance of social and religious duties. Such a discussion recalls Bourguiba's claim that the fast of Ramadan should not be observed because Moslems are mounting a "holy war" against poverty and, by tradition, those engaged in battle are not required to fast.

Solidarity with traditional cultural symbols and bases of identity may often be expressed by national leaders out of necessity, but it would be erroneous to conclude that these men and women only grudgingly allow themselves to reinforce or even employ aspects of tradition. First, there is widespread agreement, backed by considerable evidence, that many elements of the traditional cultures in their societies are in no sense incompatible with contemporary needs. Second, when inconsistencies do arise, leaders may sometimes deem it more important to retain traditional patterns for expressive or identity-related needs than to besiege them in search of material advantage. So, once again, the advent of independence and the possession of powerful political and social mechanisms for regulating social change do not mean that the legacies of Africa's past will soon fade beyond recognition. In Tunisia we have seen a determination to revitalize the Arabic language, noting that this is a pattern characteristic of all the North African countries. We have also seen a determination to preserve Islam as a pillar of national identity, even though change with respect to many specific aspects of the religion is being promoted. The review of Tanzanian politics in Chapter 5 shows that the situation in that country is similar. A national, non-European language, Swahili, is being emphasized, although the colonial language is still the principal vehicle of secondary and higher education. Tanzanian history prior to the colonial period is being avidly written and there is even a distinctive national dress. Tanzania is not pursuing socialism; it is pursuing *ujamaa* socialism.

The emphasis on *négritude* by Senegal's President, Leopold Sedar Senghor, and on Pan-Africanism by the late Kwame Nkrumah are reflections of similar concerns, being philosophies and programs that strive to go forward without denying one's heritage (Quaison-Sackey 1963). To nation-builders concerned with national or even international unity, these ideological options hold out the possibility of transcending divisive parochial loyalties. Yet they offer in their stead an identification that is unassailably African, providing continuity with a heritage that most are determined not to disavow. A study of political development in India by Lloyd and Susanne Rudolph (1967) provides additional illustrations of the ways in which traditional social codes have been productively incorporated into programs designed to meet the needs of a contemporary nation-state. The Rudolphs show that traditional patterns of social stratification associated with caste have been used to promote political mobilization and political development in India. They also show that traditional ideals having to do with courage, honor, morality, conflict resolution, and the like provided an ideological base for modern and successful political leadership, and that the form and structure of Brahmanic law, if not always the substance, played an important role in legal modernization in India. Additional African examples of these kinds of processes are also available. The Restatement of African Law Project in East Africa is codifying and standard-izing traditional African customary law in a form amenable to incorporation in national legal systems (Allott 1960). Different bodies of customary law are recorded by trained personnel and submitted to local officials for authentication. The various approved records are then presented to an assemblage of knowl-edgeable persons from different areas, and inconsistencies and discrepancies among the records are discussed and reconciled. The result is a restatement of traditional African customary law, a unified body of codes that may be incorporated into existing bodies of written law in order to render the latter more consistent with traditional African values.

All of this points to the conclusion that, new or old, nation-states, like the other sociopolitical entities examined in this book, desire to maintain their identification with ancient and venerable traditions. In some cases, of course, practical problems and pressing material needs may make it impossible to realize desires for identity and continuity in the fullest measure. But the diffusion of a world culture based largely on Western technology and organizational modes can no longer take place without the media-tion of a conscious process of cultural management (Fallers 1961:677–678), and this will assuredly mean that the traditions of African and other non-Western nation-states will retain a place in the world of tomorrow.

PATTERNS OF CONTINUITY AND CHANGE

For many individuals, changing conditions portend a welcome liberation from the constraints by which their lives have tradi-tionally been bound. Until recently, the majority of Africa's peo-ples had a relatively limited knowledge of other cultures. Nor had the idea gained widespread acceptance that a society's institu-tions and normative patterns could be restructured if they were injurious to the society's welfare. Today, however, change is ubiquitous and most Africans find a growing number of options and alternatives open to them. As a result, people are making choices, weighing alternatives to their traditional social codes and considering, though not always accepting, the possibility of change. Apter suggests that change itself becomes an institution to the extent that the members of a society are able and willing to evaluate and choose among alternatives (1965). Continual transformation becomes assured at this point. The majority of the people in most African societies do not at present think in these terms, but the number who do is growing rapidly. Change is becoming a part of the way of life of an increasing number of Africans.

Willingness to compare traditional and nonindigenous psychological and behavioral models does not mean that the latter will be preferred in all cases. A consideration of alternatives is likely to lead in many instances to the conclusion that traditional social codes are well suited to the needs of the society. Moreover, in at least some instances, the members of a society may disagree among themselves about which social and cultural norms are most desirable, either because some persons are too wedded to traditional values to honestly consider the possibility of change or because rational men and women sometimes simply disagree about what is desirable. In any event, increasing familiarity with other cultures and a growing willingness to consider aspects of these cultures as alternatives to one's own traditions are likely to lead to extensive change in some areas and to little or no change in others. It is this situation that has produced the duality of Africa's social revolution, the juxtaposition of old and new that has been such a prominent feature of all of the societies examined in this book. Many Africans desire certain kinds of changes, particularly those material changes which make their lives easier and more comfortable. But many are also desirous of preserving aspects of their traditional cultures, believing them preferable to the alternatives available to them. There are disagreements among Africans as to which forms of coexistence between traditional and nonindigenous patterns are most desirable. There are also disagreements about how to solve practical problems associated with the juxtaposition of old and new. But there is increasing agreement that the essential question to be answered by all societies in contemporary Africa is how some things but not all things can be changed.

Traditional and nonindigenous social codes exist side-by-side in most African societies. But the form of this coexistence differs greatly, both between and within societies. Six patterns of interaction between traditional and introduced normative modes may be discerned, examples of each pattern being found in stateless societies, state societies, and nation-states. First, there are instances where new cultural orientations overpower old ones, bringing about their demise. Second, there are traditions that, for the present at least, are almost totally impervious to change. In these cases, it is the nonindigenous alternatives to established patterns that are overpowered. A third situation involves the employment of traditional social and cultural institutions to accomplish tasks whose legitimacy derives from new values. When this occurs, traditions are maintained; but their historic purposes and significance are modified. The converse of this pattern, the co-optation of new roles and institutions by traditional society for its own purposes, constitutes a fourth possibility. Nonindigenous elements of culture are made the servants of long-standing institutions in such situations, and the latter are frequently stronger as a result. A fifth possibility is for old and new cultural orientations to coexist with relative harmony, each claiming precedence over a certain functional or normative domain. Cases of this sort are frequently described as examples of compartmentalization. Traditional and nonindigenous options are both available to the members of a society and opportunities for demand satisfaction thereby increase. A sixth pattern is also one of coexistence, but this time with tension rather than with harmony. Here the availability of alternative models for thought and action poses dilemmas for individuals and for a society. There is no consensus about what models are most appropriate in particular sets of circumstances. Indeed, conflicting pressures are exerted on the society by those who favor different alternatives.

These six categories describe the most important ways that old and new elements of culture come together, affecting the life styles and identities of societies in the process. An examination of the way that salient aspects of culture in Pare, Bornu, and Tunisia are distributed across these six categories provides another way of highlighting differences and similarities between the three societies in a systematic fashion, and will set the scene for a comparative analysis of the cases in the next section. Then, we will point to some more general conclusions about the future of ancient traditions and identities in those parts of Africa where social transformation has essentially become institutionalized.

In Pare, as in the other two cases, the patterns of change cover almost the entire range of combinations just outlined, although the distribution across the six categories is not even. It is difficult, for example, to find aspects of Pare culture that have not changed at all. Similarly, there are relatively few instances of traditional practices being carried out for new ends, though the adoption of circumcision by Moslems is an example of this, as is the legitimization of bridewealth institutions by Christians, Moslems, and

the civil authorities of Pare. The converse of this, the achievement of traditional goals by means of new cultural patterns, is
illustrated by the men who migrate to cities in search of wages.
Here, the old patterns of exploiting different ecological zones in
farming and herding has been maintained by attempting something new—seeking wage-labor jobs in the cities.

More important for the Pare, however, are the patterns of
change associated with the old life-crisis rituals. For the most
part, they have been replaced by the new rituals of Islam and
Christianity. The Pare language, a most important symbol of their
identity, is being used alongside of Swahili, the symbol of national, Tanzanian identity. With functional domains clearly established, there is neither serious tension between the two languages
nor indications that one is winning out at the expense of the
other. Farming and association with the highlands, the other major
constellation of Pare ethnic symbols, persists despite the fact
that many men spend much of their lives in nonfarming occupations away from the highlands. There could be an easy coexistence between the two interests were it not for the increasing
population pressure and governmental policies discouraging
migration to urban areas. But in general, the predominance of
change and coexistence over the stability of symbols of Pare
identity may be expected to continue in the foreseeable future.

The case of Bornu contrasts with Pare. Here the concern of
people is not the erosion of most major symbols of their individual and collective identity as Kanuri. To be sure, examples of
all six patterns of interaction between old and new social codes
are to be found; but examples of some of them are relatively rare.
Recent instances where old cultural orientations have been or
are being replaced totally by new ones are few, although this will
almost certainly happen in the near future for the inequitable relationship between men and women. Also rare are instances where
traditional attitudes and behavioral norms remain virtually unchanged, although the basic character of life cycle rituals and
religion has changed little in recent decades, especially in comparison to the Pare and Tunisian cases. Many important symbols
of Kanuri identity continue to exist alongside new elements, but
for the moment, they appear to be coexisting in relative harmony.
The Kanuri language and kingship are examples of this pattern.

The key area of change in Bornu centers around clientship and
corresponding patterns of social mobility. At present, there is a
quiet but tense disharmony between old patterns of clientship

and the new demands for the norms of a bureaucracy or meri-
tocracy. This is especially true in the case of the young and the
educated who seek to be mobile on the basis of newly acquired
technical skills rather than on the basis of personal client ties.
However, this change is not total in all cases. Many students,
for example, hope to utilize client relationships as at least a par-
tial means of fulfilling what are essentially nontraditional goals.
And, moreover, there is a traditional and locally well-known interpersonal style of behavior which is the opposite of clientship
(i.e., hyena-ism or self-reliance) and it is possible this will be
utilized more often for a variety of new goals. Thus, rather than
predicting the imminent demise of the clientship system, it may
be that social relationships in Bornu in the future will preserve
fundamental aspects of clientship and self-reliant achievement.

Tunisia contrasts with both Pare and Bornu on a number of
dimensions. In the first place, its identity as a cohesive unit is at
once both more established and more buffeted by change. Indeed, patterns of change found in Tunisia illustrate almost the
entire range of interaction between traditional and nonindigenous
norms, although some are of course more prominent than others.
There are only a few instances where new cultural patterns are
being employed to accomplish old ends, but there are many
instances of the converse. The use of Islamic sentiments to build
national solidarity during the colonial period provides a good
illustration of this pattern. So too do contemporary efforts to
interpret development programs to the populace as part of a
jihad, or holy war, against ignorance and poverty. In other domains, old and new norms are both well entrenched and exist
side by side, sometimes in harmony and sometimes not. The
most important case of the former concerns the roles of the
Arabic and French languages in contemporary Tunisia. French is
the language of education and the educated, of science and technology; Arabic is the language of conversation, literature, religion,
and, increasingly, of politics. It appears this pattern of coexistence will continue for some time. But, in the case of the relationship between women and men, the coexistence of old and
new is characterized by disharmony. Equality is coming to some
women; for others, it will remain a distant goal. For many men,
the former trend represents a loss of significant proportions. The
latter trend represents a tension-point for many of both sexes.

Patterns of child-rearing and, especially, professional practices
are examples of changes where the new replaces the old more

completely. The role of fathers in child-rearing is becoming more nurturant and supportive, with the authoritarian patterns of old slowly diminishing. Similarly, Tunisians are increasingly oriented to the demands of a modern industrial economy, being more concerned with wages, savings, and technology, and with traditional professions falling into disrepute. As in the case of the Pare and to a lesser extent the Kanuri, there are almost no examples of changes in Tunisia where the old has completely resisted the new, and indeed, for the foreseeable future, this situation may be expected to continue.

COMPARING THE CASES

There are at least two important differences between Bornu and Pare that are related to the way in which each responded to changes during and after the colonial period. First, the two societies had vastly different abilities to resist change. Bornu's societal complexity and sheer size provided an organizational framework that was more effective in resisting unwanted changes than Pare, a smaller-scale society whose greatest organization emerged only when it was mustered to resist colonial incursion, and even then was a far cry from the complex administrative structure of the Kanuri kingdom.

Another significant difference between the two cases is the degree to which traditional culture was really institutionalized. Kanuri traditions were the products of a millennium's cultural development, a millennium whose shape and general importance is known and appreciated locally. Kanuri identity was well developed, had important symbols like the *Shehu*, Islam, and clientship, and was institutionalized continually through important rituals. In contrast to this, Pare, as a cultural entity, developed essentially in response to the changes of the colonial period. But while ancient symbols were employed to serve as icons of the newfound identity, Pare tradition hardly had been institutionalized before additional pressures of colonialism and other forces for change began to undermine even this nascent identity. Thus, the degree of institutionalization of the traditional culture appears to have played an important role in the responses of Pare and Kanuri to threats to their collective identities.

The Pare and Kanuri material also provide empirical data which are related to the question of whether indigenous states or stateless societies are more easily incorporated into new national entities. Moreover, additional evidence from other parts of Africa suggests that these cases are representative and thus provide a general answer to the question. Stateless societies like Pare have little structure to resist change and/or incorporation. Indeed, their greatest structure emerges as a situational response to such pressures from the outside. In attempting to incorporate such societies into nation-states, the greatest problem is mobilizing them and creating structures that can articulate with the administrative framework of the nation. Indigenous states like Bornu already have complex structures and these can be employed in the service of the new nations. Indeed, it was the recognition of this fact that, in part, gave rise to Lord Lugard's policy of "indirect rule." The greatest problem faced in incorporating indigenous states into the new nations is overcoming the resistance that the already existing structures can muster. Thus, neither state nor stateless societies have a clear advantage that allows them to be incorporated more easily into a new nation. Each has certain characteristics that help in the process and each presents certain obstacles to be overcome.

A related question that a comparison of these cases introduces is why some societies seem to change so readily while others prove to be quite resistant. Two important factors must be examined to answer this question. First of all, some societies were more exposed to contact and change than others. Pare, for example, lay in the path of caravans making their way to the interior of Tanganyika. It was close to Mt. Kilimanjaro, which since explorers first reported the existence of such a mountain has held no small fascination for Europeans. Its location simply made it more vulnerable to agents of change than were many other African societies. Bornu, and the other Emirates in the northern part of Nigeria, enjoyed special protection during the colonial period which provided them greater refuge from such forces. Lord Lugard disallowed Christian missionizing in northern Nigeria and called for a maintenance of the traditional social structure. Such differences in contact histories and degrees of exposure are important factors in explaining differential responses of African societies to change.

But another and perhaps more important difference among societies is what is actually asked of them in the change process. For example, Ottenberg (1959:142) remarked that the Igbo, during the colonial period, "probably changed the least while changing most." What he meant was that many of the characteristics of

Igbo society were those that the colonists sought to encourage and develop. Before it even began to change, Igbo society was already closer to the model for African development held out by the British in Nigeria. The Masai of East Africa provide a case at the other end of the continuum. Continual efforts to transform the mobile Masai pastoralists into sedentary agriculturalists have failed. British colonial officers attributed this failure to the inherent conservatism of the Masai. But if we compare what was asked of the so-called resistant and conservative Masai with the so-called forward-looking and progressive Igbo, the principal fact we see is that there were significant differences in the degree to which each society was asked to change. Very little was required of the Igbo in contrast to the revolution of cultural styles which the Masai were asked to make. With respect to indigenous states within Africa, similar sorts of variation among societies resulted in differential ease of incorporation into colonial and national structures. The mobility system of the Kanuri, for example, differed significantly from the British model of bureaucratic behavior whereas among the Baganda there was much greater correspondence. Such differences in the preadaptedness of traditional societies to change programs is another significant factor in comprehending differences in patterns of incorporation of such societies into larger structures.

A comparison of rates and degrees of change in Bornu and Tunisia is also instructive as to the ways in which various African societies responded to the stimuli for change that entered their environments during the colonial period. Both Bornu and Tunisia had strongly institutionalized traditional cultures. The Arabo-Moslem heritage was as important a symbol of identity in Tunisia as the *Shehu* and clientship were to the Kanuri. Moreover, each shared Islam and the associated cultural complex as well-entrenched and important bases of identity. And each cultural tradition was supported by a fairly elaborate, though different, social organizational base. Yet why did Tunisia change more than Bornu during the colonial period? There are at least two interrelated syndromes of factors that account for the differences in response patterns. First, and most obviously, Tunisia's location on the Mediterranean, its proximity to Europe, its attractiveness to settlers, and the sheer intensity of contact with other cultures made it more vulnerable to outside forces than Bornu. Many Europeans settled in Tunisia, motivated primarily by proximity and climate. And once there, they exerted pressure on the colonial government to provide them with the economic and cultural institutions of the metropole. Schools, hospitals, ports, roads, and the like were built, affecting the lives of Tunisians as well as settlers. The result was greater exposure than ever of Tunisia to the outside world, and the modification of the structure of the entire society. In northern Nigeria, on the other hand, neither location nor colonial policy tended to result in the arrival of large numbers of European settlers.

The second constellation of factors responsible for differences in the patterns of change in the two societies has to do with the objectives of French versus British colonial policy. In most French territories, including Tunisia, a policy of political and cultural assimilation sought to persuade Africans to think as Frenchmen in order to bind them permanently to France. And in Tunisia, as elsewhere in the French empire (especially during the first quarter century of colonialism), quite a few persons did seek to borrow French cultural ways. British colonial policy, by contrast, was characterized by indirect rule. While admiring the intricate organization of the kingdoms of the Sudanic region, the British never assumed that Africans could become English and thus were more content to leave indigenous societies like Bornu more or less intact.

Nation-states, like stateless and state societies, also show vast differences in rates and modes of change. Some, like Tunisia and Tanzania, present cogent plans for rapid sociocultural change. Others, like Nigeria and Kenya, are also changing rapidly, but tend to rely upon less dramatically articulated philosophies of development. And in still other nations, the pace of change is slow by comparison. There are at least three important reasons for these differences. First, colonialism has not been of constant intensity across the African continent. Some contemporary African nation-states like Ethiopia and Liberia, for example, experienced neither the infrastructural development that was usually a by-product of colonialism nor the intense contact with Europeans that disrupted traditional life and stimulated change. Other nations, however, had more intense colonial experiences. Tunisia, Kenya, Nigeria, and Senegal are examples of this pattern. Each of these nations had a relatively large Western-educated élite at the time of independence. Each also had a comparatively well-developed economic and administrative base, attributable in a large measure to colonialism. This infrastructure is now in the hands of national leaders seeking development, and enables them to carry out their programs more effectively. A second factor accounting for differences between the way nation-states attempt to incorporate change and engineer cultural reforms results from differences in the personalities and philosophies of nationalist leaders. Nyerere and Bourguiba, though quite different in the specifics of their political and cultural goals, show great concern for Africanizing the politics of their nations in the postindependent period and for reviving the finest parts of the African heritage that were dislocated during the colonial period. In contrast to these leaders, there are others like Houphouet-Boigny and Banda, whose attempts to develop their countries and incorporate change have not been based, so far, on a call for such great breaks with the goals of the colonial period.

A third factor that shapes the direction in which nation-states change has to do with the nature of their traditional culture and its availability as a symbol of national identity and integrity. The nations of Tunisia, Nigeria, and Tanzania are very different in this regard. Tunisia has a stronger base of historical integrity prior to the colonial period than either of the two other cases. It has been more-or-less a cultural and political entity for nearly two thousand years. Following independence from French colonial rule, the symbols chosen for national identity were readily available from this shared history. In many ways, Bornu is similar to Tunisia in this respect. Its recorded history extends for more than a millennium and the symbols of its collective identity are ancient ones. But instead of developing into a nation-state in modern Africa, Bornu like many other Sudanic kingdoms has been incorporated into a nation which was carved out of the African continent during the colonial period. Integrating Nigeria and its indigenous cultures is a very different problem than that which Tunisia faces. Not only are the kingdoms in the northern part of the country strong subnational forces to be reckoned with, but the Yoruba kingdoms in the West and the large collectivity of Igbos and other stateless societies in the East gave Nigeria a very different set of problems and priorities than either Tunisia or Tanzania. It is a modern nation with strong subnational cultures and units. Tanzania is altogether different from the other two. Like Nigeria, it is an amalgam of indigenous societies brought together as a unit during the colonial period, but individually, they are not as strong, generally, as those of which Nigeria is composed. Therefore, like Tunisia, Tanzania's cultural policies seeking to develop among the various groups within the nation a strong national identity which will take precedence over regional attachments have had far less difficulty than similar policies undertaken in Nigeria (as the recent civil war attests). But unlike Tunisia, Tanzania's cultural unity is more an incipient than ancient reality. Nevertheless, since there were no large politically dominant ethnic groups within Tanzania, forging a nation has been easier than in many other African states. Indeed, because the cultural differences of most of its peoples are relatively minor, Tanzania has been able to seize upon such indigenous values as egalitarianism and cooperation which were widespread prior to the colonial period and elevate them to new positions of national cultural foci. In many respects, Tanzania and Tunisia are quite similar in the degree to which cultural engineering is taking place. The differences lie mostly in the degree to which the traditional cultures provided ready bases for the development of national cultures. Tanzania forged from indigenous raw materials what Tunisia already knew in its past but which colonialism made it necessary to revitalize.

THE FUTURE OF IDENTITY

The cultures of traditional African societies are being transformed by social, political, and economic change. But the societies themselves are flourishing, and normative systems that underlie them continue to owe much to age-old patterns of thought and action. Certainly some traditional foci of ethnicity and nationalism are waning as a result of changing conditions. And still others, though they remain, are being robbed of their historic significance. Nevertheless, traditional cultural symbols of solidarity are surviving Africa's social revolution, some of them in fact stronger because of it. Moreover, new integrating mechanisms are developing in response to social change, and though these mechanisms are not themselves indigenous, they play no less vital a role in the maintenance of traditional collectivities. In short, substantive change in the sociocultural identities of traditional African societies is occurring but neither is the scope of this change total nor are the societies necessarily weakened by the replacement of some old cultural symbols with new ones.

Yet the changing environments within which most Africans live require them to operate in a world growing ever wider. Members of nation-states in Africa increasingly feel a commonality with other peoples in their part of the continent. For some there is a growing sense of identity with Africa as a whole and the Third World generally. Individuals are more cognizant of these wider arenas for action and are coming to view them as related to their own lives. Members of subnational social and cultural entities are under even greater pressure to assume new identities. Nation-builders seek to foster solidarity among peoples living within their borders and possess powerful tools for mobilizing the populace and educating them to particular sets of values. And finally, all peoples of Africa increasingly share in a technological revolution and a world culture—a culture which may be of largely Western origin, but which today is an amalgam of contributions by peoples from all parts of the globe.

Cultural change and growing interaction with others produce new loyalties in Africa, but for the most part these new identities reside alongside old ones. Relatively small-scale societies are maintaining themselves in a changing world. In larger political units, especially nation-states, nationalism is in fact growing more rapidly than internationalism, despite the fact that the latter is uniquely a product of the modern age. Thus most Africans belong to an expanding number of social networks, some of which are traditional and some of which are not; and increasing compartmentalization is the result. Individuals comprehend and participate in different reference groups with mounting frequency, sharing certain bonds with each and permitting the norms of each to guide their behavior in appropriate settings. But prominent among these multiple loyalties and cultural associations are ancient values that allow Africa's peoples to identify with aspects of their proud past and to achieve a renewed sense of their own identities.

References

Abou, Selim
  1962 Bilinguisme au Liban: la recontre de deux cultures. *Esprit,* November, 753–769.
Abun-Nasr, Jamil M.
  1965 *The Tijaniyya: A Sufi Order in the Modern World.* London: Oxford University Press.
Ahmed, J. M.
  1960 *The Intellectual Origins of Egyptian Nationalism.* London: Oxford University Press.
Aldaba-Lim, Estefania, and Gloria V. Javillonar
  1968 Achievement Motivation in Filipino Entrepreneurship. *International Social Science Journal,* 20(3):397–411.
Allott, A. N.
  1960 *Essays in African Law.* London: Butterworth.
Amin, Osman
  1953 *Mohammed Abduh.* Washington, D.C.: American Council of Learned Societies.
Andreski, Stanislav
  1968 *The African Predicament: A Study in the Pathology of Modernization.* New York: Atherton.
Apter, David
  1963 Political Religion in the New Nations. In Clifford Geertz, ed., *Old Societies and New States: The Quest for Modernity in Asia and Africa.* New York: Free Press.
  1965 *The Politics of Modernization.* Chicago: University of Chicago Press.
Ardant, Gabriel
  1961 *La Tunisie d'Aujourd'hui et de Demain.* Paris: Calmann-Levy.
Atkinson, John W., ed.
  1958 *Motives in Fantasy, Action and Society.* New York: Van Nostrand Reinhold.
Atkinson, John W., and Norman T. Feather
  1966 *A Theory of Achievement Motivation.* New York: Wiley.
Attia, Abdelmajid
  1966 Différents registres de l'emploi de l'arab en Tunisie. *Revue Tunisienne de Sciences Sociales,* 3:115–149.

1967 Éducation et loisirs. *Éducation Intégrale,* 2:20–24.

Bardin Pierre
1965 *La Vie d'un Douar.* Paris: Mouton.

Barnett, Homer G.
1953 *Innovation: The Basis of Cultural Change.* New York: McGraw-Hill.

Barrett, S. R.
1968 The Achievement Factor in Igbo Receptivity to Industrialization. *Canadian Review of Sociology and Anthropology,* 5:68–83.

Barth, Fredrik
1967 On the Study of Social Change. *American Anthropologist,* 69:661–669.

Barth, Heinrich
1857 *Travels and Discoveries in North and Central Africa.* London: Frank Cass & Co., Ltd. Centenary Edition in three volumes, 1965.

Beidelman, T. O.
1966 *Utani:* Some Kaguru Notions of Death, Sexuality, and Affinity. *Southwestern Journal of Anthropology,* 22:354–380.

Bennett, John W., and Iwao Ishino
1963 *Paternalism in the Japanese Economy: Anthropological Studies of* Oyabun-kobun *Patterns.* Minneapolis: University of Minnesota Press.

Berque, Jacques
1960 *Les Arabes d'Hier à Demain.* Paris: Seuil.

Bertrand, Louis
1926 Devant L'Islam. Paris: Plon.

Blondel, Anne Marie, and Francis Décorsière
1962 Une possibilité d'enrichissement. *Esprit,* November, 787–790.

Boahen, C. F. A.
1964 *Britain, the Sahara and the Western Sudan, 1788–1861.* Oxford: Clarendon.

Botha, Elize
1971 The Achievement Motive in Three Cultures. *The Journal of Social Psychology,* 85:163–170.

Bouhdiba, Abdulwahab
1966 La conscience religieuse dans la société d'aujourd'hui. *Institut des Belles-Lettres Arabes,* 29:217–237.

Bourguiba, Habib
1961a *Building a New Tunisia.* Tunis: Secretary of State for Cultural Affairs and Information.

1961b *Doubler le Nombre des Citoyens.* Tunis: Secrétariat d'État aux Affaires Culturelles et à l'Information.

1962 *Introduction to the History of the National Movement.* Tunis: Secretary of State for Cultural Affairs and Information.

1963a *Dimensions of Underdevelopment.* Tunis: Secretary of State for Cultural Affairs and Information.

1963b *L'Usine de Kasserine: un Centre de Rayonnement.* Tunis: Secrétariat d'État aux Affairs Culturelles et à l'Information.

1963c *Toward True Socialism.* Tunis: Secretary of State for Cultural Affairs and Information.

1963d *Transcending Individualism in Outlook.* Tunis: Secretary of State for Cultural Affairs and Information.

1965 *L'Enseignement, Fonction Sociale.* Tunis: Secrétariat d'État à l'Information et à l'Orientation.

1966a *Contre Toute Hégémonie.* Tunis: Secrétariat d'État à l'Information et à l'Orientation.

1966b *Discours Prononcé à l'Occasion du Mouled le 29 Juin 1966.* Tunis: Secrétariat d'État à l'Information et à l'Orientation.

1966c *Édifier une Société Saine et Équilibrée.* Tunis: Secrétariat d'État à l'information et à l'Orientation.

1969 *Youth Problems in Their True Perspective.* Tunis: Secretary of State for Cultural Affairs and Information.

Bovill, E. W.
1933 *Caravans of the Old Sahara.* London: Oxford University Press.

Brenner, Louis
1973 *The Shehus of Kukawa: A History of the al-Kanemi Dynasty of Bornu.* Oxford: Clarendon.

Brown, Leon Carl
1964 Stages in the Process of Change. In Charles A. Micaud, ed., *Tunisia: The Politics of Modernization.* New York: Praeger.
1966 The Role of Islam in Modern North Africa. In Leon Carl Brown, ed., *State and Society in Independent North Africa.* Washington: Middle East Institute.

Brown, Roger
1965 *Social Psychology.* New York: Free Press.

Bryan, M. A.
1959 The Bantu Languages of Africa. *In* The Handbook of African Languages, vol. IV. London: International African Institute.

Burnstein, Eugene
1963 Fear of Failure, Achievement Motivation and Aspiring to Prestigeful Occupations. *Journal of Abnormal Psychology,* 67:189–193.

Camilleri, Carmel
    1966   Maintien de l'action éducative de la famille et recherche de l'équilibre familial dans les relations parents-jeunes en Tunisie. *Éducation Intégrale,* 1.23–31.
    1973   Jeunesse, Famille, Développement. Aix-en-Provence: Éditions du CNRS.
Cansever, Gokçe
    1968   The Achievement Motive in Turkish Adolescents. *Journal of Social Psychology,* 76:269–270.
Carlyle, Thomas
    1897   *On Heroes, Heroworship and the Heroic in History.* London: Chapman and Hall.
Caudill, William, and George A. DeVos
    1956   Achievement, Culture, and Personality: The Case of the Japanese Americans. *American Anthropologist,* 58:1102–1126.
Central Statistical Bureau, Government of Tanzania
    1967   Preliminary Results of the Population Census Taken in August, 1967. Dar es Salaam: Ministry of Economic Affairs and Development Planning.
Childe, V. Gordon
    1946   *What Happened in History.* Baltimore: Penguin.
    1951   *Man Makes Himself.* New York: Mentor.
Cliffe, Lionel
    1969   From Independence to Self-Reliance. In Isaria N. Kimambo and A. J. Temu, eds., *A History of Tanzania.* Nairobi: East African Publishing House.
Cohen, Abner
    1968   The Politics of Mysticism in Some Local Communities in Newly Independent African States. In Marc J. Swartz, ed., *Local-Level Politics: Social and Cultural Perspectives.* Chicago: Aldine.
    1969   *Custom and Politics in Urban Africa: A Study of Hausa Migrants in Yoruba Towns.* Berkeley: University of California Press.
Cohen, Ronald
    1960   The Structure of Kanuri Society. Unpublished Ph.D. dissertation, University of Wisconsin.
    1966   Power, Authority and Personal Success in Islam and Bornu. In M. Swartz, V. Turner, and A. Tuden, eds., *Political Anthropology.* Chicago: Aldine.
    1967   *The Kanuri of Bornu.* New York: Holt, Rinehart, & Winston.
    1970a Social Stratification in Bornu. In A. Tuden and L. Plotnicov, eds., *Social Stratification in Africa.* New York: Free Press.

1970b The Kingship in Bornu. In M. Crowder and O. Ikime, eds., *West African Chiefs*. New York: Africana Publishing Corp.

1971a From Empire to Colony: Bornu in the 19th and 20th Centuries. In V. Turner, ed., *The Impact of Colonialism on Africa*. Stanford: Stanford University Press for the Hoover Institute.

1971b *Dominance and Defiance: A Study of Marital Instability in an Islamic African Society*. Washington, D.C.: American Anthropological Association.

1971c Bornu and Nigeria: Political Kingdom in a Troubled Nation. In Robert Melson and Howard Wolpe, eds., *Nigeria: Modernization and the Politics of Communalism*. East Lansing: Michigan State University Press.

1973 Selecting Respondents for a Study of Divorce in Nigeria. In William M. O'Barr, David H. Spain, and Mark A. Tessler, eds., *Survey Research in Africa: Its Applications and Limits*. Evanston, Ill.: Northwestern University Press.

Colson, Elizabeth

1967 Competence and Incompetence in the Context of Independence. *Current Anthropology*, 8:92–111.

1968 Contemporary Tribes and the Development of Nationalism. In June Helm, ed., *Essays on the Problem of Tribe. Proceedings of the 1967 Annual Meeting of the American Ethnological Society*. Seattle: University of Washington Press.

Congrès de l'Afrique du Nord

1909 Paris: Comité d'Organisation du Congrès.

Cragg, Kenneth

1956 *The Call of the Minaret*. New York: Oxford University Press.

Crockett, Harry J., Jr.

1962 The Achievement Motive and Differential Occupational Mobility in the United States. *American Sociological Review*, 27: 191–204.

1966 Psychological Origins of Mobility. In Neil J. Smelser and Seymour M. Lipset, eds., *Social Structure and Mobility in Economic Development*. Chicago: Aldine.

Demeerseman, André

1947 *L'Évolution Féminine Tunisienne*. Tunis: Publications de l'Institut des Belles-Lettres Arabes.

1957 *Tunisie: Sève Nouvelle*. Paris: Casterman et Tournoi.

1967 La Famille Tunisienne et les Temps Nouveaux. Tunis: Maison Tunisienne de l'Édition.

Denham (Major) and Clapperton (Captain)

1826 *Travels and Discoveries in Northern and Central Africa*. London: Murray, 2 vols.

Department of Local Government
1971   *Northern States of Nigeria Local Government Year Book.* Zaria, Nigeria: Institute of Administration, Ahmadu Bello University.

Deuxième Seminaire du Linguistique
1968   *Revue Tunisienne de Sciences Sociales,* vol. 13.

DeVos, George A.
1960   The Relation of Guilt Towards Parents to Achievement and Arranged Marriage Among the Japanese. *Psychiatry,* 23:287–301.
1965   Achievement Motivation, Social Self-Identity and Japanese Economic Development. *Asian Survey,* 12:575–589.
1968   Achievement and Innovation in Culture and Personality. In *The Study of Personality: An Interdisciplinary Appraisal.* Edward Norbeck, Douglass Price-Williams, and William M. McCord, eds., *The Study of Personality: An Interdisciplinary Approach.* New York: Holt, Rinehart & Winston.

DeVos, George A., and Hiroshi Wagatsuma
1961   Variations in Traditional Value Attitudes Toward Status and Role Behavior of Women in Two Japanese Villages. *American Anthropologist,* 63:1204–1230.

Doob, Leonard W.
1960   *Becoming More Civilized.* New Haven, Conn.: Yale University Press.

Durkheim, Emile
1938   The Rules of the Sociological Method. S. Solovay and J. Mueller, trans. New York: Free Press (orig., 1895).

Duvignaud, Jean
1970   *Change at Shebika.* New York: Pantheon.

El-Arbi, Tahar
1966   L'authorité familiale qu'elle est vue par les parents. *Education Intégrale,* 1:11–18.

Elayeb, A.
1968   Contribution à l'étude des fautes d'arabe chez les élèves du secondaire en Tunisie. *Revue Tunisienne de Sciences Sociales,* 13:63–91.

Engels, Friedrich
1942   *The Origin of the Family, Private Property, and the State.* New York: International Publishers.

L'Enseignement du Français
1972   An-Nachra At-Tarbaya, Nos. 5–6.

Epstein, Scarlett
1964   Social Structure and Entrepreneurship. *International Journal of Comparative Sociology,* 5:162–165.

Evans-Pritchard, E. E.
1940 *The Nuer.* Oxford: Clarendon.

Fabian, Johannes
1971 *Jamaa: A Charismatic Movement in Katanga.* Evanston, Ill.: Northwestern University Press.

Fallers, Lloyd
1956 *Bantu Bureaucracy; A Century of Political Evolution Among the Basoga of Uganda.* Chicago: University of Chicago Press.
1961 Ideology and Culture in Uganda Nationalism. *American Anthropologist,* 63:677–686

Fanon, Frantz
1959 *Studies in a Dying Colonialism.* New York: Grove.

Fayerweather, J.
1959 *The Executive Overseas.* Syracuse, N.Y.: Syracuse University Press.
1960 *Management and International Operations.* New York: McGraw-Hill.

Field, Arthur J.
1967 Urbanization and Work in Modernizing Societies: A Working Paper. Detroit: Glengary.

Filali, Mustapha
1966 Les Problèmes d'integration posés par la sedantarisation des populations nomades et tribales. *Revue Tunisienne de Sciences Sociales,* 3:83–114.

Finney, Ruth S.
1971 *Would-Be Entrepreneurs? A Study of Motivation in New Guinea.* Canberra: Australian National University. (New Guinea Research Bulletin, No. 41.)

Fisher, R. A.
1942 *The Design of Experiments,* 3rd ed. Edinburgh: Oliver and Boyd.

Foa, Uriel
1971 Interpersonal and Economic Resources. *Science,* 171:345–351.

Fortes, M., and E. E. Evans-Pritchard, eds.
1940 *African Political Systems.* London: Oxford University Press.

Frank, André Gunder
1969 *Capitalism and Underdevelopment in Latin America.* New York: Modern Reader Paperbacks.

Fried, M.
1967 *The Evolution of Political Society.* New York: Random House.

Gal, Ladislas
1955 Whither Arabic. *Islamic Culture,* 29:32–53.

Gallagher, Charles
  1966   Language and Identity. In Leon Carl Brown, ed., *State and Society in Independent North Africa*. Washington: Middle East Institute.

Ganiage, Jean
  1959   *Les Origines du Protectorat Français en Tunisie*. Paris: Presses Universitaires de France.

Garmadi, S.
  1968   La situation linguistique actuelle en Tunisie. *Revue Tunisienne de Sciences Sociales*, 13:13–32.

Geertz, Clifford
  1968   *Islam Observed: Religious Development in Morocco and Indonesia*. New Haven, Conn.: Yale University Press.

Gibb, H. A. R.
  1926   *Arabic Literature*. London: Oxford University Press.
  1953   *Mohammedanism*. London: Oxford University Press.

Goodenough, Ward Hunt
  1963   *Cooperation in Change: An Anthropological Approach to Community Development*. New York: Russell Sage Foundation.

Gordon, David C.
  1962   *North Africa's French Legacy: 1954–1962*. Cambridge, Mass.: Harvard University Press.
  1968   *Women of Algeria*. Cambridge, Mass.: Harvard University Press.

Guth, E.
  1932   Die sippe bei den Vaasu. *Evangelischer Missionsmagazin*, 78:387–391.

Gwassa, G. C. K.
  1969   The German Intervention and African Resistance in Tanzania. In Isaria N. Kimambo and A. J. Temu, eds., *A History of Tanzania*. Nairobi: East African Publishing House.

Hagen, Everett E.
  1962   *On the Theory of Social Change*. Homewood, Ill. Dorsey.

Hahn, Lorna
  1960   *North Africa: Nationalism to Nationhood*. Washington, D.C.: Public Affairs Press.

Haim, Sylvia
  1962   *Arab Nationalism*. Berkeley: University of California Press.

Harris, John R.
  1968   Nigerian Enterprise in the Printing Industry. *Nigerian Journal of Economic and Social Studies*, 10:215–227.

Harris, Marvin
  1968   *The Rise of Anthropological Theory*. New York: Crowell.

Heckhausen, H.
1967 *The Anatomy of Achievement Motivation.* New York: Academic.
Hitti, Philip K.
1962 *Islam and the West.* New York: Van Nostrand Reinhold.
Hochschild, Arlie
1966 Women at Work in Modernizing Tunisia: Attitudes of Urban Adolescent Schoolgirls. Unpublished master's dissertation, University of California at Berkeley.
Hussein, Taha
1954 *The Future of Culture in Egypt.* Washington, D.C.: American Council of Learned Societies.
Imam, Ibrahim
1969 Kanuri Marriage. *Nigeria Magazine,* 102:512–515.
Inkeles, Alex
1962 The Modernization of Man. In Myron Weiner, ed., *Modernization.* New York: Basic Books.
1966 Participant Citizenship in Six Developing Nations. *American Political Science Review,* 63:1120–1141.
Johnson, Frederick
1939 *A Standard Swahili-English Dictionary.* Oxford: Oxford University Press.
Julien, Charles-André
1961 *Historie de l'Afrique du Nord,* vol. 1. Paris: Payot.
Kahl, Joseph
1964 Some Measures of Achievement Orientation. *American Journal of Sociology,* 70:669–681.
Kechrid, Salaheddine
1971 *Le Vrai Visage de l'Islam.* Tunis: En-Najah.
Kemper, T. D.
1968 Reference Groups, Socialization and Achievement. *American Sociological Review,* 33:31–45.
Khairallah, Chedley
n.d. *Le Movement Jeune Tunisien.* Tunis: Bonici.
Kilby, Peter
1969 *Industrialization in an Open Economy: Nigeria 1945–1966.* Cambridge: Cambridge University Press.
Kimambo, Isaria N.
1968 The Pare. In Andrew Roberts, ed., *Tanzania Before 1900.* Nairobi: East African Publishing House.
1969a *A Political History of the Pare of Tanzania c. 1500–1900.* Nairobi: East African Publishing House.
1969b The Interior Before 1800. In Isaria N. Kimambo and A. J.

Temu, eds., *A History of Tanzania*. Nairobi: East African Publishing House.

1971 *Mbiru:* Popular Protest in Colonial Tanzania. Historical Association of Tanzania Paper, No. 9. Nairobi: East African Publishing House.

Kimambo, Isaria N., and A. J. Temu, eds.

1969 *A History of Tanzania*. Nairobi: East African Publishing House.

Kirk-Greene, Anthony H. M.

1968 The Merit Principle in an African Bureaucracy: Northern Nigeria. In Arnold Rivkin, ed., *Nations by Design*. Garden City, N.Y.: Doubleday.

Kotz, Ernst

1922 *Im banne der furcht*. Hamburg: Advent Verlag.

Kumalo, C.

1966 African Elites in Industrial Bureaucracy. In P. C. Lloyd, ed., *The New Elites of Tropical Africa*. London: Oxford University Press for the International African Institute.

Laroui, Abdallah

1967 *L'Ideologie Arabe Contemporaine*. Paris: Maspero.

La Tunisie au Travail

1960 Tunis: Secrétariat d'État à l'Information et à l'Orientation.

Lazarus, J. R., F. S. Kessel, and E. Botha

1969 Cultural Differences in *n* Achievement Externality Between White and Colored South African Adolescents. *Journal of Social Psychology*, 77:133–134.

Leach, E. R.

1964 *Political Systems of Highland Burma*. Boston: Beacon Hill Press (orig. Cambridge, Mass.: Harvard University Press, 1954).

LeLong, Michel

1957 Le séminaire Internationale de la culture nordafricaine. *Institut des Belles-Lettres Arabes*, 20:239–268.

Lerner, Daniel

1958 *The Passing of Traditional Society: Modernizing the Middle East*. New York: Free Press.

LeVine, Robert A.

1962 Wealth and Power in Gusiiland. In P. J. Bohannan and G. Dalton, eds., *Markets in Africa*. Evanston, Ill.: Northwestern University Press.

1966a *Dreams and Deeds, Achievement Motivation in Nigeria*. Chicago: University of Chicago Press.

1966b Outsiders' Judgments: An Ethnographic Approach to Group

Differences in Personality. *Southwestern Journal of Anthropology,* 22:101–116.

LeVine, Robert A., Nancy H. Klein, and Constance R. Owen
1967   Father-child Relationships and Changing Life-styles in Ibadan, Nigeria. In Horace Miner, ed., *The City in Modern Africa.* New York: Praeger.

Lewis, I. M.
1959   The Classification of African Political Systems. *Rhodes-Livingstone Journal,* 25:59–69.
1966   Introduction to *Islam in Tropical Africa.* I. M. Lewis, ed. London: Oxford University Press.

Lloyd, Peter C.
1965   The Political Structure of African Kingdoms: An Exploratory Model. In Michael Banton, ed., *Political Systems and the Distribution of Power.* ASA Monographs, #2. London: Tavistock Publications.
1967   *Africa in Social Change: Changing Traditional Societies in the Modern World.* Baltimore: Penguin.

Louis, André
1965   Greniers fortifiés et maisons troglodytes: Ksar Djouama. *Institut des Belles-Lettres Arabes,* 28:373–400.

Magnin, Père J. G.
1961   Problèmes de la santé publique. *Institut des Belles-Lettres Arabes,* 24:337–347.

Maine, H. S.
1861   *Ancient Law.* London: Murray.

Marriott, McKim
1963   Cultural Policy in the New States. In Clifford Geertz, ed., *Old Societies and New States.* New York: Free Press.

Marx, Karl
1936   *Capital: A Critique of Political Economy.* New York: Modern Library (orig. 1867).
1957   *The Eighteenth Brumaire of Louis Bonaparte.* New York: International Publishers (orig. 1852).

McClelland, David C.
1961   *The Achieving Society.* New York: Van Nostrand Reinhold.
1963   Motivational Patterns in Southeast Asia with Special Reference to the Chinese Case. *Journal of Social Issues,* 19:6–19.
1965a   *N* Achievement and Entrepreneurship. *Journal of Personality and Social Psychology,* 1:389–392.
1965b   Achievement Motivation Can Be Developed. *Harvard Business Review,* 43(6):6–24.

1966 The Achievement Motive in Economic Growth. In J. L. Finkle and R. W. Gable, eds., *Political Development and Social Change*. New York: Wiley.

McClelland, David C., John W. Atkinson, Russell A. Clark, and Edgar L. Lowell
1953 *The Achievement Motive*. New York: Appleton-Century-Crofts.

McClelland, David C., and G. A. Friedman
1952 Child-Training Practices and the Achievement Motivation Appearing in Folk Tales. In T. M. Newcomb, E. L. Hartley, and G. E. Swanson, eds., *Readings in Social Psychology*. New York: Holt, Rinehart & Winston.

McClelland, David C., and David G. Winter
1969 *Motivating Economic Achievement*. New York: Free Press.

Mead, Margaret
1956 *New Lives for Old: Cultural Transformation—Manus, 1928–1953*. New York: Morrow.
1964 *Continuities in Cultural Evolution*. New Haven, Conn.: Yale University Press.

Memmi, Albert
1966 *La Statue de Sel*. Paris: Gallimard.

Micaud, Charles A.
1964 *Tunisia: The Politics of Modernization*. New York: Praeger.

Monteil, Vincent
1960 *L'Arabe Moderne*. Paris: Klincksieck.

Moore, Clement Henry
1965 *Tunisia Since Independence*. Berkeley: University of California Press.
1970 *Politics in North Africa*. Boston: Little, Brown.
1971 On Theory and Practice Among Arabs. *World Politics*, XXIV:106–126.

Morgan, J. N.
1964 The Achievement Motive and Economic Behavior. *Economic Development and Cultural Change*, 12:243–267.

Morgan, L. H.
1877 *Ancient Society*. New York: World Publishing.

Moris, Jon R.
1972 Administrative Authority and the Problem of Effective Agricultural Administration in East Africa. *The African Review*, 2:105–146.

M'Rabet, Fadela
1964 *La Femme Algérienne*. Paris. Maspero.

Mukherjee, B. N., and S. Verma
1966 A Cross-cultural Comparison of Judgments of Social Desir-

ability for Items of a Forced-choice Scale of Achievement Motivation. *Journal of Social Psychology,* 69:337–338.

Murdock, G. P.
1959 *Africa: Its Peoples and Their Culture History.* New York: McGraw-Hill.

Nachtigal, G.
1879 *Sahara und Sudan: Ergebnisse Sechsjähriger Reisen in Afrika.* Berlin: Weidmannsche Buchhandlung.

Nash, Dennison, and Louis C. Shaw
1965 Achievement and Acculturation: A Japanese Example. In M. E. Spiro, ed., *Context and Meaning in Cultural Anthropology.* New York: Free Press.

Nash, Manning
1961 The Social Context of Economic Choice in a Small Society. *Man,* 61:186–191.

Nyerere, Julius K.
1966 Dibaji (Preface). In Peter Temu, ed., *Uchumi Bora.* Nairobi: Oxford University Press.
1967a *Education for Self-Reliance.* Dar es Salaam: Government Printer.
1967b *Socialism and Rural Development.* Dar es Salaam: Government Printer.
1969 *Ujamaa: Essays on Socialism.* Dar es Salaam: Oxford University Press.

O'Barr, William M.
1973 Genealogy-based Samples for African Research. In William M. O'Barr, David H. Spain, and Mark A. Tessler, eds., *Survey Research in Africa: Its Applications and Limits.* Evanston, Ill.: Northwestern University Press.

Ostheimer, John M.
1969 Measuring Achievement Motivation Among the Chagga of Tanzania. *Journal of Social Psychology,* 78:17–30.

Ottenberg, Simon
1959 Ibo Receptivity to Change. In W. R. Bascom and M. J. Herskovits, eds., *Continuity and Change in African Cultures.* Chicago: University of Chicago Press.

Pellat, Charles
1956 *Introduction à l'Arabe Moderne.* Paris: Adrien–Maisonneuve.

Peshkin, Alan
1970 Education and Modernism in Bornu. *Comparative Education Review,* 14:283–300.
1971 Education and National Integration in Nigeria. In Robert Melson and Howard Wolpe, ed., *Nigeria: Modernization and*

the Politics of Communalism. East Lansing: Michigan State University Press.

1972   Kanuri Schoolchildren. New York: Holt, Rinehart & Winston.

Pickthall, Marmaduke
1930   The Meaning of the Glorious Koran. London: Knopf.

Proehl, Paul O.
1965   Foreign Enterprise in Nigeria. Chapel Hill: University of North Carolina Press.

Prothero, Edwin Terry
1961   Child-Rearing in the Lebanon. Cambridge, Mass.: Harvard University Press.

Pye, Lucien
1962   Politics, Personality and Nation-Building. New Haven, Conn.: Yale University Press.

Quaison-Sackey, Alex
1963   Africa Unbound. New York: Praeger.

Raymond, André
1961   La Tunisie. Paris: Presses Universitaires de France.

Riguet, Maurice
1972   Étude sur un Échantillon d'Adolescents Tunisiens. Unpublished thesis for Doctorat 3e Cycle, Université de Lyon II.

Riahi, Z.
1968   Le français parlé par les cadres tunisiens. Revue Tunisienne de Sciences Sociales, 13:195–217.

Rogers, Everett M.
1962   Diffusion of Innovations. New York: Free Press.
1969   Modernization Among Peasants: The Impact of Communication. New York: Holt, Rinehart & Winston.

Rogers, Everett M., and T. E. Neill
1966   Achievement Motivation Among Columbian Peasants. East Lansing: Michigan State University, Department of Communication.

Rosen, Bernard C.
1956   The Achievement Syndrome: A Psychocultural Dimension of Social Stratification. American Sociological Review, 21:203–211.
1959a   Race, Ethnicity, and the Achievement Syndrome. American Sociological Review, 24:47–60.
1959b   The Psychosocial Origins of Achievement Motivation. Sociometry, 22:185–218.
1961   Family Structure and Achievement Motivation. American Sociological Review, 26:574–585.

1962 Socialization and Achievement Motivation in Brazil. *American Sociological Review*, 27:612–624.

1964 The Achievement Syndrome and Economic Growth in Brazil. *Social Forces*, 42:341–354.

1971 Industrialization, Personality and Social Mobility in Brazil. *Human Organization*, 30:137–148.

Rudolph, Lloyd, and Susanne Rudolph
1967 *The Modernity of Tradition.* Chicago: University of Chicago Press.

Sahlins, M. D.
1961 The Segmentary Lineage: An Organization of Predatory Expansion. *American Anthropologist*, 63:332–345.

Saumagne, C. H., and A. Cardoso
1950 Le Protectorat: l'organisation politique et administrative. In J. Despois, ed., *Initiation à la Tunisie*. Paris: Adrien-Maisonneuve.

Schumpeter, Joseph A.
1934 *The Theory of Economic Development.* Cambridge, Mass.: Harvard University Press.

Schuon, Frithjof
1963 *Understanding Islam.* New York: Roy.

Sebag, Paul
1950 *La Tunisie.* Paris: Éditions Sociales.

Service, E.
1962 *Primitive Social Organization.* New York: Random House.

Sherrill, Kenneth S.
1969 Attitudes of Modernity. *Comparative Politics*, 1:184–210.

Shils, Edward
1958 The Concentration and Dispersion of Charisma: Their Bearing on Economic Policy in Underdeveloped Countries. *World Politics*, 11:1–19.

Shrable, Kenneth, and Lawrence H. Stewart
1967 Personality Correlates of Achievement Imagery: Theoretical and Methodological Implications. *Perceptual and Motor Skills*, 24:1087–1098.

Singh, N. P.
1969 *N* Achievement Among Successful-unsuccessful and Traditional-progressive Agricultural Entrepreneurs of Delhi. *Journal of Social Psychology*, 79:271–272.

Smith, M. G.
1959 The Hausa System of Social Status. *Africa*, 29:239–252.

1960   *Government in Zazzau, 1800–1950.* London: Oxford University Press.

Smock, Audrey
1971   *Ibo Politics.* Cambridge, Mass.: Harvard University Press.

Southall, Aidan W.
1956   *Alur Society.* Cambridge: Heffer.
1965   A Critique of the Typology of States and Political Systems. In Michael Banton, ed., *Political Systems and the Distribution of Power.* ASA Monographs, #2. London: Tavistock Publications.
1970   The Illusion of Tribe. In P. C. W. Gutkind, ed., *The Passing of Tribal Man in Africa.* Leiden, The Netherlands: E. J. Brill.

Spain, David H.
1971   The Conflict Between 'Ranky-Daddy' and 'Hyena': Reflections on Some Causes of Civil Wars, Riots, and Intra-office Squabbles. Paper presented at the Center for Afro-American Studies at the University of Wisconsin-Milwaukee, May, 1971 (mimeo).
1973   Developing a New TAT for Studying Achievement Motivation in Africa. In William M. O'Barr, David H. Spain, and Mark A. Tessler, eds., *Survey Research in Africa: Its Applications and Limits.* Evanston, Ill.: Northwestern University Press.

Spicer, Edward H.
1971   Persistent Cultural Systems: A Comparative Study of Identity Systems That Can Adapt to Contrasting Environments. *Science,* 174:795–800.

Stambouli, Fredj
1964   Ksar Hillal et Sa Région: Contribution à une Sociologie du Changement dans les Pays en Voie de Développement. Unpublished thesis for Doctorat 3e Cycle, Université de Paris.

Stenning, Derrick J.
1959   *Savannah Nomads.* London: Oxford University Press for International African Institute.

Steward, J.
1955   *Theory of Culture Change.* Urbana: University of Illinois Press.

Stopler, Wolfgang F.
1962   The Main Features of the 1962–1968 National Plan. *Nigerian Journal of Economic and Social Studies,* 4:85–91.

Strodtbeck, Fred L.
1958   Family Interaction, Values and Achievement. In D. McClelland, A. Baldwin, U. Bronfenbrenner, and F. Strodtbeck, eds., *Talent and Society.* New York: Van Nostrand Reinhold.

Tabouret-Keller, Andrée
  1961 Vrais et faux problèmes du bilinguisme. In I. Lézine, F. Kocher, A. Brauner, L. Lentin, and A. Tabouret-Keller, *Études sur le langage de l'Enfant*. Paris: Les Éditions du Scarabée.
  1968 Le bilinguisme à l'age scolaire. *Revue Tunisienne de Sciences Sociales*, 13:149–171.
Tedeschi, J. T., and M. Kian
  1962 Cross-cultural Study of the TAT Assessment for Achievement Motivation: Americans and Persians. *Journal of Social Psychology*, 58:227–234.
Tessler, Mark A.
  1969 The Nature of Modernity in a Transitional Society: The Case of Tunisia. Unpublished Ph.D. dissertation, Northwestern University.
  1970 A Cultural Basis for Arab-Israeli Accommodation. *World Affairs*, 133:183–200.
  1971a Interviewer Biasing Effects in a Tunisian Survey. *Journal of Social Psychology*, 84:153–154.
  1971b Cultural Modernity: Evidence from Tunisia. *Social Science Quarterly*, 52:290–308.
  1973a Measuring Abstract Concepts in Tunisia. In William M. O'Barr, David H. Spain, and Mark A. Tessler, eds., *Survey Research in Africa: Its Applications and Limits*. Evanston, Ill.: Northwestern University Press.
  1973b Response Set and Interview Bias. In William M. O'Barr, David H. Spain, and Mark A. Tessler, eds., *Survey Research in Africa: Its Applications and Limits*. Evanston, Ill.: Northwestern University Press.
Tessler, Mark A., and Mary E. Keppel
  n.d.   Change in Tunisia: Essays in the Social and Health Sciences. In John Simmons and Russell Stone, eds., *Social Science Research in Tunisia*. Forthcoming.
Tillon, Germaine
  1966 *Le Harem et les Cousins*. Paris: Seuil.
Tönnies, Ferdinand
  1957 *Community and Society (Gemeinschaft und Gesellschaft)*. Translated and edited by Charles P. Loomis. East Lansing: Michigan State University Press. (orig. 1887).
Trabelsi, Mohammed
  1966 Les jeunes devant l'autorité. *Éducation Intégrale*, 1:19–22.
  1967a L'éducation sociale. *Éducation Intégrale*, 2:14–19.
  1967b Recherche scientifique et éducation. *Éducation Intégrale*, 3:55–57.

Trimingham, J. Spencer
    1959 *Islam in West Africa.* London: Oxford University Press.
    1968 *The Influence of Islam upon Africa.* New York: Praeger.
Tukur, Mahmud
        n.d. Philosophy, Goals, and Institutions of the Sokoto Caliphal
              Administration: A Preliminary View. In *Nigerian Administra-
              tion Research Project: First Interim.* Institute of Administra-
              tion, Ahmadu Bello University, Zaria, Nigeria.
UNESCO
    1961 Development and Education in Africa: Final Report of the
          Addis Ababa Conference, May 15–25, 1961. New York:
          UNESCO Publications.
Vansina, Jan
    1962 A Comparison of African Kingdoms. *Africa,* 32:324–335.
Vaughan, James H., Jr.
    1970 Caste Systems in the Western Sudan. In A. Tuden and L.
          Plotnicov, eds., *Social Stratification in Africa.* New York:
          Free Press.
    1962 *Modern Islam: The Search for Cultural Identity.* New York:
          Knopf. (Vintage ed., 1964).
von Grunebaum, G. E.
    1955 Islam: Essays in the Nature and Growth of a Cultural Tradi-
          tion. *American Anthropologist,* 57 (2, part 2, Memoir No. 81).
    1961 Nationalism and Cultural Trends in the Arab Near-East.
          Studia Islamica, 14:121–153.
Weber, Max
    1930 *The Protestant Ethic and the Spirit of Capitalism,* Talcott
          Parsons, trans. New York: Scribner.
    1947 *The Theory of Social and Economic Organization.* Translated
          by A. M. Henderson and Talcott Parsons; edited with an
          Introduction by Talcott Parsons. New York: Oxford University
          Press. (Free Press ed., 1964).
White, Leslie A.
    1959 *The Evolution of Culture.* New York: McGraw-Hill.
Williams, John S.
    1960 Maori Achievement Motivation. Victoria University of Welling-
          ton Publications in Psychology, #13. Department of Psy-
          chology, Victoria University of Wellington, N.Z.
Winterbottom, M.
    1953 The Relationship of Childhood Training in Independence to
          Achievement Motivation. Unpublished Ph.D. dissertation, Uni-
          versity of Michigan.

1958 The Relation of Need for Achievement to Learning and Experiences in Independence and Mastery. In J. W. Atkinson, ed., *Motives in Fantasy, Action and Society.* New York: Van Nostrand Reinhold.

Yacine, Kateb
1962 Jardin parmi les flammes. *Esprit,* November: 771–773.

Zajonc, Robert B., and N. Kishar Wahi
1961 Conformity and Need-Achievement under Cross-cultural Norm Conflict. *Human Relations,* 4:241–250.

Zamiti, Khalil
1971 Problématique de la contradiction survenue entre la formation professionelle et l'emploie en Tunisie. *Revue Tunisienne de Sciences Sociales,* 25:9–53.

Zghal, M.
1966 Cadres agricoles et ouvriers qualifiés dans le nouveau systeme agricole. *Revue Tunisienne de Sciences Sociales,* 3:137–152.

Ziadeh, Nicola
1957 *Whither North Africa.* Aligarh, India: Institute of Islamic Studies.
1962 *Origins of Nationalism in Tunisia.* Beirut: American University of Beirut Press.

Index